# School Library Management

## SIXTH EDITION

## Judi Repman and Gail Dickinson

Professional Development Resources for
K-12 Library Media and Technology Specialists

Library of Congress Cataloging-in-Publication Data

School library management notebook. -- 6th ed. / edited by Judi Repman and Gail Dickinson.
    p. cm.
  Rev. ed. of: School library management. 5th ed. c2003.
  Includes bibliographical references and index.
  ISBN 1-58683-296-4 (pbk.)
  1. School libraries--United States--Administration. I. Repman, Judi. II. Dickinson, Gail K. III. School library management.
ment.
  Z675.S3S354 2007
  025.1'978--dc22

2006103468

Published by Linworth Publishing, Inc.
3650 Olentangy River Road, Suite 250
Columbus, Ohio 43214

ISBN: 1-58683-296-4

5 4 3 2 1

# Table of Contents

# Table of Contents continued

# About the Editors

**Judi Repman** is a Professor of Instructional Technology at Georgia Southern University, where she teaches courses related to school library media certification. She holds B.A., M.L.S. and Ph.D. degrees from Louisiana State University, Baton Rouge. Judi is also the Associate Editor for Linworth Publishing. Judi is a frequent presenter at library and instructional technology conferences and has also published articles in both fields.

Judi is married to Duane and they have one son, James. Two dogs and a cat round out the family. Judi's hobbies include reading, travel, and cooking.

**Gail Dickinson** is Associate Professor of School Librarianship at Old Dominion University in Norfolk, Virginia. She teaches courses in school library administration, reference, and collection development. Her research interests are school library budgeting and collections and the National Board for Professional Teaching Standards certification for school librarians. Gail lives in North Carolina with her husband, Michael Colson.

Their almost-grown-up children are Margaret and Beth Ann Dickinson and Michael and Alex Colson. Gail and Mike spend part of their time relaxing on the Eastern Shore of Virginia overlooking the Chesapeake Bay.

# Introduction

Multitasking is the watchword for the 21st century school library media specialist. Managing shrinking budgets, collaborating with teachers, serving as webmasters for school and/or school library web pages, helping students pick out a great book to read, and processing new materials are examples of some of the range of tasks that fill the media specialist's days. Just as media specialists multitask, this book serves multiple purposes for a variety of audiences.

*For the media-specialist-in-training or the novice media specialist* this book serves as an experienced mentor who is always available with advice and strategies for dealing with a range of media center issues. The articles included represent the best-of-the-best of *Library Media Connection* (LMC); they present best practices and concrete examples to bring the ideas, goals and strategies outlined in *Information Power: Building Partnerships for Learning* (AASL & AECT, 1998) to reality. The ideas described have been tested in media centers around the country and the articles provide blueprints for developing a strong media center program. This book also allows the novice media specialist to meet some of the leaders in our profession: Mike Eisenberg, Carol Simpson, Gary Hartzell, Toni Buzzeo, Ross Todd, and Gail Dickinson. But just as many articles are written by building level media specialists who have worked hard to build outstanding media programs and who then shared those ideas through the pages of LMC.

*For the experienced media specialist* this book is like attending a national conference with only the best presenters. The articles showcase creative ways to ensure the continued viability of media center programs and give practicing media specialists a chance to learn the nuts and bolts of many innovative media center programs. This book can also be used as a resource for professional learning communities. The articles in *School Library Management* provide perspectives from urban, rural and suburban schools and for elementary, middle/junior high and high school media centers in one handy volume.

*For school library media faculty* this book can be a supplement to courses such as Administration of the School Library Media Center or Current Issues in School Libraries. As experienced school library educators, we know how valuable it is for students to be able to see beyond *Information Power* and read examples from media specialists who are actually implementing its principles. The range of ideas presented here will provide excellent foundations for class discussions and help to bridge the gap between theory and practice. The list of additional resources in the appendix points faculty and students to other sources with information about the topics presented.

## The Article Selection Process

In 2002, two well-known Linworth Publishing periodicals, *Library Talk* and *The Book Report*, merged into *Library Media Connection (LMC)*. The goal of *LMC* remained the same as the goals of *Library Talk* and *The Book Report*: to provide school library media and technology specialists with practical advice and descriptions of best practices to create effective media and technology programs in K-12 schools. As we reviewed the first four volumes of LMC we found a wide range of excellent articles on just about any topic related to school library practice. We immediately made some difficult decisions. This compilation does not include any lesson plans nor does it include articles directly related to books and authors. With very rare exceptions we limited ourselves to a single article on a topic. For topics like advocacy, collaboration and information literacy, if we determined that the articles included enough different information or a new approach, we included multiple articles. Both editors have experience as building level media specialists and currently work as school library educators. We have been active in school library associations, attended many conferences, and visited media centers around the country. Our selection criteria were developed from these experiences. We chose articles that demonstrate best practices, that are practical, and that will encourage reflection. By sharing these articles, we hope to inspire media specialists to reflect on their current practice and get fired up to try something new.

## How This Book Is Organized

The sixth edition of *School Library Management* is organized into five sections. This broad, thematic approach makes it easier to see the interrelationships between all aspects of media center programs and operations. Each section begins with a brief introduction highlighting key issues represented by the articles. A list of print and web-based supplemental resources can be found in the Appendix and an author/title/subject index provides quick access to specific articles.

**Section I: Before You Start** covers the basics. This section includes articles on time management, the role of the media specialist in the instructional program of the school, and how to communicate effectively with administrators and parents. This section also includes several "Hands-on Handouts" and "Tools of the Trade", one page ready-to-use documents that can be put to immediate use in the media center.

**Section II: The Big Ideas** brings together key articles on topics that are at the foundation of our changing profession and widely discussed whenever media specialists gather. Here you'll find a thought-provoking article with practical implications for media specialists on topics ranging from ethics and plagiarism to helping increase student learning as reflected on standardized test scores.

**Section III: Program Administration** is the section to turn to if you have a media center renovation project in your future. This section also includes strategies for leadership, advocacy and budgeting, critical ideas that go hand-in-hand in our current era of NCLB and accountability.

**Section IV:  Professional Growth and Staff Development** makes a good starting point if you need some new ideas for working with the teachers at your school. This section explores electronic portfolios as a tool for professional growth and describes the National Board for Professional Teaching Standards process for media specialists.

**Section V: Where Do We Go Next?** looks into the future. Change is a constant in all of our lives. These articles explore new technologies and how they can be used in the media center, and describe ways that media specialists can document the impact of their programs on student learning.

Whether you start at page one of this book or turn directly to a section that interests you, we hope you'll find an article that will inspire you, make you think, or help you develop a new approach to ensure that "all students and staff are effective users of ideas and information" (*Information Power*, p. 6).  After all, that's what we're all about!

### *Reference*

AASL & AECT, (1998). *Information Power: Building partnerships for learning.* Chicago: ALA.

# Before You Start

## Introduction

"You only get one chance to make a good first impression" sets the tone for Section I. No matter how experienced (or inexperienced) you are, when that first day of school comes around we all get a chance to make a fresh start. Situational changes like moving from a classroom to the media center or changing schools bring their own unique challenges and hearing the voices of experience can help calm the jitters that come with change. In this section you will also find current information about topics like teaching reading in the media center or communicating about the media program with your principal in the era of *No Child Left Behind* (NCLB). For media specialists knowledge is power and this focus on issues related to the instructional role of the media specialist "before you start" gives you the background you need from your first day on the job.

This section opens with a one page list by Carl Harvey that answers the critical question *"What Should a Teacher Expect a School Library Media Specialist to Be?"* Expectations become a theme that runs through several articles that follow. There is practical advice from Sue Howard just for new media specialists along with tips for getting ready before the first day of school. Students, teachers, and administrators expect the media center to be well organized and developing useful policies and procedures is a critical organizational strategy. Colleen MacDonell's comprehensive list of essential procedural documents will make your life easier and allow you to focus on what's really important in your media center. How much time should you spend collecting those two-cent a day fines? Pam Bacon's tips about overdues should ease your mind about what you should (and should not) spend your time doing.

Time management is consistently identified as a challenging area for media specialists. Mary Ann Fitzgerald and Andrea Waldrip's helpful techniques related to planning and prioritizing can be used by even the most experienced media specialists. Their discussion is the perfect lead for Gail Dickinson's article about how to avoid burn out. Dickinson provides a reality check about the personal and professional impact of running a busy media center. Dickinson's article reinforces Sue Howard's closing point in "Librarians Behind the Scenes Before the Year Starts." Howard reminds all of us that "as librarians we try to be all and do all for our clients, but when we find that we are staying late every afternoon and working until bedtime, it is time to say no. You can always pick up where you left off the following day." (p. 6)

People skills and communication skills go hand-in-hand and are the focus of *"The Principal Component: Bringing Your Administrator on Board"* by Marla McGhee and Barbara Jansen. This principal-media specialist team provides a wealth of practical advise about building this critical relationship. If you want your principal to recognize you as a member of the school's instructional team, articles by Michael Eisenberg on reading advocacy, Donna Miller on supporting standards-based instruction through the media center, Peggy Milam on models for teaching information literacy, Crystal Barringer and Marilyn Joyce on teaching reading in the media center, and Karen Larsen on differentiated instruction provide you with up-to-the-minute background information on each of these topics. These articles also address the challenges media specialists face when adapting these popular school or district-wide initiatives into the media center program.

# What Should a Teacher Expect a School Library Media Specialist to Be?

## By Carl Harvey II

- **A Library Media Specialist is a teacher.** They work with students in the library media center, the computer lab, and the classroom. They help teach students how to be information literate.

- **A Library Media Specialist is a collaborator.** They work with teachers to plan, intruct, and evaluate student learning.

- **A Library Media Specialist is a resource locator.** They help you find answers to questions and help find resources (all kinds) to support instruction in the classroom. They may not always be able to succeed, but they always try their best.

- **A Library Media Specialist loves literature.** They enjoy sharing great books with students and teachers. They help entice students to have a lifetime love of reading. They have ideas on incorporating great books into a variety of curriculum topics. Share with them the great books you find, too.

- **A Library Media Specialist is technology literate.** They work with students to use technology in the library media center, the computer lab, and the classroom.

- **A Library Media Specialist is a staff developer.** They help teachers learn new technologies and how to use them with students.

- **A Library Media Specialist is an innovator.** They are quick to come up with ideas and are open to new ideas from others, too.

- **A Library Media Specialist is a manager.** With the assistance of many people, the library media specialist makes sure the library media center runs effectively and efficiently.

- **A Library Media Specialist lends a helping hand.** They are always willing to help out when needed even with it isn't their "job." Ask for their help when needed. It makes them happy to be of service

- **A Library Media Specialist is flexible.** They are very willing to make changes when changes need to be made. Although they are planners, they are able to see that sometimes adjustments in plans are necessary.

- **A Library Media Specialist loves to learn.** They love to hear about the great books people are reading and new ideas and strategies for working with students. Share with them the new things you learn, too.

- **But most of all, the Library Media Specialist does not work alone.** For a school to have a successful library media program it takes everyone (the library media specialist, teachers, administration, and the library media staff) working together for the benefit of the students.

---

*Carl A. Harvey II is the library media specialist at North Elementary School in Noblesville, Indiana.*

Harvey, C. (2005). What should a teacher expect a school library media specialist to be? *Library Media Connection*, 23(5), 23.

# Tips For New Librarians

## By Sue Howard

You have just been given your first position as a library media specialist. You are eager to get started and want to do the best job possible. The following tips will help you get started.

- **Find a mentor**. Having a seasoned library media specialist to ask for help when problems arise is a good idea. Your mentor can be a good friend and sounding board, as well as a treasure trove of information.

- **Form a library advisory committee if there is not one already in place.** Ask for volunteers during a faculty meeting. Try to recruit a volunteer from each grade level. This committee includes the administrator, and is the one that works on Children's Book Week and Read Across America activities.

- **Look at the existing library rules and procedures.** If there are changes you need to make, you might want to present them to the library advisory committee. These can be added to the first library newsletter.

- **Prepare a handbook or folder for teachers showing services, collections, policies, and other informational items.** Teachers use this to keep newsletters and other communications from the library.

- **Devise a form for teachers to request books, materials, unit collaborations, and use of the library.** Put these in teachers' boxes throughout the year to remind them to schedule in advance.

- **Ask the curriculum coordinator for extra curriculum guides so you can become familiar with what subjects and units the teachers will be teaching.** Be sure to check the bibliographies at the end of each lesson or unit. If there is not a curriculum coordinator, ask teachers to see their curriculum guides. They are usually happy to share when they know you are interested.

- **Ask if you may participate in grade level meetings**. You will be able to find out what lessons or units teachers are planning, which makes it easier to collaborate on lessons or units of instruction. It will give you a chance to distribute materials, promote the library and its resources, and explain how you are able to assist them.

- **Invite new teachers to an orientation.** Although you are a new library media specialist, you can still make the other new teachers aware of the different media and services that are available. This can be done individually or at a special afternoon meeting. Go exploring together!

- **Promote the library media program.** A good relationship with all clients helps to promote your program. Make the library a pleasant place where people want to come. Make announcements at the faculty meeting. You could also devote an afternoon meeting to library news and business. This could also be tied in to American Education Week or Children's Book Week. Be sure to provide refreshments.

- **Develop a "Professional Library" and keep it current.** Even if you do not have a separate room for the professional collection, you can keep it in a certain area. Purchase professional books, materials, and magazines that will contribute to professional instruction and growth. If you have a separate room, invite teachers to have their meetings there. Keep it attractive with displays of interest. Put in a copy machine, microwave, or whatever it takes to motivate teachers and staff to use the professional library and its resources.

- **Acquire technology skills so that you can plan and implement staff development workshops.** These skills will be needed for project assignments that you will be doing with classes.

- **Get to know students and parents.** During registration and open house, get to know as many parents as possible. Ask for volunteers to assist in the library. Students' behavior is much better when you have developed a partnership with their parents. Take the extra time to get to know the students. It shows you care.

- **Join professional associations.** Go to meetings to learn about new trends in the library and technology field. Get to know your colleagues in other parts of the city, state, and country. Develop a partnership with the local public library.

- **Join a library e-mail list**. You can gain a storehouse of knowledge.

- **Volunteer to take your program to the classroom.** This is especially important in secondary schools, as many teachers only bring their classes for reference projects. You can also make a contribution to study hall. Take advantage of every opportunity to work with teachers.

- **Recognize teachers who have made the library a part of their lessons or units.** This recognition will encourage other teachers to participate. Giving certificates and trophies can be a strong motivator.

- **Familiarize yourself with the collection and the arrangement of the library.** If needed, rearrange the furniture to make it more welcoming and functional. Check the climate: Is it conducive to learning and growth? Make adjustments as needed.

- **Stay focused on the task.** You may not always have adequate time to complete tasks. Relax; sometimes the solution is simple.

- **Connect more with teachers who are positive than teachers who are negative.** Positive teachers are usually the ones who will want you to work and collaborate with them on lessons and units. They are usually ready to get involved in new learning adventures.

- **Remember that attitude is important.** Don't intimidate the teachers, but do speak up. Keep things in perspective. It has been said that laughter is the best medicine. The next time you feel stressed, have a good laugh!

*"Experience is not what happens to a man. It is what a man does with what happens to him."*

—Aldous Huxley

*Sue N. Howard is the library media specialist at Locke Elementary School in Memphis, Tennessee.*

Howard, S. (2004). Tips for new librarians. *Library Media Connection, 23*(3), 17.

# Librarians Behind the Scenes Before the Year Starts

## By Sue Howard

In thinking about the new school year, I always remind myself to keep a sense of humor, be positive, be flexible, get to know the students, and maintain a life outside of the workplace. Many times this is hard to do as we work with many personalities and have so many various duties to perform in a limited time. The following list includes tasks to try to accomplish before classes start:

**1 Update the bulletin boards and displays before students start coming to class.** Summer is a good time to find ideas. Use folders to collect ideas for each month, holiday, or theme. At the beginning of school, put up a welcome board until you find out what themes or units the teachers will be using. Sometimes do displays for these special themes and save the bulletin boards for literature genres or other library skills or promotions.

**2 Set up the calendar and automation system information before entering client names and information.** Library cards can be made and distributed to students.

**3 Have the Acceptable Use Policy ready to distribute to clients.** This policy also can be available for parents to sign during registration. Usually, the return is greater by having it done at this time.

**4 Purge library computers of old data and downloads.** Start the school year off by getting rid of old files that clients have saved or downloaded. Computer disk space fills up quickly and lack of space can be the root of some problems.

**5 Meet with new teachers and students for library orientation.** Set up an orientation time for new teachers and students to tour the library. Give the new teachers a handbook or a library folder with the AV collection, the copyright policy, library rules and procedures, and other informational items. This is a good time to get to know the new students.

**6 Meet with teachers for collaboration on units or themes and participation in reading programs.** I have had more success in meeting with the teachers at grade-level meetings. Information can be gathered about the type of reading program teachers would like to be involved in for the coming year. Special projects for the year, particular reading literature in the units, and author studies can be discussed.

**7 Prepare and enter new materials and equipment into the computer system's database.** This activity might not be possible depending on when your new books and materials arrive. However, the sooner you get this done, the more time you can devote to your program.

> In thinking about the new school year, I always remind myself to keep a sense of humor, be positive, be flexible, get to know the students, and maintain a life outside of the workplace.

**8 Prepare new books and materials for preview.** As new books and materials arrive, find a time for teachers to preview them. Having them available for preview before or after a faculty meeting or a special afternoon meeting with refreshments is a hit with most teachers.

**9 Prepare the first newsletter for teachers, parents, and students to include rules and procedures.** Sending home a newsletter to parents is good public relations and lets them know you care.

**10 Prepare portfolios, folders, etc. for students' work and assessment.** If you are bad about learning names, take a picture of students and put it on the front of their portfolios. Put previous years' work on one side of the portfolio so that you can refer back to grades, etc. When they leave school, they will be very excited about seeing their old school work and pictures. Though this activity is time consuming, it is well worth it.

**11 Establish protocol for entering and leaving the library, library behavior, and other library rules and procedures.** Be consistent. Be sure to check with the teachers as some teachers want students to line up in a certain order.

**12 Work on long term and short term goals and objectives for the school year.** Review previous goals and objectives and adjust them to fit the coming school year. Review the school's improvement plan and the state test scores. Know what it is that you want to accomplish this year and build on it.

**13 Work on the grade book and lesson plan book.** In getting the grade book ready, put all your library skills at the top. By doing this, it is readily available and you don't have to keep referring back to the curriculum book. Use a separate sheet for the Information Literacy Skills. The first week of library can be preplanned if you do a PowerPoint library orientation presentation and a story.

**14 Update the library's Web site.** Change the Calendar, Goals and Objectives, Advisory Committee, Library Club Members, etc. to reflect the current year.

**15 Gather all library forms that you will use.** These will include forms such as the communications log, library use schedule, computer repair forms, etc. and keep them in a prominent place in your **clean** office.

There are other activities that come up from time to time that I try to complete and I'm sure that others could add to the list. However, with the previous activities completed, you can now concentrate on lesson planning and teaching. When other duties or activities come up, make a to-do list that ranks in order of importance or urgency.

With so many roles to fill, being a librarian can sometimes be very stressful. As librarians we try to be all and do all for our clients, but when we find that we are staying late every afternoon and working until bedtime, it is time to say no. You can always pick up where you left off the following day. On days that I feel overwhelmed with the various tasks before me, I close the door at the end of the day. I take a walk, get in the hot tub, do my hair, relax, or go shopping. By doing this I feel I am keeping my life in balance and doing a better job.

Throughout the school year, remember to keep library issues before the faculty, keep the administrator informed of the library's activities, maintain a good working relationship with the administrator and staff, and involve the community in your program.

*Sue N. Howard is a library media specialist at Locke Elementary in Memphis, Tennessee and can be reached at howards@k12tn.net.*

Howard, S. (2004). Librarians behind the scenes before the year starts. *Library Media Connection*, 23(1), 44.

# Essential Documents for School Libraries: Do You Have Them?

## By Colleen MacDonell

Essential documents answer questions and comments that continually arise in school libraries. Ask yourself if you've ever heard the following:

- "This book is filth!"
- "Doesn't a librarian just check out books?"
- "Why are you throwing away these good books?"
- "Tell me, how many books [videos, visits per day] do you have in your library?"
- "I've downloaded five articles. I've finished my research!"
- "I have a paper due tomorrow. Can you help me do a bibliography?"
- "If I think a student plagiarized, what do I do?"
- "Can I check my e-mail?"
- "Shouldn't we have an Internet filter on these computers?"
- "What does the library do for my child?"
- "How did we do that last year?"

Library policies, guides, brochures, procedure sheets, and handouts can come to your aid when administrators want an answer, when students need help, when teachers look to you for advice, and when parents come to visit. If you recognize which documents you need, write them clearly, and promote them well, many potential problems, misunderstandings, and stereotypes can be vitiated before they get out of hand.

If you are lucky, you have a district supervisor who has already done most of this work for you. All you need to do as a teacher-librarian is to have this information ready-to-hand when crucial questions arise and to promote the content of the documents as widely and effectively as possible. More on that in a minute! For those of you who do not have officially approved library documents, you'll need to play a bit of catch-up. Here's how.

## Planning and Writing Essential Documents

As a library administrator in an international school, I have had to plan and write all of our essential documents. This is my "can't live without" list:

**Library Programming** documents justify your very existence in the school. It is *the* answer to the question of what you do as a teacher-librarian to facilitate inquiry-based learning and promotion of reading.

A. Mission Statement
B. Cooperative Planning Policy
C. Internet Acceptable Use Policy
D. Statement on Plagiarism
E. Library Skills Continuum

> *All you need to do as a teacher-librarian is to have this information ready-to-hand when crucial questions arise and to promote the content of the documents as widely and effectively as possible.*

**Collection Development** documents justify the way you spend your money. They give clear guidelines as to what resources are considered necessary to answer the information and pleasure-reading needs of your students and teachers.

A. Collection Development Policy
B. Book Challenge Policy & Procedure
C. Donations Policy & Procedure
D. Weeding Policy & Procedure
E. Budget Formula Guidelines

**Library Rules and Regulations** are clear statements of the responsibilities of anyone who uses the library. Although rules can always be broken or bent when

situations warrant, we can't function without them.

A. Library Borrowing Rules
B. Library Fines
C. Hours of Operation
D. Guidelines for Student Behavior

**Procedures** should be clearly and concisely written on single sheets, for easy use when doing non-routine technical tasks. At our main library, we write up step-by-step instructions for tasks that are not detailed in current user manuals—the sorts of things that involve minute details that are easy to forget if you don't do them often. If you have a high turnover of staff—often the case with volunteers—this can be another reason for writing up some procedures in an easy-to-follow format.

A. Inventory
B. Acquisitions
C. Book Processing

**Planning** documents help remind you of your short-term goals so that they are accomplished in a timely fashion and allow you to sit back to assess your overall progress from time to time. A good strategic plan can be updated periodically for brief presentations to administration and staff.

A. Strategic Plan (2-year)
B. Operational Plan (annual)

**Reporting and Publicity** is where you get to accentuate the positive. Any documents that promote what the library does for administrators, teachers, parents, and even students, should be upbeat, focusing on how the library contributes to the school as a whole.

A. Annual Reports
B. Brochures for Parents
C. Flyers for New Teachers
D. "Quick Picture" Statistics

Teaching documents answer questions that come up in almost every teaching situation in the library. We place our essential teaching handouts in plastic display cases in our libraries. Teachers and students have come to depend on them. As with other documents, they are available through the library website in pdf format, for printing at home.

A. Research Process Handout
B. Fill-in Bibliography Forms
C. In-text Citation How-To
D. Online Searching How-To

Even if you are part of a large school district, it doesn't hurt to ask yourself the same questions that someone without that support must ask:

What documents do you have now?

A. How old are these documents?
B. Have they received official approval?
C. Are they widely circulated?
D. Is the content of these documents already a part of the school culture?

If you are starting from "scratch," seek help. There are many excellent examples of these policies and forms available through school district Web sites, school library associations, teacher-librarian homepages, and library management handbooks. Read as many examples of what others have done and apply these ideas to your particular needs.

Once you have written your own documents, make sure they receive the imprimatur of an official Library Committee, which should include representatives from every group you serve: teachers, students, administrators, library staff, and parents. In fact, all documents should be presented as drafts to your committee so they can help you tailor these policies and guidelines to your school community.

## Promoting and Applying Essential Documents

Many library management handbooks suggest that you collect your policies and procedures in a Library Management Manual (Markuson) or Handbook (Where do I start?). While this is excellent advice, you can't stop there. I have a lovely Library Management Manual. It has every essential document in a neatly classified arrangement. *No one has ever asked to see this document.* And they never will.

If you believe in the content of your essential documents, you will make sure that they don't just gather dust on a shelf, but become living documents which affect real change in the culture and behavior of your school's learners and teachers. For example, you have an approved Statement on Plagiarism and an Internet Use Policy. Have you asked your principal to include it in the student handbook? Do students sign a form saying they have read and understood these documents? Do you refer to them during cooperative lessons? Do you tell new teachers about them? Are they made accessible through your school's Web site?

On the Web, through your Library Committee, in your Student Handbook, in school-wide published policies, in speeches to teachers, in reports to administrators, and in everyday conversations with colleagues and students, you can make this important information a part of your school culture. As the content of these documents becomes common knowledge, you are sure to see a real effect on learning. And you'll notice you haven't heard some of those old questions and comments for a long time.

### Bibliography

Markuson, Carolyn. *Effective Libraries in International Schools.* London: John Catt, 1999.

*Where Do I Start? A School Library Handbook.* Worthington, OH: Linworth, 2001.

*Colleen MacDonell is currently working at the Raha International School in Abu Dhabi and is author of* Project-Based Inquiry Units for Young Children: First Steps to Research for Grades Pre-K-2, *(Linworth Publishing, Inc., 2007) and of* Essential Documents for School Libraries: "I've Got-It" Answers to "I-Need-It-Now" Questions *(Linworth Publishing, Inc., 2005).*

MacDonell, C. (2004). Essential documents for school libraries: Do you have them? *Library Media Connection, 22*(7), 18-19.

# Tools of the Trade:
# Library Schedule & Attendance Statistics Form

*By Jacquie Henry*

## Library Schedule & Attendance Statistics

Today's Date_____

| Period | Classes/Activities |
|---|---|
| Homeroom | |
| 1 | |
| 2 | |
| 3 | |
| 4 | |
| 5 | |
| 6 | |
| 7 | |
| 8 | |
| After School | |

A. _____ # of students using the library media center independently **BEFORE SCHOOL, DURING HOMEROOM, and LUNCH**

B. _____ # of students using the library media center independently during **STUDY HALL PERIODS**

C. _____ # of students using the library media center independently **AFTER SCHOOL**

D. _____ Total # of **STUDENTS** using the library media center **INDEPENDENTLY** (lines A + B + C)

E. _____ # of **CLASSES** in the library media center

F. _____ Total (estimated) # of **STUDENTS IN RESEARCH CLASSES** (line E x 25*) *average # of students per class

G. _____ Grand Total # of **STUDENTS USING THE LIBRARY MEDIA CENTER TODAY** (lines D + F)

*Jacquie Henry is a library media specialist at Ruben A. Cirillo High School, Ganada Central School District, in Walworth, New York, and can be reached at jhenry@gananda.org.*

Henrie, J. (2006). Library schedule & attendance statistics form. *Library Media Connection, 24*(4), 25.

# Tools of the Trade: Copyright Do's and Don'ts

## By Carol Simpson

**DO** make sure that all audiovisual material shown to students is directly related to the curriculum. Be especially aware of film ratings (G, PG, R).

**DO** sign your copyright compliance agreement.

**DO** write the recording date on all videos you record. Consult your librarian to find out how long you can use home-taped video (it varies with the program).

**DO** write the required erase date on all videos you record. This date will vary with the program. See program advertisement or flyer from producer, or calculate fair use date.

**DO** keep receipts and purchase orders for all videos and computer software. Keep the catalog (or pertinent pages) to verify purchase of public performance rights.

**DO** write for permission to retain recordings of useful programs. The worst a copyright holder can do is say no.

**DO** ask the librarian to record programs for you. Requests to record programs must come from a teacher in advance and in writing.

**DO** keep a copy of Kidsnet or Access Learning to verify taping rights from the various networks. Kidsnet also lists supporting materials and addresses where inexpensive copies of nonrecordable programs can be obtained. Both Kidsnet and Access Learning have online counterparts.

**DO** use fast forward on the VCR. Often only a portion of a video will make as effective a point as an entire film. Also, some producers will allow use of excerpts when they will not allow use of an entire program. Write for permission.

**DON'T** show films or videos for reinforcement or reward. Try popcorn and soda parties, games, stickers, or free time. You may rent movies for reward performances, paying a minimal public performance fee, from suppliers such as Movie Licensing USA. Video rental stores cannot authorize you to give public performances.

**DON'T** copy commercial computer software, except to make an archival copy (one that isn't used).

**DON'T** copy cartoon, TV, or film characters for decorations, bulletin boards, or handouts. Purchasing clip art, duplicator books, and bulletin board figures is acceptable, but you may not enlarge, modify, or change the medium (e.g., make slides or coloring sheets).

**DON'T** record programs from cable television without investigating the recording rights first. Only programs recorded off the air (VHF and UHF channels) can be recorded without express permission. Look for this permission in teacher's guides that the various networks and program producers send out. These guides will also tell you the retention rights (e.g., seven days plus fair use, one year, life of tape or disk). Keep a photocopy of the permission with the recording at all times, and make sure there is a copyright notice on each copy.

**DON'T** create anthologies on tape, disk, or the photocopier. Copying an article, poem, or excerpt is fine, but combining them into a new work is not permitted.

**DON'T** apologize for obeying federal law. If you would like a free copy of the law, visit the U.S. Copyright Office Web site for a copy of Circular 92

*Carol Simpson, Ed.D., is an associate professor in the School of Library and Information Sciences at the University of North Texas. She is also editorial director at Linworth Publishing, Inc., and author of Copyright for Schools: A Practical Guide, 4th Edition (Linworth Publishing, Inc., 2005) and Ethics in School Librarianship: A Reader (Linworth Publishing, Inc., 2003).*

Simpson, C. (2006). Copyright do's and don'ts. *Library Media Connection*, 24(6), 45.

# Don't Overdo Worrying about Overdues!

## By Pamela S. Bacon

At the end of the school year, my overdue count was staggering—410 books missing in action (yikes!). Not all of these overdues were mine. (Our circulation system carries over books from the junior high. Much to the dismay of many a senior, the system even includes books long since forgotten from elementary school!) I had to admit, though, the bulk of the overdues were MIA's from our high school library media center shelves. Granted, we have almost 3,000 students . . . but 410 overdues was still a whopping figure, no matter how you looked at it.

The more I thought about it, I realized I could reduce the number of overdues without assessing hefty fines or assigning lifetime detentions—if I was willing to change my entire non-traditional library media specialist philosophy. All I had to do was change every mindset and belief I had about creating and maintaining a positive library media center environment. If I could just make myself follow the 10 tips below . . . I knew my future would hold fewer overdues. But should I be careful what I wished for?

### Tip #1

Whatever you do, do *not* encourage students to check out books—especially high-priced reference books. Work especially hard to keep all shelves completely full. Since shelving books will no longer be a time-consuming task, spend that extra time dusting your precious collection.

### Tip #2

Do not have hours before school, after school, or at lunch—or any other time that might possibly be convenient for students to check out books. Keep students out to keep books in!

### Tip #3

If a student asks for a book you don't have, never offer to order a copy—and don't borrow one from another library. These habits encourage more reading and, as a result, more checkouts.

### Tip #4

No matter the question . . . always say no first. Say yes only when forced to do so. Like the Capital One® commercial, no is always the answer. For those of you who have a difficult time saying no, practice aloud on your way to work.

### Tip #5

Never allow a student to renew a book. Snatch the book back immediately from the eager reader and reshelve carefully (after dusting, of course!).

### Tip #6

Do not, under any condition, agree to sponsor a book club. Talking about books and authors will make students want to read (i.e., check out books) more! If your principal forces you to hold a book club, always hold your meetings at inopportune times. (6:00 a.m. on Monday morning or 5 p.m. on Friday nights have shown to be inconvenient for sleepers and daters).

### Tip #7

Always frown when students come into the library media center. (Thick glasses perched on the end of the nose are also a nice feature if you can manage it.) Students who are intimidated are less likely to approach the counter and, inadvertently, check out a book.

### Tip #8

Practice saying "shhh" with as much resentment as you can manage. If positive noise (or any enjoyable activity) is heard in the vicinity of the library media center, other students may work up the courage to enter (i.e., check out a book).

### Tip #9

Do not allow browsing . . . students may stumble upon an author, book, or (heaven forbid!) an entire series!

### Tip #10

Whenever a student asks for help finding a book, tell him or her without hesitation that it's checked out. If a student can't find a book, then it can't be checked out!

*Note*: Always do the opposite of Tips 1–10 to promote a positive academic climate in which students want to read!

Obviously, you've figured out by now that no practicing library media specialist would ever follow these 10 tips. But the more I thought about it, the more I decided that overdues weren't so bad after all. Didn't the fact that students were reading more than ever (my circulation counts were skyrocketing) make up for the lost books? Were books that were currently overdue making the rounds this summer between friends? I certainly hope so. Sure, overdues still bother me—but, given the alternative, I wouldn't have it any other way!

*Pamela S. Bacon is a part-time freelance writer and full-time library media center director at Ben Davis High School (Indianapolis, Indiana). Bacon is the author of 100 Library Lifesavers, 100 More Library Lifesavers, and Creating Online Courses and Orientations: A Survival Guide (forthcoming) by Libraries Unlimited (www.lu.com). She can be reached at psbacon@aol.com.*

Bacon, P.S. (2005). Don't overdo worrying about overdues! *Library Media Connection*, 24(3), 45.

# Not Enough Time in the Day: Media Specialists, Program Planning, and Time Management, Part I

## By Mary Ann Fitzgerald and Andrea Waldrip

### Introduction

Today media specialists operate in an environment of challenge, controversy, and daily travail. Budgets have been slashed, and programs and personnel are being cut in schools and media centers all over the country. The No Child Left Behind legislation has established new mandates that public school educators are scrambling to fulfill.

Technology continues its rapid advance, and schools must keep pace despite budget decreases. In response, media specialists have added responsibilities to an already long list of daily tasks. In view of these new and continuing challenges, this two-part article revisits the essential task of program planning, incorporating a discussion of time management in light of new priorities. Part I focuses on the systematic creation of a Media Plan. Part II discusses how to keep the Media Plan on track in the face of the realistic challenges faced by media specialists each day.

### No time to think

We could construct a long list of events, tasks, and projects making up a media specialist's typical day, but such a list would consume most of the space for this article. The traditional challenges -equipment maintenance, copyright compliance, collection maintenance, student and teacher assistance, lesson planning, staff development, and many others-remain. This endless list varies from school to school. Further, budget cuts often mean that paraprofessional assistance is cut.

A new and particularly challenging trend makes media specialists responsible for teaching classes, especially in reading, or to hold a spot on the so-called "specials" rotation. In other words, teachers in elementary school are given planning time only through the "babysitting service" of "special" classes such as physical education, music, art, and often "library time." Classes appear at the door like clockwork. No pretense of collaborative planning is made, because this time is the only release time given to teachers for planning. In middle and high school, an emphasis on reading skills or the inability to hire enough qualified teachers often prompts principals and systems to use the media specialist as a classroom teacher.

While we understand that administrators are struggling in desperate circumstances, there is no question that media specialists in these situations must rearrange their priorities significantly in order to accomplish their four intended roles. What media specialist has not wondered on the drive home from school: "How on earth am I supposed to be a program administrator, teacher, instructional

> When the job begins to seem impossible, it's time to reassess priorities and work styles.

consultant, and information specialist all at the same time? When am I going to have time to move our media program toward the goals set forth in *Information Power*? I don't have time to think, much less plan and implement a program based on lofty goals and standards."

These questions are legitimate and troubling. They echo the frustrated struggles of people in many professions today, in which it seems that more productivity is demanded despite reduced resources. In the media center, what can be done to address the struggle of time management? How can a media program make progress in these challenging times? In some cases, how can media programs continue to operate?

### Helpful Tools

When the job begins to seem impossible, it's time to reassess priorities and work styles. Media specialists have several tools available that will help them work through these challenges. These tools include planning, prioritization, and a workflow management system that keeps priorities clearly in front of them at all times. We now turn our attention first to a few reminders about program planning.

We are often dismayed to learn that many school library media programs have no working plan in place. Although most media specialists are well aware of what their job entails, the place to start when making a plan is to revisit what *Information Power* tells us the school library media program mission is supposed to be: "The mission of the library media program is to ensure that students and staff are effective users of ideas and information." It is worthwhile to print this statement in an attractive and eye-catching font and post it as a mantra on the refrigerator or office door. When business really gets crazy, a moment to breathe deeply and reread this mission is in order. This sounds simplistic, but only by keeping the mission in front of our eyes will we be able to establish priorities properly. There are many times when choices must be made in the moment, and keeping the mission in the forefront will help this choice be the proper one.

Furthermore, each library media program should have its own mission statement. This should be *one sentence* that expresses the active mission of this school's library media program. It may be very similar to the one expressed in *Information Power* and should at minimum contain the major idea of promoting information literacy. Some media specialists and media committees find it useful to write out a formal philosophy statement of school library service, and then to condense this philosophy down into a single mission statement. Only after doing this kind of thinking can program planning logically proceed. It is also useful to note all of the tasks performed in a typical day that have nothing to do with the media center mission.

## Steps in Program Planning

### Step 1. Assess the current situation.

A number of stimuli will help you do this. Think about the following:

- In your day-to-day activities, what events frustrate you or even anger you? Carefully collect these events as signals of conditions that need to change.

- Of your current programs, projects, and practices, which really work? Are there any that do not achieve the desired result? It may be necessary to backtrack and consider whether or not the desired result of each project is clearly in view. For example, are the desired outcomes of your Story Time for kindergarten clearly written down somewhere as objectives? If so, are these objectives being met, and how do you know? If the objectives are not being met, then the program should either be revised or scrapped-there is no need to spend your time carrying out an ineffective process!

- How do you spend your time now? Choose between two and five typical days in your media center, and conduct a time study on yourself, and have your staff do the same. Studies show that media specialists often do not spend their time in the ways they think they do, and self-analysis can help you identify time drains. Regardless of what your priorities are supposed to be, the way you choose to spend each moment, or in the way this choice is dictated, indicates where your real priorities are.

- Is student learning prominently represented in your day? How much of your time directly supports student learning and achievement, and of that proportion, how much is spent in teaching the information literacy curriculum you are responsible for?

- How well do your activities and stated mission fit into the mission of your school? Each school should likewise have a mission statement and your school system may have one as well. Your planning priorities should directly reflect the major components in this mission. Make sure that your priorities align with the current political priorities-whatever they are-and use similar vocab-ulary to make this relationship obvious and direct. Use these priorities and accompanying language in all requests and program initiatives.

### Step 2: Set goals.

Based on your assessment, identify goals that are already in place. If old goals need to be abandoned, this is the time to do it. Next, identify new goals.

Start by convening the Media Committee. It is imperative that they have a say in this goal-setting process. When representative committees have input into decisions, all members of the learning community are better served. The committee will help show how your program is seen in relationship to other parts of the school. Groups also are much better at brainstorming than individuals and can generate a greater list of possibilities.

> Choose between two and five typical days in your media center, and conduct a time study on yourself, and have your staff do the same. Studies show that media specialists often do not spend their time in the ways they think they do, and self-analysis can help you identify time drains.

It may not be possible to address all of the tasks identified as possible goals. Identify the most important and set the rest aside for revisiting later, perhaps one year from now. Choose a set of goals that is challenging yet attainable within a given time frame.

Even if you did not consult your media committee to brainstorm goals it is imperative that you obtain their buy-in at the goal adoption stage. Consensus-based goal setting empowers other members of the learning community to participate and have a greater stake in your program. More practically, committee endorsement of library media program goals covers you and dilutes blame if things go wrong. Remember that media committees should be representative of all the school-teachers, parents, students, and administrators. The presence of at least one administrator on the committee helps keep goals within school goals and guidelines, and publicizes your program to a very important group.

*A word about the structure of goals.* Read a standard text on goal-setting, because this is an important activity. Goals should be large targets and may well be vague. They will probably take at least a year to accomplish, and may take more than a year-even three to five years. Goals are useless without objectives spelled out to support them. Unlike goals, these objectives should not be vague-they should clearly describe an observable action, indicate who will carry them out, establish a deadline, and give a measure to indicate success. As you establish each goal, plan how you will evaluate its accomplishment. What evidence will you have to show when a goal has been accomplished? In other words, it is important to be able to know when an objective has been accomplished and can be checked off the list. For example, if your goal is to increase the number of research group visits to the media center, have the children sign in at the door and keep this log as evidence.

*What about the Technology Plan?* Many schools and school systems have formalized Technology Plans. In our opinion, it is most logical and helpful if the Media Plan and Technology Plan are parts of the same integrated plan, generated by a Learning Resources Committee (instead of a Media Committee or a Technology Committee). If this level of collaboration is not possible, then we recommend that media specialists do everything in their power to coordinate the two plans. Find out what the Technology Plan requires and avoid working at cross-purposes. We believe it is time for Media Centers to morph into Learning Resource Centers that incorporate all technologies; keeping print and digital sources of information separate is not progressive. Many times, work is duplicated between the two committees where two exist, or they work in conflict with each other. Turf wars may rage between media specialists and technology coordinators. Take steps to avoid these counter-productive situations.

### Step 3: Make the budget.

Budgets should never be arbitrary wish lists. Arrange your list of goals in order from most to least important. Next, assign a percentage to each one indicating its importance. For example, if the most important goal for next year is to encourage reading in your students, assign a large figure (perhaps 40%) to that goal. Divide the remaining 60% among the other goals. If you have standing encumbrances such as supplies or telecommunication fees, incorporate these into the figures. Keep in mind that some goals may require no dollar expenditures, but instead take up considerable time resources. As you lay out the budget, reference each expenditure item to a goal and underlying objective(s). Be as specific as possible. You should not spend any substantial amount of money on items or activities that are not spelled out in the Media Plan. Each goal and objective should contribute to student learning in some way.

### Step 4: Implement the plan.

This step is easy to describe, but the real work starts here! Implement the Media Plan, tracking progress as you go. Document all accomplishments through photographs, sign-in sheets, circulation reports, artifacts, and any other kinds of relevant evidence. Documentation will add work to your day, but only through it will you able to convince yourself, the Media Committee, and the members of your learning community that you are making progress.

### Step 5: Evaluate.

Documentation will go a long way toward evaluating progress. Read a text on library media program evaluation, such as Everhart's *Evaluating the School Library Media Center: Analysis Techniques and Research Practices* (1998, Libraries Unlimited). Ideally, both the processes of documentation

> *Make sure to publicize and celebrate all accomplished goals, especially those involving learning and students directly.*

and evaluation should be ongoing. However, discipline yourself by scheduling a time on the calendar to conduct formal and informal evaluation, coinciding in a natural way with the endpoints of major goals. Otherwise, the rush of daily activities will completely overwhelm this vital activity. In the goal-planning stage, you indicated what evidence would document each goal. Now is the time to gather and interpret that evidence. Ready sources of evaluation data in media centers include circulation statistics, information about the collection itself from the catalog, surveys of students, faculty, and parents, suggestion box data, and ongoing lists of unfulfilled requests.

### Step 6: Celebrate.

Make sure to publicize and celebrate all accomplished goals, especially those involving learning and students directly. Track them publicly on a bulletin board or Web site. Announce when a goal has been accomplished. Plan parties or staff receptions for major accomplishments.

For more information and detail about the complex process of program planning, we highly recommend AASL's *A Planning Guide For Information Power: Building Partnerships For Learning With School Library Media Program Assessment Rubric For The 21st Century* (1999, ALA).

**Acknowledgment:** We would like to thank Terrie Gribanow for her contributions to this article.

*Mary Ann Fitzgerald is an Associate Professor at The University of Georgia, where she teaches school library media courses.*

*Andrea Waldrip is Media Specialist at West Jackson Intermediate School in Hoschton, Georgia, where she teaches third through fifth grades.*

Fitzgerald, M.A., & Waldrip, A. (2004). Not enough time in the day: Media specialists, program planning and time management, part I. *Library Media Connection, 23*(1), 38-40.

# Not Enough Time in the Day: Media Specialists, Program Planning, and Time Management, Part II

## By Mary Ann Fitzgerald and Andrea Waldrip

### Editor's Introduction

In Part I of this article, authors Mary Ann Fitzgerald and Andrea Waldrip outlined systematic steps to create a Media Plan. Now they provide us with "the rest of the story," discussing how to keep the Media Plan on track in the face of the realistic challenges faced by media specialists each day.

### Prioritizing and Workflow Management: Making it all fit

In Part I of this two-part series, we described how to plan and carry out a media program. Reading that article may have seemed like a flight of fancy to you. You may be thinking: "there is no way that I have time to achieve all of the goals in my plan!"

A sparkling new Media Plan will shift to the bottom of your desk pile when Mr. Jones needs a new overhead lamp, when a video needs to be started in the media retrieval system immediately, when Mrs. Nelson needs *Brown Bear, Brown Bear* within five minutes, and when Suzie squeals that her laboriously read book does not show up in the *Accelerated Reader* test list. How can you keep these kinds of tasks from swamping progress toward goals? First, you need a system for prioritizing tasks, both planned goal-related tasks and tasks that walk in the door in varying degrees of emergency status. Second, you need one or more time management strategies. In this final installment, we describe both of these survival tactics.

### Prioritizing

Retrieve three tools from earlier planning: the mission statement, a list of your goals in priority order, and the Media Plan itself.

1. Construct a Gantt chart (one that plots time across the X-axis and activities along the Y-axis). Plot each goal on this chart over time (weeks or months), indicating when it should start and when it should finish. Be very generous in the amount of time you allow to accomplish each objective, within the overall time frame allotted. It should be possible to see which goals are to be worked on at any given time.

2. Set up goals and objectives as projects. Break projects down into pieces of the smallest possible size. Create a folder (either electronic or paper) to keep all related items together. Keep a list of specific actions to be done in relation to the project, and check off completed tasks as you go. Expect to have three or four projects going simultaneously. Have them set up so that you can

> *Our jobs are unique in that we have a mixture of scheduled tasks (like classes and meetings), a set of planned goals to carry out, normal in-the-minute service requests (like assisting students), but also daily "fires" that erupt and must be extinguished.*

easily shift from task to task and use every five minutes. Some projects might be easy to work on as 10-minute chunks in between students, while others need stretches of 45 minutes or more.

3. At the end of each day, or the very beginning (depending on your energy level and preference), choose daily priorities. Consider the known items on the agenda first, and select a number (perhaps just one) of projects for work.

4. Set up a stack of Action Cards. Different from project action lists, this is the definite set of tasks to accomplish today, including "load the coffee maker," "prepare lesson plan for kindergarten," and "brainstorm three new reading promotion strategies." Cards from multiple projects along with routine tasks will mingle together in this stack. Make one special card that marks the place in the stack of tasks that you need to finish today. There will always be more tasks in the stack than you can possibly do. The special card will encourage you by marking the place where you have achieved a significant amount of work for the day.

5. Finally, place the Action Cards in priority order. "Load the coffee maker" may come first, but once the routine preparations for the day are finished, you can start tackling goal-related items bit by bit as you have time.

### Time management strategies

Many books have been written on time management, and we recommend that you read one like *Getting Things Done* by David Allen (Penguin, 2001). However, few seem to apply directly to the library media context. Our jobs are unique in that we have a mixture of scheduled tasks (like classes and meetings), a set of planned goals to carry out, normal in-the-minute service requests (like assisting students), but also daily "fires" that erupt and must be extinguished. To keep things moving smoothly, you must manage all four of these types of tasks. The following strategies will help:

- Use your Action Cards as your daily organizer. As new tasks come in, write them down and place them in the stack *according to their importance and priority*. If you are in the middle of assisting a student in assembling a set of resources, a teacher's request to laminate something needed for Friday should not interrupt you. As you jot the task on a card, record when it is needed.

Then, return to helping the student. Go about your day, scratching off tasks as you accomplish them. Use your cards to delegate tasks when possible. When you are interrupted, which will be often, the cards will help you re-focus.

- Save time by recycling Action Cards that represent routine tasks. Simply turn them aside or to the back of the stack, ready to be used again the next day. These recycled cards will faithfully remind you to do each routine task.

- Do teachers stop you in the hall asking for services? Don't pressure your memory to keep track of these tasks. Write them down immediately, along with a due date. This procedure will help you feel in control and assure the person who is requesting the service that you won't forget.

- Some media specialists wear aprons with lots of pockets. Not only do these protect your clothes as you crawl beneath tables to hook up equipment, but pockets hold cards and a pencil for jotting notes about new tasks. Carry the little tools that you always seem to need at hand.

- Delegate tasks as often as you can, consciously counteracting the compulsion to do everything yourself. Think of yourself as a project manager. During the planning process, consider which tasks can be done by paraprofessionals, volunteers, and perhaps students as learning activities. If a media center task can teach a child something, try to make this happen. Verley Dotson, media specialist at Greene County High School in Greene County, Georgia, engages two to four student workers per class period. Using occupational learning objectives, she trains them to be reliable assistants. This program is beneficial to all participants - the media specialist receives valuable help, while the students learn how to conduct customer service, run a dedicated computer system, carry out important responsibilities, and manage their time - all transferable workplace skills.

- Set up your media center so that patrons can do as many things as possible for themselves. Usually, it is in their best interest not to have to

wait on you to accomplish something. Think of yourself as an enabler rather than a concierge! Some simple improvements will help: signs to help people locate things; job aid sheets to help people operate equipment, such as the scanner and fax machine; and a Web page that organizes library computers for easy navigation to often-requested services. Note the queries that come up repeatedly and try to design a self-help feature to make the process self-explanatory.

## When you are asked to do something new

For the purposes of community spirit and collaboration, it is probably wise to accomplish as many low-cost, one-time-only services as you can in support of teaching and learning. However, reconsider when a request becomes a standing order or when a new task is

*Delegate tasks as often as you can, consciously counteracting the compulsion to do everything yourself. Think of yourself as a project manager.*

added to your list of responsibilities. Also, do not allow the lack of preparation on the part of a staff member to become an emergency for you. It is one thing to help someone out in a pinch with an educational video to replace an outdoor science activity when it's raining. It is another to find a movie to babysit students because a teacher failed to make a lesson plan for a Friday afternoon.

Sometimes an administrator approaches a media specialist with a request for a new service that represents a long-term standing commitment. You may not have the option of saying no. However, think carefully before you meekly say "yes." If this task harmonizes with your Media Plan or otherwise represents some part of the four media specialist roles as laid out in *Information Power*, then you should probably agree to take on the task - editing the Media Plan if necessary.

However, if the task does not correspond with your Media Plan, or it has nothing to do with the four roles, think carefully. Is the administrator asking you to do this task because no one else is available? It may be in the best interest of the school for you to do the task, but the reverse may instead be true. If so, suggest that the principal find some other person to do it. Your bargaining chip is this: What part of your Media Plan will go unaccomplished if you take on this new job? What part of your job as a media specialist must be given up in order for you to accomplish this new job?

Accepting new responsibilities without this consideration increases the perception that media specialists have nothing to do. Make it clear that you have an ongoing program of goals and expectations that will increase student learning. If you can argue that the new requirement to do bus duty every morning from 7:30 to 8:00 will decrease student learning because no one will open the media center for early students hoping to work on the computer, then the administrator will have to choose. Naturally, you must conduct these negotiations with diplomacy and in an obvious spirit of putting the children's needs above all others.

## When things are seriously wrong

If you find that your media program is dreadfully off course, then a stronger remedy than one year of thoughtful planning and work to reform the program may be needed. For example, let's say you are in the situation of having to be the Story Lady for four hours per day in order for teachers to have planning time. Using half your time this way is likely to seriously impede collaborative planning and other essential tasks that are a part of your job. Yet, teachers desperately need planning time. For the time being, you should use this burden to accomplish as much as you can, according to the information literacy standards. (In other words, do more than tell or read stories. Design lessons that link the students' current content with an information literacy skill in those stories and through other activities as much as you can.) Give this dilemma some thought and put together a package of arguments for a well-planned presentation to the principal. Include:

- An explanation of media specialist roles according to *Information Power.*
- The Media Plan along with a vision of what your media program could do if given a chance.
- Examples of other fine media programs.
- A demonstration of how the plan aligns with the school plan and supports student learning, supported by research showing the value of good school library media programs.
- A list of things you are NOT able to do because you're the Story Lady instead.
- At least one alternative approach to the problem of inadequate teacher planning time (or whatever the problem may be).
- A plan for moving from where you are right now to where you want to be, with examples.

Make an appointment ahead of time. Remember to be brief! Use all of the interpersonal communication skills you can muster. Do not be defensive or angry. Present yourself as a team player, a collaborator, and a professional with vision. Also emphasize your flexibility. You must not whine or complain. Do not expect immediate results - transformation may take several years. Three years is not an unreasonable span for completely overhauling seriously impaired programs.

If a major obstacle is school tradition ("we have always done it this way!") then first try to enlist administrative support for change. As part of your plan for change, include a substantial avenue for working on attitudes. One strategy would be to enlist several key teachers to help you lead the way. After initial success with these key teachers, present the plan to the faculty. Remember that they are

> *In education, change tends to come slowly and at the mandates of higher authority. Program planning for media specialists is an opportunity to be proactive and implement change from the bottom up.*

always being buffeted by new reforms, so make sure to show what's in it for students and for them. Your goal is not to make their jobs more difficult, but to show how their jobs will become easier. Answer questions. Take baby steps to implement your plan. Try not to become frustrated, and remember from the outset that you will never please everyone.

## Conclusion

It is our experience that media specialists, in their desire to serve and be helpful, will tolerate unworkable situations for years with an attitude of martyrdom. Or, when frustration becomes intolerable, they seek out new jobs, leaving behind a legacy of a non-functional media program. In the long run, students suffer from perpetually poor media programs. Even good media programs can be improved, and planning is the key to improvements large and small.

In education, change tends to come slowly and at the mandates of higher authority. Program planning for media specialists is an opportunity to be proactive and implement change from the bottom up. Always remember that your program impacts the entire school. If it is not having this level of impact, then change is imperative.

**Acknowledgment:** We would like to thank Terrie Gribanow for her contributions to this article.

*Mary Ann Fitzgerald is an Associate Professor at The University of Georgia, where she teaches school library media courses.*

*Andrea Waldrip is Media Specialist at West Jackson Intermediate School in Hoschton, Georgia, where she teaches third through fifth grades.*

Fitzgerald, M.A., & Waldrip, A. (2004). Still not enough time in the day: Media specialists, program planning and time management, part II. *Library Media Connection, 23*(2), 26-28.

# Doing the Job Without the Job Doing You In

## By Gail K. Dickinson

It's the closing day of library school. You are one of the lucky ones, with both diploma and job in hand. You are not going to spend your days at the academic reference desk, in the back rooms of technical services, or in the children's room of the public library. You are going to do it all; you are a library media specialist!

The question of exactly *how* you are going to do it all is probably starting to emerge from the first flush of excitement. If your school is like most, there is only one library media center position. More than likely, there will be no one to ask, no one to learn from, and no one to either laugh or cry with who truly understands your work, your mission, and your passion for libraries. You will be the only library professional in your institution.

The library media specialist profession wears many hats, has many hands, and is shod in everything from tennis shoes to chase down classroom teachers for possible integrative activities to high heels to make budget presentations to sensible shoes for working with today's children and youth. There are library media specialists in the latest jeans and those who have worn the same shirtwaist and bowtie since 1972. There are those who walk the halls with students, listening for every child's emotional heartbeat, and those who never leave the library media center and would be happiest if no one entered. Who will you be as a library media specialist?

You already know from library school some things that you should do as a library media specialist, namely collaborate with teachers to integrate information skills instruction with classroom content, encourage reading, teach wise use of technology, and advocate for the library media center program. Maybe what isn't talked about as much is what a library media specialist should *not* do.

## Eight Things Library Media Specialists Do to Lose Friends and Decrease Influence

1. **Complain about working hard**.
   Whether unintended or not, when someone complains about his or her workload, the person may be interpreted as hinting that he or she works harder than anyone else. A teacher's lounge may not take those words lightly. Elementary classroom teachers barely have time for a bathroom break, and secondary teachers usually see over 100 students a day. Sure, there are teachers, including library media specialists, who do next to nothing all day long and seem to breeze through the day. In general, though, teachers in all aspects of school life are hard-working, take work home, and care about what they do. Library media specialists work hard, but they do not have as much student work to grade at home, and they do not receive nor make nearly as many parent phone calls. Remember that the grass is always greener and classroom teachers may think you have the best pasture of all. Show that you work hard; don't talk about it.

2. **Sit in a dark and empty library media center.** Dark means closed. It doesn't matter if it is much cooler that way or if the light will fade the carpet or if the hall gets noisy. Your harried peers in the school community, whether they are classroom teachers, bus drivers, parents, or school administrators, will resent your ability to emerge cool and collected from the library media center castle. Perception is the only reality that we have. Worry when the library media center is empty. Figure out ways to keep students in the library media center, visibly using resources at all times. Make sure that you are visible as well even if you are doing seat work. Stand in the hall as students change classes and hold up the latest magazines or new books as if you were hawking newspapers on a street corner.

3. **Pretend that the school year starts two weeks later than it does for everyone else.** I know that the patron database is not running, the technicians haven't reconnected the wires, and the collection is not ready. Yet classroom teachers have had to walk in the door on the first day of school, knowing that in a matter of minutes they would have 25 smiling, crying, groaning, silly, shining, and surly faces rushing in to meet them. They would like a few weeks of silence as well! The one day that library media specialists will find it easiest to entice classes to the library media center is the first day of school. Worst case scenario: use a two-column notebook to record barcodes of books and patrons to be entered later when the system is up. Ask the teachers to start the year off reading. Encourage classes to come in to get books on Day 1. Show your principal the first day circulation, and discuss the technical obstacles you have had to hurdle to make the students' first day a reading day. You might find a few phone calls may be made on your behalf.

4. **Close the library media center at the times when everyone can use it.** Students in busily scheduled schools are free before school, after school, and at lunch. Classroom teachers are available before school, after school, and at lunch. Administrators are less hamstrung before school and after school. Therefore, logical reasoning would have it that if the library media center were open at all, it certainly should be open before and after school and during student and teacher lunches. This is not a call to martyr yourself for the cause (see #1). But there has to be a way to make the library media center and its resources available to match patron time. If there is another person in the library media center, whether it is a paraprofessional or a partner library media specialist, see if you can stagger

your hours so that one person can come in earlier than the other and leave earlier. Ask the principal, school-based team, and media advisory committee to help you solve this problem. An unacceptable answer is for you to arrive at work under cover of darkness, eat a bite of a sandwich every 15 minutes in between interruptions, and stay until you are the last car in the parking lot. It does mean that you continually talk to others about a way to open the library media center and its resources. This may mean letting go of the keys to the castle and allowing the library media center to be a teacher duty before school, after school, and at lunch. Yes, someone may mess something up. That is the definition of "used" (see #2 and #5).

5. **Care more about the books than about kids reading.** Wash your hands. Never read with food. Sit up straight with the book flat on a table. Practice the correct way to turn a page. Use a bookmark. These and other rules taught to kindergartners place how a book is used far above whether or not it is used. Readers read messily. They read in the tub, on the bus, on the playground, sprawled in a chair, and at the dinner table. They read while they drink, eat, slurp, and spill. They do this because they can't put the book down. This is the goal we should aim for. It's ironic that we preach care of books at the same time that we complain about needing to weed. Books not only need to be used, they need to be used up. They need to be literally read to death. I know that budgets fall far short of replacing books, but I've never seen a library media center that had the dire threat of completely empty shelves come to pass. Wouldn't it be wonderful if the PTA council walked in to their meeting at the library media center and that actually happened? When they asked where all the books were, the library media specialist could say wearily, "They have been all read up." Instead the PTA members hear complaints of how the library media center budget is so small while they see shelves that seem to have too many books still on them. The creation of readers is a dirty business. Our job is to wallow in it!

6. **Impose rules to limit the access of all, rather than work to change the behavior of a few.** Food in the library media center: Students made such a mess we had to stop. Allowing student access to videos: Teachers complained so we had to stop. The above examples show the difficulty in separating the behavior of few from the behavior of many. Most students behave, but some don't—just like the rest of us. There are two ways to create opportunities for changing a situation. One is to enforce structure, hoping that a global rule will solve a problem. Unfortunately, this forces everyone to follow a procedure. If 3 teachers out of 30 are consistently late to work, the principal has solved nothing by forcing teachers to sign in when they arrive. For 27 teachers, this is yet another morning task they will dutifully follow. For the three who were late to begin with, they will ignore the procedure, falsify their arrival time, or blatantly write that they were 15 minutes late. The same is true in the library media center. Most students will be respectful of resources, their peers, and their teachers. Most will be able to do self-checkout of resources consistently, and most will use technology responsibly. We need to deal with the few who choose not to follow our simple rules, rather than create more rules for the masses to follow. Changing a situation by changing behavior is messy, can create conflict, and is time-consuming. Situations can only truly change when the behaviors that caused them are targeted and dealt with fairly, swiftly, and consistently.

7. **Say no first**. "No. No, we can't. No, policy prevents it. No, absolutely not. Well, maybe. We'll see. I don't think so, but I suppose we could try although we tried that before and it didn't work. If I let you, then I would have to let everyone. Well, just this once." And so a "no" becomes a "yes," slowly, painfully, and in the most time-consuming way possible. Rules are made to increase access, not deny it. If you are saying no more than you are saying yes, it's a problem. And if you are overriding a rule every time you are asked to, then eliminate the rule. Rules need to make sense—first and foremost. We can't continually bemoan that children aren't reading at the same time we have limits on resources to be checked out. Obviously, limits exist to prevent overindulgence or enforce safety procedures. Treating books as if they were deep-fried Twinkies would indicate that middle schoolers were reading at such an alarming rate we had to limit them to only two at a time, hence "readobesity" would follow. Teachers have to sign up to bring their class in because if they didn't and arrived at the door and the library media center was full, well . . . come to think of it . . . what would happen if they arrived and the library media center was full? I suppose they could just turn around, march the students back down the hall, and admit they forgot to reserve a space. If there's another class, but there's still room in the library media center, then there's room in the library media center for the unexpected class. Either way, it's not a problem unless we work to make it one.

8. **Allow noninstructional use of the library media center without complaint.** It is tempting for a harried principal searching for space to hold an event to use the large open space in the library media center. Although we may lose the battle, we cannot achieve our goals if students are prevented from using the library media center and its resources. The reasons why library media centers are closed range from testing to meetings to senior pictures and even scheduled health visits such as hearing tests and hepatitis B shots. If possible, maintain normal operations even if a section is cordoned off for special use.

If the library media center must remain silent and undisturbed, then make a written plan for how the library media center services will continue. This is done for two reasons. If the library media specialist is perceived as only having the function of running the library media center, then he or she may be assigned extra duties or even be used as test proctor. Second, it is imperative that the principal understand the effect of closing the library media center on the instructional life of the school. Keep charts to show the dip in circulation and library media center use. Note the instructional opportunities that have to be lost.

Some ways that the library media center can continue to operate is to take carts of books to the hall to check out and return. Treat the library media center as a closed stack, in which the library media center staff will have to retrieve resources for students. Try putting a computer terminal in the hall or in a storage room that opens to the hall so that students and teachers can still research without disturbing the library media center. Go to the classrooms instead of the classes coming to you. This is a great time to do booktalks, poetry readings, or instruction in specific databases that have been distributed to classrooms. And above all, work to find a solution that allows the library media center to stay open. The statistics on library media center use should write the story. Then the story needs to be told.

## A Note about Access

Access to services and resources is the key to lifelong learning. There are four types of access:

### ■ Physical
Students and staff must be physically able to use the library media center and its resources. This means compliance with the issues in the Americans with Disability Act (ADA) such as having wheelchair access for computers, doors that open automatically, and adaptive or assistive technology as needed. It also means shelving books at a height reachable by students or making sure that the library media center's electronic resources are available in the classroom, at home, and possibly other community spaces such as the public library.

### ■ Emotional
Each student and staff member must feel that the library media center is a

welcoming place. The presence of adults has a calming effect on student behavior and is a good model for the use of library media centers. Allowing school support staff to read newspapers and magazines in the library media center on breaks or between shifts sends a positive message to students. Students should be proud of the appearance of the library media center and feel that it has been designed with their interests in mind. Some library media centers are putting in café tables, along with browsing furniture, to capture the mood of a coffeehouse. Elementary library media centers have reading and browsing corners that invite students to be comfortable while reading.

The atmosphere must be welcoming as well. Students and teachers need to feel that the library media center staff likes their job and that they want to be in the library media center. Library media center staff should actively welcome visits from all patrons and be creative in finding ways to make the library media center more inviting to students and staff.

### ■ Intellectual
The use of library media centers must be taught. Students need to know what they can do in a library media center and know how to use the resources. The instruction behind intellectual access to the library media center ranges from whole-class instruction for a collaborative integrated information skills unit to simple displays or signs highlighting new books or magazines. Do students and staff know the resources they can access through the library media center, and does the library media center staff constantly seek ways to open intellectual access to resources for students and staff? The curse of "I didn't know you had this" is a worst-case scenario for library media center use.

### ■ Economic
The only way to never have an overdue book is never to check one out. This shouldn't be the first lesson that we teach students about the library media center. There are stories of library media specialists who even charge teachers overdue fines for resources, thus guaranteeing that a teacher will work hard to avoid that

situation for the following year and will think twice about checking out resources. Asking for donations rather than charging for copies, establishing amnesty days when materials can be returned without penalty, and enforcing a generous forgiveness policy ensures equitable economic access to library media center resources. Some children and some school staff members live a life of disarray. The only purpose resources have is to be used (see #5).

## Turning It Around

For those who seek to become the center of the school, and become directly involved in the achievement, then the Hippocratic Oath for Library Media Specialists should be Do Not Deny Access. There are two possibilities for the power of the library media center. One is the power to say yes, which opens the library media center, its use, and its resources to all students and staff. The other is the power to say no, to close off use, and to eventually make the library media center a useless appendix to the body of the school. It becomes an organ that has lost its function, is no longer central to the school operation, and can be casually snipped off with only a small scar to show that it ever existed.

What kind of library media specialist will you be? Will you be the one to say yes or the one to say no? Will you seek ways to encourage access or allow the existence of policies and procedures to deny it? Will you be the one who greets every day in the library media center as a new experience, or will you be the one who rules with an iron hand to ensure as few students as possible enter?

You have your diploma, your job, and the keys that open the library media center door. Fling it wide open. Let the adventure begin!

*Gail K. Dickinson, Ph.D, is an associate professor in the Department of Educational Curriculum and Instruction, Darden College of Education at Old Dominion University in Norfolk, Virginia. She can be reached at gdickins@odu.edu.*

Dickinson, G.K. (2006). Doing the job without the job doing you in. *Library Media Connection, 24*(5), 20-22.

# The Principal Component: Bringing Your Administrator on Board

## By Marla W. McGhee and Barbara A. Jansen

What administrators know and understand matters when it comes to organizing a school for teaching and learning. When principals and assistant principals discourage the use of practices unfamiliar to them or do not support best practices, they can actually hamper student achievement and professional growth. This is especially true when it comes to the library media center, where front office decisions directly affect program budgets, the master schedule, and your overall role as library media specialist.

On the other hand, when you and your administrators share a philosophy of supported practice, the results can be tremendous. As you probably already know, a series of research findings from around the country have clearly shown that reading scores improve as quality characteristics of the library media center program increase. "When factors such as *program development* (staffing, spending, print and digital titles per student), *information technology* (databases and access to the free Web), *collaboration* (library media specialists planning, teaching, and professionally learning alongside teachers), and *library media center visitations* (number of individual visits per student) rise, so do student performance indicators" (6). Most of these factors are more achievable if administrators and library media specialists are on the same page.

Since you are reading this article, chances are your principal does not support the kind of library media center you envision. Clearly, some aspects of your program and duties, such as programming and literature promotion, supervising staff and volunteers (if you are fortunate enough to have them!), bibliographic instruction, selecting print titles and electronic databases, and the day-to-day administration of the library media center, can function well without the direct involvement of your principal.

Other aspects of the library media center program, however, are best accomplished with specific involvement of the principal, both administratively and instructionally. Our story is proof-positive that when library media specialists and administrators work together, good things happen!

### A Daring Duo

Our partnership began in 1989 at a central Texas elementary school (when Barbara assumed the post of library media specialist at the school where Marla was principal). From that point on, learning at the school was not the same. As a school community, we began to view the library media center program differently as we worked together to learn and apply best practices in the library media center

> When principals and assistant principals discourage the use of practices unfamiliar to them or do not support best practices, they can actually hamper student achievement and professional growth.

program. We viewed planning, co-teaching, and technology differently. Barbara worked alongside teachers and students, facilitating critical thinking, creating meaningful research, and constantly promoting a love of literacy throughout the school. Marla provided strong instructional leadership, allowing for the integration of the library media center program across and into the curriculum—something the school had not experienced under the previous library media specialist (nor had Marla learned in her principal preparation program). We worked together for the benefit of teaching and learning, each supporting programs the other valued.

So, how do you gain the support needed for those areas that result in increased learning and achievement? How do you move toward more promising practices: collaborating with teachers, scheduling for optimal learning, adequately funding for collection development, and appropriate professional appraisal? We offer thoughts on each of these themes from *our* latest collaboration—a text to help principals become more familiar with the role of the library media specialist and library media center program. *The Principal's Guide to a Powerful Library Media Program* was created to help educate principals on areas that require support for success. Based on practical experience, professional literature, and state and national standards for library media centers, this handbook can help your principal (and assistant principals) better understand best practices for the library media center program and help you gain their enthusiastic involvement.

### Collaborating with Teachers

It is not easy to convince some teachers, especially those with many years experience, that by collaborating with you to integrate the critical literacies of information, communication, and technology (ICT) skills into their curriculum, they will increase student learning, achievement, and foster positive attitudes. By working together, time is actually maximized by combining subject area curriculum standards with ICT skills. And, if taught through a consistent information search process, students increase efficiency by applying those skills in a transferable method to learn the subject content. Teachers often view collaboration as an intrusion or "one more thing" that is added to their already full curriculum. Or they may see it as an enrichment activity that is easy to skip when time is short and high-stakes tests are looming.

Getting those reluctant teachers to plan and teach with you will probably require the involvement of your principal. By setting an expectation of meaningful integration of the library media center program into the classroom course of study, the principal demonstrates the value that collaboration adds to teaching and student learning. How can you persuade the principal to set this expectation? Presenting results from the studies mentioned above shows how collaboration increases student learning before giving specific details in the collaboration process and its benefits to students and faculty. Discussing with your principal the reasons for collaboration—combining the expertise of teachers and library media specialists, in addition to curriculum support—will help convince him or her to encourage the practice among the faculty. "Bringing the brightest minds together for the sake of teaching and learning makes good sense. Teaming the library media specialist with the classroom teacher puts the person who is the most knowledgeable about resources and information skills with the person who is the subject-area expert." And, when "taught at time of need, students make connections between the content area objectives and the information search process that facilitates the transfer of the information search process to other subjects" (20).

## Scheduling

Central to collaborating with teachers is a schedule that allows for teaching at point of need in the subject area curriculum. If your principal has the library media center scheduled to provide teachers with a conference period, you need to convince him or her to remove you from that rotation. As you well know, this is easier said than done! Take a positive approach, discussing with your principal the advantages of keeping a flexible schedule. By integrating the library media center program with the content standards, you will help increase learning and achievement. If the library media center program cannot be completely removed from the rotation for teacher conference periods, provide alternatives to the existing schedule as described in *The Principal's Guide* and come armed

with a plan of action. Some alternatives you may consider include having volunteers or paraprofessionals read to classes or simply sit with them while each student reads self-selected books for pleasure, freeing you to plan and teach with faculty as needed.

"By implementing a flexible schedule, teachers and their students will effectively use print and electronic resources, and students will know how a school library can be used. When they move from the elementary school to a middle school and high school with an open-access schedule, they will be more likely to use library materials and services as a natural extension of their educational process" (72).

## Budgeting

When campus leaders allocate funds to various programs and purposes, the library media center program should be included. "Each year the library media

> Getting reluctant teachers to plan and teach with you will probably require the involvement of your principal.

specialist should come to the budget-planning table to present funding needs, explain budget requests, and advocate for a share of available resources" (67). Because school-level administrators and campus colleagues may not be familiar with general library media center needs, you should share funding requirements with your principal and others. As you prepare the annual budget request, keep in mind the following examples of regular yearly expenditures: general supplies, books and periodicals, audiovisual equipment, online subscription reference databases, bookbinding, equipment repairs and cleaning, support agreements for circulation and cataloging software, on-site professional collection, conference registrations and travel, promotional and special reading events, and professional organization membership dues.

*The Principal's Guide* provides two valuable working documents in

the appendix. The Budget Proposal Worksheet offers 12 categories to consider when planning the fiscal proposal. This worksheet also provides three columns to use in organizing the budget request: one for the current year's amount, another for the coming year's request, and a third space for noting the rationale for each requested sum. The other form, the Annual Budget Worksheet, can aid you in keeping track of expenditures throughout the school year, noting allocated amounts for each category as well as totals spent.

## Appraisal

Principals and assistant principals have the important responsibility of appraising staff performance, annually or biannually, for the purpose of contract renewal or extension. As a teacher, your professional performance should be examined with the same school, district, or state appraisal instrument used for the regular instructional faculty. Due to the unique nature of your work as a library media specialist, your appraisal experience should include your library-related tasks such as collaboration with teachers, integrating information and technology skills across the curriculum, collection development, cataloging, and supervision of your paraprofessional staff.

A well-orchestrated, productive appraisal cycle includes a series of steps that may span the entire academic year. These steps are:

- a pre-observation conference to discuss issues and expectations and set goals for the process,
- on-site visits to the instructional setting by your appraiser for in-class data gathering and on-the-job observation, and
- a post-observation or end-of-cycle conference to recap results and findings and clarify any questions.

In the pre-observation conversation, it may be helpful to review your roles and responsibilities with the appraiser early in the process. You can accomplish this by examining your job description or sharing examples of the tasks you are or should be performing. Another tool included in *The Principal's Guide* may be quite useful. The Quality Continuum of Instructional Time for Library Media Specialists offers an overview of how the library media specialist may choose to use his or her time. On the left side of the document is a list of tasks that should most consume your professional time (e.g., collaboration, collection development, literacy program, reader guidance) while on the right side appears the tasks that should get the least amount of time and attention (e.g., collecting fines, managing electronic reading incentive programs).

## Conclusion

A quality library media center program has the potential to impact student learning like no other support program. In fact, the importance should move the library media center program from "support" to "critical" status by its ability to bring those real-world critical information, communication, and technology skills into the more traditional content area curriculum standards. Along with your efforts, the principal is the other critical force to ensure the library media center program takes its appropriate place in the school's course of study. Bringing the administrator on board may be your most important challenge, but it will be well worth the effort!

## Work Cited

McGhee, Marla W., and Barbara A. Jansen. *The Principal's Guide to a Powerful Library Media Program.* Worthington, Ohio: Linworth Publishing Inc., 2005.

*Marla W. McGhee is an assistant professor at Texas State University–San Marcos. Barbara A. Jansen is the library media specialist and technology coordinator at Saint Andrew's Episcopal High School in Austin, Texas.*

McGhee, M.W., & Jansen, B.A. (2006). The principal component: Bringing your administrator on board. *Library Media Connection, 24*(4), 34-35.

# Reading Advocacy: Creating Contagious Enthusiasm for Books and Reading K-12

## By Michael B. Eisenberg

What's this? Mike Eisenberg is writing an article on books, literature and reading? Is this that Mike Eisenberg? You know, Big6 Mike Eisenberg? Is it information technology (IT) Mike Eisenberg and the Mike Eisenberg who writes about library media program management and planning? What's going on? Has Mike finally seen the light?

Well yes, it is that same Mike Eisenberg, and no, Mike hasn't finally seen the light because he always saw it. It's a little known fact that as a building-level library media specialist in the 1970s, Mike wrote his very first article for publication—and it was on the topic of booktalking for teens (Eisenberg, 1978). Furthermore, for many years, one of Mike's mainstay teaching assignments at Syracuse University was "Media for Young Adults."

So, don't turn the page; read on and see what Mike has to say in this first of three articles on the roles of the 21st century teacher-librarian.

—Carol Simpson

## Introduction: The Mission and Roles of Library Media Programs and Teacher-Librarians

To me, it's really quite simple: it all stems from the mission statement of the library media program from *Information Power*:

"The mission of the library media program is to ensure that students . . . are effective users of ideas and information." (AASL/AECT, 1988, 1998)

Read this statement carefully a couple of times. Turn it over in your mind and think about what it means and the implications for library media programs and the professionals who run them, teacher-librarians (aka library media specialists).

What I like best about this mission statement is that it's bold and ambitious "the mission . . . is to ensure." Wow, that's powerful. No wishy-washy-ness here. We're not talking about facilitating, helping, guiding, encouraging, or assisting. Library media programs and teacher-librarians need to step up to the plate.

And, what is it that we are ensuring? We are ensuring that students are effective users of two things: ideas and information.

Let's start with the latter, "effective users of information," because it's straightforward in terms of implications for library media programs and teacher-librarians. Ensuring that students are effective users of information calls for the library media program to fulfill a teaching role. Teacher-librarians have a clear instructional mandate to ensure that all students gain the requisite knowledge and skills in order to use information and technology effectively.

> It is through books and reading that students become effective users of ideas. Library media programs enrich curriculum through literature and motivate students through reading promotion activities.

While the next article in this series will focus on the teaching role and how to fulfill this role in more depth, let me point out a few key aspects here. First, the charge is to teach all essential information and technology skills. We're not just talking about "library skills" or even "research skills." Students must learn to use the full range of information problem-solving skills. Bob Berkowitz and I have explained these in terms of the Big6 approach, but others have done so as well (e.g., Kuhlthau, 1993; Pappas, 2001). Second, students should be able to apply information and technology skills across situations, not simply write papers or reports or projects. *Information Power* doesn't say, "ensure that students are effective users of information for papers and reports." It doesn't even say "in school" or "in the library." This broadens the scope of the charge to library media programs and professionals. We must ensure that students are effective across settings— after-school, home, recreation—as well as library and classroom.

Lastly, we know that the most effective way to implement the information and technology skills instruction program is through integration with subject area curriculum and through collaboration with classroom teachers, or, information in context. But, let's not forget that this is a *means*, not an end. The ultimate measure of success of the library media program is not the degree to which there is collaboration with classroom teachers; it's whether or not students are effective users of information.

OK, enough on information and technology teaching for now. Let's back up to the other part of the mission statement: to ensure that students are effective users of *ideas*. Again, if you consider this statement carefully, you'll realize that it too is bold, broad, and ambitious. Certainly, one could say that the role of every teacher, regardless of setting or specialization, is to ensure that students are effective users of ideas. But, I think the statement makes a very unique and powerful connection for teacher-librarians because it directly relates to our traditional efforts to promote books and reading. That's because it is through books and reading that students become effective users of ideas. Library media programs enrich curriculum through literature and motivate students through reading promotion activities.

## Reading Advocacy: Bold and Active

Take a moment and ponder "books." What is it about books that is so special and unique? Through books, students travel beyond their own environment, across our world as well as to worlds beyond. The book is the original virtual reality technology. Books challenge students to think and to imagine, to wrestle with ideas, and to dream. Our goal as teacher-librarians is to get kids excited about reading, books, and media for two major reasons: (1) reading is the baseline skill for success in all human endeavor, and (2) through reading students learn, grow, and develop.

Reading proficiency is widely recognized as the No. 1 predictor of student success. From *The Power of Reading: Insights from the Research* by Stephen Krashen: "in-school free reading programs [or voluntary reading] are consistently effective. In 39 out of 41 comparisons (93 percent), readers do as well or better than students who were engaged in traditional language arts programs" (pp. 3). "The California Assessment Program (CAP) reported a clear positive relationship between the amount eighth graders said they read per day and their scores on the CAP test of English and Language Arts. These tests cover reading comprehension; both "basic skills" and "critical thinking"; as well as writing (punctuation, word choice, sentence style, paragraph development)" (pp. 6). This is also included in the "independent learner" part of the *Information Power* standards for student learning that states "[t]he student who is an independent learner is information literate and appreciates literature and other creative expressions of information."

As noted by Cullinan (2000), many teachers of language arts, recognizing the value of independent reading, immerse students in real literature from their earliest encounters with print and establish sustained silent reading time in their classrooms. Cullinan, citing Anderson, Fielding, and Wilson (1988), says students who begin reading a book in school are more likely to continue to read outside of school than students who do not begin a book in school. However, research also suggests that some teachers are not knowledgeable about children's literature; they are not able to introduce students to the wealth of books available, and they may not rec-

ognize the effects of their teaching methods on students' attitudes toward reading (Short and Pierce, 1990).

Clearly, a key role for the library media program and teacher-librarian is to advocate books and reading. And, not just for K-8. The mission doesn't stop at the high school doors. The implementation may change, but the role remains the same.

Regardless of grade level, reading advocacy is not an easy task today. Students face lots of distractions including television, computer games, movies, the Web, e-mail, and instant messaging. There are also sports, family, hobbies, and, oh, yes, school. That's right, school too can be a distraction from books and reading because it gobbles up time, effort, and energy. Just ask high school students about how much time they have to read and why they don't read more. They'll tell you it's because they're so busy, and part of that is the busyness of school. And, while we are concerned about shortened attention spans in the classroom, our society seems to be encouraging "multi-processing" jug-

gling a number of things at the same time. All of these make the task of promoting reading difficult, but more important than ever.

So, if teacher-librarians are serious about the reading advocacy role, they need to get organized and active. Passive reading guidance when students ask for help just won't cut it. And, simply providing reading appreciation opportunities isn't enough either.

Teacher-librarians need to capture students' imaginations. We need to understand and apply all the tools of student motivation. One of the most effective motivation approaches is the ARCS model, developed by Keller (1987) and applied to the library and information science field by Small (1997) <http://www.ed.gov/databases/ERIC_Digests/ed409895.html> and one of her students, Chemotti (1992). ARCS stands for **A**ttention, **R**elevance, **C**onfidence, and **S**atisfaction, and these four criteria can be applied to any learning situation:

- Attention means gaining and sustaining students' attention. This

## FIGURE 1: FORMAL READING/MEDIA ACTIVITIES

*Note:* This is only a partial list of reading advocacy actions. It is not meant to be comprehensive or selective in terms of best or recommended actions.

### Formal Reading/Media Activities

- Reading clubs
- Reading contests
- Everyone reads the same book
- Storytelling
- Booktalking
- Special reading program (e.g., Accelerated Reader)
- Write a diary as a book character
- Theme-based group reading, e.g., "Climb the Glass Hill" Reading Club, based on reading Scandinavian folktales
- Skits based on books
- Puppet shows based on folktales, fairy tales

- "Researchers Incorporated," choose a topic and read to answer questions and receive a "Researchers Incorporated" card or badge
- Poetry Club to memorize a poem a month (voluntary)
- Reading "contests," e.g., challenge a teacher to read a set number of pages or books (Never based on time because it penalizes slower readers)
- Trivia based on novels

### Resources and Facilities Provision

- Special reading or media area
- Displays targeted to specific needs or assignments
- Unique collections

### Informal Reading/Media Activities

- One-on-one guidance
- Peer reading advisory service
- Collecting and sharing student reviews

requires getting students excited, and equally important, keeping their attention over time. This is a definite challenge considering shrinking attention spans. Reading advocacy activities that focus on attention include reading contests, "everyone read the same book" programs, booktalking, and storytelling.

- Relevance means directly relating to the students' needs and interests—either school or personal. Relevance is not always apparent, so teacher-librarians can work to make the connection between a reading activity and the student. Booktalking that focuses on books for school assignments is an effective technique for highlighting books relevant to school interests (more on this in the next section). Booktalking or storytelling can also easily be targeted to personal interests.

- Confidence refers to making sure that the students are comfortable with the level of information being presented. First, can they "get it?" Is the presentation or language too sophisticated? Are they able to understand and respond appropriately to what's being presented? Conversely, is the material or approach too simplistic for them? For reading advocacy activities, this means making sure that the books or media presented are at the students' level and also that the students have confidence that they can attain what is being encouraged (e.g., reading a book a week for the next month).

- Satisfaction is a summative criteria that focuses on how the students feel about the reading activity. Was the experience satisfying and was it worth the time and effort devoted to it? Satisfaction is based on both the content of the reading activity as well as the approach.

Motivation as reflected by ARCS should be a prime consideration when deciding on which reading advocacy options to employ (see Figure 1). Being able to respond affirmatively to each of the ARCS criteria will ensure a successful reading advocacy activity. That is, you are guaranteed success if you can say, "yes, the activity grabbed students' attention, was clearly relevant, was at their level of comfort and

confidence, and was ultimately satisfying to the students."

All these options seek to motivate and guide students to read. The purpose is to get students focused on reading and to keep their interest. My favorite technique is booktalking, which can take many different forms. The next section focuses on one style of booktalking, mine.

## Booktalking Eisenberg Style

In one of my past lives, I had the good fortune to be a high school teacher-librarian in a school of 1,500 students. As you can imagine, we built a program that stressed information-skills instruction fully integrated with the subject area curriculum. In one of our library media program planning sessions, we lamented that the fiction collection seemed under-utilized; the students didn't seem to be reading very much—especially for pleasure.

So, we decided that promoting reading and books would be a major goal for the year. We started talking to teachers, particularly those in the English Department, and found that students did have a substantial number of outside reading assignments. Ah ha! Clearly, an opportunity. What if we implemented a booktalking program—one where we targeted our talks about books to specific assignments requiring outside reading?

While we didn't know it then, we were analyzing the need and opportunity from the ARCS perspective. The assignment was the relevance part of ARCS, as many students have a specific need for selecting books for reading. Our challenge then was to grab their attention, match books to their confidence level, and provide a satisfying experience.

So, we surveyed the English Department for specific assignments and scheduled booktalks. After a few of these we hit our groove in terms of structure and format:

- A 20-30 minute booktalk in the classroom.

- Linked to a specific assignment, which was explained and discussed at the beginning of the booktalk, and made sure that we were on the same page as the classroom teacher.

- Selected 15-20 books (or media, if

acceptable) that met the criteria of the assignment.

- Talked briefly (2-4 minutes) about each book:
  - Talked about something special about the book. This could be the plot, characters, author, setting, the link to something the students are familiar with (e.g., a television show, current event).
  - Made the link between the book and the assignment.
  - If I was actually unfamiliar with the book, I would say so while explaining why I selected the book (e.g., from a review, familiar with the author, recommendation from someone else, nice cover).
  - If I hadn't read the book, I would say so as it is critical to be straightforward and honest with the students.
  - Students could sign out a book on the spot. In fact, as soon as a student indicated that they wanted a book, I would stop talking and give it to them. Usually, for the first few books, there were no takers so I passed the books around but they rarely made it around the room. Later in the talk, sometimes all I had to do was hold up a book and a student would want it.

- Set up a display of additional books relevant to the assignment in the library media center.

Again, we found that we could easily cover 15 to 20 books in 30 minutes. Because there were usually more students than 20, that created demand and kept their attention. We stressed that if they hadn't selected a book, there were more on display in the library media center and we were available for additional assistance.

This high school booktalking program really took off! We started with a few teachers in the English Department and it quickly spread to almost all teachers in the department. We then surveyed other departments to see who was or might be able to require students to read outside materials. We found opportunities throughout the school including:

- A social studies teacher who was interested in teaching concepts (e.g., exploration, conflict, war, social welfare) through literature. We jointly planned an assignment and a reading list matching the concepts.

- Two art teachers who were interested in having students read biographies of famous artists. We were able to get full classes interested in Time-Life and other series on artists.
- Coaches who wanted physical education students as well as sports team members to read books about the nuances of a sport, personal fitness, or overcoming challenges.
- The reading specialist who wanted to introduce high interest books-on-tape to students needing special assistance.

Although not required for the booktalk experience, we delivered these booktalks in the classroom because it dramatically extended the library media program throughout the school and also allowed the library media facility to be used for other needs. We arranged for two teachers per period to be scheduled into the library media center to provide supervision, even when a teacher-librarian was available.

At the peak of the program, we averaged one booktalk per day for 180 booktalks in one year. Later, we scaled back a bit because students now knew about us and were able to be given an assignment and directed to the library media center for books on display and one-on-one guidance.

## Ensuring Success and Recognition through Systematic Planning and Documentation

The importance of reading advocacy mandates that teacher-librarians carefully plan and document the full scope of the reading advocacy function of the library media program. I recommend that you systematically plan and document in the following ways:

1. Work with administrators and key teachers in the school (preferably through a building-level planning team if it exists) to determine what is already taking place in the school in terms of reading programs. It is important to determine a baseline, as it is crucial that the reading advocacy actions of the library media program fully integrate with those of the classroom and the reading program.

2. Work with this same group of administrators and key teachers to establish priorities for the nature and scope of the reading advocacy actions of the library media program. Time and effort are limited. Where is the greatest need for library media involvement and what program actions are likely to have the most impact?

3. Plan the reading advocacy program in advance (e.g., monthly, every 10 weeks, or by marking period) by matching classroom and curriculum need to formal reading advocacy activities as much as possible. Document these plans on a chart.

4. Update the chart each week to document what was accomplished and what actually took place. Library media programs have too few output measures of performance. The completed chart is a firm record of the extent of the reading advocacy program.

5. Provide a brief report to the principal, as well as the group of administrators and key teachers every marking period on the reading advocacy program. Briefly review the goals and objectives, describe what the chart shows in terms of activity, outline plans for the next marking period, and raise any issues or concerns.

This approach will raise awareness of the library media program and teacher-librarian role in promoting reading in your school. It also will provide opportunities for buy-in by administrators and teachers and facilitate careful analysis and planning. This is crucial in order to coordinate the library media efforts with others and to maximize impact of time and effort allocated to reading advocacy.

## Summary

Reading advocacy is an important and fundamental function of the library media program and the role of the teacher-librarian. However, today's demands on schools and library media programs call for a more highly active and engaged reading advocacy program than ever before. The nature and extent of the reading advocacy program, as well as the time and effort allocated, should be directly tied to the needs and situation of the school. Teacher-librarians can facilitate this by involving key administrators and teachers in the decision-making process, as well as by systematically planning and documenting the reading advocacy program.

### Bibliography

Chemotti, J.T. (June 1992). "From nuclear arms to Hershey's kisses: Strategies for motivating students." *School Library Media Activities Monthly*, 8(10), 34-36.

Cullinan, B.E. (2000). "Independent Reading and School Achievement." *School Library Media Research Online*, Vol. 3. http://www.ala.org/aasl/SLMR/vol3/independent/independent.html

Eisenberg and Miller (September 2002). "This man wants to change your job." *School Library Journal*, 48(9), 46-52.

Keller, J.M. (October 1987). "Strategies for stimulating the motivation to learn." *Performance and Instruction*, 26(8), 1-7.

Kuhlthau, C.C. (Fall 1993). "Implementing a Process Approach to Information Skills: A Study Identifying Indicators of Success in Library Media Programs." *School Library Media Quarterly*; Vol. 22, n1, 11-18.

Pappas, M.L. (October 2001). "Teaching Information Skills: Perspective." *School Library Media Activities Monthly*, Vol. 18, n2, 25-28.

Small, Ruth V. (1997). "Motivation in Instructional Design." *ERIC Digest*, ED409895. ERIC Clearinghouse on Information and Technology Syracuse, New York. www.ed.gov/databases/ERIC_Digests/ed409895.html .

*Mike Eisenberg is Dean Emeritus and Professor in the Information School of the University of Washington. Prior to his role as Dean, Mike Eisenberg worked for many years as Professor of Information Studies at Syracuse University and as Director of the Information Institute of Syracuse (including the ERIC Clearinghouse on Information & Technology, AskERIC, and GEM).*

Eisenberg, M. (2003). Reading advocacy: Creating contagious enthusiasm for books and reading K-12. *Library Media Connection*, 21(5), 22-27.

# Integrating Library Programs Into the Curriculum: Student Learning Is the Bottom Line

## By Donna Miller

Those who have been in education for any number of years can readily testify that educational trends come and go as quickly as the seasons, and many times, they make less sense. Most of us can identify with the phrase "this year's new thing." As a result, we're suspicious of the latest educational innovation. Before we embark on the next journey of change, educators expect — no, we demand — to know what makes the new idea better than the tried and true. In addition to other on-going changes, the current emphasis on standards and standardized testing makes it imperative for educators to create learning environments that are both efficient and effective. Thus, our library programs must offer resources and services that align with and support required curriculum to positively impact student learning. One sound approach to creating such a learning environment is implementing a fully integrated library program. The time is ripe for this philosophy to be embraced as we meet the mandate to incorporate standards into all learning environments to prepare students to take standardized tests that are regarded as the major measure of learning in most states and districts.

Audrey Church, in her book *Leverage Your Library Program to Raise Test Scores: A Guide for Library Media Specialists, Principals, Teachers, and Parents* (Linworth, 2003) states that the best way to achieve the dual goals of helping students perform well on standards-based tests and producing independent, lifelong learners is to create a library program in which the library media specialist collaboratively partners with teachers in " . . . relevant, authentic instruction." (34) In addition, one of the roles for library media specialists mandated in *Information Power* (ALA/AECT, 1998), that of a full instructional partner with teachers, is clarified. "As instructional partner, the library media specialist joins with teachers and others to identify links across student information needs, curriculum content, learning outcomes, and a wide variety of print, nonprint, and electronic information resources." (4) A fully integrated library program meets these requirements and provides just such an environment to foster this partnership between teachers and library media specialists.

The question arises, "What is a fully integrated library program?" Consider the following definition. A fully integrated library program is one in which

- Teachers and library media specialists plan together to develop instructional units. (The program works for grades K-12.)

> The current emphasis on standards and standardized testing makes it imperative for educators to create learning environments that are both efficient and effective.

- Library and information skills taught are standards-based.
- Students practice direct, hands-on application of information skills and research processes.
- Library use is based on need rather than on a rigid schedule.
- The library becomes an extension of the classroom, with some projects taking place in the classroom and others taking place in the library as appropriate.
- All team members within the school provide reading guidance and motivation.

## How Does It Work?

Just as the "what" is straightforward, so is the "how" for implementing an integrated library program. The program works as follows.

- Library media specialists and grade-level or subject area teachers meet to brainstorm, plan, and teach units and lessons, many of which can be interdisciplinary.
- The library media specialist gathers and presents to teachers library and information resources and other materials to be used within the units and lessons.
- Teachers and the library media specialists develop a schedule of library visits in which students are served on an as-needed basis to complete projects and assignments.
- Standards-based inquiry-focused learning events are planned in which students become active participants.
- Teachers and the library media specialist teach units and lessons using the library's resources as well as other learning materials.
- The library media specialist and teachers evaluate units and assess student learning so that future units and lessons can be refined and modified as needed.

The model described above results in exciting, interactive learning experiences for students that result in improved achievement. With teachers and library media specialists partnering to plan and deliver standards-based lessons that incorporate a wide variety of resources and projects, the library becomes a critical factor in the overall educational experiences of students. Thus, the library's use is no longer driven by the school's schedule but instead is a center of learning used on a just-in-time basis!

## What Does It Look Like?

Below is a sample third grade unit.
**NOTE:** for elementary students, "task cards" provide specific instructions to guide them through the research process. Older students will not need such detailed instructions, as they should be more fluent in conducting research. Since most state and local standards are derived from national standards, the unit incorporates national standards from the following organizations, the text of which can be found on the Web sites of the organizations:

National Council of Teachers of English – NCTE
http://www.ncte.org/about/over/standards/110846.htm

National Council of Teachers of Mathematics – NCTM
www.nctm.org/standards/standards.htm

National Science Education Standards (created by the National Science Teachers' Association and now owned by National Academy Press) - NSES
http://books.nap.edu/html.nses/

National Center for History in the Schools – NCHS
http://www.sscnet.ucla.edu/nchs/standards/

National Geographic Society's Standards – NGS
http://www.nationalgeographic.com.xp editions/standards/matrix.html

International Society for Technology in Education's Standards for Students – ISTE
www.iste.org

AASL/AECT's Information Literacy Standards for Student Learning from *Information Power* – AASL
www.ala.org/aasl/ip_nine.html

## Third Grade Endangered Animals Unit

### Standards addressed:
NCTE: 1,3,4,5,6,7,8,11,12
NCTM: 1,5,10
NSES: C,F
NCHS: 7
NGS: 1,4,8,14,17,18
ISTE: 1,3,4,5,6
AASL: 1,2,3,5,6,7,8,9

### Prior to Week 1

*Objectives*
Develop enthusiasm for the unit.

---

> **Task Card** — **Let's Find Out About The Grasslands**
>
> 1. Using the *World Book Encyclopedia* online at one of the library computers, look up the word "grasslands." Find the average summer and winter temperatures for this region. Make a bar graph showing both of these temperatures on the paper at your table.
>
> 2. Use the computer to search the World Wide Web for grasslands and use Encarta online at <http://encarta.msn.com> to find as many different plants as you can that are found in the grassland regions. Make a list of these plants. Write the names of the plants that your animal eats on the chart paper provided at your table.
>
> 3. Using all of the above resources, list as many reasons as you can find for your animal's endangerment. Place these reasons on your chart paper in the right column.

Emphasize the importance of the topic, its relevance, and its place in the curriculum.

Develop interest by showing an example of a finished product for the unit (student made books).

*Time Frame*
One, 45-minute library visit

*Procedure*
Read to the class the book *And Then There Was One* (Little, Brown, and Co., 1993) by Marjory Facklam, stressing the importance of protecting animals from extinction so that nature remains balanced.

Assign students to an ecosystem (arctic, desert, forest, wetland, grassland, mountain), about which they will conduct research throughout the unit.

### Week 1

*Objectives*
Learn to use various maps in an atlas to find the location, topography, and climate of assigned ecosystems.

Use indexes and tables of contents of nonfiction books, as well as reference sources such as encyclopedias to find and incorporate information about assigned ecosystems.

*Time frame*
Two, 45-minute library visits

*Procedure*
Develop six centers, one for each ecosystem. Place task cards at each center to direct the students to the information needed. At each center, place a list of animals representative

---

> **Task Card** — **Guide for Observing Your Animal**
>
> Using the nonfiction books at your table, the *World Book Encyclopedia,* and the Web site for endangered animals at <http://eelink.net/EndSpp/specieshighlights-mainpage.html>, locate the following information about your animal, and record it on your response sheet.
>
> **Physical Appearance**
> - Body texture of your animal
> - Color
> - Weight at birth
> - Weight at adulthood
> - Life expectancy
>
> **Habits**
> - How does your animal move?
> - What does it like to eat?
> - Where does it live?
> - Does it communicate through movement? How?
> - How and when does it rest?
> - How does it defend itself?
> - Is this animal used by man? If so, how (for food, for clothing, pets, transportation)?
> - Is the animal independent, or does it live with a group of animals?
> - Look for any other information that you find interesting about your animal and write it on your response sheet.

1. Using the *World Book Encyclopedia* online, the *EBSCO Searchasaurus* database, and the nonfiction books on your table, take notes on the primary producers, primary consumer, secondary consumers, and third consumers of the plants and your animal of the wetland habitat. Put your notes on the information chart at your table.

2. Create a living pyramid for your endangered wetland animal to include the animals in each group listed above. Use the paper at your table to create your pyramid. Be sure to label each level of the pyramid, draw pictures of the animals, and put the animals' names underneath each one.

of the endangered animals of that particular ecosystem. Let students select which animal they want to study. Once students have conducted research about their ecosystem's features, ask students to determine the reasons why their chosen animal is endangered based on the information they find about the location, topography, and climate of their ecosystem. Students will stay in their designated center the entire time, becoming experts on their ecosystem. Provide a chart for each group with a column labeled "Foods of the _____ Region" and one labeled "Why the _____ is Endangered"

**NOTE:** A list of endangered species within the United States can be found at <http://endangered.fws.gov/>.

After returning to the classroom, each group of students will give oral reports about their ecosystem.

**NOTE:** This unit is particularly suited for the Big6 information problem-solving model. Students can follow the steps in the Big6 to discover why their animal is endangered and complete their reports.

Online resources will vary depending upon availability.

Following is a sample task card for the grasslands ecosystem center.

### Week 2

*Objectives*
Learn to use various kinds of maps to find information about the animals of each ecosystem.

Use indexes and tables of contents in nonfiction books and encyclopedias to locate information about the animals.

*Time frame*
Two, 45-minute library visits

*Procedure*
Using the same six centers as before, have groups use the Guide For Observing Your Animal task card at each center to answer questions about the animal they have selected.

### Week 3

*Objectives*
Use indexes and tables of contents of nonfiction books to find information about the food chain of an animal.

Use the online encyclopedia and reference database to find information about the food chain of an animal.

Take notes using the information found in all resources.

Synthesize the information by creating a living pyramid using the information found.

*Time frame*
Two, one-hour library visits

*Procedure*
Student groups will use the same ecosystems as before. Tell them that after taking notes on the food chain of their animals, they will build a living pyramid to indicate the third consumer, secondary consumer, primary consumer, and primary producers. Computer generated charts (or

hand written ones) with the previous headings will need to be prepared and placed at each center on which students will write their notes. Following is a sample task card for a wetland animal. Other task cards will follow this pattern. Online resources will vary depending upon availability.

### Week 4

*Objective*
Use nonfiction books, *Zoobooks* (or other magazines), print encyclopedias, online encyclopedias and databases, and other reference sources to find more information about endangered animals.

Design a brochure to convince consumers about the importance of saving a specific endangered animal.

*Time frame*
Two, 1-hour library visits

*Procedure*
Each group will use all resources available to tell how to help their endangered animal recover. Students will go to the same centers as before and, using the resources, will look for animals in their region/ecosystem that have begun to recover and what is being done to help them. Students will discuss and brainstorm in their groups ways we can help endangered animals to recover.

*Donna Miller is Library Media Coordinator for the Mesa County Valley School District in Grand Junction, CO and is author of* The Standards-Based Integrated Library: A Collaborative Approach for Aligning the Library Program with the Classroom Curriculum, 2nd Edition *(Linworth Publishing, Inc. 2004) and and co-author with Karen Larsen of* Day by Day: Professional Journaling for Library Media Specialists *(Linworth Publishing, Inc. 2003).*

Miller, D. (2004). Integrating library programs into the curriculum: Student learning is the bottom line. *Library Media Connection*, 22(7), 34-36.

Since people have become concerned about what is happening to wildlife, many people, governments, and other organizations have tried to help save them. Using all of the

resources you have used before for this unit, locate the following information and record it on your response sheet.

# Destination Information: A Road Map for the

## By Peggy Milam

Pitts (1995
Libra

With the current emphasis on standards-based curriculum and student performance indicators, students need to demonstrate competency with information literacy skills. Many information literacy models exist, but which one is best for your students? The process of developing a research question, searching for information, organizing the information, and sharing and evaluating the results is comparable to a journey; arriving at the desired destination can be daunting for students, especially if they encounter roadblocks along the way. A road map outlining various models for information literacy skills instruction allows teachers and media specialists to compare and contrast the features of each model and determine which matches the needs of his or her students, a particular project, and the curriculum. This article highlights eight paths to choose from on the road to information literacy.

### Project 1: The Big6™ Skills

**ROUTE BIG6**

**Authors:** Michael B. Eisenberg and Robert E. Berkowitz

**Concept:** This widely used model represents a non-linear process that is applicable to a variety of information problem-solving situations.

Six Steps:
1. Task definition (defining the problem and identifying its information requirements)
2. Information-seeking strategies (determining possible sources and evaluating their priority)
3. Location and access (locating the sources and then locating information in them)
4. Information usage (reading information and then extracting details)
5. Synthesis (organizing and presenting information)
6. Evaluation (judging the product and the process)

**Web site:** http://www.big6.com/

> *"Ensuring that students are effective users of ideas and information is not optional,"* said Mike Eisenberg in a presentation given to media specialists at the 2003 National Education Computing Conference in Seattle, Washington.

**Discussion:** The popular Big6™ model supports critical thinking skills and is based on the six levels of Bloom's taxonomy: Task definition can be compared to knowledge; information-seeking strategies can be compared to comprehension; location and access can be compared to application, and so on. In addition, every two steps in the Big6™ model roughly relate to one of Piaget's three stages of cognitive development: pre-operational, concrete-operational, and formal operational. Students achieve information literacy skills with the Big6™ model based on their level of cognitive development. Noting that younger students have not yet achieved the formal operations stage, Eisenberg and Berkowitz created the Super3 Model containing the steps Plan, Do, Review. Prepared lessons are available on the Big6™ website and in various publications in support of both models.

**Publication(s):**

Eisenberg, M. and Berkowitz, R. (1996). *Information problem solving: The Big Six Skills approach to library and information skills instruction.* Norwood, NJ: Ablex

Eisenberg, M. and Berkowitz, R. (1999). *Teaching information and technology skills: The Big6 in elementary schools.* Worthington, OH: Linworth

Eisenberg, M. and Berkowitz, R. (2000). *Teaching information and technology skills: The Big6 in secondary schools.* Worthington, OH: Linworth.

### STRIPLING PITTS PARKWAY

**Authors:** Barbara K. Stripling and Judy M. Pitts

**Concept:** Authors Stripling and Pitts identify six levels of student research: fact-finding, asking/searching, examining/organizing, evaluating/deliberating, integrating/concluding, and conceptualizing. These categories are somewhat similar to Bloom's Taxonomy, and they identify six responses to research endeavors entitled REACTS (Recalling, Explaining, Analyzing, Challenging, Transforming, Synthesizing). The Thoughtful Learning Cycle encompasses these levels and reactions and is also metacognitive, as students reflect on their learning as they progress.

10 Steps plus reflection points after most steps:

- Choose a broad topic
- Get an overview of the topic
- Narrow the topic; reflection point: Is my topic a good one?
- Develop a thesis statement or purpose; reflection point: Does my thesis statement represent an effective concept for my research?
- Formulate questions to guide research; reflection point: Do the questions provide a foundation for my research?
- Plan for research; reflection point: Is the research plan workable?
- Find/analyze/evaluate sources; reflection point: Are my sources adequate?
- Evaluate evidence/take notes/compile bibliography; reflection point: Is my research complete?
- Establish conclusions/organize information into an outline; reflection point: Are my conclusions based on researched evidence?
- Create and present final product; reflection point: Is my project satisfactory?

**Discussion:** Judy M. Pitts' extensive research on the cognitive aspects of student research concludes that media specialists need to base instruction on the ways students learn, integrating research with the curriculum. An important feature of the model is that the authors believe instruction should be based on how students learn best and have concluded that more new learning occurs when connected to previous learning, a precept of constructivist learning theory.

### Publication(s):

Stripling, B. and Pitts, J. (1988). *Brainstorms and blueprints: Teaching library research as a thinking process*. Littleton, CO: Libraries Unlimited.

Pitts, Judy M. (1995). Mental models of information: The 1993-94 AASL/Highsmith research award study." *School Library Media Quarterly, 23*, 177–84.

Stripling, Barbara K. (1995). Learning-centered libraries: Implications from research." *School Library Media Quarterly, 23*, 163–70.

### KUHLTHAU CONNECTOR
### Project 3: The Information Seeking Process (ISP)

**Author:** Carol Collier Kuhlthau

**Concept:** Kuhlthau's model is effective in that it focuses on students' feelings throughout the research process, while applying constructivist principles of building on prior learning.

### Seven Stages:

1. Initiating a topic
2. Selecting a topic
3. Exploring information
4. Forming a focus
5. Collecting information
6. Preparing to present
7. Assessing the process

### Web site:

http://www.scils.rutgers.edu/~kuhlthau/

**Discussion:** Kuhlthau's model is based on extensive observation of students in various stages of research process. Kuhlthau noted the feelings of student researchers at various stages, beginning with confusion and frustration and ending with confidence. Kuhlthau's model is rooted in constructivist theory, or building knowledge by activating prior learning.

### Publication(s):

*Kuhlthau, C. (1987). Information skills for an information society: A review of research.* ERIC Clearinghouse on Information Resources, Syracuse, University.

Kuhlthau, C. (1989). "Information search process: A summary of research and implications for school library media programs." *School Library Media Quarterly, 19*, 25.

Kuhlthau, C. (1993). *Seeking meaning: A process approach to library and Information services.* Norwood, NJ: Ablex.

Kuhlthau, C. (1994). *Teaching the Library Research Process*, 2nd ed. The Center for Applied Research in Education. Metuchen, NJ: Sacrecrow Press.

### I-SEARCH INTERSTATE
### Project 4: The I-Search Process

**Author:** Ken Macrorie

**Concept:** Designed to promote interest in research and support a student's choice of a compelling topic, this affective model requires students to describe their search process in first person. The final product requires meshing student's own thoughts and ideas with research and includes student reflection on process.

Five Steps:

- Let a topic choose you
- Search for information
- Test the information
- Write the paper in first person, including the following
  - What I want to know about my topic
  - Why the topic is important to me
  - The story of my search for information
  - How I applied the information I found to answer my question
- Edit the paper

**Web site:** (not author's site) http://www.edc.org/FSC/MIH/i-search.html

**Discussion:** The I-Search model was originally created by Ken Macrorie, but Joyce and Tallman researched and publicized its use. Especially appropriate for students who find research intimidating or who have learning difficulties, the model is motivating to students who select a topic in which they have a strong interest. The final product is less threatening because students are encouraged to include their own thoughts and feelings along with their research.

### Publication(s):

Macrorie, K. (1988). *The I-Search paper*. Portsmouth, NJ: Heineman.

Joyce, M. and Tallman, J. (1997). *Making the writing and research connection with the I-Search process: A how-to-do-it manual.* New York: Neal-Schuman.

### RESEARCH CYCLE RACEWAY
### Project 5: The Research Cycle

**Author:** Jamison McKenzie

**Concept:** McKenzie's inquiry-based model repeatedly cycles through seven steps while refining a research question, the search process, and the final results.

Seven Steps:

- Questioning
- Planning
- Gathering

- Sorting and Sifting
- Synthesizing
- Evaluating
- Reporting

**Web site:** www.fromnowon.org

*McKenzie (2000) says in Beyond Technology that "... without strong questioning skills, you are just a passenger on someone else' tour bus. You may be on the highway, but someone else is doing the driving."*

**Discussion:** McKenzie recognizes that students need to refine, revise, and revisit sources repeatedly before a research project yields optimum results. He notes that questioning is an essential skill in the research process and that a question may not be refined until a student begins to research and revise the search repeatedly to maximize results. McKenzie's model helps students to become independent users of information as it requires more intensive research efforts and more critical evaluation of results before the product is finalized. For example, a student might Determine essential questions, Determine subsidiary questions, Develop a research plan, Gather information, Sift to refine results, Synthesize and evaluate findings, Revise questions, Revise plan/revisit sources, Gather information again, Sort and sift again, Synthesize again, Evaluate again, Revise questions and focus, Revise plan, Gather more precisely, Sort and sift again, Synthesize to infer and evaluate, Report findings.

**Publication(s):**
McKenzie, J. (2000). *Beyond technology: Questioning, research and the information literate school.* Bellingham, WA: FNO Press.
McKenzie, J. *From Now On: The Educational Technology Journal.* Available online at http://fno.org

**FLIP-IT FREEWAY** / **Project 6: Flip-It!**

**Author:** Alice Yucht

**Concept:** Yucht's problem-solving model utilizes a mnemonic device to help students recall stages in process. The model has been successfully implemented with a variety of age levels. Four Steps, plus Two final steps:
- **F**ocus (specifying)
- **L**ink/Logistics (strategizing)
- **I**nput/Implementation (sorting, sifting, storing)
- **P**ayoff/Proof (solving, showing)
- **I**nformation (facts and prior knowledge)
- **T**actical maneuvers and thinking strategies

**Web site:** http://www.aliceinfo.org/

*Alice Yucht's motto as posted on her web site is: "Show, Help, Accept, Reach out, Engage others—that's been my personal and professional motto for over three decades as a librarian (public, school, corporate), teacher (Pre-K to post-grad), staff developer, curriculum consultant, humorist and storyteller and even lunchroom overseer."*

**Discussion:** Yucht noted that students not only need a research model, but also need a means of recalling its steps. With the help of her students, she developed a mnemonic device to assist students in recalling steps in her information problem-solving model. The model is simple to implement and easy for students to remember.

**Publication(s):**
Yucht, A. (1997). *FLIP IT! An information skills strategy for student researchers.* Worthington, OH: Linworth.

**PATHWAYS TO KNOWLEDGE** / **Project 7: Pathways to Knowledge**

**Authors:** Marjorie Pappas and Ann Tepe

**Concept:** Created for the Follett Company, Pathways to Knowledge focuses not only on the steps in the research process, but also on constructing knowledge from findings. The model encourages students to become adept at constructing knowledge using a number of sources and creating a variety of end products.

Six Steps:
- **Appreciation:** students explore topics about which they are curious as an introduction to information-seeking through sensing, viewing, listening, reading, and enjoyment.
- **Presearch:** students explore what they already know and what they want to know about a topic and establish a focus—develop an overview and explore relationships.
- **Search:** students seek appropriate sources and plan and implement a search strategy—identify information providers, select information resources and tools, and seek relevant information.
- **Interpretation:** students assess usefulness and reflect on research results to develop personal meaning and interpret information.
- **Communication:** students organize and apply their research in an appropriate format.
- **Evaluation:** thinking about product and process—evaluate process and product; this ideally occurs at each stage as needed.

**Web site:**
http://www.pathwaysmodel.com/

**Discussion:** This model is based on a variety of options for student researchers. Students gather information from a number of sources and utilize multiple formats to present findings. This constructivist model is inquiry-based, and acknowledges that students work best when building on previous knowledge.

**Publication(s):**
Pappas, M. and Tepe, A. (1997). *Pathways to Knowledge. Follett's*

*Information Skills Model Kit.* McHenry, IL: Follett Software.

## Project 8: InfoQuest S.T.A.I.R.S. (Steps To Achieving Independent Research Skills)

**Author:** Peggy Milam

**Concept:** This inquiry-based model is designed to ignite curiosity and develop research skills in even the youngest students by asking challenging questions in a game format. InfoQuest is a process-oriented model and is easily connected to the curriculum.

Four Steps:

1. Inquiring: determine keywords and related topics in research question.
2. Searching: select and utilize specific resources to gather information.
3. Organizing: logically organize results, discarding unrelated information, and retaining most pertinent data.
4. Sharing: communicate results of search from a simple "I found it!" to a formal presentation. This is a process-based more than product-based process, so sharing need not be formal.

**Web site:** www.infoquestonline.net

*Milam (2002) noted in InfoQuest that "questioning is the key that unlocks the door to wonder. Research carries students through that door and into different rooms in the house of knowledge."*

**Discussion:** InfoQuest is easily adapted to all ages, from primary grades to college. The model is intrinsically motivating as students search because they wish to know more about a research question. InfoQuest is based on the need to know information in real-life situations. Students benefit from experience with the model's steps without being required to create a product with their research results. The model is designed around four levels of researchers: preliminary, beginner, intermediate, and advanced. InfoQuest is both process-oriented and resource-based. A key concept is that the model uses repetition to develop expertise in a wide variety of research techniques and sources.

**Publication(s):**

Milam, P. (1999). "The influence of InfoQuest." *Library Talk, 12*(1), 12–14.

Milam, P. (2002). *InfoQuest: A new twist on information literacy.* Worthington, OH: Linworth.

Milam, P. (2003). "How to create a standards-driven, technology based, collaborative media program." *Multimedia Schools, 10*(5).

### References

Callison, D. (2002). "Information use models." *School Library Media Activities Monthly, 19*(2), 36-39.

Shannon, D. (2002). "Kuhlthau's Information Search Process." *School Library Media Activities Monthly, 19*(2), 19–23.

Stripling, B. (1995). "Learning-centered libraries: Implications from Research. *School Library Media Quarterly, 23*(3).

Tallman, J. (1998). "I-Search: An inquiry-based, student-centered, research and writing process." *Knowledge Quest, 27*(1).

Yucht, A. (1999). "Flip-It! For information skills." *Teacher Librarian, 26*(3), 37–38.

Zimmerman, N. (2002). "Pappas and Tepe's pathways to knowledge model." *School Library Media Activities Monthly, 19*(3), 24–27.

*Peggy Milam, Ed.S., is a library media specialist at Compton Elementary School in Powder Springs, Ga. She serves on the Media Leadership Team for her district and is an assessor in Library Media for the National Board of Professional Teaching Standards.*

Milam, P. (2004). Destination information: A road map for the journey. *Library Media Connection, 22*(7), 20-23.

Figure 1. **Relationships Among Information Literacy Models**

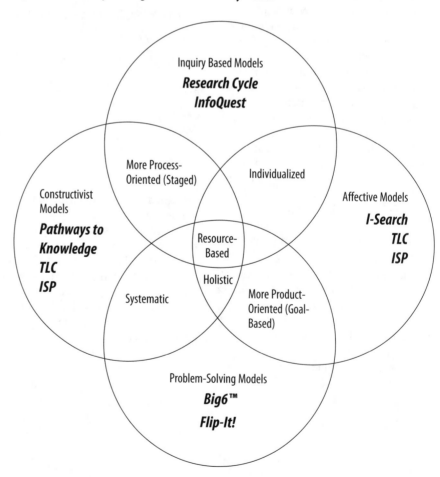

# Teaching Beginning Reading Strategies in the Library Media Center: A "How To" Guide

## By Crystal Barringer

### Why Teach Reading in the Library Media Center?

Library media specialists have been collaborating with classroom teachers for years and have long been advocates for tying the classroom curriculum to the library media center in real-world ways. In the past, however, this collaboration has focused almost exclusively on upper-elementary, middle, and high school students as it involved only research and information skills.

The idea of teaching reading is not so much a shift in philosophy as it is a new perspective. This "old" form of collaboration should not be discontinued. On the contrary, we know through well-established research that the more connections students can make, the more meaningful their learning becomes. The No Child Left Behind Act makes it clear that we should all be working together, collaborating and making strong connections, to reach this goal.

Library media specialists are not reading teachers, nor should they be. And library media specialists should not spend all of their time engaged in reading instruction. However, as teaching professionals, we are all responsible for helping students succeed academically. After all, finding information in the library media center doesn't do a student a whole lot of good if he or she can't read or understand it.

Current reading research focuses on the many aspects of learning to read, including phonics and alphabet recognition, vocabulary building, fluency, and the motivation to read. All of these skills work in combination to increase reading comprehension.

### Phonics

Phonemic awareness occurs when students realize that spoken language is actually made up of individual sounds, and traditional phonics instruction focuses on the relationship between those sounds and the letters of the alphabet. These strategies will most likely be introduced and taught by classroom teachers yet they are easily reinforced in the library media center simply by using a good alphabet book. For example, a library media specialist can use careful pronunciations and a chalkboard or projector to write out spoken, but possibly unfamiliar or difficult, words as he or she shares a read-aloud. Many library media specialists may already be teaching letter recognition or alphabetical order activities. To build on these, have students match uppercase letters to their lowercase counterparts, or share alphabet books with children such as:

- *Alphabet City* is a great book for getting students to identify letters and then trace them with their fingers as they say the corresponding sounds.

> To build fluency, students need good reading modeled for them. And who is better than the library media specialist to model an expressive, fluent voice?

- *Alphabatics* is a fun book to share aloud with a class because they get to interpret what happens to each letter.
- *The Z Was Zapped* is a wonderful book that builds vocabulary.

### Vocabulary Building

Building a child's vocabulary may be the single most important way to increase comprehension. The more words a child hears and understands, the better off that child will be when it comes time to actually read and recognize words. Build vocabulary using these strategies with any book:

- *Previewing*: Pull out words that might be new or troubling, spell those words, and define them. With *Score One for the Sloths,* you might preview the words *chortle, louts, amble,* and *vitality*. When the students later hear these words in the context of the story, they will be better prepared to understand their meanings.
- *Make a Word Splash*: Simply fold a sheet of 11" x 18" construction paper into fourths. Write the new word in the middle of the paper. In one quadrant you can write the definition, in another you can paste pictures that go along with the word, in another you can write synonyms, and in the last antonyms. This technique will build a more thorough understanding of a word. Again, pull the word from any that you have read aloud.
- *Utilize Nonfiction*: Almost all high-quality, current nonfiction is appropriate for introducing new and interesting content-area words. Teach students how to read captions and headings, and explain why such printing techniques as italics and boldfaced print are used. This also is a natural way to teach parts of a book such as glossary, index, and table of contents.

### Fluency

*Fluency* is the ability to read text accurately and quickly. Fluent readers recognize words automatically and effortlessly construct meaning from the text. Fluent readers read with expression and don't stop to sound out words. To build fluency, students need good reading modeled for them. And who is better than the library media specialist to model an expressive, fluent voice? To practice fluent reading, share books with repetition and have students join in reading. *Brown Bear, Brown Bear What Do You See?* and *The Napping House* are good examples of books that can build fluency.

### Motivation

This is a natural place for library media specialists to fit in the teaching of reading because most library media specialists already consider motivating students to read a big part of their job. We want to encourage students to read but not just to read anything. We want students to read books that are on their reading level—not so difficult that they can't process the text and not so easy that they're not challenging themselves. We also want students to read quality literature: books that are interesting and help students develop higher-order thinking skills. Here are some techniques:

- *Book Displays*: You can build a display around movie tie-ins such as *Because of Winn-Dixie* and *Holes*. Or you can make suggestions based on popular themes, "If you like adventure stories, you might like *Island of the Blue Dolphins*."

- *Feature Readers*: If a student reads an award-winning book, have him or her write a summary and a recommendation. Then take digital pictures of the student and the book cover and feature them prominently on a bulletin board.

- *Reading Incentives*: Some library media specialists use and enjoy Book It®, Advantage Learning System's Accelerated Reader®, Parents As Reading Partners (PARP), Scholastic's Reading Counts! and other well-known reading programs. Or invent your own reading incentive program. Giving away trinkets, such as stickers, pencils, or bookmarks, for so many books read is a surefire way to get kids reading.

## Teaching Reading Comprehension

The area of reading comprehension includes many well-documented strategies that classroom teachers have used for years and that library media specialists can easily reinforce during storytime. These strategies are listed in no particular order:

- *Building background knowledge:* This may include gathering nonfiction to accompany a fiction

read-aloud or having students look up their own information, in print or nonprint sources.

- *Determining the main idea:* After reading, have students discuss with a partner what the story was mostly about. Then ask for pairs who would like to share their ideas with the whole group.

- *Sequencing:* Read the book *How to Make an Apple Pie and See the World*. After sharing the story with the class, ask them to sequence the order in which the girl gathers her ingredients for the pie. Another option is to ask your class to sequence an apple pie recipe.

- *Comparing and contrasting:* Read several versions of the same story such as *Lon Po Po, Flossie and the Fox*, and *Little Red Riding Hood*. Have students find story elements that are alike and different.

- *Visualizing:* Help students practice seeing a picture in their mind's eye. Select a story and read it aloud, without showing the pictures. Then, supply paper and crayons and let students create their own pictures that go with the book. *Wild About Books* may be a good choice to practice visualizing.

- *Predicting:* This skill can be taught with any story. Simply have students guess what the book will be about by the cover illustration or title. Or, with a chapter book, stop at a predetermined place and have students write the next chapter.

## In the End

Teaching reading in the library media center can be a way to strengthen your overall library media center program. It certainly shouldn't be the main focus of the library media center, but it will be another way that you can connect with your colleagues: the teachers in your building. It may also be a good way to promote your program with your administrator. After all, we are all responsible for helping students succeed academically, and reading is the first step on the road to academic success.

## Bibliography

DiCamillo, Kate. *Because of Winn-Dixie*. Massachusetts: Candlewick Press, 2000.

Johnson, Stephen T. *Alphabet City*. New York: Viking Children's Books (Penguin Putnam), 1995.

Lester, Helen. *Score One for the Sloths*. New York: Houghton Mifflin, 2001.

MacDonald, Suse. *Alphabatics*. New York: Bradbury Press, 1986.

Martin, Jr., Bill and Eric Carle. *Brown Bear, Brown Bear, What Do You See?* New York: Henry Holt & Company, 1992.

Marzollo, Jean. *Happy Birthday, Martin Luther King*. New York: Scholastic Inc., 1993.

McKissack, Pat. *Flossie and the Fox*. New York: Dial Press (Penguin Putnam), 1986.

O'Dell, Scott. *Island of the Blue Dolphins*. New York: Houghton Mifflin, 1960.

Priceman, Marjorie. *How to Make an Apple Pie and See the World*. Dragonfly Books, 1996.

Sachar, Louis. *Holes*. New York: Farrar, Straus & Giroux, 1998.

Sierra, Judy. *Wild About Books*. New York: Knopf, 2004.

Van Allsburg, Chris. *The Z Was Zapped*. New York: Houghton Mifflin, 1987.

Wood, Audrey. *The Napping House*. San Diego: Harcourt, Brace & Jovanovich, 1984.

Young, Ed. *Lon Po Po: A Red Riding Hood Story from China*. New York: Philomel (Penguin Putnam), 1989.

*Crystal Barringer is a library media specialist at Christopher Columbus Elementary School in Utica, New York.*

Barringer, C. (2006). Teaching beginning reading strategies in the school library media center: A "how to" guide. *Library Media Connection*, 25(1), 34-35.

# A Niche for Library Media Specialists: Teaching Students How to Read Informational Texts

## By Marilyn Z. Joyce

With all the high-stakes testing required by state mandates and No Child Left Behind (NCLB), improving reading scores is a top priority for many K–12 educators. What is the role of the library media specialist? We teach students how to read informational texts.

Recently I was given the opportunity to serve on the Planning Committee for the 2009 revision of the National Assessment of Educational Progress <http://nces.ed.gov/nationsreportcard/> in reading, part of "the Nation's report card." I helped to draft the test framework and specifications. One of the questions the committee discussed was "Who is responsible for teaching students how to read informational texts at the middle and high school level?" English courses tend to emphasize reading literature. Moreover, teaching students how to read science, social studies, and math belongs in those content area classrooms. But teachers in those fields frequently lack the background in reading instruction to accomplish this task. Here is the perfect niche for library media specialists. We teach skills for reading informational texts as part of the research process, and we do it by collaborating with teachers.

How can we build the case that library media specialists teach students how to read informational texts? We need to "talk the talk and walk the walk." We can

- adopt and use the vocabulary of reading specialists,
- study the scientifically-based research on reading, and
- select the best practices in reading to integrate into our instruction.

With this knowledge, we can design and implement collaborative research units with strong reading components and demonstrate our role in teaching students how to read informational texts.

## Scientifically-Based Research

NCLB legislation calls for using teaching practices supported by scientifically-based research or "research that involves the application of rigorous, systematic, and objective procedures to obtain reliable and valid knowledge relevant to education activities and programs" (2001). This is also known as evidence-based research. The Partnership for Education <www.nifl.gov/ partnershipforreading> is an excellent place for accessing publications for teachers and parents on the current, evidence-based research and practice on reading. It is a collaborative effort of the National Institute for

> *Text comprehension contributes to students' ability to apply information as they solve problems and make decisions.*

Literacy (NIFL), the National Institute of Child Health and Human Development (NICHD), and the U.S. Department of Education. Much of the scientifically-based research on this Web site comes from the findings of the National Reading Panel <www.nationalreadingpanel. org/>, a committee convened by Congress to evaluate the effectiveness of different approaches of teaching reading.

I highly recommend the reader-friendly pamphlet, *Put Reading First: The Research Building Blocks for Teaching Children to Read* <www.nifl.gov/partnershipforreading/publications/k-3.html>. Although earmarked for grades K–3, *Put Reading First* reviews effective areas of reading instruction that apply to a range of grade levels. The five essential areas of instruction are phonemic awareness, phonics, fluency, vocabulary, and text comprehension.

Text comprehension has the greatest connection to the research process. Instruction in effective comprehension strategies helps students understand and remember what they read. It contributes to their ability to apply information as they solve problems and make decisions. In the age of high-stakes testing, it also leads to improvement in test scores.

## Strategies for Reading Informational Texts

The scientifically-based research reveals a number of effective strategies for improving reading comprehension. As teachers of information literacy, we already incorporate many of these strategies into our instruction. A review of the research supports our case that we teach students how to read informational texts and gives us a common vocabulary for discussing reading instruction with other educators.

The scientifically-based research confirms five major strategies for improving text comprehension: monitoring comprehension, using graphic and semantic organizers, answering and generating questions, recognizing story structure, and summarizing. Integrating these strategies into research-process instruction strengthens students' reading and information literacy skills.

The first strategy, **monitoring comprehension**, tracks understanding of text. Students who monitor their comprehension are aware of what they understand and do not understand. When they have trouble making meaning of text, they know how to apply a number of "fix-up" strategies. For example, successful readers reread confusing text, consult a dictionary when confronted with an unfamiliar word, and try to restate difficult passages in their own words.

The second strategy, **using graphic organizers and semantic organizers,** helps students visualize the relationships among key concepts and terms in informational texts. Webbing diagrams, concept maps, flowcharts, matrices, and other visual aids assist students in understanding the content and structure of informational texts. The use of graphic organizers and semantic maps increases students' ability to learn when reading science, social studies, and other content area texts.

The third strategy focuses on **answering and generating questions**. A teacher or library media specialist asks students questions to monitor their understanding. These questions also provide students with a purpose for reading and help them focus on what they need to learn. In addition, students can generate their own questions using a variety of questioning strategies that range from 5W+H (who, what, when, where, why, and how) to Bloom's Taxonomy to McTighe and Wiggins' Six Facets of Understanding. (For an excellent review of questioning strategy models, see Jill B. Slack, *Questioning Strategies to Improve Student Thinking and Comprehension* <www.sedl.org/secac/rsn/quest.pdf>.)

The fourth strategy is **recognizing story structure**. This strategy applies to reading fiction, but comparable strategies exist for informational texts. Students need to recognize the structure of informational texts. This includes understanding different organizational patterns (e.g., compare and contrast, cause and effect, problem and solution) and using graphic features (e.g., headings and subheadings, italics and bold type, photos and illustrations, charts and tables) to locate information within texts.

The final strategy is **summarizing**. Summarizing is an effective strategy because it requires the synthesis of information. In order to condense information, students must understand main ideas, determine the supporting details, and state them in their own words.

## The Reading-Research Connection

Search library literature or the Internet and you can find numerous examples of research units that feature effective strategies for helping students make meaning of informational texts. Here are some of my favorite tools recom-

mended by reading specialists for improving students' reading comprehension and research skills.

Students need a purpose for reading and research. That is why pre-reading and presearch are critical phases of their related processes; they prepare students for the work that lies ahead. An effective tool for facilitating both pre-writing and presearch is a variation of the K-W-L chart. K-W-L, when applied to reading an informational text, is a chart with three columns: "What I Know, What I Want to Learn, and What I Learned." When used for research, a variation has the following columns: "What I Know, What I Don't Know, What I Want to Learn through My Research."

> Search library literature or the Internet and we find numerous examples of research units that feature effective strategies for helping students make meaning of informational texts.

K-W-L incorporates effective strategies for monitoring comprehension and developing questions. The "What I Know" component asks students to activate their prior knowledge, and the "What I Don't Know" component helps them recognize gaps in that knowledge. Activating prior knowledge helps students connect new information to past learning and facilitates memory of new material. Identifying gaps in prior knowledge is a valuable "fix-up" strategy. Students understand that they need to do some background reading or find the definitions of unfamiliar vocabulary words to better understand a challenging text. K-W-L also facilitates question generation. When combined with background reading, students can use a variety of questioning strategies to brainstorm a list of questions for the "What I Don't Know" column. Then students can select three or four related questions for the "What I Want to Learn through My Research" column. These focus questions guide their research and provide a purpose for reading.

"Think-aloud" is an excellent tool for modeling how a good reader uses text structure and features to make meaning of text. During a "think-aloud," library media specialists and partner teachers can verbalize how they use text structure and features to preview a text, determine key words and concepts, and predict main ideas and supporting details. Then they can ask students to verbalize their thinking through conferences or a "pair-share" activity with another student.

Double-entry journals are effective tools for improving comprehension and taking notes. Students create a chart with two columns: one for content and one for response. In the content column, students can summarize important parts of the text, note answers to their questions, and pinpoint unfamiliar words and confusing passages. In the response column, they can discuss the significance of information in the content column. This might include

- a paraphrase of a complex segment of text,
- a possible explanation of confusing material,
- a main idea from the resource and why it is important,
- a strong positive or negative reaction and an explanation of that reaction,
- a reason for agreeing or disagreeing with the author,
- a comparison or contrast of a passage with another resource or with prior knowledge,
- a prediction based on evidence from the resource, or
- a question generated as a result of reading.

Double-entry journals help the library media specialist and partner teacher monitor students' comprehension and content learning. During conferences with students, teachers can reinforce valid interpretations of text and intervene when the students encounter problems.

Learning logs are powerful tools for reflecting on both content and process. Reading specialists frequently use learning logs as a metacognitive tool to help students think about their thinking throughout the reading process. They use learning logs to monitor comprehension, a critical part of metacognition. In their learning logs, students can summarize text, compare and contrast text from different resources, and discuss their "fix-up" strategies. Library media specialists and partner teachers can use learning logs, as well as double-entry journals, to track students' understanding of both reading and content learning and can intervene when students need assistance. Moreover, double-entry journals and learning logs serve as deterrents to plagiarism. When students make their own meaning of text, they do not resort to cutting and pasting from resources. Students learn content when they write in their own words.

K-W-L charts, "think-alouds," double-entry journals, and learning logs are only a few examples of tools that connect the scientifically-based research to the research process. Teaching students how to read informational texts is not an addition to our curriculum but an integral part of what we already teach.

## Components of Reading Instruction

According to the scientifically-based research, effective reading instruction is "explicit" or direct. It includes four key components to incorporate into our research units.

- Provide **direct explanations** of how a strategy works and why the strategy helps readers understand.

- Use "think-alouds" to explain the process or **model** how we, as good readers, make meaning of informational texts.

- Allow for **guided practice** where students have the opportunity to practice effective reading strategies with our support.

- Give students the opportunity to **apply** the strategy until they have mastered how to use it.

Library media specialists have the unique opportunity, through their collaboration with content area teachers, to provide the explicit instruction that leads to reading achievement.

## The Next Steps

So many times reading instruction in the content areas is done in a hit-and-miss fashion. Content area teachers, when they do incorporate reading instruction into their lessons, tend to use different strategies. Frequently there is no common vision within a school. With little consistency and reinforcement across the disciplines, students receive mixed messages about how to read informational texts. Library media specialists can solve that problem by consistently applying the best practices as we collaborate with teachers.

Imagine a school where students have the opportunity to learn, practice, and perfect their reading skills in a consistent, focused fashion through all subject areas. Think of the improvement in reading achievement. Library media specialists have the power to create such a school.

*Marilyn Z. Joyce is a library media specialist at Brewer (Maine) High School and can be reached at mjoyce@breweredu.org.*

Joyce, M.Z. (2006). A niche for library media specialists: Teaching students how to read informational texts. *Library Media Connection, 24*(7), 36-38.

# Sink or Swim?
# Differentiated Instruction in the Library

## By Karen Larsen

I am absolutely terrified of swimming. The mere thought of putting my head underwater makes me nauseated. I had to be rescued during a water aerobics class because I drifted over to where my feet didn't touch and I panicked. I am in awe of people who just jump right into the pool instead of slowly easing in one toe at a time as I do. My husband and daughters are on the other end of the spectrum. They rival Shamu in their ability to swim. The girls are swim team members and love to snorkel. My husband is certified in scuba diving and can dive off the high board. Even our Pekingese can swim better than I.

- Now imagine you are a swimming instructor for all of us.

- Would you put us all in the same class?

- Would it bolster my confidence to see others diving like porpoises while I clutch the side of the pool and cry?

- Should we form a cooperative learning group where my team's grade depends on how well I learn to swim?

- Should others be used as unpaid tutors to teach me how to swim?

- Should others wait for instruction until I catch up to their abilities?

Of course the answer to all the above questions is a resounding "no." The logical way to teach us would be to divide us into needs-based instructional groups. My husband could be in the deep-sea dive instruction group, the girls could be learning how to start off the blocks more efficiently, and I could be in the group with other terrified people and we could learn to let go of the wall. We would all be working on the concept of "swimming," just at our own instructional level.

Now imagine you are working with a group of second grade students who are learning about magnets. Some of the students can read at a sixth grade level, have a passion for magnets, and have already read several books about magnets. Others have never even played with magnets, and barely know how to read. Then there is the group in the middle who reads on grade level and has had some experience with magnets. Should these children all be in the same instructional group? Again the answer is "no." Each child should be allowed to learn at a level appropriate to his or her ability level. If the instruction is too high, the learner is frustrated. If the instruction is too low, the learner is bored. It is impossible to design a one-size-fits-all curriculum.

> One question that people ask about differentiation is: don't the students wonder why they are not doing the exact same lesson?

## Enter Differentiation

This is where differentiation comes in. Differentiation is " . . . a way to get students to wrestle with profound ideas, call on students to use what they learn in important ways, help students organize and make sense of ideas and information, and aid students in connecting the classroom with the wider world," according to Carol Ann Tomlinson (2000, 6).

The goal of differentiation is to bring the ideas and concepts of the curriculum to the learner at a pace and depth that is appropriate for the ability of each student. For example, in our magnet lesson, one of the broad concepts that might be taught in this unit is that magnets stick to some objects and not to others. In a whole group instruction method, all the children would be given a variety of magnets (bar, horseshoe, ring, disc, wand, and sheet magnets) and a variety of objects (foil, nails, pennies, tin cans, aluminum cans, paper clips, fabric) and

the students would experiment with the magnets to see which objects stick to the magnets. The teacher would record the results on chart paper and they would discuss as a whole group with a few children dominating the discussion. For the children who have had experience playing with magnets, this lesson is too easy. For the children with little experience with magnets, this lesson is just right. For all the rest, it is somewhere in between.

In a differentiated lesson, Group One would be given the magnets and objects and a sheet with not only the name of the object, but also a picture clue and the students would make a check under the "yes" or "no" boxes; then see which objects stick to the magnets. The small group is led by a teacher who encourages the children to experiment as much as they need to until they start to see patterns of why some objects stick and other do not. Then as a group, they write a sentence or two at the bottom of their worksheets describing the results of their experimentation.

Group Two would be given the same objects and magnets. Their worksheets would not have the picture clues and would have an additional column labeled "Hypothesis." The teacher would teach the children what a hypothesis is and they would proceed with the activity in a more formalized manner using a beginning version of the scientific method. The students would record their guesses and see if they were accurate. Their conclusion would discuss which objects stuck and which ones did not, and why they were correct or incorrect in their guessing.

Group Three would also receive the same objects and magnets, and books about magnets. Their worksheet would be a template of the scientific method and the group would design an experiment using the materials they have. The teacher would lead them through the scientific method and the students would complete the sections for Title, Hypothesis, Procedure, Materials needed, Experiment results, and Conclusions. One group I have worked with decided to do an experiment to see if the shape of the magnet made a difference as to the type of objects it would or would not pick up. Another group wanted to know if different shapes of magnets were more powerful than others. The students design their experiment, conduct it, and record their results.

All students in the above lesson are working on the concept of "what do magnets stick to," just at a different pace and depth. They are learning at their own pace and at their instructional level. The classroom teacher works with one group, the library media specialist works with another group, and a parent volunteer or student teacher works with the third group. In my own library media center, I am fortunate enough to have a clerk and she has taken a group at times.

## Learning Options

With older students, you can devise a menu of choices of varying difficulty. For example, if the assignment is to read *To Kill a Mockingbird*, the choices could be as follows:

- Look up the vocabulary words from the book and define them.

- Read the book and answer the comprehension questions on the worksheet.

- Find three Web sites that discuss *To Kill a Mockingbird* and compare them on content.

- Taking a chapter from the book, write a play script for the scene.

- Film and edit the scene using iMovie® adding in at least one special effect.

- Read *To Kill a Mockingbird* and *Peace Like a River*. Compare and contrast the two books looking at theme, plot, setting, and characters.

- Design and conduct a Socratic Seminar about *To Kill a Mockingbird*.

- Design your own final product that demonstrates your knowledge of the book using different levels of Bloom's Taxonomy.

Choices 1 and 2 are more suitable for the struggling learner while choices 6, 7, and 8 are more appropriate for the advanced student. Some choices can be worth more points or even extra credit points. All students can succeed using differentiation and all students can be challenged at their learning level.

One question that people ask about differentiation is: don't the students wonder why they are not doing the exact same lesson? After using differentiated instruction for years, I have never had a student ask this question. I always start the lesson with, "We are going to be working in three different groups. It is boring if we are all doing the same thing. If you feel you are not being challenged enough in your group, please let me know and I will make an adjustment."

## An Added Benefit

One of the unexpected benefits of doing differentiated instruction in the library media center is that teachers are very open to doing collaborative lessons. It is much more efficient to teach a differentiated lesson with two of you in the room. Once the teachers see how much more effective differentiated instruction is, they will want to collaborate with you all the time. I have found differentiation to be the "hook" to get teachers on board with co-planning and co-teaching.

Almost every school and school district has a mission statement that says something like, "We at ABC School District uphold high standards and expectations which challenge each student to reach his or her potential." Using differentiated instruction, we as educators can help each child achieve his or her potential.

The students prefer this type of instruction as they all have success. The teachers like it, as it is much more effective to work with a small group, and the library media specialists like it because they are being used for collaborative instruction. It is a Win-Win-Win situation all the way around. With differentiation, all students can succeed—even those who are terrified of the water!

### Good resources for your professional collection:

*The Differentiated Classroom: Responding to the Needs of All Learners* by Carol Ann Tomlinson. Association for Supervision & Curriculum Development, 1999. 0871203421.

*Differentiation in Practice: A Resource Guide for Differentiating Curriculum, Grades 5–9* by Carol Ann Tomlinson and Caroline Cunningham Eidson. Association for Supervision & Curriculum Development, 2003. 0871206552.

*Fulfilling the Promise of the Differentiated Classroom: Strategies and Tools for Responsive Teaching* by Carol Ann Tomlinson. Association for Supervision & Curriculum Development, 2003. 0871208121.

*How to Differentiate Instruction in Mixed-Ability Classrooms* by Carol Ann Tomlinson. Association for Supervision & Curriculum Development; 2nd edition, 2001. 0871205122.

*Leadership for Differentiating Schools and Classrooms* by Carol Ann Tomlinson and Susan Demirsky Allan. Association for Supervision & Curriculum Development, 2000. 0871205025.

### Bibliography

Tomlinson, Carol Ann. (2000). Reconcilable Differences? Standards-Based Teaching and Differentiation. *Educational Leadership*, 58 (1), 6–11.

*Karen Larsen is a teacher-librarian at Cotton Creek Elementary School in Westminster, Colorado. She can be reached at larsenfam@mho.net. Karen is also the co-author of* Day-by-Day: Professional Journaling for Library Media Specialists *(Linworth Publishing, Inc., 2003).*

Larsen, K. (2004). Sink or swim: Differentiated instruction in the library. *Library Media Connection*, 23(3), 14-16.

# The Big Ideas

## Introduction

Sometimes doing the tasks of the job of being a school librarian becomes so overwhelming, we forget what the job is. This happens frequently in all work environments, for instance when grocery clerks are so busy restocking shelves that they neglect to notice that the cash registers are understaffed. The job of a grocery store employee is to sell groceries. The task may be to stock the shelves, but the importance of the task pales in comparison with the importance of the job. The same is true of the library media center. We achieve our mission by encouraging children to love to read, to become skilled users of technology, and to develop a lifelong library habit, among others. The tasks of the job may be circulation, collaborative teaching, and managing the program, but the tasks cannot detract from the successful achievement of the mission.

In circulation, for instance, it is important for students to return books on time so that they learn responsibility and so that other students can read those books. While denying access to children who have one overdue book may help to better implement the task of circulation, it may do nothing to ensure that the child will learn to love to read. In fact, it most likely will achieve the opposite.

The day of the school library media specialist is comprised of making management decisions, teaching information skills, interacting with patrons from the youngest children in the school to the oldest teacher, and a host of other tasks. The authors of the articles in this section remind us that the tasks have to relate back to the big ideas of our profession, to access, intellectual freedom, legal and ethical issues, and evidence-based planning for collaborative teaching and learning.

We start with teaching and learning, because school librarians as teachers is the heart of what we do. Articles by Michael Eisenberg and Toni Buzzeo address the importance of collaboration. Violet Harada and Joan Yoshima take us further down that path as they explore inquiry learning, and Jennifer Youssef provides a case study of her first collaborative experience. Beth Yoke combines advocacy with collaboration, and Carol Simpson, Julieta Fisher, and Ann Hill address several aspects of ethical and legal issues. Julie Scordato looks at combined school and public libraries. Melissa Gardner seeks to define the technology role of the media specialist in terms of access to resources, services, and instruction. Jon Mueller explores critical aspects of assessment. This section concludes with Fay Shin's strong statement about the relationship between access to books and student reading achievement.

# It's All About Learning: Ensuring That Students Are Effective Users of Information on Standardized Tests

## By Michael B. Eisenberg

This article describes and advocates for taking the next step in connecting school library media programs to student learning and academic achievement. It's time to get specific and detailed in terms of the examining and documenting the relationship between library media program services, particularly information skills instruction, and student performance as measured on standardized tests. Making this connection is crucial if school library media programs are to thrive in an educational system increasingly focused on accountability and measured achievement through examination by standardized testing.

### Where the Action Is

It's pretty obvious. The bottom line in K-12 education today is student achievement, and, like it or not, increasingly that achievement is defined by standardized testing and the No Child Left Behind act. For example, an August 2003 poll on the Big6.org Web site asked, "Starting the 2003-04 school year, what is the new initiative in your district?" Of the almost 700 responses, 86% indicated No Child Left Behind/ Standardized Testing! Standardized testing is the overwhelming educational focus around the country. We as educators need to take action to ensure success for all students.

No Child Left Behind, President Bush's education agenda, is designed to improve student achievement in all schools across the United States. The Act is intended to guarantee quality education for all children—with an emphasis on increased funding for poor school districts, higher achievement for poor and minority students, and new measures to hold schools accountable for their students' progress. The Act significantly expands the role of standardized testing in American public education.

The bill mandates that states develop and implement "challenging" academic standards in reading and math, set annual statewide progress objectives to ensure that all groups of students reach proficiency within 12 years, and then test children annually in Grades 3 through 8, in reading and math, to measure their progress. The bill specifically prohibits any "national testing" or "federally controlled curriculum." It is up to the states to select and/or design their own tests, and to make sure that the tests are aligned with the state curriculum standards. (U.S. Department of Education 2003; Public Broadcasting System, 2003) The test results are made public in annual "report cards" on how schools are performing and how states are progressing overall toward their proficiency objectives.

> Targeting library media information skills instructional programs to standardized testing is not an add-on to existing programs. Rather, it is a long-term commitment to targeting the focus of instruction to school and district priorities

Before continuing, let me be very clear about one thing: I am not a proponent of standardized testing. Standardized testing has its place, but the "testing movement" seems overboard to me. As library and information professionals, it is our job to fight for true education reform (e.g., focusing on higher-level thinking skills) rather than simply testing. At the same time, we need to help students succeed at whatever has been set before them. Today, that means focusing on standardized tests and the relationship between information literacy skills instruction and student performance on these standard tests.

### What This Means for Library Media Programs

In considering a more direct connection between library media programs and standardized tests, it's important to remind ourselves of our ultimate purpose and goal: "the mission of the library media program is to ensure that students…are effective users of ideas and information." (*Information Power*, 1998) Our work is founded on a fundamental conviction—the more skilled that students are in gathering, processing, evaluating, and applying information, the more they will be able to achieve on any task. Thus, it is essential that we direct our attention to student success as measured by standardized tests.

The school library media field appears to be increasingly aware of this need to focus on achievement and standards. Over the past 10 years, much progress has been made in focusing programs on student performance and the connection to state and subject area standards. Teacher-librarians recognize that the key to providing a meaningful program is the direct connection to curriculum and the classroom.

The library media field has also made progress in recognizing that it's not enough to simply "say" that we are important and make a difference. Ross Todd nailed it on the head in his August/September 2003 article in *Library Media Connection*. It's right on the cover, "It's not enough to say that school libraries contribute to learning. Now you have to prove it." Exactly, and as Todd implies, we need to focus on what it all means for students—how does an effective school library media program help students? What does it enable them to do and to become? What does it mean in terms of student learning? (p. 13).

Among the research that Todd reviews are the well-cited studies conducted by Keith Curry Lance and colleagues. (Lance 2001) These studies empirically analyzed the connection between student achievement and school library media programs. As recently reported in an Association of Supervision and Curriculum Development Research Brief (ASCD 2003), the Lance studies confirmed a correlation between the presence of a library or librarian and higher student achievement, especially in reading. Among other findings, studies in Alaska, Colorado, Oregon, and Pennsylvania found that professionally trained and credentialed teacher-librarians have a positive effect on student achievement.

The Smith (2001) study of Texas school library media programs looked specifically on the effects of school libraries on student achievement as measured by the reading portion of the Texas standardized test, the Texas Assessment of Academic Skills (TAAS). The study found that school library media programs do have a measurable effect on student achievement. At the elementary and middle school levels, library media programs could account for approximately 4% of the variance in TAAS scores; at the high school level, 8.2% of variance. Furthermore, at the middle school level, two variables stood out, including "providing information skills instruction to students." At the high school level, seven variables were noted including "units planned with teachers."

This is great news, right? Isn't this is the evidence that we've all be waiting for? We should be shouting the news from roof-tops and on street corners! Better yet, the eyes of administrators and school boards should be finally opened and the money and support for library media programs should be flowing.

Well, not so fast. While these results are encouraging, they are not overwhelming in any sense. First, these studies are correlational, not causal. It appears that effective library media programs have a positive impact on student performance, but there are no studies that demonstrate a direct causal effect. Second, we are talking potential impact in the 4–8% range, and that pales before the strongest predictor of academic success, socioeconomic factors. Lastly, as the ASCD piece asks, how much does a 4–8% variance cost a district? What is

the cost-benefit analysis, and what specific aspects of the library media program account for the variance?

A missing element is a direct connection between core library media functions (specifically information skills and reading advocacy) and performance on standardized tests. We do have valuable and important studies on the nature and impact of information skills instruction. Kuhlthau (2001, 1993), Todd (2003), and others investigate student performance on papers, projects, and reports. These are certainly important pieces of the evidence puzzle. But, we need to go one step further; we need to address the specific questions of performance on standardized tests.

Therefore, I propose that we complete the picture by taking the next, bold step—to get detailed and specific in focusing our attention on state standards and tests and the connection to core library media functions. I propose that we move from broad, sometimes vague correlations to specific and direct connections.

Specifically, that means:

- analyzing state standards and test items to determine direct connections to information skills instruction.

- targeting information skills instruction actions to specific standards and test items.

- evaluating the impact of these interventions on student performance on test items.

Today's library media program encompasses three important functions: reading advocacy, information skills instruction, and information management. While there are direct connections between all of these functions and standardized tests, we are limited as to what can be covered because of time and space constraints. Therefore, the focus for the remainder of this article will be on information skills instruction and testing.

## Information Skills Instruction

There's an extensive body of literature on the information skills instruction and information literacy (see Eisenberg, Lowe, and Spitzer, 2004) including the empirical work of Carol Kuhlthau (1993), various state standards (e.g.,

Wisconsin 1998), the national AASL/AECT standards (AASL/AECT 1998), and my Big6 problem solving skills approach, developed in conjunction with Bob Berkowitz. (Eisenberg and Berkowitz, 1990)

I have previously written on a number of occasions about the commonalities among these models. (see Figure 1, based on Eisenberg and Lowe 1996; also in Spitzer, Eisenberg, and Lowe, 1998). From this side-by-side view, we see a process unfold—that information skills are connected activities that flow from identifying a task through gathering, evaluating, use, synthesis, and assessment of information.

More recently, Janet Murray went even further, matching the Big6 model, the AASL/AECT national standards, Information Literacy Standards, and the National Educational Technology Standards for Students (NETS) developed by ISTE. Murray documented the relationship between the Big6 and specific state information and technology skills standards, with examples from Washington, North Carolina, Colorado, and Missouri. (see Murray, 2002)

What all this means is that, regardless of the information skills curriculum, model or standards used, you can make the connection to other models and standards, including the AASL/AECT framework and the Big6 approach. Because it is the most widely used approach to information literacy instruction in K-12 schools and because of my familiarity with it, I will use the Big6 process to explore the relationship of information skills instruction and standardized tests. The Big6 is a process model of how students solve an information problem. From practice and study, we found that successful information problem-solving encompasses six stages with two sub-stages under each (see Figure 2).

Students go through these Big6 stages—consciously or not—when they seek or apply information to solve a problem or make a decision—both on a personal level and with school work. It's not necessary to complete these stages in a linear order, and a given stage doesn't have to take a lot of time. We have found that in almost all successful problem-solving situations, all stages are addressed.

## Content Area Standards and the Information Skills Connection

State and subject area standards are now part of the fabric of K-12 education and define the goals of education across the United States. McREL, the Mid-Central Regional Education Lab, has compiled content for K-12 curriculum (see McREL 2003). According to McREL, in the 1980s and 1990s, most national subject-matter organizations sought to establish standards in their respective areas, including mathematics, science, civics, dance, theater, music, art, English/language arts, history, and social studies. "Since 1990 the movement has acquired considerable momentum at the state level as well. As of 1999, the District of Columbia, Puerto Rico, and every state except Iowa have set or are setting common academic standards for students." (American Federation of Teachers, 1999 quoted on the McREL Web site).

Much has been written about the importance of connecting library media programs to school and classroom curriculum. We talk about context and collaboration, and one important tangible way to do this is to make the connection between information skills instructional programs to state content area standards. Furthermore, this connection is essential when we turn to focusing on standardized tests. Tests are developed to assess student performance on state standards, and individual test questions are referenced to the state standards (this is explained in more detail in the next section). The connection between information skills standards and state content standards allows us to make the necessary connection and target information skills instruction to student achievement as measured on the standardized tests.

Fortunately, we have a number of excellent models of how to make the connection between state content standards and information skills. Wisconsin (1998) was one of the first states to develop combined information and technology skills standards. The heart of these standards, "Information and Inquiry" is based directly on the Big6 approach. Wisconsin also led the way in fully integrating information and technology skills standards with content area standards and offers an extensive set of matrices connecting information technology literacy standards to content area standards. (Wisconsin

### Figure 2: The Big6

1. Task Definition:
   1.1 Define the problem.
   1.2 Identify the information needed.
2. Information Seeking Strategies:
   2.1 Determine all possible sources.
   2.2 Select the best sources.
3. Location and Access:
   3.1 Locate sources.
   3.2 Find information within sources.
4. Use of Information:
   4.1 Engage (e.g., read, hear, view).
   4.2 Extract relevant information.
5. Synthesis:
   5.1 Organize information from multiple sources.
   5.2 Present information.
6. Evaluation:
   6.1 Judge the result (effectiveness).
   6.2 Judge the process (efficiency).

### Figure 1: Comparison of Information Skills Process Models

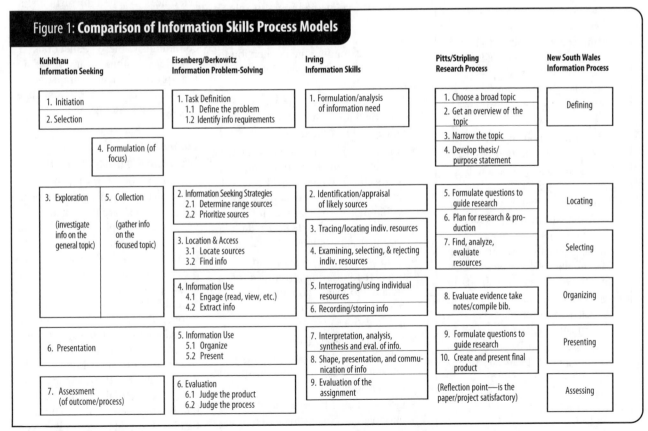

| Kuhlthau Information Seeking | Eisenberg/Berkowitz Information Problem-Solving | Irving Information Skills | Pitts/Stripling Research Process | New South Wales Information Process |
|---|---|---|---|---|
| 1. Initiation<br>2. Selection | 1. Task Definition<br>1.1 Define the problem<br>1.2 Identify info requirements | 1. Formulation/analysis of information need | 1. Choose a broad topic<br>2. Get an overview of the topic<br>3. Narrow the topic<br>4. Develop thesis/purpose statement | Defining |
| 4. Formulation (of focus) | | | | |
| 3. Exploration (investigate info on the general topic)   5. Collection (gather info on the focused topic) | 2. Information Seeking Strategies<br>2.1 Determine range sources<br>2.2 Prioritize sources<br>3. Location & Access<br>3.1 Locate sources<br>3.2 Find info<br>4. Information Use<br>4.1 Engage (read, view, etc.)<br>4.2 Extract info | 2. Identification/appraisal of likely sources<br>3. Tracing/locating indiv. resources<br>4. Examining, selecting, & rejecting indiv. resources<br>5. Interrogating/using individual resources<br>6. Recording/storing info | 5. Formulate questions to guide research<br>6. Plan for research & production<br>7. Find, analyze, evaluate resources<br>8. Evaluate evidence take notes/compile bib. | Locating<br><br>Selecting<br><br>Organizing |
| 6. Presentation | 5. Information Use<br>5.1 Organize<br>5.2 Present | 7. Interpretation, analysis, synthesis and eval. of info.<br>8. Shape, presentation, and communication of info | 9. Formulate questions to guide research<br>10. Create and present final product | Presenting |
| 7. Assessment (of outcome/process) | 6. Evaluation<br>6.1 Judge the product<br>6.2 Judge the process | 9. Evaluation of the assignment | (Reflection point—is the paper/project satisfactory) | Assessing |

*(Adapted from Eisenberg, M. and Brown, M., 1992 and Spitzer, Eisenberg, and Lowe, 1998)*

2000). See Figure 3 for more information on these connections.

The state of Missouri also fully documents the relationship between state information and technology literacy skills standards and the state content standards, as well as more general process/performance standards. (Missouri 2001) Figure 4 illustrates how, under the broad information skill of "Access of Information," the specific skill of "Determine purpose" links to Process/Performance Standards 1.1 and 3.1. The even more detailed sub-skill "Brainstorm" links to Process/Performance Standards 3.6 and Science Content/Knowledge Standards SC 7. Figure 4 illustrates the similarities between the Missouri program and the Show-Me Standards.

If your state does not have a linking document, it is relatively easy to do so. Sue Wurster and I (Eisenberg and Wurster 2002) created a matrix aligning the Florida Language Arts Standards with the Big6 Skills. We paid particular attention to Language Arts Standards that are tested on the Florida FCAT exams (see Figure 5).

## The Final Chapter: Making the Connection to Standardized Tests

Making the connection between information skills standards to state content standards is essential to the task of making library media programs relevant to educational priorities, but it is not the end of the story. The last part of the plot is extending the connection to the state tests themselves. This requires:

- Becoming familiar with various state tests (including the nature, format, and content of the tests)

- Analyzing the tests and individual test questions from an information perspective (i.e., identifying relevant information skills standards or skills within models such as the Big6 that would help students to succeed on specific test questions).

- Collaborating with classroom teachers to offer opportunities for students to learn and apply the relevant information skills to specific test questions.

- Designing and delivering lessons that help students to learn and apply the relevant information skills to specific test questions.

- Documenting actions taken to connect information skills instruction to tests, test questions, and standards.

- Assessing success by looking at the test results (as provided in the various state "report cards").

- Revising and planning for future instruction.

This is clearly a long-term commitment and effort. One-shot lessons and interventions will probably not result in any measurable improvement in student performance. However, over time, teacher-librarians can make a difference by working with classroom teachers to integrate information skills instruction into subject area learning that is targeted to performance requirements on standardized tests. This is not "teaching to the test." It is "teaching skills that allow students to perform better on tasks as measured by standardized tests."

Information on tests is readily available from most states on the Web. These include sample exams across subject areas and grade levels. Most samples also include references to the related state content standards. These references provide useful insights into how standards are translated into test items as well as the style and format of test questions. Unfortunately, I have not found any references to state information skills standards. It is up to us—the library media field—to begin to make and communicate these connections.

Here are three examples of what I am proposing using sample test questions from three different states, subject areas, and grade levels.

### Example 1:
### Wisconsin 4th Grade Mathematics

Sample test questions for the "Wisconsin Knowledge and Concepts Examinations" are presented by subject, grade, and proficiency category (minimal performance, basic, proficient, and advanced). The questions provided are edited and are intended as samples only. Actual questions are available to Wisconsin educators through the local district or school.

Mathematics Question 9 from the Wisconsin Department of Public Instruction, Office of Educational Accountability (1997, ) reads:

"The tree in the picture is 10 feet tall. Next to the tree, draw another tree that is 20 feet tall. Explain how you

---

### Figure 3: Wisconsin 4th Grade Examples of Connections: Mathematics

#### A. Mathematical Processes

Students in Wisconsin will draw on a broad body of mathematical knowledge and apply a variety of mathematical skills and strategies, including reasoning, oral and written communication, and the use of appropriate technology, when solving mathematical, real-world and nonroutine problems.

#### ITL Performance Indicators

- formulate initial questions to define what additional information is needed—B.4.1

- determine a specific focus for the information search questions—B.4.1

- recognize that materials in the school library media center are organized in a systematic manner —B.4.3

- locate materials using the classification system of the school libarary media center—B.4.3

- identify new information and integrate it with prior knowledge —B.4.6

- determine if information is relevant to the information question—B.4.6

- select information applicable to the infomation question—B.4.6

- seek additional information if needed—B.4.6

- apply the information gathered to solve the information problem or question—B.4.6

- recognize the three common types of communication or presentation modes (written, oral, visual)—B.4.7

- choose a presentation format (e.g., speech, paper, web page, video, hypermedia)—B.4.7

- develop a product or presentation to communicate the results of the research—B.4.7

*(from Combined Matrix, Model 2, B. Information and Inquiry ITL Content Standard: p. 179-180)*

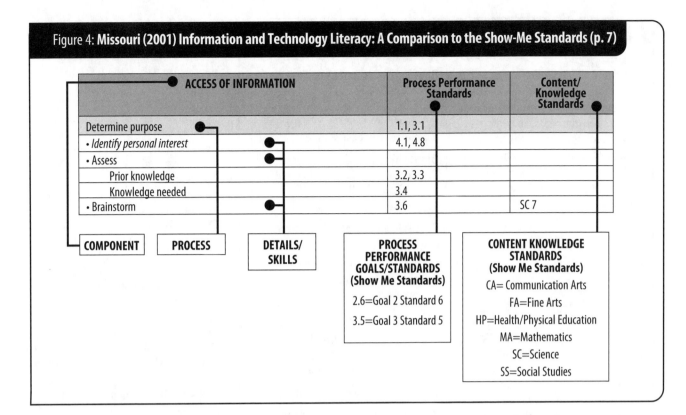

**Figure 4: Missouri (2001) Information and Technology Literacy: A Comparison to the Show-Me Standards (p. 7)**

| ACCESS OF INFORMATION | Process Performance Standards | Content/ Knowledge Standards |
|---|---|---|
| Determine purpose | 1.1, 3.1 | |
| • Identify personal interest | 4.1, 4.8 | |
| • Assess | | |
| Prior knowledge | 3.2, 3.3 | |
| Knowledge needed | 3.4 | |
| • Brainstorm | 3.6 | SC 7 |

COMPONENT    PROCESS    DETAILS/ SKILLS

**PROCESS PERFORMANCE GOALS/STANDARDS (Show Me Standards)**

2.6=Goal 2 Standard 6

3.5=Goal 3 Standard 5

**CONTENT KNOWLEDGE STANDARDS (Show Me Standards)**

CA= Communication Arts

FA=Fine Arts

HP=Health/Physical Education

MA=Mathematics

SC=Science

SS=Social Studies

decided how tall to draw your tree."

This question is followed by a picture of a tree with a ruler next to it noting its height as 10 feet. Blank spaces are provided below for students to show and explain their answers.

According to the scoring explanation provided, this item tests two objectives: Measurement and Communication. For Measurement, the student demonstrates an understanding of scale by drawing the second tree twice the height of the first. The student can use the ruler provided or another strategy. Communication objectives include relating daily vocabulary to mathematical terminology and relating models, diagrams, and pictures to mathematics. Students validate their solutions by explaining their decision-making process.

Looking at this question from an information perspective, it appears to relate to two Big6 skills:

Big6 #1: Task Definition—recognizing that the question has two parts to it. It's not enough to just draw a tree, the student must also explain his or her decision-making process.

Big6 #6: Evaluation—reflect on decision-making process. "Explain how you decided how tall to draw your tree" is asking students to describe and reflect on their decision-making process.

Task Definition lessons may include: Recognizing multiple parts of questions. Assignments and questions frequently have multiple components, and students need to learn to focus on this. Using existing homework, tests, and other assignments, students can be asked to break them down and identify the parts—and the relative importance of each part to the assignment or question.

Learning key words in questions. Bob Berkowitz works with high school students to highlight and define the key verbs in questions. Students make flash cards to help them study and remember the terms. For example, in the question above, the key terms are "draw " "explain" and "decided." Most students will understand "draw" but they may have more trouble with knowing what is required for "explain" and also that "decided" means that they are to reflect on their decision-making process.

For Evaluation, students should be able to reflect on their process and communicate what they did:

Teacher-librarians and classroom teachers can teach students how to break down their actions into steps, for example, by listing them one-by-one or writing them on cards.

Students can practice this type of

written self-reflection if they are sometimes required to include an explanation of their work when they turn in assignments.

### Example 2:
### Florida (FCAT) 8th Grade Reading

Florida provides extensive sample information for its FCAT. (Florida's Comprehensive Assessment Test Keys (2002–2003). A series of questions, including #16, follows a 900+ word reading passage, *America's Saltiest Sea: Great Salt Lake* by Angela B. Haight, illustrations from the Utah Division of Wildlife. *Cricket Magazine*, April 1996. Question 16 (from Florida's Comprehensive Assessment Test FCAT Sample Test Books and Answer Keys (2002–2003) Grade 8 Reading, 2003, p.12):

Question 16: Using details and information from the article, summarize the main points of the article.

For a complete and correct response, consider these points.

- its history

- its interesting features

- why it is a landmark.

A Scoring Rubric for Question 16 is provided in the Grade 8 Answer Key Book (p. 11). It refers to the passage as an "informational text" and refer-

| 3rd grade - 5th grade<br>LA.A.2.2.8: The student selects and uses a variety of appropriate reference materials, including multiple representations of information, such as maps, charts and photos, to gather information for research projects. **(Tested on FCAT)** | **Big6 Skill #2: Information Seeking Strategies**<br>2.1 Determine the range of possible resources<br>2.2 Select the best sources<br><br>**Big6 Skill #3 Location and Access**<br>3.1 Locate sources (intellectually and physically)<br>3.2 Find information within sources<br><br>**Big6 Skill #4: Use of Information**<br>4.1 Engage (e.g., read, hear, view) the information in a source<br>4.2 Extract information from a source |
|---|---|
| 6th grade - 8th grade<br>LA.A.2.3.5: The student locates, organizes, and interprets written information for a variety of purposes, including classroom research, collaborative decision making, and performing a school or real-world task. **(Tested on FCAT)** | **Big6 Skill #3 Location and Access**<br>3.1 Locate sources (intellectually and physically)<br>3.2 Find information within sources<br><br>**Big6 Skill #4: Use of Information**<br>4.1 Engage (e.g. read, hear, view) the information in a source<br>4.2 Extract relevant information from a source<br><br>**Big6 Skill #5: Synthesis**<br>5.1 Organize information from multiple sources<br>5.2 Present information |

Note Standard LA.A. = Reading

ences it to the following Language Arts Benchmark:

Benchmark: LA.A.2.3.5 The student locates, organizes, and interprets written information for a variety of purposes, including classroom research, collaborative decision-making, and performing a school or real-world task. (Includes LA.A.2.3.6 uses a variety of reference materials, including indexes, magazines, newspapers, and journals, and tools, including card catalogs and computer catalogs, to gather information for research projects; and LA.A.2.3.7 synthesizes and separates collected information into useful components using a variety of techniques, such as source cards, note cards, spreadsheets, and outlines.)

According to the Rubric, "a top-score response will include information about the Great Salt Lake's history, interesting features, and why it

is a landmark."

From the Eisenberg/Wurster chart (see Figure 5), we see that Florida Benchmark: LA.A.2.3.5 is linked to Big6 Skills #3, Location and Access, #4, Use of Information, and #5, Synthesis. Therefore, in considering this question and the rubric from an information perspective, and by analyzing the question and information skills required of students more carefully, it seems that students will be successful if they are able to:

- effectively and efficiently extract relevant information (Big6 #4.2 , Use of Information).

- organize and present complete information (Big6 #5, Synthesis)

Use of Information lessons related to this need might include:

Teaching students how to skim and scan a text. One key element of

this is helping students to learn to read for a purpose (i.e., to look at the questions being asked of them *before* they start reading the text) so that they know what to look for.

Highlight relevant parts of a reading passage. Again, students should learn to first look at the questions being asked and then how to read a text and highlight key parts.

Another possible approach to this question combines Task Definition, Use of Information, and Synthesis. Devised by Bob Berkowitz, students learn to analyze the parts of a question, create a chart that outlines the parts, read the text and take notes on the chart, and finally to write the full answer from the chart.

For example, Question 16 requires three information items about the Great Salt Lake: its history, its interesting features, and why it is a landmark. Before even reading the passage, students can create the following blank chart:

| History | |
|---|---|
| Interesting Features | |
| Why a Landmark | |

Then, if they come across any information on the aspects when reading the passage, they can simply enter the information into the chart, for example:

| History | - In 1847, settlers arrived in Salt Lake City<br>- Once, during a swarm of crickets, seagulls saved the settlers' crops |
|---|---|
| Interesting Features | 25 percent salt<br>- 75 miles long by 50 miles wide<br>- the largest body of water west of the Mississippi River. |
| Why a Landmark | - the largest body of water west of the Mississippi River. |

With this chart in hand, it's a straightforward matter to write a complete response that directly answers the question. Students are able to draw the relevant facts out of the passage before having to worry about the writing process.

## Example 3:
## Missouri 10th Grade Science

The Missouri State Department of Elementary and Secondary Education provides up-to-date examples of the Missouri Assessment Program (MAP). Question 2 on the 2003 Grade 10 Science test (Missouri State Department of Elementary and Secondary Education 2003 Science Released Items Grade 10, p. 3) asks:

Each of the three main particles that make up a neutral atom has mass and either a positive (+), negative (–), or neutral (0) charge.

List the three main particles found in a neutral atom.

1. _____
2. _____
3. _____

Show the charge on each of these three particles by writing a symbol (+, –, or 0) to the right of its name Circle the name of the particle that has the least mass.

The Scoring Guide for Question 2 notes that this relates to Missouri Standard: III.A.4 (Std 1) Goals: 1.10. The answer should include the following elements:

- electron, proton, neutron (in any order)
- – with electron, + with proton, 0 with neutron
- Electron is circled.

Students receive the following scoring points:
3 points three key elements
2 points two key elements
1 point one key element
0 points other

Analyzing this question from an information perspective, we again see that a key to this question is Big6 #1, Task Definition as well as Big6 #6, Evaluation, for which students are able to judge and score answers themselves.

For question 2, Students must include all three elements to receive the 3 maximum possible points. Teacher-librarians can work with classroom teachers to design learning experiences that help students learn to recognize the requirements of a complete answer and to make sure that students do, in fact, include all of the requirements in their answer. These learning experiences can include:

Lessons that teach students how to analyze questions and identify the requirements.

Exercises and homework that have students practice analyzing questions and identifying requirements.

Having students create their own rubrics for questions, homework, and assignments.

## Summary: Putting It All Together

The three examples presented in the previous section demonstrate how it is possible to not only link information skills standards to content area standards, but to get much more specific in providing meaningful information skills instruction that helps students to succeed on standardized tests. I recognize that one lesson here and there will not have much of an impact on student performance. However, over time, repeated lessons that focus on the same information skills—targeted to questions in the same format and style that appear on statewide tests, taught collaboratively by the teacher-librarian and classroom teacher—can make a difference.

To review the recommended approach:

- Become familiar with various state tests.
- Analyze and break down the tests and individual test questions from an information perspective.
- Collaborate with classroom teachers to offer opportunities for students to learn and apply the relevant information skills to specific test questions.
- Design and deliver lessons that help students to learn and apply the relevant information skills to specific test questions.
- Document actions taken to connect information skills instruction to tests, test questions, and standards.
- Assess success by looking at the test results.
- Revise and plan for future instruction.

While not discussed in detail in this article, these last three bullets—document, assess, and plan—are as important as the others to overall success. Documentation (through charts, sched-ules, or reports) of specific information skills instructional efforts provides evidence of the involvement of the library media program in the effort to improve student achievement. Documentation also provides a baseline for assessing any potential impact on test scores. In addition to assessing success, examining test results will point to problem areas for student performance, and future information instructional efforts can be targeted to the most problematic areas. Lastly, revisions in the instructional efforts should be systematically planned and communicated to administrators and school decision makers.

The targeting of library media information skills instructional programs to standardized testing is not an add-on to existing programs. Rather, it is a long-term commitment to targeting the focus of instruction to school and district priorities. It is fully consistent with the mission and goals of the library media program as it takes a systematic approach to "ensuring that students are effective users of ideas and information."

The potential result is for library media programs to make a difference in student performance and to finally gain the deserved recognition that library media programs are vital to education in an information society.

### Bibliography

American Library Association and Association for Educational Communications and Technology (1998). "Information Literacy Standards for Student Learning," In *Information Power: Building Partnerships for Learning* (Chapter 2).

Association for Supervision and Curriculum Development (ASCD) (2003). *School Libraries and Their Impact on Student Performance.* Research Brief (September 2, 2003, volume 1, number 18), Available online: www.ascd.org/publications/researchbrief/volume1/v1n18.html

Eisenberg, M. and Berkowitz, R. (1990). *Information Problem-Solving: The Big6™ Skills Approach to Library & Information Skills Instruction.* Norwood, NJ: Ablex.

Eisenberg, M. and Brown, M. (1992). "Current Themes Regarding Library and Information Skills Instruction: Research Supporting and Research Lacking." *School Library Media Quarterly* 20(2): 103–109.

Eisenberg, M., Lowe, C., and Spitzer, K. (In press). *Information Literacy: Essential Skills for the Information Age*. Westport, CT: Libraries Unlimited.

Eisenberg, M. and Wurster, S.L. (2002). Florida State Language Arts Standards Aligned with Big6™ Skills. Available online: http://www.big6.com/showarticle. php?id=151

Florida's Comprehensive Assessment Test FCAT Sample Test Books and Answer Keys (2002–2003). Available online: http://www.firn. edu/doe/sas/fcat/fcatit02.htm

Florida's Comprehensive Assessment Test FCAT (2002). Grade 8 Reading 2003. Available online: http://www.firn.edu/doe/sas/fcat/ pdf/fc8rib2a.pdf p.12

Florida's Comprehensive Assessment Test FCAT (2002). Grade 8 Reading 2003. Grade 8 Answer Key Book. Available online: http://www.firn.edu/doe/sas/fcat/p df/ fc8rik2a.pdf p.11

International Society for Technology in Education (2003). National Educational Technology Standards NETS. Available online: http://cnets.iste.org/students/s_stan ds.html

Kuhlthau, Carol C. (2001). Rethinking libraries for the information age school: vital roles in inquiry learning. Keynote Address, International Association of School Librarianship Conference & International Research, Forum on Research in School Librarianship, July 9, 2001 Auckland, New Zealand. Available online: www.scils.rutgers.edu/ ~kuhlthau/Presentations.htm

Kuhlthau, Carol C. (1993). *Seeking meaning: a process approach to library and information services.* Norwood, NJ: Ablex, 1993.

Lance, K. (2001). *Proof of the power: Recent research on the impact of school library media programs on the academic achievement of U.S. public school students.* Syracuse, NY: ERIC Digest: ERIC Clearinghouse on Information & Technology. Available online: http://ericit.org/ digests/EDO-IR-2001-05.shtml

McREL. (2003) *Content Knowledge.* 3rd Edition. Available online: http://www.mcrel.org/standards-benchmarks/

Missouri State Department of Elementary and Secondary Education (2001). *Information and Technology Literacy: A Comparison to the Show-Me Standards.* Available online: http://dese.mo.gov/ divimprove/curriculum/literacy/doc-ument.pdf

Missouri State Department of Elementary and Secondary Education (2003). Missouri Assessment Program Spring 2003 Science Released Items Grade 10. Available online: http://www.dese. state.mo.us/divimprove/assess/ science/releaseditems/2003/sc10re leased2003.pdf

Murray, J. (2002). *Big6™ and State Standards.* Big6 eNewsletter 3(2). Available online: http://www.big6. com/showarticle.php?id=339

Murray, J. (2003). *Apply Big6™ Skills to Integrate Content Standards in the Curriculum,* Big6 eNewsletter 4(1). Available online: http://www. big6.com/showarticle.php?id=325

U.S. Department of Education (2003). *No Child Left Behind.* Available online: www.ed.gov/ nclb/landing.jhtml

Public Broadcast System (2003) *Frontline: The New Rules.* Available online: www.pbs.org/ wgbh/pages/frontline/shows/schoo ls/nochild/nclb.html)

Smith, E. G. (2001). Texas school libraries: Standards, resources, services, and students' perform-ance. Austin, TX: Texas State Library and Archives Commission. Available online: http://www.tsl. state.tx.us/ld/pubs/schlibsurvey/ survey.pdf

Spitzer, K., Eisenberg, M., and Lowe, C. (1998). *"Information Literacy: Essential Skills for the Information Age."* ERIC Clearinghouse on Information & Technology ED427780.

Todd, Ross (2003). *"School Libraries & Evidence: Seize the Day, Begin the Future"* Library Media Connection 22(1): 12-18.

Wisconsin Department of Public Instruction, Office of Educational Accountability (1997). Sample Test Questions, MATHEMATICS Proficiency Category: BASIC Elementary School Level at Grade 4. Available online: http://www.dpi. state.wi.us/dpi/oea/math4bas.html

Wisconsin Department of Public Instruction (2002). Curriculum Alignment Resources for Wisconsin's Model Academic Standards An Information Technology Literacy (ITL) Resource http://www.waunakee.k12. wi.us/DPI_Standards/index.htm

Wisconsin Department of Public Instruction (2000), "B. Information and Inquiry ITL Content Standard: Information and Inquiry, Combined Matrix, Model 2," Curriculum Alignment Resources for Wisconsin's Model Academic Standards An Information Technology Literacy (ITL) Resource p. 179-180. Available online: http://www.waunakee.k12. wi.us/DPI_Standards/ITL%20Stand ards%20Matrix/Matrix%20Model% 202.doc

Wisconsin Department of Public Instruction (1998). Model Academic Standards for Information and Technology Literacy, Available online: http://www.waunakee.k12. wi.us/DPI_Standards/Academic%2 0Standards/Info%20Tech%20Liter acy.doc

*Mike Eisenberg is Dean Emeritus and Professor in the Information School of the University of Washington. Prior to his role as Dean, Mike Eisenberg worked for many years as Professor of Information Studies at Syracuse University and as Director of the Information Institute of Syracuse (including the ERIC Clearinghouse on Information & Technology, AskERIC, and GEM). Mike and his co-author Bob Berkowitz created the Big6 approach to information problem solving, and he has worked with thousands of students (preK through higher education) as well as people in public schools, business, government, and communities to improve their information and technology skills. Mike has written numerous books and articles on aspects of information science and librarianship, information literacy, library media work, and information technology.*

Eisenberg, M.B. (2004). It's all about learning: Ensuring that students are effective users of information on standardized tests. *Library Media Connection*, 22(6), 22-30.

# Collaborating from the Center of the School Universe

## By Toni Buzzeo

Imagine the school as a universe. Like our own universe, it will either continue to grow and expand forever or it will be gravitationally slowed and eventually collapse back upon itself in a "big crunch." There is a temptation to wonder whether we've reached the time of that collapse in schools as federal law drives our practice and measures our outcomes. Yet insofar as space science is concerned, current evidence suggests an accelerating universe, dictating that the expansion of the universe will accelerate for eternity. Perhaps our schools, along with their educational programs, will also continue to expand and grow in positive ways, with our students' learning and achievement accelerating. If so, what role will we as library media specialists play in the newly expanded universe of our schools? How can we influence and benefit the achievement of our students? And what will be our vehicle of influence? The answer is as simple and complex as collaborative practice.

### The Changing World

School librarianship has definitely changed in the accelerating school universe since the publication of *Information Power: Guidelines for School Library Media Programs* in 1988. That document clearly defined our roles as library media specialists: information specialists, teachers, and "instructional consultants" to our classroom colleagues. For the first time, we were instructed to create flexible schedules and engage in collaborative teaching. Library media centers had entered an age of collaborative practice!

When I finished my master's degree in Library and Information Science and landed a full-time position in an elementary school with a professional title and professional pay, I worked in a library media center created from leftover space in the basement of a lovely old school. You note that I do not write, "in the lovely old basement of a school." In fact, that basement was a horrible place. It

smelled funny, especially when it rained for more than one day. The windows were sealed shut due to a radon problem (common in Maine cellars), and the abatement system would not work unless we kept the space airtight.

The library media center itself was exceedingly small for my population of 500 students and failed to meet even one state facilities guideline. It was the much neglected stepchild of the school, and it was completely invisible, out of sight there in the malodorous basement. My library media center was *not* at the center of the school universe.

Luckily, I was hired to bring my vision (the reason, in fact, that I agreed to accept this basement job), and my vision was to move that library media center, both physically and metaphorically, to the heart of the school, to

> Just as it isn't possible to ignore the sun, our primary source of energy and light, my new faculty couldn't ignore the library media center with collaborative energy powering the program.

make it the center of a universe I knew existed on the two floors above: the accelerating universe of learning and student achievement. Moving the physical library media center proved to be a daunting goal not much in my control, for we needed to wait four long years until two contiguous classrooms could be freed up on the main floor directly across from the office. Fortunately, moving the library media center program to the center of the school universe could begin immediately—and did.

### Collaboration as a Mission

Schooled in the age of *Information Power 1*, I have believed from the outset of my library career in the mission and mandate to deliver instruction collaboratively as equal partners with our colleagues—fellow specialists and

classroom teachers alike. Therefore, moving the library media center program to the center of the universe began precisely there for me, with collaborative practice that involved me with my teaching colleagues in a visible and meaningful way. Just as it isn't possible to ignore the sun, our primary source of energy and light, my new faculty couldn't ignore the library media center with collaborative energy powering the program.

Of course, the analogy is off here, for our solar system isn't the center of the universe. It isn't even the center of our galaxy. In fact, at the center of the Milky Way is a great black hole sucking everything into it—not quite the image I am after, except on my darkest and most hopeless days. Nor is our galaxy the center of the universe, my scientist and space aficionado husband informs me. There *is* no center of the universe, he says, as it is ever-expanding and the galaxies are spinning farther and farther apart. So I continue with apologies to those who know anything about space and want their analogies arrow straight and true. You'll understand that I am an English major and a writer. I claim poetic license!

Sometimes, galaxies collide, though, which is both true and useful information for my purposes. In fact, they may even exchange stars in their collisions! Collaboration, of course, is all about productive collision courses: the combination of one or more curriculum content areas with information literacy skills; the intersection of two or more great minds, intent on creating and delivering something bigger and better than they might create and deliver alone; the juncture of educational standards, mandates, and federal requirements with our desire for our students to learn, to know, and to achieve. We collaborate because, unlike the explosive scenes of made-for-TV disaster movies, this collision is a source of energy, a source of light, and a surefire method for influencing student achievement as the school library impact studies of Lance, Rodney, and Hamilton-Pennell has shown us over and over again.

## Styles of Collaboration

Another truth about galaxies in our universe is that they come in a variety of shapes and sizes, just as our teachers have a variety of teaching styles and levels of involvement. Our challenge is to practice responsiveness and respect for those individual strengths and differences while holding fast to our goal of collaboration. My job as a new library media specialist in my basement library media center that first year was to look for the "Oh Yeah's!" on my staff, the risk takers, the open-minded and undefended teachers willing to try something entirely new with someone entirely new. I reasoned that success with the few would breed interest among the many, and that did prove to be true.

Even when we are no longer new to our buildings, we must continue to practice responsiveness and respect for those different teaching styles and levels of involvement as we push forward toward our goal of full collaborative practice. Collaborations with our long-standing and highly organized veteran collaborative partners (our "Oh Yeah's!") might be smooth and well-rehearsed while, simultaneously, our work with novice teachers—or at least novice collaborators (our "Yeah, But's")—might require more leadership, instruction, and hand-holding. And should we be lucky enough to convince our administrators to lend their support by requiring our truly collaboration-resistant colleagues (our "No Way in Heck's") to engage in a team-planned, team-taught, and team-assessed project. The level of delicacy and light-handed humor required to find common ground might challenge even the expert collaborators among us. But, as Ann Carlson admonished us in her winningly titled 2001 *School Library Journal* article, "Stop the Whining" and get on with an activist approach. We must take every step necessary to put our library media centers at the center of the school universe—and the most essential step of all is collaboration.

## The Impact of Standards

I will admit that the world of education has changed enormously since my early days in that basement library media center. Those were the days when the standards movement was new in Maine, when we were only beginning to articulate what we expected our students to know and be able to do. As in our educational communities then, in the universe there are large volumes of empty space between areas of accumulated matter. Writing the standards was akin to the pioneering work of defining the location and extent of that matter!

I remember long, confusing meetings in my former district at which all teachers were challenged to identify essential knowledge in their subject areas, the results of which would be sent to the state for aggregation. Although it was challenging work, amazingly, it resulted in a functional state document called "The Maine Learning Results." A few years later, in my subsequent school district, I had the privilege of sitting on the committee that wrote our district information literacy standards. Our team of five worked tirelessly. We argued over language, ideology, student abilities, and educational expectations. In a new age of accountability, we created a document we were all proud to share, teach from, and be accountable to.

That seems so long ago. Now, learning standards are not only a part of our educators' vocabulary, but they are also the vocabulary of our students and the community at large. We have gone beyond identifying learning standards—and learning to design instruction to target and meet them—to an age of high-stakes testing, a completely different model of collision course quite a bit more reminiscent of those made-for-TV movies. The stakes are so high, the accountability so strict that just as stars can sometimes be ejected from a galaxy, administrators can be ejected from schools that do not make Adequate Yearly Progress (AYP). In these times, education can sometimes feel a less friendly place.

## NCLB and the Library Media Center Program

A colleague of mine, Debbie Fisher, is employed as a library media specialist in an underperforming school in Rhode Island. On the one hand, her library media center is the fortunate recipient of one of this year's Literacy through School Libraries grants. "I have to say," Debbie writes, "that in terms of [the sense of] making some funding available for libraries that were traditionally under-funded in high poverty areas, NCLB has been [is] good."

In fact, under Resources for Literacy, Learning, and Teaching, Part B—Student Reading Skills Improvement Grants, Subpart 1—Reading First, Section 1202, NCLB outlines the acceptable use of funds and thereby makes explicit the need for quality library media center materials: "promoting reading and library programs that provide access to engaging reading material."

As library media specialists, this is a potentially enormous benefit of the federal law. It is our responsibility to maintain a focus on this mandate for quality library media center materials. Additionally, in NCLB Subpart 4—Improving Literacy through Schools Libraries, Section 1251, the need for excellent library media centers is emphasized: "The purpose of this subpart is to improve literacy skills and academic achievement of students by providing students with increased access to up-to-date school library materials, a well-equipped, technologically advanced school library media center, and well-trained, professionally certified school library media specialists."

## Conflicts Within

However, NCLB has also created competing priorities. Fisher notes, "Until three years ago, my library did receive some funding. However, as the mandates for our low performing, not-improving school kicked in, the priorities shifted to literacy programs and training for the teachers in those programs. Thus, the negative side of NCLB. The result of this shift in priorities is that the libraries in the district lost all funding. No books, no magazines, no newspapers. I ended up spending about $2,000 per year of my own money on books, barcodes, and miscellaneous library media center expenses. I paid for my own travel and registration for professional conferences. Needless to say, that was definitely a negative impact of NCLB. Again, this will change for the coming year, but most likely only for this coming year." As the money for the grant comes in, Fisher anticipates that the library media center will be conducting its usual work: supporting the faculty and students through the curriculum, encouraging independent reading, and teaching information literacy skills.

Another Pennsylvania colleague, working as an experienced reading specialist in her elementary school, is a newly certified library media specialist without a library, she says, thanks to NCLB. Despite her request for a transfer to a library media center position, and despite the fact that a district decision had been made to increase time spent on third grade information literacy skills in the library media center from 30–40 minutes per week, her skills were more highly valued as a reading specialist than as a library media specialist. This reveals a lack of understanding of the role of the library media specialist! While none of us would deny that learning to read is essential, we know as well that, once the first task is accomplished, reading to learn is the work of the student through all of the remaining years of his or her education. From my perspective—and hers—my colleague would have been equally valuable at the helm of a collaborative library media center program, designing, teaching, and assessing units of study that infused information literacy skills into content area curriculum and supporting students as they continued to read to learn. Unfortunately, her district interpreted NCLB guidelines differently.

## A More Positive View

Parson Hills Elementary School (Springdale, Arkansas) library media specialist Kriste Rees is, on the other hand, having a much more positive experience as a result of NCLB. This summer she spent time with colleagues in a workshop about using

data to help students meet NCLB standards. Additionally, this year for the first time Rees's library media center will be flexibly scheduled (with the exception of kindergarten), an enormously positive result of the efforts to meet NCLB guidelines! Rees writes, "I also work with a committee of nine other teachers who will be peer coaches with 2–3 other teachers in our building. We are reading books about teacher leadership, action research, and Robert J. Marzano's book, *Classroom Instruction That Works: Research-Based Strategies for Increasing Student Achievement*, about high-yield strategies in preparation for our work." Rees's district is taking seriously the direction under Section 1251 of the law for use of funds to "provide professional development for school library media specialists, and activities that foster increased collaboration between school library media specialists, teachers, and administrators." As Rees comments, "All of this collaboration is to improve student learning in our building and help students meet NCLB standards."

So, whether we view NCLB as a comet momentarily streaking across our solar system's planetary orbits in a long elliptical orbital path of its own—then disappearing again for 100 years—as evidence that our current educational system is going supernova (the death of a star that has run out of fuel), or as a purely scientific space probe sent out to gather reliable data, it is a part of our current universe and one to which all educators must respond. Fortunately, the essential response of the library media specialist has not changed, nor should it. The American Association of School Librarians points out in its exceptional brochure addressed to principals, "Many state tests ask students to apply skills as well as recall facts. School

library media specialists, by designing and teaching information literacy units tied to the classroom curriculum, help all students learn to not only memorize information, but also to use it in meaningful and memorable ways. Which, of course, leads to higher test scores. We want to produce critical readers, real-world math users, and passionate, effective writers. Project-based learning that is planned, co-taught, and assessed by your school's library media specialist will always ask children to go beyond the minimum, and in doing so they will have no difficulty in passing tests that measure just the minimum" (AASL 2005). Our essential response to the need to both raise and document student achievement is, first and foremost, collaborative practice. If you have not yet begun true collaboration, team-designed, team-taught, and team-assessed units of study that integrate information literacy skills into content area teaching, now is the time to begin collaborating from the center of your school universe.

*Toni Buzzeo MA, MLIS, is an author as well as a career library media specialist and member of the Maine Association of School Libraries Executive Board. She is the author of four picture books and several professional books, including the Linworth Publishing titles Collaborating to Meet Standards, Teacher/Librarian Partnerships for K–6 and Collaborating to Meet Standards, Teacher/Librarian Partnerships for 7–12 (2002). Visit her Web site at www.tonibuzzeo.com.*

## Work Cited

AASL. (2005). *Your School Library Media Program and No Child Left Behind.* Chicago: American Association of School Librarians.

Buzzeo, T. (2006). Collaborating from the center of the school universe. *Library Media Connection, 24*(4), 18-20.

# Moving from Rote to Inquiry: Creating Learning That Counts

## By Violet H. Harada and Joan M. Yoshina

Today's schools face enormous challenges in implementing high standards that demand greater rigor and relevance in their curricula. Unfortunately, the norm in many classrooms remains teaching practice that results in rote learning and regurgitated facts. In this article, we describe inquiry-focused learning as a process that provokes deeper thinking and investigation and greater student motivation to learn.

## Picture This

Does the following scenario sound familiar? We share this from one of the schools where our graduate students engage in their practicum experiences.

*Fourth graders are doing a research project on animals living in different habitats. The teacher assigns each student a different animal to study. She hands out the questions that every student must answer, including questions that deal with the animal's physical appearance and characteristics, living conditions, and eating habits. The class visits the library media center for an hour where they learn how to access information from both print and online encyclopedias. Students continue their research independently as homework. At the end of two weeks, they turn in booklets that contain text and illustrations of their animals. The teacher grades the booklets and returns them to the students.*

We conducted an informal interview with the teacher at the end of the project to discuss her perceptions of its overall effectiveness. She indicated that the booklets were disappointing and mediocre in quality. Regardless of the animal studied, the reports "all sounded alike" and much of the information was regurgitated. She said that her students had made little effort to use sources beyond the encyclopedia, and that she should have involved the library media specialist in planning this assignment.

Even more telling was a focus group session with some of the students in this fourth grade class. They said this was an "easy" assignment since all of the information they needed was "right there in the encyclopedia." As one student noted, "All I had to do was copy the stuff." Being an easy assignment did not necessarily mean that students were motivated to work on it. They unanimously agreed the project was "really boring" because they "just had to answer the teacher's questions."

In the above scenario, neither the teacher nor students felt that the project had generated excitement or produced high-quality results. Yet similar projects yielding similar results are repeated year after year in hundreds of classrooms. What is lacking in these projects? What would make such experiences truly meaningful?

> The norm in many classrooms remains teaching practice that results in rote learning and regurgitated facts.

## Creating Meaningful Teaching

Research conducted by educators, such as Perkins (1992), Newmann (1996), Stiggins (1997), Wiggins and McTighe (1998), and Marzano (2003), indicate learning that works must reflect authentic and rigorous practices. We (Harada and Yoshina, 2004, 2–3) have distilled the following key points from these various research studies:

### #1 Questioning is at the center of the learning experience.

Real learning involves questions—more than simply the answers (McKenzie 2000). Students' own curiosity and wonder should provide the seeds for meaningful learning. At the same time, students need assistance in shaping an essential or over-arching question that drives their investigations and creating relevant and higher-order questions.

### #2 Students help to negotiate the direction of the learning.

Students work with their instructors to shape the learning experience. Instructors are less directors, and more facilitators, in negotiated learning situations. While direct teaching is still valued, instructors spend more time listening to and observing what students do and asking questions that help students gain confidence in finding their own answers.

### #3 Learning is social and interactive.

Students work in groups—and so do teachers and other members of the professional staff. The synergy of these exchanges brings substance and richness to the entire learning project. By working cooperatively and collaboratively, people discover creative solutions to difficult situations and develop respect for diverse points of view on a topic or an issue.

### #4 Solving problems is an integral part of the process.

The ability to recognize problems and devise strategies confronting them is an essential life skill. Students must challenge themselves with questions such as, "Why didn't this work?" and "What can we do next?" Applying systematic reasoning strengthens their abilities to distinguish causes from symptoms. It also fosters thoughtful consideration of alternative strategies to resolve problems.

### #5 Students learn by doing.

Rather than learning solely through lectures and exercise sheets, students are engaged in hands-on and minds-on interaction. They perform tasks that require higher-order thinking. Students frequently construct things and do live performances that demonstrate their understanding of concepts

### #6 Products and performances reflect application and transfer of learning.

In their performances, students not only demonstrate what they understand from their readings, discussions, and observations, but they also display how they might transfer this learning to different situations. By applying their understanding, students exhibit the depth of their own newly acquired knowledge.

### #7 Assessment is ongoing.

Assessment is done continuously, not just at the end of a project, and both students and instructors engage in this crucial aspect of learning. Students assess to see what they are doing well and where they might improve in a specific phase of their work. Instructors assess to determine what's working and where they might modify their teaching. The tools used can take many forms, including observations, conferences, graphic organizers, and journals. The critical point is that the tool selected must clearly address the learning target.

### #8 Learning is authentic.

The learning experiences are linked to issues and situations about which students are genuinely curious. In addition, they are often connected to larger social themes and problems. Importantly, students' performances are intended for audiences other than the teacher. The students wrestle with questions such as, "How does this influence my own life?" and "How can I share what I know with other people?" In short, students believe that what they are learning truly matters.

## Inquiry as a Way of Knowing

Inquiry is a process of learning that embraces all of the features described above. It embodies an educational philosophy that directly responds to the national emphasis on high standards and is bolstered by an expanding body of research about learning and the brain (Stripling, 2003; Marzano, Pickering, and Pollock, 2001; Senge et al., 2000; Bransford, Brown, and Cocking, 1999). It involves students in a spiraling cycle of questioning, investigating, verifying, and generating new questions

(Harada and Yoshina, 2004). Pappas and Tepe (2002) describe this type of learning as "an investigative process that engages students in answering questions, solving real world problems, confronting issues, or exploring personal interests" (27).

Stripling (2003, 8) succinctly outlines the inquiry process as follows:

- Connect—connect to self and previous knowledge, gain background knowledge, observe and experience to gain an overview

- Wonder—develop questions, make predictions and hypotheses

> *Library media specialists are potentially powerful partners in designing and implementing an inquiry approach to learning*

- Investigate—find and evaluate information to answer questions and test hypotheses, think about the information to illuminate new questions and hypotheses.

- Construct—build new understandings, draw conclusions about questions and hypotheses.

- Express—communicate new ideas, apply understandings to a new context or situation.

- Reflect—reflect on one's own process of learning and new

understandings gained from inquiry, pose new questions.

The benefits for students engaged in this type of learning are:

- Increased self-direction
- Higher levels of comprehension
- Growth in interpersonal skills and teamwork
- Greater motivation about what they are learning (Harada and Yoshina, 2004)

## Revisiting Our Scenario

Returning to our earlier scenario, how might we reshape the fourth grade assignment to reflect an inquiry approach to learning? Here is a modified example taken from *Inquiry Learning Through Librarian-Teacher Partnerships* (Harada and Yoshina, 2004). We encourage our readers to create other possibilities.

*Students visit the local zoo and return with many questions about where these animals originally came from and what the animals' lives would be like if they were back in their real homes. Back in the classroom, they generate a number of questions that center on the relationship between living things and their habitats. With the teacher's help, they settle on the following as key questions they want to study:*

- *Which plants and animals live in a particular habitat?*

- *How do plants and animals survive in that habitat? What challenges do they face?*

### Figure 1: Example of Inquiry Process in Action

| Inquiry process | Example |
|---|---|
| Connect | Students visit zoo to gain background knowledge. |
| Wonder | Students generate questions about the animals and their habitats. |
| Investigate | Students organize in teams and plan strategies to find information that answers their questions. |
| Construct | Students collect and synthesize their information. |
| Express | Students apply their information by creating various products for an exhibit. |
| Reflect | Students assess their progress and performance throughout the project. |

- *How does the habitat help plants and animals meet their needs?*
- *What body parts and behaviors help animals survive?*

*Students decide that they want to create an exhibit that combines murals, animals, and posters describing their various animals. The teacher involves the library media specialist in the project. Working together, they help students organize themselves in teams to plan their information-search strategies and assign responsibilities for the exhibit's products. Throughout the project, students assess their progress, along with the teacher and the library media specialist. The month-long study culminates in an exhibit that is staged in the library media center. Students invite the entire school and their parents to visit the exhibit and they serve as the guides for this three-day event.*

The figure below summarizes how this particular scenario is an example of inquiry learning.

## Role of the Library Media Specialist

Library media specialists are potentially powerful partners in designing and implementing an inquiry approach to learning. They are strategically positioned to work with entire school populations and examine curriculum from a big-picture perspective (Harada, 2003). Stripling (2003) maintains that library media specialists can "teach inquiry skills to all students and across the curriculum" (33).

In the fourth grade scenario, the enterprising library media specialist has numerous opportunities to integrate information literacy skills. The figure below poses examples of what she or he might do as a collaborative partner in the project.

## Conclusion

Inquiry places students at the center of the learning process. The power of inquiry is that it is a way of "respecting, building upon, and supporting all learners, tall and small" (Mills and Donnelly, 2001, xix). When the library media specialist is a collaborative partner in inquiry learning practices, the division disappears between what happens in the classroom and in the library media center (Harada and Yoshina, 2004). Even more important, the boundaries vanish between the school and the outside world. When instructors and students create such communities of inquiry, Stripling (2003) maintains that we "have the potential to change the national conversation from 'All students *can* learn' to 'All students *will* learn'" (36).

## Works Cited

Bransford, J. D., Brown, A. L., and Cocking, R., eds. 1999. *How People Learn: Brain, Mind, Experience, and School.* Washington, DC: National Academy Press.

Harada, V. H. 2003. "Empowering Learning: Fostering Thinking across the Curriculum." In *Curriculum Connections Through the Library,* eds. B. K. Stripling and S. Hughes-Hassell. Westport, CT: Libraries Unlimited, pp. 41–65.

Harada, V. H., and Yoshina, J. M. 2004. *Inquiry Learning Through Librarian-Teacher Partnerships.* Worthington, OH: Linworth Publishing.

Marzano, R. 2003. *What Works in Schools: Translating Research into Action.* Alexandria, VA: Association for Supervision and Curriculum Development.

Marzano, R., Pickering, D. J., and Pollock, J. E. 2001. *Classroom Instruction That Works.* Alexandria, VA: Association for Supervision and Curriculum Development.

McKenzie, J. 2000. *Beyond Technology: Questioning, Research, and the Information Literate School.* Bellingham, WA: FNO Press.

Mills, H., and Donnelly, A. 2001. *From the Ground Up: Creating a Culture of Inquiry.* Portsmouth, NH: Heinemann.

Newmann, F. M., ed. (1996). *Authentic Achievement: Restructuring Schools for Intellectual Quality.* San Francisco: Jossey-Bass.

Pappas, M. L., and Tepe, A. E. 2002. *Pathways to Knowledge™ and Inquiry Learning.* Englewood, CO: Libraries Unlimited.

Perkins, D. N. 1992. *Smart Schools: From Training Memories to Educating Minds.* New York: Free Press.

### Figure 2: Example of LMS Involvement in an Inquiry Project

| Inquiry process | What the LMS might do |
| --- | --- |
| Connect | Expand on zoo field trip by taking students on an Internet field trip to explore how animals survive in different environments. |
| Wonder | Help students generate higher-order questions using a webbing technique. |
| Investigate | Work with students on keyword searching strategies. Brainstorm with them the various types of resources that might be useful for their investigation including community and online sources of information. |
| Construct | Model effective note-taking strategies (e.g., highlight key ideas). |
| Express | Help students synthesize their information using graphic organizers (e.g., create concept maps of information to include in their posters). |
| Reflect | Collaborate with the teacher and students in designing rubrics that assess students' performance throughout the inquiry process as well as the students' culminating products. |

Senge, P. et al. 2000. *Schools That Learn.* New York: Doubleday.

Stiggins, R. J. 1997. *Student-Centered Classroom Assessment.* Columbus, OH: Prentice-Hall, Inc.

Stripling, B. K. 2003. "Inquiry-Based Learning." In *Curriculum Connections Through the Library*, eds. B. K. Stripling and S. Hughes-Hassell. Westport, CT: Libraries Unlimited, pp. 3–39.

Wiggins, G., and McTighe, J. 1998. *Understanding by Design.* Alexandria, VA: Association for Supervision and Curriculum Development.

*Violet H. Harada is a Professor in the Library and Information Science Program at the University of Hawaii. She coordinates the school library preparation program there. Joan M. Yoshina is a recently retired Library Media Specialist whose last assignment was at Mililani Mauka Elementary in Hawaii. Harada and Yoshina are co-authors of* Inquiry Learning Through Librarian-Teacher Partnerships *(Linworth Publishing, Inc., 2004). The authors may be contacted at vharada@hawaii.edu.*

Harada, V.H., & Yoshina, J.M. (2004). Moving from rote to inquiry: Creating learning that counts. *Library Media Connection, 23*(2), 22-24.

# Tools of the Trade: Comparison of Conventional and Inquiry-Focused Schools

## By Violet H. Harada and Joan M. Yoshina

This chart compares a traditional approach to instruction and learning versus an inquiry-based approach; and it is found on page 4 (Figure 1.1) in *Inquiry Learning Through Librarian-Teacher Partnerships* by Violet H. Harada and Joan M. Yoshina (Linworth Publishing, Inc. 2004).

| Attributes | Conventional school | Inquiry-focused school |
|---|---|---|
| Students | Passive learners | Active, engaged learners |
| Teachers, Library Media Specialists | Content-oriented<br>Teacher as information provider | Student-oriented<br>Teacher as facilitator |
| Scheduling | Rigid | Flexible |
| School culture | Bureaucratic | Collaborative |
| Curriculum and instruction | Textbook-driven<br>Teacher-focused<br>Breadth emphasized<br>Topic-oriented<br>Fragmented | Standards-driven<br>Student-negotiated<br>Depth emphasized<br>Thematic or problem-based<br>Integrated |
| Assessment | Evaluation at the end<br>Right answers are stressed<br>Teacher assesses<br>Grading is the goal<br>Asks, "What do we know?" | Assessment is ongoing<br>Diverse responses are encouraged<br>Students and teacher assess<br>Goal is improving learning and teaching<br>Asks, "How do we come to know?" |
| Resources | Restricted to resources available in the classroom | Expands to resources beyond the school |
| Technology | Focus on learning about technology | Use of technology as a tool for learning |

*Violet Harada is an Associate Professor in the Library and Information Science Program at the University of Hawaii where she also coordinates the specialization for school library media preparation.*

*Joan Yoshina recently retired from the Hawaii Department of Education after thirty-four years as an Elementary and High School Teacher, a Language Arts Specialist, and a Library Media Specialist.*

Editor's Note: Each issue will feature reproducible items that are designed for you to share with your school community. It might be a tool to help manage the library media center or an executive summary of an important library-related issue for your administrator or colleagues. Each carries permission for you to reproduce the material within the building in which you work.

Harada, V., & Yoshina, J. (2004). Tools of the trade: Comparison of conventional and inquiry-focused schools. *Library Media Connection*, 23(2), 25

# Collaboration: It Really Does Work!

## By Jennifer L. Youssef

## A Teacher's Perspective

As a teacher after the "No Child Left Behind" program has been established, I feel a little overwhelmed with all of the pre-testing, quizzing, testing, writing portfolios, projects, post-testing, and state and nationally mandated tests. On top of the weeks lost to testing, we have a very rigid curriculum in which to teach an abundance of objectives in a little amount of time. How can teachers help students not just learn, but understand what we teach in so short of a time span? One strategy that I found to work very well is collaboration between a classroom teacher and a library media specialist.

## Team Building

Sixth grade students are often required to write an in-depth research paper with a thesis statement, supporting details, note cards, and a bibliography. This assignment is often stressful and overwhelming for all involved: teachers, parents, and students.

The research objective in the state curriculum may be vague about topics and the how-to steps to get to the end result. Normally, it is the responsibility of the classroom teacher to comprehend the curriculum and construct a project to teach the skills that enable the students to complete the task. However, many classroom teachers are not trained in the area of information skills and research.

This year I tried something new to alleviate the stress on myself and benefit my coworkers. First, I thought of what associates I could collaborate with on this project. I worked with a sixth grade English teacher who is new to the grade level and has never completed the research paper. A sixth grade social studies teacher, also the curriculum leader for the grade and department chair, worked with me to determine a list of appropriate topics. Also, I worked with our school's library media specialist for her expertise in helping to guide me in the collaboration. I explained my goal for the collaboration to the cooperating teachers and asked for any input.

After our initial meetings, we had a plan. The social studies teacher helped identify famous historical people in the curriculum (figures who would be included on the state-wide assessment test in May). The English teacher and I worked together to identify the steps and goals we wanted the students to accomplish with their research paper. The library media specialist and I worked together to strategize what information skills they needed to learn to research their famous person in history. Second, I contacted the local public library and explained the research project so they would be able to help students. The local librarian was also sent a copy of the project with a name and contact number for any questions. The local librarian was very receptive and extremely appreciative with our conversation.

> How can teachers help students not just learn, but understand what we teach in so short of a time span?

## Let the Collaboration Begin!

With a plan in hand, we were ready to collaborate. Upon briefly explaining to the students in a letter to their parents the requirements on the paper, we began the process of instructing the students in research. The role of the classroom teacher was to teach the students the lessons on how to write a thesis statement and supporting details prior to researching in the library media center. The students are not required to know everything or even anything about their topic, but they need to think about a thesis statement and three supporting details as they are acquiring new information. The library media specialist and I worked together and produced several PowerPoint presentations on paraphrasing, Big 6™, research, taking notes, plagiarism, citations, online

subscriptions, and CD-ROMs. We incorporated worksheets, such as graphic organizers, and several Kagan strategies to ensure that the students practiced the skills. Following three days of PowerPoint mini-lessons, the students selected a famous person in American history and began their guided research with the assistance of the library media specialist and the classroom teacher. We were very excited to see that the students applied content from the mini-lessons in the library media center. As the students were researching, we reminded them to think about their thesis statement and three supporting details, and to look for pertinent information. After four days of dedicated research time in the library media center, we noticed a considerable difference between the previous years of researching, without the collaboration between classroom teacher and library media specialist, and this school year. The students were very eager to take their research and form a paper detailing the facts about their famous person in American history.

## Back to the Classroom

As we moved from the library media center back into the classroom, we focused on writing a thorough research paper. The English teacher and I worked with each student to compose a thesis statement and three supporting details. Many students surprised us because their thesis statements and supporting details were so well written. Most of the students did not require as much one-on-one conferencing as previous years. After we determined if they acquired enough information on each detail, we focused on writing a bibliography. This task was a little more difficult for the students to grasp, especially with Internet sites, but we were elated that the majority of the students retained what they learned from the mini-lesson and cited their sources effectively. It only required one class block time to complete the lesson. In previous years, it has taken two or more class blocks because many students forgot to write down information, such as author or contributor, article title, publisher, publication city, publication date, and page numbers, from encyclopedias. I attribute the success this time to the collaboration between the library media specialist and the classroom teacher working so well together and providing meaningful minilessons on citations.

Next, the English teacher and I provided a step-by-step outline for the students to fill in, along with a completed example outline to demonstrate the process. It showed the thesis statement and three supporting details, and adding detail sentences under each of the three supporting details. From the outline, the students were able to write a rough draft. After reviewing the outline handout with the students, they had a very clear idea of what to include. Finally, the students wrote their research paper from their guided outline. To complete the project, each student typed the handwritten research paper on an AlphaSmart® (small replica of a computer keyboard with a tiny screen to view as you are typing). After checking their paper on the computer, they printed it out with a title page, table of contents, and correctly written bibliography, and placed it in a folder ready to be graded. In the end, the students were so proud of their research papers. They couldn't wait to see the grade they received and placed the papers in their writing portfolio as one of their best works ever.

## Collaboration Works!

Working collaboratively with other classroom teachers and the library media specialist can transform a tedious assignment into an exciting, memorable project. Not only did the students learn a new skill, but all who were involved learned something new, too. Learning can be fun, especially when everyone joins together and helps out one another. As a result of the collaboration on the research paper, the other five English teachers on the grade level have met with us and signed up with the library media specialist to start their research papers. Yeah for collaboration!

---

*Jennifer L. Youssef is a grade 6 social studies and English teacher at Corporate Landing Middle School in Virginia Beach, Virginia. She has a Master's Degree in Elementary/Middle School Education from Old Dominion University and is seeking a license endorsement as a library media specialist.*

Youssef, J.L. (2005). Collaboration: It really does work! *Library Media Connection, 24*(1), 40-41.

# Open Doors to Collaboration With an Open House

## By Beth Yoke

Does your long-range plan contain something like "Build a better relationship with the school faculty"? Does the task seem almost too daunting to accomplish? As library media specialists, we know we should collaborate with teachers, but this is not an easy undertaking and it doesn't happen overnight. A good first step towards collaborating with faculty is a library open house. Teachers and staff will appreciate the attention and the chance to interact in a relaxed atmosphere instead of a stuffy inservice workshop. You will be thankful for the chance to meet and greet teachers. These informal interactions will help pave the way to building the kind of professional relationships you need in order to successfully collaborate with your faculty.

### Careful Planning Is the Key to Success

The goal is an experience that blends relaxation and fun with information and resources about you and your library program. The first thing to do is schedule a date. The end of September is a great time to host such an event. Most teachers have settled into their routine, and it is too soon in the school year for report cards and exams to occupy much of their time. Look closely at the school calendar and pick a day when the fewest after-school activities are going on. Try to avoid Mondays and Fridays, as these days are usually busy days for everyone. Checking with the school secretary is recommended. Schedule the event to begin just after the end of the school day. Allow yourself enough time so that you have a full four weeks to plan the event.

### Work out the Details

Food is a must. If you are on a tight budget, recruit parents and library supporters to furnish some of the refreshments. Try to offer a variety of munchies and drinks to satisfy different tastes, but keep it simple and don't kill yourself whipping up gourmet dishes.

You may want to consider serving "mocktails," or cocktails without the alcohol, but check with your principal to be sure this concept is acceptable with him or her. Fruity drinks complete with little umbrellas help promote a festive atmosphere and add some fun to the occasion. Bring in a blender and recruit a parent or teacher to be the "bartender."

Besides refreshments, it would be beneficial to offer other enticements, such as a door prize. Local businesses are often more than willing to donate an item as long as you provide them with some documentation so they will be able to deduct it from their taxes. Usually a thank-you letter on your letterhead that states what the donated item was will suffice.

> Secretaries, cafeteria workers, and custodial staff are a vital part of the school, and they can be important library supporters if you get them involved in your program.

Entertainment of some sort is also a good idea. Perhaps some of the school's band members can be recruited to play some background music. If that proves too complicated, a CD player and a variety of CDs will do just fine.

Once you've made plans for the fun part of the open house, it's time to think about what educational items and resources you want to make available. Setting up different stations in your library is an effective way to organize the event. You can create displays for new books and videos that you want teachers to know about. You can set up a TV and VCR so teachers can preview the videos. On one table have vendor catalogs that teachers can peruse; furnish wish lists that can fill out for items they would like the library to consider purchasing.

Another station could be your computer area. Boot up any new online resources you've acquired and provide simple "how-to" sheets for faculty and staff so they can get hands-on experience with the new resource. Inviting your local public librarian is a great idea, too. Provide him or her with a space to spread out some resources and talk with teachers about the library's services for educators. If you have any new equipment, be sure it is on hand for teachers to examine as well.

Locating the food in areas near these various stations will help ensure that teachers and staff take advantage of both the fun and informational aspects of your open house. If you have a small library and space is at a premium, you may need to get creative with your physical arrangement. It might also be beneficial to consider holding your open house in shifts, perhaps by grouping teachers by academic areas or grade levels.

### Advertise your Event

Pick a theme for your open house that helps convey the message that this event will be fun—for instance, a tropical theme with the message "We survived September." If your budget allows and if you're so inclined, purchase decorations to go with your theme or recruit art students or service groups to create them. You can also use clip art on your invitations to represent your theme.

Invitations created with a desktop publisher work well. You can place them in mailboxes or hand deliver them yourself or through a student helper. You may want to ask teachers to RSVP so you'll know how much food to provide. Be sure to invite your building administrators as well, and don't forget another important group: school staff. Secretaries, cafeteria workers, and custodial staff are a vital part of the school, and they can be important library supporters if you get them involved in your program.

Another simple way to advertise is to make colorful buttons or tags for the library staff. They can say something simple like "I'll see you at the Open House!" Posting flyers in faculty areas such as the lounge or departmental offices can serve as colorful reminders about the open house.

Perhaps the best form of advertising is simply word of mouth. Talk with your teachers, staff, and administrators and encourage them to come. A personal invitation from you will mean a lot.

## On the Big Day

Be sure to clear your afternoon schedule to give yourself some time to set up. If this isn't possible, recruit parents, teachers, or other library supporters to help set up while you handle your regular library duties. Ask a responsible student or library supporter to be the photographer for the event. Try and greet teachers as they arrive, and make an effort to talk to as many people as you can. Be sure to thank them for coming. Think of the open house as a way to expose your faculty, staff, and administrators to what it is that you and your library program have to offer. Instead of getting bogged down in detailed discussions about a particular question a person may have, schedule a later date and time with him or her so the two of you can meet without the distractions or interruptions of the open house.

## After the Open House

Be sure to follow up on any appointments you scheduled. It's also a great idea to follow through on less formal requests that you may have received. Perhaps a teacher expressed a passing interest in learning how to create Web Quests. Send him or her an article or a URL for a Web site about Web Quests. The extra effort you take after the open house will remind teachers that you are not only willing to help them but have the training and skills to do so.

Another important thing to do after the open house is promote your success. Place pictures and a brief article about the event in your library and school newsletters, or post them on the school's Web site. This shows parents, community members, and faculty who couldn't attend the event the positive things that are going on in your library. Most important, don't forget to thank all those who lent their time to help you plan and carry out the event.

*Beth Yoke is Executive Director of the Young Adult Library Services Division, American Library Association, 50 E. Huron Street, Chicago, IL, 60611.*

Yoke, B. (2003). Open doors to collaboration with an open house. *Library Media Connection, 22*(1), 44-45

# School Library Ethics—A Battle of Hats

## By Carol Simpson

One must go backward to understand the concept of ethics. Originating with the Greek word *ethos*, meaning character, ethics follows only philosophy in guiding a profession. Philosophy gives a profession its foundation, whereas ethics gives the profession its walls. Most trace contemporary ethics to the writings of Immanuel Kant who wrote, "Treat every human person whether in your own person or that of another as an end and never merely as a means" (in Froehlich, 264). Essentially Kant was making a case for the Golden Rule.

Professional ethics, however, extend far beyond the "do unto others…" philosophy. Froehlich (2000) reports that "…ethical principles are called into play when deliberating about values, particularly when values may run into conflict…and when one value may take priority over another." (p. 267) When one is forced to defend one's profession and one's program, it is quite likely that the values of various stakeholders will clash. Karen Adams (2001) defines professional ethics as "rule ethics, as they prescribe an external standard for the conduct of one's profession." She continues, "Professional codes of ethics give practitioners material for internal reflection to encourage self-criticism by the practitioner." (p. 7) Lindsey (1985) finds that a code of ethics is reflective of a profession's attitude toward service and the responsibility it feels toward the clients it serves.

In the US, the American Library Association (ALA) has established a code of ethics for the profession in the United States. Analogous to the code of ethics established by the National Education Association, or the American Medical Association, this statement of principles shapes the practice of the profession in that political arena. In Canada, The Canadian Library Association has a similar document.

The ALA code of ethics has been revised several times. The latest revision was in 1995 (with an explanatory statement passed in 2001). However the concepts presented in the code are central to the profession and have remained unchanged since 1939, save for changes in wording meant to clarify the concepts to both the profession and to the general public. In fact, the preface of the 1981 version states: "Since 1939, the American Library Association has recognized the importance of codifying and making known to the public and the profession the principles which guide librarians in action." (ALA, History) These principles are the heart and the foundation of the profession. They are the tenets that one adopts to become part of the profession. Whether you agree with all the political machinery of the Association or not, the foundation principles remain the same. This is what librarianship is all about.

> Information Power *gives us standards, but it doesn't give us ethics.*

## Many Hats, Many Points of View

The school library is not only affected by the ethical code of the American Library Association, however. Both the American Library Association and the Association for Educational Communications and Technology (AECT) are responsible for the national standards set for the profession. Both ALA and AECT have highly considered and carefully worded statements of ethics. While not completely parallel, there are distinct similarities between the two codes. As members of the faculty, school librarians are educators. In fact, many, if not most, school librarians are also credentialed teachers. Since teachers have their own codes of ethics, librarians have now assumed yet another mantle of ethical responsibilities under which to labor. Adding personal and religious ethical values to the mix yields a melt-ing pot of behaviors that may be in total conflict.

Taking on multiple ethical frameworks assumes that all the codes have similar goals and intentions. Since each of these roles has its own point of view, it is reasonable to expect there will be times when the various roles will conflict. What the National Education Association perceives as appropriate behavior for a teacher to follow when communicating with parents, for example, may be diametrically opposed to what the American Library Association endorses as ethically correct practice. The many state library associations and state education groups each has some type of statement of ethical behaviors that may or may not be congruent with that of its national cousin.

Knowing what is the ethical framework of a profession gives members of that profession a playing field and rulebook. Can you imagine the medical profession without the Hippocratic Oath? The entire subset of medical ethics stems from that short, simple mission statement for the profession. Alas, librarianship, and more specifically school librarianship, has no such concise statement. *Information Power* gives us standards, but it doesn't give us ethics.

Many people disagree with the code of ethics of the profession. Interestingly, the longer-acknowledged professions, such as medicine, law, the priesthood, and the military, have far less dissent about ethical baselines than does librarianship. In those professions, generally only new advances in technology produce loud and animated debate about the application of ethical principles. For example, cloning—a cutting edge technology—has stirred extensive debate in medical, legal, and ecclesiastical circles over the ethics of the practice. The law finds ample debate fodder when new technologies are applied to old legal understandings. Apparently business has not arrived at a generally accepted code of ethics when one considers the recent accounting scandals and insider trading reports. Interestingly, in January 1990, Lillian Gerhardt wrote:

> The word 'ethics' is on every newspaper's front page and in the lips of every newscaster. This ethical din arises from grand scale thievery by legislators and stock manipulators and all the many commissions created to scrutinize big money scandals. It really ignores the fact that ethics go beyond monotonous, Gargantuan greed. (p. 4)

Ethics is simply the character of the profession. It is what one may count on, what one finds true and right, what one believes. It is the religion of the practice. While even true believers may quibble over the details, the basic concepts stay rooted in the basic belief. This is the ethic of any profession.

There are naysayers in any group. Robert Hauptman has taken the role of one who promulgates a contrarian view of the ALA code of ethics. He believes that one should pay more attention to one's personal ethical beliefs than to a rigid and possibly compromised code. He states:

> To act ethically is to consider basic principles, a course of action, and the potential results, and then to act in a responsible and accountable way. The ethical professional does not simply follow the mandates and fiats of the controlling organization or ethos, especially since the rules are sometimes formulated to protect the practitioner and not the client. (p. 13)

## The High and the Low of It

There are several views of most ethical codes. Librarianship is no exception. One might describe them as "high ethics" and "low ethics," or "preceptual ethics" and "survival ethics." The profession without question embraces some ethical concepts. Resistance to censorship is generally one of the most accepted. However, along with a resistance to improper *removal* of materials from the library

should go a resistance to *adding* improper materials to the collection by those who would promote a specific point of view; however, this important distinction isn't even mentioned in the 1989 Code of Ethics. (Gerhardt Ethical II, p. 4) One might consider that "high ethics" is a broad view of an ethical precept as applied to all aspects of the profession. "Low ethics" would be the application of the ethical principle with a strong dose of reality thrown in. Bodi (1998) finds that ethics is ambiguous because there are wars among competing interests. The fact may be, however, that it is competing ethics that cause the problem.

"Ethics matters because it helps us to act responsibly." (Hauptman, 139) Not having a standard by which to judge is the ethical dilemma. Without such a standard, we are free

> *Ethics is simply the character of the profession. It is what one may count on, what one finds true and right, what one believes. It is the religion of the practice.*

to apply ethics from other value systems, other aspects of our lives, and we all view things differently. A shared set of values gives us a basis on which to coalesce as a profession, a community. It also gives us a set of standards against which to judge the professional behavior of our peers. As Lillian Gerhardt wrote: "You can't accept reproach if you don't know why what you've done is reprehensible." (Nuts, p. 4)

### Works Cited

Adams, Karen Gunhild. "Ethics in librarianship: an overview." *PNLA Quarterly*. 65(3) (2001): 6–7.

American Library Association. "History of the Code of ethics: Statement on Professional Ethics." 6 December 2002 <www.ala.org/alaorg/oif/1981code.html>.

Association for Educational Communications and Technology. Code of Ethics. http://www.aect.org/About/Ethics.htm

Bodi, Sonia. "Ethics and information technology: some principles to guide students" *The Journal of Academic Librarianship* 24(6) (November 1998): 459–63. Library Literature and Information Science Full Text.

Froehlich, Thomas J. "Intellectual freedom, ethical deliberation and codes of ethics." *IFLA Journal* 26(4) (2000): 264–72.

Gerhardt, Lillian N. "Ethical back talk: chewing on ALA's Code". *School Library Journal* 36(1) (1990): 4.

Gerhardt, Lillian N. "Ethical back talk: II." *School Library Journal* 36(4) (1990): 4.

Gerhardt, Lillian N. "Nuts in May: wedded to confidentiality: the Unabomber and you." *School Library Journal* 42(5) (1996): 4.

Hauptman, Robert. *Ethics and Librarianship*. Jefferson, NC: McFarland, 2002.

Kant, Immanuel. *Foundations of the Metaphysics of Morals, 1959*. Translated by L.B. White. New York: Library of Liberal Arts. Quoted in: Froehlich, Thomas J., "Intellectual freedom, ethical deliberation and codes of ethics." *IFLA Journal* 26(4) (2000): 264–72.

Lindsey, Jonathan A. and Ann E. Prentice. *Professional ethics and librarians*. Phoenix: Oryx, 1985.

*Dr. Carol Simpson is Associate Professor in the School of Library and Information Sciences at the University of North Texas, and a Fellow in the Texas Center for Digital Knowledge. She is also the Editorial Director for Library Media Connection and the author of* Ethics in School Librarianship: A Reader *(Linworth, 2003) and* Copyright for Schools: A Practical Guide, 4th Edition *(Linworth, 2006).*

Simpson, C. (2004). School library ethics: A battle of hats. *Library Media Connection*, 22(4), 22-23.

# Tools of the Trade:
# Copyright Suggestions for Administrators

## By Carol Simpson

- **Model copyright compliance**. Request permission before photocopying copyrighted materials for your faculty. (There is limited fair use for copying for staff, anyway). Mark the copies as "Reprinted with permission from . . . ."

- **Be aware of video use in your building**. How much video is used? Is it related directly to instruction? Is it appropriate? Teachers rarely have enough instructional time. Can students afford to spend an hour and a half watching an entertainment video?

- **Have teachers document each video performance in their lesson plans**. There should be a close correlation between the current lesson and district and state curriculums.

- **Require teachers to clear all video use through your office or designated emissary**. Develop a form that identifies the teacher, video, and purpose of the showing. Teachers are less likely to use time-wasting videos if they feel the administrator is aware of what is being shown.

- **Know your curriculum**. If the fourth grade studies volcanoes, why is the third grade teacher showing a video about them?

- **Watch extracurricular activities**. The fair use exemption permits limited use of copyrighted materials in classroom situations. That exemption does not permit free use of copyrighted materials for student council dances, cheerleading posters, or video yearbooks.

- **Look around your building**. What type of decorations do you see? Are they bought from school suppliers, created by teachers, or copied from greeting cards, cartoons, or movie characters?

- **Enlist the assistance of staff members who are aware of copyright violations.** Teacher aides know what types of materials are being photocopied. Library media specialists know what videos are shown and what multimedia is appropriated. They can assist you with recordkeeping, but they shouldn't be put into the role of copyright police.

- **Help teachers find other creative ways to reward students.** Reward videos are public performances and require payment of royalties or written exemption from the copyright holder. Some videos in your collection may already have the necessary rights.

- **Keep accurate purchase records for audiovisual materials and computer software.** These records should be retained as long as the materials are in use. The records may be needed if there should be a question of legality. They also document performance rights.

- **Purchase a performance license for your building.** You can show some noninstructional videos for rewards or as quick fill-ins when events get rained out or teachers are involved in conferences.

- **Assist staff in their efforts to stay copyright compliant**. Make sure there are enough copies of computer software (or appropriate licenses) to cover each machine that will use the software. Budget for recordkeeping supplies, compliance reminder stickers for equipment, and sufficient consumables.

- **Keep an upbeat attitude**. Long-held habits die hard. Commiserate with those who complain that their favorite items are no longer permitted. Look on the bright side: You'll see how creative your teachers can be!

- **Remember that a good faith effort and an honest accounting can go a long way when someone does slip up.** Everyone makes occasional mistakes. Learn from them and go on.

You can find these tips and other useful information in Carol Simpson's book *Copyright for Schools: A Practical Guide,* 4th Edition (Linworth Publishing Inc., 2006).

*Dr. Carol Simpson is Associate Professor in the School of Library and Information Sciences at the University of North Texas, and a Fellow in the Texas Center for Digital Knowledge. She is also the Editorial Director for Library Media Connection and the author of* Ethics in School Librarianship: A Reader *(Linworth Publishing Inc., 2003) and* Copyright for Schools: A Practical Guide, 4th Edition *(Linworth Publishing Inc., 2006) and c-author of* Internet for Schools: A Practical Guide, 3rd Edition *(Linworth Publishing Inc., 2006).*

Simpson, C. (2005). Copyright suggestions for administrators. *Library Media Connection, 24*(5), 5.

# Plagiarism in an Electronic Age

## By Julieta Dias Fisher and Ann Hill

### How Big Is the Problem?

Doris Kearns Goodwin and Stephen Ambrose were recently in the news for "sloppy research." A *New York Times* reporter was forced to resign when the articles he had supposedly written on the sniper episodes in Washington D.C. and the war in Iraq were found to be plagiarized. These well-known authors are not the only ones accused of plagiarism. According to *Who's Who Among American High School Students,* "80% of the country's best students cheated to get to the top of their class and 53% say it is no big deal."

In the article "Academic Honesty: Teaching Kids Not to Take the Easy Way Out," Patricia J. Harned and Kathryn M. Sutliff (Our Children, 27(4), p. 4-5; Jan-Feb 2002) quote statistics taken from a 2001 survey conducted by Donald McCabe of Rutgers University and founder of the Center for Academic Honesty. Of 4,500 high school students interviewed by McCabe, 97% admitted to questionable academic honesty, 50% admitted to downright plagiarism, and 52% copied Web site information without using citations.

Plagiarism is not a new phenomenon. With the Internet, however, it is just easier to copy and take credit for work that belongs to someone else. The Internet has changed the rules and the perception of what is acceptable and what is not. "Basically our teachers are clueless about the Internet" is what students told McCabe. They found it easy to copy sentences, paragraphs, even full page papers from the Net, and use them without documentation and with a low probability of being caught. McCabe also found a perceived lack of consequences – 47% of students said teachers ignore cheating and do not want the aggravation of having to report and deal with the administration, parents, and students. Last year in Kansas, Christine Pelton, with the support of her administration failed 28 of her sophomores for cheating. When the parents complained, the school board intervened and asked the teacher to be more lenient. She resigned instead. Many teachers do not want to deal with this type of situation. Since they know that their academic integrity policies will wilt under parental criticism and subsequent lack of support from the administration, they in turn become lenient with these policies, thus giving students carte blanche to cheat.

### What's Out There and How Students Find It

Students can sit at their computers and with a click of a mouse find paper mills where they can download free papers and complete research assignments without strenuous thought. The following are just a few of the many Internet paper mill sites:

> *Students can sit at their computers and with a click of a mouse find paper mills where they can download free papers and complete research assignments without strenuous thought.*

www.gradesaver.com/ClassicNotes.html
www.cheater.com
www.cyberessays.com

Original papers can be purchased for a nominal fee of around $25.00 per page at these sites where credit cards are cheerfully accepted!
www.genuispapers.com
www.cheathouse.com
www.houseofcheats.com

Students can also search Google, Yahoo and Dogpile for term papers. All they have to do is put in their topic and the word "essay." For example, a search for *Crime and Punishment* will garner over 901,000 hits. This makes it easy for students to copy, paste, add a few personal touches, and then hand in a ready-made paper.

Students offer many reasons for cheating. Many state that they lead busy lives and don't have time. Pressure for good grades comes from both parents and peers. Some students feel they have to cheat in order to compete to get good grades and/or go to college, while others are either procrastinators or lazy. Some students cheat because of low self-confidence, while others do it for the thrill of testing boundaries by breaking rules.

### Options for Media Specialists and Teachers

So how can teachers win the fight against plagiarism in the face of such odds? Here are some tips to help prevent plagiarism:

- At the beginning of the year, ask the students for a writing sample and put it on file. Alert the students that this will serve as a barometer for their upcoming research paper.

- Follow the steps of the research process. As a part of the research process, the librarian and teacher should define plagiarism. Consider taking students on a virtual tour of the paper mills to show them the "quality" of the papers available.

- Give the students an academic honesty quiz and discuss the results with them.

- Use peer groups to evaluate rough drafts of essays and papers.

- Require that copies of Internet and database sites be submitted with final papers.

- Vary the topics from year to year or provide a list of specific topics; don't allow students to choose a topic.

- Require specific components as part of the process, such as two Internet sources, two books, two articles, etc.

- Vary the format of the final product; instead of a formal written paper ask for PowerPoint presentations, Web pages, speeches, and oral presentations.

- Require a bibliography or works cited page for all assignments regardless of whether the format is electronic or written.
- Create an archive of all students' papers by having the students e-mail the papers to you or hand in a disk with their papers. Organize your archive by topic so that if a paper looks suspicious, you can easily locate the topic in your archive. Do this by using the "Edit—Find in Page" command to locate distinctive words and phrases.
- Set up student conferences to discuss the topics and the students' progress.
- Ask the students to evaluate the research process on the day they hand in their finished work. This evaluation should include what they learned from the assignment, the problems encountered, and the resources used.

If all else fails, here are some tips to detect plagiarism:

- Check for unusual formatting. This could mean that the students have cut and pasted the information into their papers without matching the fonts.
- Compare the in-text documentation with the works cited list and see if they match. The sources from paper mills are usually older, sometimes not in print, nor available in most libraries. If your school requires a certain style, check to see if the correct citation style has been used; for instance, if you require MLA and the paper is in APA this will be another indicator of a stolen paper.
- Since students usually write their own introductions and conclusions, you can use the Internet to locate certain passages that do not seem to match these sections. Phrase searching in several search engines can help to verify the validity of a paper by looking for distinctive phrases from the middle of the paper.

You can spend your life trying to track down students who plagiarize, but who has time for that? Simplify your life by taking a proactive approach. Which is better: prevention or detection? The best, of course, is prevention as it is proactive. To use an old cliché by one of our founding fathers, an *ounce of prevention is worth a pound of cure!*

*Julieta Dias Fisher and Ann Hill are Library Media Specialists at Washington Township High School in Sewell, New Jersey. They are also the authors of* Tooting Your Own Horn: Web-Based Public Relations for the 21st Century Librarian *(Linworth Publishing Inc., 2003).*

Fisher, J.D., & Hill, A. (2004). Plagiarism in an electronic age. *Library Media Connection, 23*(3), 18-19

# A Tale of Two Libraries: School and Public Librarians Working Together

## By Julie Scordato

You may have thought of, or actually created partnerships with public libraries in the areas of book talking, author visits, or summer reading program promotion; but have you thought of teaching online research classes with the help of a public librarian? Finding a public librarian who enjoys working with teens and has solid research skills may help you and teachers convince students that no, one can't find everything needed for a term paper on Google. There are some specific steps to building a partnership with your public library to bring further research instruction into the classroom. The public librarian can round out your instruction and encourage students to get a public library card.

The right public librarian can talk about a range of relevant research topics for your middle and high school students. More and more small to medium sized public libraries offer their catalogs online and most public libraries offer links to various reliable, comprehensive research databases like EBSCOhost or ProQUEST. According to the 2001 NCES Public Library Survey, 96% of public libraries offer direct Internet access to patrons and 90% offer other electronic resources. Public librarians can also provide a new angle on searching school resources. The key, of course, is finding a public librarian who is open, if not outwardly enthusiastic about working with teens. This could be either a children's or adult services librarian. Focusing on what the public library can offer in electronic and other resources can be useful in several ways. Students who may not value the public library for traditional materials may be enticed to get a library card. Students who already use the public library may be motivated to use it more often. For teachers who live out of town or just haven't utilized the local library, the library can introduce them to pertinent resources. *http://nces.ed.gov/surveys/libraries/highlights.asp

## Motivating the Motivators

In a perfect world teachers would be aware of all of the resources available to them in both the school and public library. Teaching creates a demanding schedule and for as many instances of teachers being inquisitive, open, and interested in new opportunities and resources, there are just as many instances of teachers feeling burned-out, overwhelmed, and unmotivated in learning about new things to use in the classroom. School and public librarians can work together to help teachers and students deal with information overload by introducing high quality information and ways to access it quickly and conveniently. By setting up research classes in the media center or computer lab, busy instructors can see firsthand another librarian enthusiastic to help teens become better readers and researchers and the partnerships can start to grow.

Word of mouth is the tool for building these kinds of partnerships. Once one teacher agrees to give a whole class period to a research class, the positive results will reverberate throughout the halls. When a few teachers can vouch for the program, others will be more interested in similar classes for their own students and the original teacher will be open to other activities, like tours of the public library, booktalks, and coordinating author visits.

Do you ever feel like a broken record when talking about expanding/narrowing the search, not relying on a quick Internet search and the first results on the list? Having someone else to reiterate these points can help convince students that thoughtful strategies are important and necessary when searching any electronic resource. For the school librarian, having another person willing to help teach students can be a real morale booster.

### The public librarian and the high school student

When I teach a research class at Marysville High School. I always describe my job as "the person you go to for books on C+ programming, engine diagrams for a 1986 Camaro, the average rainfall of the Amazon forest, and a recipe for vegetarian chili." I then remind students that the library is a great place to earn volunteer service hours whether for National Honor Society, Student Council, or "other" things, and I'll exchange sly looks with some of the more sheepish teens. The final, and for me, most important thing I talk about before launching into instruction is the subject of fines and lost items on library card records. For some teens, the guilt, and, it wouldn't be an exaggeration to say anxiety, has kept them out of the library. Teens can have hefty charges of $50.00 or more, but I insist that this too can be corrected. I try to make it very clear that at our library, we do not want such charges or even fear of such charges to keep students from using our library. I assure them that most library users rack up fines at some point and also lose/break items. I use myself as an example to reiterate that arrangements can always be made, such as installment payments, working the charges off by volunteering, or a combination of both. Admittedly, not every public library may be so flexible with charges on teens' library cards. A survey, however (even as informal as the school librarian asking around), will reflect reasons for not using the public library (charges, transportation, uncomfortable around staff etc.), and this can help the public library develop strategies to counter these issues.

## View from Across the Street

From a public librarian's perspective, teaching research classes is a good way to re-establish the library with teens. There seems to be more interaction with public librarians and schools on the elementary level than in the higher grades. Building a public library presence in older students' minds is just as important, whether it is to prepare them for college with stronger research skills or whether it is to help those non-college track teens develop a better sense of information literacy. For all students, it's an opportunity to build their association of the public library with free access to quality information.

I tell teens that what I am about to tell them will help them get their homework, especially big projects, done easier and faster, and, for many, from home. The fact that teens can access both our online catalog and electronic databases from home is a real selling point right from the beginning. When I started these classes, I would model where to navigate on my own computer with the screen projected. I found though, that it is much easier, to simply talk the teens through it without using a computer myself. Teens know how to use a mouse and by not having the visual to refer to, teens must actively listen to my instruction to follow along. This also enables me to walk around the classroom or lab and make sure students are keeping up with me and not playing solitaire.

Research starts with a brief overview of our library's homepage and then I get them into the online catalog and guide them through a couple of popular materials searches to show them how to read a catalog entry, to spot where an item is in the system and to discern how to place reserves. If the teacher gives me a list of research topics beforehand, I then shift to more purposeful searches using the relevant topics. After a couple of these searches, I turn the class loose to search for books relevant to their topic and float around the room to troubleshoot. At this point there are usually a handful of teens that have their card and they began reserving items for their project. Of all the things that go on during my instruc-tion, this may be the one thing that motivates other teens to pick up applications for cards; seeing other teens use their cards immediately for their projects. This immediate, tangible benefit really stirs up the interest. Students who are 18 can sign up for a card on the spot and I have returned to the library with as many as 30 or 40 applications to add to the system.

After catalog searching, I take the class into the Web page listing all of our electronic databases. Generally, we have time to focus on one resource. I choose the database based on the class and assignment and often introduce EBSCOhost. I think it is important to capture students' attention by helping them appreciate the enormity of these resources. In EBSCOhost, for example, I will guide the teens through a layered search through the title list

> *I tell teens that what I am about to tell them will help them get their homework, especially big projects, done easier and faster and for many, from home.*

feature for a specific issue of a title. By getting teens to choose the magazine, from a list of hundreds or thousands, then choosing a single year and finally a single issue to review the articles therein, teens really grasp the breadth and depth of this resource they can access for free with a library card. After I talk about the importance of reviewing the different databases within the EBSCO collection, and how to choose the best combinations based on search topic, I choose a subject (ideally from the teacher's pre-submitted list) and we all do the same search from the basic search screen. I'll dissect the basic search screen and explain the full text, and all the search quali-fiers like "any word" searching versus "all word" searching etc. Even though I explain the importance of choosing search terms and what to think about when choosing them, it is best to illustrate.

## Shotgun Searching

Many teens want to search by long, too-specific phrases or full sentences like "Americans' fascination with the Jeep." It takes some time and persuasion to get students thinking in terms that are smaller, and more specific. Letting them conduct a couple of searches their way and getting frustrating results brings them around to follow my advice. Once we've done some practice searches with my suggestion, teens start actively pursuing their own subjects as I advise them on examining the results list, the choice between HTML and PDF formats, and the various pros and cons of e-mailing, linking, saving, and printing the article. The class ends with students independently searching their topics, asking questions specific to their topic and orienting themselves with the process. It's a far cry from typing in a phrase or sentence in Google.

Students continue to use these resources after the classes. Teachers tell me they notice a marked improvement in the information and references in the students' papers. Students also e-mail me or come to the library later with questions for other homework needs or suggestions to search for the next research topic. It is extremely gratifying as a public librarian to cultivate this relationship with the local high school. We are able to bring teens into the library (virtual or physical), to encourage teachers to see the public library as a rich, convenient resource, and to build a partnership with the high school librarian/media specialist in meeting teens' research needs.

*Julie Scordato is a Young Adult Librarian at the Reynoldsburg Branch of the Columbus (Ohio) Metropolitan Library System.*

Scordato, J. (2004). A tale of two libraries: School and public librarians working together. *Library Media Connection, 22*(7), 32-33.

# The Role of the Library Media Specialist in School Technology

## By Melissa E. Gardner

In March 2003, a total of 394 media specialists throughout the state of Kentucky completed an online survey regarding their professional development needs. The Public Relations subcommittee of the Kentucky School Media Association Board of Directors generated the questions and collected data from the three parts of the survey—demographics, professional development, and technology (see Appendix).

The committee designed the survey with two purposes in mind. The first purpose was to collect data regarding the professional development needs of media specialists throughout the state, their preferences as to what format this professional development should take, and when the professional development should be offered. The second purpose was to analyze the role of media specialists in technology integration. Results from the technology portion of the survey as well as discussion based on additional research follow.

### The Media Specialist as School Technology Coordinator

In most school systems across the state of Kentucky, school library media specialists are a valued part of the school technology team, or what Mike Eisenberg and Carrie Lowe (1999) refer to as "Information and Technology Teams" (I&T). Ideally, these teams provide an "integration of information, library, and instructional technology services, systems, resources and roles" with library media specialists, technology teachers, and administrators, working for the common goal of preparing students for success in the "information age" (Eisenberg & Lowe, 1999). In many instances, however, the media specialist fulfills more than one role on the team. For example, in the survey of Kentucky school library media specialists, 34 percent of the respondents stated that they also served as their school's technology coordinator.

A full partnership and true integration of responsibilities are needed to create the technology-rich learning centers of the future espoused by Eisenberg and Lowe. According to a survey published by *Independent School* in 2001, library media specialists are "performing the bulk of information technology and information literacy integration" (Ellis, 2001). Ellis goes on to state that:

Although, the survey showed many intersections between the roles of the media specialist and the technology specialist, the structures within the schools don't emphasize the key role the media specialists fill in technology integration. Only thirty-eight percent of the schools surveyed reported having a

> *The key for the future will be for library media specialists to be recognized as a valued part of the school technology or I&T team without having to fill many of the other roles on the team.*

school-wide plan for incorporating information literacy. Seventy-five percent of the schools reported having a technology committee, but only sixty-one percent of those committees included media specialists. (2001, 3)

The key for the future will be for library media specialists to be recognized as a valued part of the school technology or I&T team without having to fill many of the other roles on the team as well. A sharing of responsibilities must exist among team members for the I&T team to be truly effective.

The media specialist's skills in technology integration not only benefit students using the library media programs of the school, those skills also benefit the media specialist as a means

of job security. Mary Alice Anderson stated that "administrators everywhere want tech-savvy media specialists; they want media specialists who welcome and embrace technology and are leaders in their schools' technology and curriculum initiatives" (2002, Share of the Blame, 6) Gary Hartzell advocates that "library media specialists should be participants in the decisions affecting technology, curriculum and resources at the school and district level" (Lowe, 2001, Challenges, 1). Media specialists need to be proactive and promote their technology skills and knowledge. Media specialists need to become involved in school technology planning and in the teaching of technology.

### The Media Specialist as Technology Integration Specialist

According to the I&T model, the media specialist brings the information component to the Information & Technology team. As described by Eisenberg and Lowe:

Information is a librarian's business, and librarians are most qualified to create and assist teachers in implementing information literacy instruction. In terms of technology, librarians have led the way in teaching students technology skills in context throughout their professional history. Clearly, the library and information professional is an essential component of the Information & Technology team. At the same time, we must stress the necessity for librarians to reinvent themselves as they face new professional challenges. (1999, 4–5)

Library media specialists must embrace technology to be effective. According to Keith Curry Lance, "[Media Specialists] must ensure that school networks extend the availability of information resources beyond the walls of the library media center, throughout the building, and, in the best cases, into the students' homes" (2001, Common findings). To benefit the most from their technology investments, schools need to ensure that the skills are in place not only for students but also for teachers and administrators to use the technology and tie it to their curriculum effectively.

Technology use has been a major predictor in all three major studies on the impact of school library media programs on the academic achievement of U.S. public school students (Alaska, Pennsylvania, and Colorado). In the Alaska study, researchers were able to tie higher test scores to the availability of Internet-capable computers for student use in the media center. Achievement levels increased in both Pennsylvania and Colorado due in part to the availability of networked computers providing access to electronic sources of information (Lance, 2001).

Two main factors contribute to the impact of media specialists on technology usage in the schools. The first factor is the two-fold teaching role of the media specialist—instructor and collaborator. Media specialists teach students and help them to develop information literacy skills. Media specialists may deliver instruction directly to students or act as support for the instruction provided by the classroom teacher. Media specialists understand the information needs of teachers and provide them with the latest in information resources and technology. Kentucky's media specialists reported an average of 3.32 hours per week spent on collaboration with teachers on technology integration. On a scale of 1 to with 5 being fully integrated, the media specialists reported an average of 3.46 for the level of technology integration in their media centers.

The second factor is the attributes that media specialists have that distinguish them from their academic peers. Doug Johnson (2003, p. 3) lists eight professional attributes that he feels make media specialists successful in technology integration. These attributes are:

- A healthy attitude toward technology
- Good teaching skills
- An understanding of the role technology plays in information literacy

and how it fosters higher-thinking skills

- Experience as skillful collaborators
- Models for the successful use of technology
- The flexibility to provide in-building support
- A whole school view
- Concerns about the ethical use of technology

School media specialists have focused for many years on integrating curriculum and information technology. Using the KSMA survey, media specialists were asked about their own comfort level in using technology. The average response was 6.98 on a 1 to 10 scale with 10 being extremely comfortable. Media specialists are comfortable with automated catalogs,

> To benefit the most from their technology investments, schools need to ensure that the skills are in place not only for students but also for teachers and administrators to use the technology and tie it to their curriculum effectively.

circulation systems, electronic resources, and computer workstations within the media center and are able to extend that comfort into other areas of the curriculum as needed.

According to the KSMA survey, only 57 percent of schools in Kentucky are served by Technology Resource Teachers. Because of their training and the attributes listed above, library media specialists are able to fill that void on the technology team and are able to ensure that technology is successfully integrated into all aspects of the curriculum.

## The Media Specialist as a Student of Technology

Not only is the school library media specialist a teacher and user of technology, but he or she is also a student. "Our profession demands a lifelong commitment to learning—and that

applies to all of us. We should think more creatively, critically, and analytically as we mine appropriate and useful information for our students and faculty" (Young, 2003, 3). When surveyed, the Kentucky library media specialists listed their top three professional development needs:

- Information literacy and core content (22%)
- Information technology (21%)
- Content and posting of library Web pages (18%)

Many opportunities exist for media specialists to continue their own learning in the area of technology. The International Society for Technology in Education (ISTE) has recently created a Special Interest Group for Media Specialists (SIGMS) to provide support for library media specialists working to integrate instructional technology into the curriculum. Group members will be able to communicate via an e-mail list and on the SIGMS website. Many states offer summer sessions for media specialists in the area of instructional technology and information literacy. State computer/technology and library conferences also provide workshops and sessions geared toward media specialists. Online courses and direct instruction in all aspects of technology are also available from the colleges and universities as well as from the American Association of School Librarians (AASL).

## Conclusion

The survey conducted by the KSMA Public Relations Committee provides some insight into the current role of the school media specialist in technology integration. Further areas of investigation in this area might include:

- The impact of technology on standardized test scores. Are schools with high levels of technology integration more successful on standardized tests?
- The impact of media specialist experience on technology integration in the media center. Does a relationship exist between the years of experience of a media specialist and the degree of technology integration in the media center?

- The availability of technology. Does a relationship exist between the number of computers and related technologies and the level of technology integration?

Media specialists throughout the state of Kentucky are actively engaged in all aspects of technology in the schools. They are providing direction and support to Information and Technology Teams, helping students make valuable connections between their curriculum and their lives, and strengthening the role of the media specialist in the school. There is evidence to suggest that many of the state's media specialists feel confident in their technology abilities and in providing help to teachers and students in the area of technology. With the training opportunities available, Kentucky's media specialists (and media specialists around the country) will be able to face the challenge as their role in technology integration continues to evolve.

## Works Cited

Anderson, M. A. (2002). Why are Media Positions Cut? How Not to Survive! *Multimedia Schools*. 9(3). Retrieved May 28, 2003 from EBSCOhost.

Eisenberg, M. & Lowe, C. (1999). Call to Action: Getting Serious about Libraries and Information in Education. *Multimedia Schools*. 6(2): 18–22.

Ellis, K. V. (2001). Libraries and Information Literacy Survey Analysis. *Independent School*. 60: 14. Retrieved June 2, 2003 from EBSCOhost.

Johnson, D. (2003). Becoming Indispensable. *School Library Journal*. 49(2), 3. Retrieved May 28, 2003 from EBSCOhost.

Lance, K. C. Proof of the Power: Quality Library Media Programs Affect Academic Achievement. *Multimedia Schools*. 8(4). Retrieved June 2, 2003 from EBSCOhost.

Lowe, C. The Role of the School Library Media Specialist in the 21st Century. *Teacher Librarian*. 29(1), 30–34. Retrieved June 1, 2003 from EBSCOhost.

Young, T. E. (2003). Greatest Challenges for 2003. *School Library Journal*. 49(1), 48-51. Retrieved June 2, 2003 from EBSCOhost.

## Appendix

### Kentucky School Media Association Professional Development Needs Survey Questions

Actual survey may be viewed at http://intercom.virginia.edu/SurveySuite/Surveys/media/index2.html

1.01 In what school district do you work?

1.02 Grade levels served

1.03 How many years experience do you have in education?

1.04 How many years experience do you have as a media specialist?

1.05 Which type of degree do you hold in library science?

1.06 Are you currently a member of the Kentucky School Media Association?

2.01 Which format would you prefer for professional development?

2.02 Which format would be your second choice for professional development?

2.03 Which format would be your third choice for professional development?

2.04 Which time of year would you prefer to have professional development opportunities?

2.05 Which of the following do you see as your biggest professional development needs? Check all that apply.

| | |
|---|---|
| 02.05.01 | information technology |
| 02.05.02 | content and posting of library Web pages |
| 02.05.03 | collection development |
| 02.05.04 | mentoring/ collaboration |
| 02.05.05 | using threaded discussions/chats |
| 02.05.06 | flexible scheduling |
| 02.05.07 | information literacy and core content |
| 02.05.08 | Other, Please Specify |

3.01 Approximately how many hours per week do you spend collaborating with teachers on technology integration?

3.02 How would you rate your comfort level in using and integrating technology. 1 is extremely uncomfortable. 10 is extremely comfortable.

3.03 At what level is the integration of technology in your media center? A rating of 5 is very high. A rating of 1 is very low.

3.04 Do you currently serve as the school technology coordinator?

3.05 Is your school served by a technology resource teacher?

*Melissa Gardner is a Library Media Specialist/Technology Resource Teacher for the Kenton County School District in Erlanger, Kentucky and can be reached at mgardner@kenton.k12.ky.us.*

Gardner, M.E. (2004). The role of the library media specialist in school technology. *Library Media Connection*, 22(5), 48-50.

# Authentic Assessment in the Classroom . . . and the Library Media Center

## By Jon Mueller

Are your students information literate? How do you know? How could you find out? You could administer a multiple-choice test that assesses students' knowledge of relevant terminology, their ability to identify appropriate sources of information for different questions, and their awareness of the need to evaluate the accuracy, currency, relevancy, and authenticity of information found in different sources. Or, you could administer an authentic assessment that requires students to select appropriate sources for a specific question, then find, access, and evaluate those sources of information to be integrated into an answer to the question (e.g., a research paper).

What would each type of assessment tell you? A well-designed, multiple-choice test could tell if your students possess the knowledge and the skills required to complete a research task. You could then attempt to infer that the students could effectively apply that knowledge to real-world tasks requiring those skills. Yet, would a filled-in circle on a Scantron sheet give you such confidence?

On the other hand, what if students successfully completed an assessment in which they were required to formulate a question (or, perhaps, start with one), find appropriate sources of information for the question, access information from the sources, evaluate the quality of the information, and, finally, determine when they had sufficient information to answer the question? Would you be more confident that the students were information literate?

Educators are struggling with such assessment questions, from mathematics departments to social science teachers to special education classrooms, from Head Start to high school, from individual teachers to state boards of education. Clearly, calls for accountability are on the rise from the No Child Left Behind Act and other state and national efforts to measure student progress. But, aside from these more formal efforts at accountability, there is considerable value in knowing how well students are meeting the goals we have set for them, including information literacy goals.

Assessment should not just serve as a vehicle for assigning grades or comparing schools and districts. Gathering meaningful information about student performance allows us to identify strengths and weaknesses. Such information can help pinpoint specific areas that have improved or need improvement. Similarly, assessment data can inform educators about need for change in instruction to better address learning goals.

We also recognize that an overreliance on traditional assessments, such as multiple-choice tests, limits the type

> Authentic assessment is a form of assessment in which students perform real-world tasks that demonstrate meaningful application of essential knowledge and skills.

and quality of information we can gather (Wiggins, 1998). It is understandable if a teacher has 150 students and very little time to grade final assignments at the end of a quarter or semester that the teacher will look for assessments that can be quickly scored. But, we have to ask what we are missing by relying so heavily on tests composed of multiple-choice, true-false, and matching questions. To answer that question, we need to better understand an alternative—authentic assessment.

## What Is Authentic Assessment?

Authentic assessment is a form of assessment in which students perform real-world tasks that demonstrate meaningful application of essential knowledge and skills. Or, as Grant Wiggins (1993) describes it, authentic measures are "engaging and worthy problems or questions of importance, in which students must use knowledge to fashion performances effectively and creatively. The tasks are either replicas of or analogous to the kinds of problems faced by adult citizens and consumers or professionals in the field." Authentic tasks include analyzing a political cartoon, making observations of the natural world, computing the amount of paint needed to cover a particular room, and performing in a chorale.

Similarly, authentic tasks can range from elaborate projects spanning several weeks to brief activities. Many teachers have mistakenly equated authentic assessment with extensive assignments requiring considerable investment of time and effort for teacher and student alike. Yet, adults often face many simpler and briefer tasks in their work or life. For example, I send my introductory psychology students to a Web page I created, <http://jonathan.mueller.faculty. noctrl.edu/100/correlation_or_causation.htm>, which lists headlines taken from scientific news stories reported in the media. If students click on the headline, it will take them to the story. I can use such a resource in a variety of ways to capture brief activities adults engage in on a regular basis. For example, I ask students to determine if a headline (e.g., "Low self-esteem 'shrinks brains'") is causal or correlational in nature. Then, I ask them to determine if the research described in the article actually justifies such a claim. (Fortunately, the research in the self-esteem article was *not* consistent with the headline's claim!)

All of these tasks replicate real-world challenges, and student performance on all of them can be assessed. Multiple-choice questions can be designed to capture some ability to apply or analyze concepts, but filling in the corresponding circle on a

Scantron sheet does not begin to have the face validity of asking students to complete engaging tasks that replicate real-world ones. Of course, capturing a more authentic performance does not ensure validity.

## Measures of Validity

A measure cannot be valid if it does not effectively address the learning goals it was designed to assess. Thus, as described in Figure 1, the development of good assessments of any type begins with the development of meaningful goals and standards. Learning goals and standards are statements of what students should know and be able to do at some time (e.g., the end of 3rd grade or the end of a course on music theory). For a given standard, an educator would ask, "What indicates students have met these standards?" which would lead to the development or selection of a relevant authentic task. Next, the teacher would ask, "What does good performance on this task look like?" Those characteristics become the criteria by which one would judge student performance. Finally, the educator would identify likely levels of performance along which he or she could judge student performance for those criteria. The criteria and accompanying levels of performance are then usually combined into a rubric, a scoring scale for the assessment. (Elaboration of the four steps of developing an authentic assessment I just outlined, along with more examples of authentic assessments, can be found at my *Authentic Assessment Toolbox* Web site at <http://jonathan.mueller.faculty.noctrl.edu/toolbox>.

## Why Do It?

### Authentic Assessments Are Direct Measures

We do not just want students to *know* the content of the disciplines when they graduate. We, of course, want them to be able to *use* the acquired knowledge and skills in the real world. So, our assessments have to also tell us if students can apply what they have learned in authentic situations. If a student does well on a test of knowledge, we might infer that the student could also apply that knowledge. But that is indirect evidence. I could more directly check for the ability to apply by asking the student to use what he or she has learned in some meaningful way. If I taught someone to play golf, I would not check what he or she learned with just a written test. I would want to see more direct, authentic evidence. I would put my student out on a golf course to play. Similarly, if we want to know if our students can interpret literature, calculate potential savings on sale items, test a hypothesis, develop a fitness plan, converse in a foreign language, or find useful information, then authentic assessments will provide the most direct evidence.

### Authentic Assessments Capture the Constructive Nature of Learning

A considerable body of research on learning has found that we cannot simply be fed knowledge. We need to construct our own meaning of the world, using information we have gathered and were taught and our own experiences with the world. Thus, assessments cannot just ask students to repeat back information they have received. Students must also be asked to demonstrate they have accurately constructed meaning about what they have been taught. Furthermore, students must be given the opportunity to engage in the construction of meaning. Authentic tasks not only serve as assessments, but also as vehicles for such learning.

### Authentic Assessments Provide Multiple Paths to Demonstration of Learning

We all have different strengths and weaknesses in how we learn. Similarly, we are different in how we can best *demonstrate* what we have learned. Regarding the traditional assessment model, answering multiple-choice questions does not allow for much variability in how students demonstrate the knowledge and skills they have acquired. On the one hand, that is a strength of tests because it makes sure everyone is being compared on the same domains in the same manner, which increases the consistency and comparability of the measure. On the other hand, testing favors those who are better test-takers and does not give students any choice in how they believe they can best demonstrate what they have learned.

Thus, it is recommended that multiple and varied assessments be

---

### Figure 1: **Steps for Creating an Authentic Assessment (Mueller, 2004)**

#### Questions to Ask:

1) What should students know and be able to do?
This list of knowledge and skills becomes your . . .

**STANDARDS**

2) What indicates students have met these standards?
To determine if students have met these standards, you will design or select relevant . . .

**AUTHENTIC TASKS**

3) What does good performance on this task look like?
To determine if students have performed well on the task, you will identify and look for characteristics of good performance called . . .

**CRITERIA**

4) How well did the students perform?
To discriminate among student performance across criteria, you will create a . . .

**RUBRIC**

---

used so that 1) a sufficient number of samples are obtained (multiple), and 2) a sufficient variety of measures are used (varied). Variety of measurement can be accomplished by assessing the students through different measures that allows you to see them apply what they have learned in different ways and from different perspectives. Typically, you will be more confident in the students' grasp of the material if they can do so. But some variety of assessment can also be accomplished *within* a single measure. Authentic tasks tend to give the students more freedom in how they will demonstrate what they have learned. By carefully identifying the criteria of good performance on the authentic task ahead of time, the teacher can still make comparable judgments of student performance even though student performance might be expressed quite differently from student to student. For example, the products students create to demonstrate authentic learning on the same task might take different forms (e.g., posters, oral presentations, videos, Web sites). Or, even though students might be required to produce the same authentic product, there can be room within the product for different modes of expression. For example, writing a good persuasive essay requires a common set of skills from students, but there is still room for variation in how that essay is constructed.

## What Roles Can Library Media Center Staff Play in Assessment Development?

### Work with Classroom Teachers

Because library media specialists are educators in schools, they should be involved in the development of a school's or district's learning goals and standards. At the very least, they should be familiar with the goals and standards teachers are supposed to be teaching and assessing. This enables staff to ask good questions of teachers regarding the assignments they are using. For example, teachers are being asked more and more to integrate technology into their instruction and assignments they give to their students. A good consequence of that practice is that teachers frequently turn to library media center personnel who often have

greater expertise in the use of information technology. Consequently, the staff members have an excellent opportunity to ask meaningful questions such as:

- Is the assignment designed (or, how can the assignment be designed) to meet one or more of your standards?
- Does it capture truly meaningful learning?
- Will students' behavior on the task be clearly observable and measurable? That is, what will be the indicators (criteria) of good performance on the task?

> There is considerable value in knowing how well students are meeting the goals we have set for them, including information literacy goals.

- Does the use of library media center tools required in the task reflect authentic and meaningful uses of those tools? For example, are students merely locating and printing out lots of pages somehow related to the topic, or are they appropriately identifying and evaluating which material is relevant?
- Does the rubric capture these essential behaviors? Students will more likely address critical skills if they know what they are and that they will be assessed on them.

## Develop Resources and Assessment Tasks for Classroom Teachers

As mentioned above, assignments do not need to be long, elaborate tasks to capture authentic learning. Teachers would appreciate ideas for shorter assignments that are quicker to assess, but still capture meaningful application of knowledge and skills. I believe this provides an excellent opportunity for library media specialists to assist classroom teachers in developing student learning in the content areas while promoting critical information literacy skills.

For example, through the simple Web page I described above listing accurate and misleading headlines, I can assign numerous brief, meaningful tasks requiring the application of scientific literacy and critical thinking. Similarly, library media specialists could generate small, content-specific print or electronic resources that are aligned with particular learning goals and standards of a school, team, or department. Teachers could then design meaningful tasks for students around these resources. Or, library media specialists could go a step further and suggest a few specific tasks students could complete with these resources that would also require some element of information literacy. A further step would be to develop a simple rubric for the task that would permit the teacher to quickly assess student performance on it. Yes, I know, "free time" is not often in the library media specialist's vocabulary. But, as I suggest with most tasks—start small. Ask a particular teacher if there might be such a resource that would be helpful. Of course, many library media specialists are already providing such resources. If you are, take it a step further by connecting it to the assessment process.

## Design Your Own Assessments

Library media specialists and library media center staff should have their own goals for student learning, particularly related to information literacy. If a goal is worth pursuing, it is worth measuring. So, design your own assessments of such skills to inform you, the students, and the other school faculty and administrators of the strengths and weaknesses of the students and the progress being made on these skills.

Information literacy skills are obviously not the sole province of library media specialists. Students should develop such skills across the curriculum and in the context of learning the content of the disciplines. However, it is not always easy to convince teachers that a) students need information literacy skills, b) these skills are best taught in the context of learning the content, c) these skills can be assessed, d) these skills can be assessed alongside the disciplinary knowledge and skills, and e) data acquired from such assessments can assist teachers and library media specialists in planning future teaching and learning.

For example, I recently consulted with the Media Information Services Department (composed of library media center staff and the information technology specialist) at a local high school. Administrators in the district wisely brought these staff members into the process of developing goals, standards, and assessments. The library media center staff identified information literacy as the target of their efforts. They were well aware that many teachers were struggling with the issues I just mentioned. So, after identifying the specific skills they wanted to address, they began creating assessments to measure them.

First, the staff developed a traditional assessment to determine the current knowledge base of students related to information literacy. A brief, multiple-choice test was administered to all freshmen at the beginning of the year in a required course, and then administered again at the end of the year. Most of the results confirmed staff beliefs about student knowledge, but there were a few surprises. For example, it was startling to see how few students knew what the term *periodical* meant.

Assessment of such knowledge was not just for the benefit of the library media center staff. The staff shared the results with the entire school so that everyone was aware of the gaps in student knowledge. This encouraged a conversation between the library media center staff and the classroom teachers about creating a collaborative effort to increase information literacy.

Second, to complement the assessment of knowledge, the staff wanted to develop a more authentic measure of information literacy to better capture the application of this knowledge. So, we worked on a meaningful and manageable task that the library media center staff could administer. Randomly sampling students who came to the library media center to work on a research paper, library media center staff completed an observational assessment that tracked a few students through the research process. The staff applied a fairly detailed rubric to each of the key steps. Now, the staff is collecting data that can also be shared with the other teachers and administrators in the building to further the development of information literate students.

Such locally developed and administered authentic assessments can guide meaningful review and improvement of teaching and learning. As Popham (1999, 2001) has so effectively argued, standardized tests created by some external agency cannot adequately measure the quality of student learning in local classrooms, particularly authentic learning. Local assessments need to be developed, and all educators in the school can and should contribute to that critical mission of improving teaching, learning, and assessment.

## References

Mueller, J. *Authentic Assessment Toolbox,* <http://jonathan.mueller.faculty.noctrl.edu/toolbox>, 2004.

Popham, W. J. "Why Standardized Tests Don't Measure Educational Quality." *Educational Leadership* 56 (1999): 8-15.

Popham, W. J. *The Truth About Testing: An Educator's Call to Action.* Alexandria, VA: ASCD, 2001.

Wiggins, G. P. *Assessing Student Performance.* San Francisco: Jossey-Bass Publishers, 1993.

Wiggins, G. P. *Educative Assessment: Designing Assessments to Inform and Improve Student Performance.* San Francisco: Jossey-Bass, 1998.

*Jon Mueller is professor of Psychology at North Central College in Naperville, Illinois and can be contacted at jfmueller@noctrl.edu.*
*http://jonathan.mueller.faculty.noctrl.edu/toolbox/whydoit.htm - top#tophttp://jonathan.mueller.faculty.noctrl.edu/toolbox/whydoit.htm - top#top*

Mueller, J. (2005). Authentic assessment in the classroom......and the library media center. *Library Media Connection, 23*(7), 14-18.

# Books, Not Direct Instruction, Are the Key to Vocabulary Development

## By Fay Shin

When a child has an extensive knowledge of vocabulary, it is most likely from extensive reading. Regardless of whether the reading is from comic books, magazines, Captain Underpants, or from the recommended reading literature list. Teachers who are always trying to find the best strategies for teaching literacy skills such as reading comprehension, vocabulary development, or spelling need to focus more on reading and access to books. Time (or opportunity to read) and access to a wide variety of reading materials is the most effective reading tool a teacher or educator needs. Access must come from the schools by focusing and promoting libraries and books, and teachers need to provide opportunities to read in their classroom. Although the research in vocabulary development (Anderson, 1996; Krashen, 1993) supports reading books for vocabulary development, it took a sixth grade student to teach me about applying the research into my classroom.

## The Research

Anderson, Wilson, and Fielding found that the average U.S. fifth grader reads about 600,000 words a year from books, magazines, and newspapers outside of school. If a student reads just 15 minutes a day in school, another 600,000 words of text could be covered. Therefore, a conservative estimate of the total volume of reading of a typical fifth grader in the United States is 1 million or more words per year. The researchers estimated that a child who reads one million words a year will encounter 20,000 unfamiliar words. With a 5 percent chance of learning a word (which is a low estimate), 1,000 words a year from reading may be learned. Even more interesting and compelling was that when self-selected or assigned material is not extremely difficult, the chances of learning an unfamiliar word rise to 10 percent or more, making a yearly total of 2,000 words. The researchers also

note that these are figures for average readers. Avid readers may be learning two or three times as many words simply from reading.

The fact that the likelihood of vocabulary learning increased 10 percent when children were reading easy narratives to near zero when they were reading difficult expositions should encourage teachers, parents, and librarians to promote "easy and fun books" over "grade level" books. I personally find this significant because, like most people who love to read for pleasure, everyone reads books that are below their academic reading level when they want to relax and enjoy the experience.

> Research widely supports children learn new words more from reading, not vocabulary instruction in school.

Obviously, if the reading experience is pleasurable, adults and children tend to read more. Also, popular children's books such as in the best-selling series of Captain Underpants, surprisingly has challenging vocabulary words in the text. For example, on page 14 in Captain Underpants and the Attack of the Talking Toilets, the words: attitude adjustment, criminally mischievous, behaviorally challenged, and disruptive are found in the text.

Another study by Nagy and Herman found that in a typical classroom a maximum of 300 words a year are covered in direct instruction aimed specifically at word learning. Therefore, even in an ideal program of vocabulary instruction, the number of words actually learned in a year will still be in the hundreds. On the other hand, the number of words learned in a year from independent reading is in the thousands for the typical child.

In conclusion, independent reading appears to be a far more impor-

tant source of vocabulary growth than direct vocabulary instruction.

## Case Study

Torl was a student in my sixth grade class. He is one of those students a teacher will always remember. Not only was he personable and intelligent, but he was constantly challenging me to become a better teacher. He taught me to re-learn and re-think what I thought I knew about being a good teacher.

It was the first day of school at an elementary school in Los Angeles. It was my fourth year as a teacher and I assigned the class to write an essay about what they did over their summer break. Torl wrote that he received $100 for his birthday and he spent it all on comic books. I thought that was very unusual at first, but as the semester progressed I realized he was no ordinary student. It turned out that Torl was a brilliant 6th grader. He was always very inquisitive and demonstrated to me that he was always critically thinking about the assignment or discussions. He also consistently turned in high-quality work. Most of all, he was an avid reader. In addition to comic books, he loved to read fiction and non-fiction popular books. His favorite part of the class was when it was independent reading time and he was able to read the book he selected.

One day during the beginning of the second semester, we were reviewing and copying down the vocabulary list for the week. I always created a list of challenging vocabulary words from the book we were reading in class. That particular week we were reading Chapters 3 through 5 from *Johnny Tremain*. I was writing the words and definitions of the words for the week, of which there were approximately 15.

Although I strongly believed in literature-based instruction and teaching the reading skills through context, I also believed students needed strong "skills and vocabulary instruction" as part of the curriculum. Every Monday we reviewed and discussed the vocabulary words, then I would have the students copy the words and definitions. Every Friday we had a test.

As the students were copying down the words, Torl raised his hand and asked, "If I know all of those words already, do I have to copy these words down and take the test on Friday?"

I was somewhat shocked that Torl was confident that he knew ALL of the words. The words I selected were challenging, and I could not believe he knew every single one. In front of the whole class I asked if he was sure that he knew the vocabulary words. He assured me that he knew them all. I said I would give him a quick quiz and he asked for one minute to review the words on the board. After 30 seconds when he said he was ready, we proceeded with the test. In front of the whole class, I asked him to turn around and I read each word in a random order. He correctly defined all of them and then I told him he did not need to copy the word list or take the test. He proudly grinned, stood up and raised both of his arms and yelled "Yeah!" in front of the class. Then he sat down in his chair, took out a paper back book from his backpack and quietly started to read—with interest and pleasure, I must note.

As I looked around the classroom, all of a sudden I started to realize that Torl was teaching me something I should have realized before. The research widely supports children learn new words more from reading, not vocabulary instruction in school. Torl was supporting and reinforcing this research.

Torl, who had an extensive knowledge of vocabulary (in addition to other necessary literacy skills), loved to read books. He thought my vocabulary lessons were boring and a waste of time. He would rather be reading. He learned his words through books, and it was easy and effortless. It didn't take memorization exercises, tests, or dictionaries to learn new words.

## The Lesson

After learning this lesson from Torl, I then started to analyze the situation. I asked myself, "Now what is wrong with this picture? Torl, a very bright and intelligent student, is doing what he wants to do, which is to read a book he wants to read. The rest of the class is copying the words and getting ready to study them for a test. A disappointing component of this was that the students who received A's and B's on the test, always got A's and B's. The students who didn't study the words and failed the tests, always failed the test. The worst part of this was that the students who did study and always got A's, seemed to FORGET the words they learned the following week! I would always "review"

> In order to promote more reading, educators need to start paying attention to the research that clearly demonstrates we need more access to books, better libraries, and more investment in promoting independent reading in schools.

the words in context as we discussed the chapters, and I would get blank stares from the class. In other words, the students who "seemed" to learn the words, actually just memorized the words right before the test, and probably forgot them as soon as the bell rang and the kids left school. This reminded me of my high school days in Spanish class. My Spanish teacher gave us a list of 25 words each week that we had to memorize. We had a weekly test. I always got a 90 or above. I even got an A in the class. What I also did was forget the vocabulary words the day after the test was over. I then realized this was happening to my students. Why did I think it would be any different?"

Since that day, I threw out vocabulary word lists and tests. I still reviewed vocabulary words and incorporated them into my literature lessons, however, not in the hopes of increasing vocabulary but as a means of reviewing important concepts and generating an interest in language and language use. Most importantly, I learned from Torl that direct vocabulary instruction was not as effective as learning words from reading. As Nagy and Herman (1987) have noted, independent reading is a far more important source of vocabulary development. Therefore, in order to promote more reading, educators need to start paying attention to the research that clearly demonstrates we need more access to books, better libraries, and more investment in promoting independent reading in schools.

### References:

Anderson, R. C. (1996). Research foundations to support wide reading. In V. Creany (Ed.), *Promoting Reading in Developing Countries* (pp. 55–77). Newark, DE: International Reading Association.

Anderson, R. C., Wilson, P. T., & Fielding, L. G. (1988). Growth in reading and how children spend their time outside of school. *Reading Research Quarterly*, 23, 285–303.

Krashen, S. D. (1993). *The power of reading: insights from the research.* Englewood, Colo.: Libraries Unlimited.

Nagy, W. E., & Herman, P. A. (1987). Breadth and depth of vocabulary knowledge: Implications for acquisition and instruction. In M. McKeown & M. Curtis (Eds.), *The nature of vocabulary acquisition* (pp. 19–35). Hillsdale, NJ: Erlbaum.

*Fay Shin is an associate professor in the Teacher Education Department at the California State University, Long Beach. She can be reached at fshin@csulb.edu.*

Shin, F. (2004). Books, not direct instruction, are the key to vocabulary development. *Library Media Connection,* 22(4), 20-21.

# Program Administration

## Introduction

The school library media specialist has many tasks similar to a library director in a large public library, and has many things in common with a CEO of a company. The school library media specialist in the program administration role plans for future success, organizes the library to operate efficiently, implements a budget strategy to ensure success, and advocates for continued support.

The variety and detail of these activities are sometimes a surprise to new library media specialists. Classroom teachers who are used to organizing their classroom space, spending a few hundred dollars on classroom supplies, and communicating with administrators, other teachers, or parents are amazed at the depth and complexity of these tasks in the school library media center.

Many of the activities detailed in the articles in this section seem to take place in the library office, away from the needs of students, demands of teachers and administrators, and interests of parents and community members. Student-centered school librarians know that when they walk into the back room, they have to be careful not to turn their backs on students, teachers, and the community. When the librarian owns the library, then decisions are made on what's best for the system. The librarian and staff make all of the decisions, which they should, since they know best. Problems are handled structurally by making rules and regulations.

But when patrons own the library, then decisions are based on patron needs and wants. Patrons are asked for input before decisions are made, and library media advisory committees share in that decision-making. Problems are handled behaviorally, by addressing student or patron conduct directly and one-on-one.

In the articles in this section, the authors review elements of the program administration role. Mary Alice Anderson and Gary Hartzell start us off with a discussion of leadership for school librarians. Mary Moyer, Rosalie Baker, Thomas Hart, and Steve Baule illustrate student-centered principles in the design of the school library media center facility. Using evidence-based practices to plan for the library media center is covered by Colleen MacDonell, Terrence Young, and Audrey Church. The important facets of advocacy are written by Amy Burkman and Sandy Schuckett. Aspects of the program such as budgeting, grantwriting, and technology leadership are covered by Gail Dickinson and Parisa Tahouri.

The important theme of these articles is not merely how to do the backroom tasks of the program administration role, but why the program administration tasks are so important, and how they can lead to improved learning and teaching within the library media center.

# Leadership: What Makes Us Tick?

## By Mary Alice Anderson

Whether it is within the library media center, the district, or the community, library media specialists accept leadership roles that expand their influence. What drives people to become leaders and move to the forefront? What makes them tick? Meet some of today's leaders and upcoming leaders and learn what they see as top issues facing our profession.

**Leaders see a job to do be done and do it!** They go beyond their job description and beyond the expectations others have of them. They're busy, but they get things done. Wendy Larson and Sue Wilmes, Minnesota library media specialists, demonstrated leadership in the district by taking their desire for improved district book collections to enviable heights. Budget cuts had hurt their collections and programs, but they knew what to do and where to go for support. They became proactive leaders instead of complainers. Using local, state, and national standards and data, they methodically met with key district officials and committees to lay the groundwork for requesting significantly increased funding for collection development. They were "inspired and nourished," accomplishing something far beyond what they had initially imagined when they received "over a half million dollars to meaningfully improve our media center collections in order to serve our students."

Wilmes, like other leaders interviewed for this article, willingly serves on key district committees. She is a "member of [the] district media/technology committee, which includes school board members where vision is developed and decisions made on direction of technology and media centers. She is also a member of the union executive board, working to investigate, organize, and communicate issues and information to members, administration, and residents."

New Yorker Carolyn Gierke supports library media specialist involvement in teacher associations. "People appreciate that you do something for the greater good, and librarians especially should have an active part of the teachers' associations. Who better to explain the nature of library concerns? Classroom teachers live in different worlds, and there are more of them in any school district. Librarians sometimes have a tougher time getting union representation. But not if you are a part of the system. You need to be active in some form that you are comfortable with."

Karen Muronaga from Hawaii cochairs a Family Involvement Committee, which plans and coordinates "monthly activities for families to attend with their children. Families learn about content standards and ways they can help their child at home. Some of the topics include technology, parenting skills, family musical talents,

> *Online learning is another avenue for leadership.*

test-taking skills and strategies, holiday crafts, math and science fun activities, and a family picnic and movie on the lawn."

Indianian Carl Harvey concludes, "A school library media specialist has to be willing to give the time on school committees to help articulate the library media program's mission, goals, and services. Eventually, once you've proven the worth of the library media program, the staff will start to be that voice for you, too, which will multiply the sphere of influence. To have a successful library media program, I don't have a choice but to be out there leading the way. It is just part of the job."

**Technology provides diverse opportunities for leadership.** Library media specialist leaders are involved members of district technology committees, participating in long-range planning and policy development. They are at the forefront of introducing new technologies, trends, and ideas in their buildings and districts. They oversee the implementation of new technology-based resources in their schools, often coordinating 21st century tools and resources such as streaming video.

A Midwestern library media specialist described an efficient idea she proposed. She had a vision for a system for one identification card for student ID, library card, and lunch card. She had presented the idea to the right people, found answers to questions, and figured out how to make it work, coordinating efforts between the lunch program, library media center, and attendance/grading program. It was a huge step for the school and gave her a leadership edge. Gierke notes, "Being a person who finds the answers or gets results doesn't hurt. When you know something that is of value to another person, your stock goes up. When you can teach it to them in a way that makes them feel empowered, you are on the road to educational leadership."

**School Web sites can be a catalyst for modeling a leadership role.** Examples include creating library media center Web sites, serving as school and district Web masters, and helping teachers create their own classroom Web sites. New York library media specialist Will Haines created an "ask a librarian feature" on his middle school library media center Web site <www.greece.k12.ny.us/ath/library/askalibrarian/default.htm>.

Online learning is another avenue for leadership. It's rapidly growing, offering opportunities for library media specialists to teach classes for K–12 and post-secondary students, coordinate online learning experiences for their students, or use tools, such as Blackboard®, to deliver instruction.

**Staff development is a familiar path to leadership and provides a high level of visibility.** It may involve one-on-one teaching, group instruction, or coordinating building and district training initiatives. Wilmes is on the district leadership committee "where decisions are made on how to allocate and expend district staff development funds to meet the needs of both the majority and the minority of the teaching staff." Jim Glazer, also a Minnesota library media specialist, completed a doctoral dissertation on the role of library media specialists in staff development. The bottom line: If library media specialists don't do it, it doesn't get done.

**Leaders extend their leadership role into their communities: participating in diverse community organizations, from public library boards to civic organizations and museums.** Some library media specialists have partnered with their county historical societies to create museum Web sites and plan educational programs. Others coach neighborhood or community athletic teams. Georgia library media specialist Pam Nutt leads in a unique way: She is on a school board in one county and a library media specialist in another. "Being on the school board has helped me see just how much money is needed in the media centers, but with cutbacks, it is hard to fund. Because of being on the board, I've helped to fund media centers at a higher rate. Our new media centers get a start-up budget spread over three years. That means money over and above their state allotment. If we are to change education, then we are going to have to be the change agent. It is not easy to work all day and then go to board meetings. But I'm helping to improve the educational system in my county."

Judy Bull, a district coordinator in Minnesota, is serving her fourth term on a city council. She views this role as somewhat natural since library media specialists "administrate a program, see the big picture, and, like elected officials, are servant/leaders. I think my education; experience as a teacher, media person, and musician; and birth order (oldest) gave me the confidence to run for office. Decision making was not threatening." Since city council meetings are reported in local newspapers and are on TV, Judy is also creating visibility for her and the library media specialist profession.

**Leaders are responsible, credible, and professional.** If we conduct ourselves in a professional manner, we will develop a strong professional reputation. Gierke observed, "It's like money in the bank. Every interaction you have with a student, parent,

teacher, or administrator is a public relations opportunity for yourself and your library. Handling it professionally will build strength for your program, and your role as a school leader will establish itself."

**Leaders have a sense of follow-through.** They make decisions; they can be counted on to get things done. Having good organizational skills helps. Carolyn Kirio from Hawaii explains, "Through the years, I've learned to keep things simple by using a planning process (assess, analyze, set goals, plan activities, implement, evaluate) to keep meetings organized and to lead with the heart and mind. I respect time, accept different personalities, delegate, and share responsibilities."

**Leaders are passionate, energetic advocates for our profession.** Peggy Milam encourages us to "do more than speak about the roles we play in student

> If we conduct ourselves in a professional manner, we will develop a strong professional reputation.

achievement to become indispensable. We must be vocal, visible, and vociferous. My work is my passion. I want to make a difference." Claire Sato, a retired library media specialist from Hawaii, believes advocacy is no longer an option but a must: "Advocacy is everything you say and do."

Gierke publishes a column in her school's parent newsletter. "This began as a way to shamelessly promote the library program to counteract a less than supportive former principal. As it turned out, the teachers loved it! Teenagers don't tell their parents much about what goes on in school. This does. The Board reads it. While on the surface it might be the library article, it really promotes the whole instructional program, so the teachers support it. Nobody views it as me bragging about my program."

**Leaders are involved in professional organizations at state, regional, and national levels.** Professional organizations provide camaraderie and opportunities to hone leadership skills that

can be applied in the daily job setting. Many people start out just wanting to be involved, but one thing leads to another. Carl Harvey wrote, "In the eight years I've been a library media specialist, I've been a committee member, committee chair, conference chair, and president of our state association. None of these were things I set out to do, but rather that first step of volunteering for a committee led to another opportunity, which led to the next, and so forth. Part of being a professional is giving back and being involved in the profession. It certainly takes time and we're all busy people, but the rewards have made me a better library media specialist for my students and staff."

**Leaders lead committees that benefit the organizations, the profession, and students.** For example, many are involved in legislative committees or groups studying the impact of library media center programs on student achievement. Kirio co-chairs the Hawaii Association of School Librarians' School Library Public Relations committee. "The goals are to gain support for legislative action, advocate our mission and goals, and survey school librarians for gathering evidence that we are impacting student achievement."

Diane Chen from Tennessee encourages "every individual to do two things this year to proactively impact our field. Write a letter or phone your representative concerning a library issue, and send someone, even a parent, from your state to represent libraries during National Library Legislative Day in May. The ALA Washington Office will provide you the leadership tools and words to communicate. You provide the passion for our students and their need for libraries."

**Dedicated leaders continue their organizational leadership into retirement.** Last spring I attended the Wisconsin Educational Media Association's annual spring conference. The number of retirees who were involved was impressive. They were contributing to the conference, their organization, and the profession as speakers and advocates, online instructors, fund-raisers, and conference worker bees.

Claire Sato is typical of active retirees. She works with the Hawaii Association of School Librarians' Buddies Program. "...we match experienced librarians with new librarians so that the new librarians have someone to call on when they have questions. For the first time this year we hope to build a stronger program." She conducts a Beginning Librarians' Seminar through the University of Hawaii's Outreach College and Library School. "The seminar is built around the needs of the participants....we cover management and address the importance of people skills." Claire also conducts a professional development course on Inquiry Learning that continues throughout the year, speaks at university classes, and works with the State Department of Education.

**What drives us?** Familiar reasons are a passionate desire to help the profession, help students, and grow personally and professionally. New Yorker Sara Kelly Johns noted that *Information Power* (1988) and a deep personal need inspired her. She explained, "I've been promoting librarians being leaders for a very long time as Educational Leadership Chair of our state affiliate since the early '90s because I know it is important and not always an innate personality trait of librarians. *Information Power* was the fuel for my crusade, but it fit right into my own 'story' of needing to be more assertive and making myself assume leadership positions when I was in my late 20s and felt I had a handicap in my profession by being shy."

**Leadership is a natural part of our jobs.** Gierke noted, "Other than the principal, the librarian is the only person who sees the entire educational program of the building in context....Librarians are the original team players, and their knowledge and expertise is valuable to teachers and students who have to pack so much learning into their school day and school year. [We] are a different breed to begin with, my colleagues seem to be more gregarious than other types of librarians, and are more willing to deal with people..."

**On a personal level, leaders hate to be left out or uninformed.** Kirio commented, "Unless you are a leader or part of the leadership team, information is not always disseminated and shared. By being active, you're constantly in the know and are aware of everything that is occurring within the school. Because of our involvement, we are highly visible." Needing to be involved also drives Carl Harvey.

"There are so many exciting things happening in my school and in the profession, that I want to take every opportunity available to be a part of it. I want to create a culture that it is just natural for the library media program to be a part of the decision-making process. The only way to do that is to be proactive and demonstrate what the library media program can do and how it can support teaching and learning in the building."

**Leaders want to leave a legacy.** Several library media specialists said they want to be remembered for positive achievements and their professional contributions. Whether it's teaching, technology, collaboration, facilities planning, encouraging students to read, or impacting change, we want to make our mark on the world. And, while not always publicly admitted, many leaders privately admit they are driven by their egos and the need to exert influence and be recognized.

**Family members, or experiences early in life, often supply a positive influence that encourages library media specialists to seek a leadership position.** Several students in the online class I teach have described how their mothers encouraged them. Laurie Conzemius, current co-president of the Minnesota Educational Media Organization (MEMO) and editor of the state media journal, wrote: "When I was a young girl my mother used to say, 'To those whom much is given, much is required.' I have been afforded the luxury of the opportunity and enough time and money to be able to attend meetings and conferences. My administration and my family have been supportive of my involvement in MEMO, and that makes a big difference. Of course, my mother also used to say that she knew how things should be done—but people didn't always listen to her! And I guess that shaped me as well! I knew that if I wanted to affect change, and have it resemble what I envisioned, I had to be a leader in that change!"

A hospitalized son influenced Diane Chen. She planned to cancel attendance at a conference. "My son told me, 'NO! Go make libraries better!' His commitment inspired me and enabled me to take up the leadership mantle on his behalf." She was elected chair of the AASL Affiliate Assembly

and will lead this group of representatives of every state-affiliated organization this year. Diane also gained inspiration from experiences as a young adult. "I attended a girls' state leadership camp, then became a presidential fellow during college to hone my leadership skills. Each of these opportunities were offered to prepare me for life because someone else cared."

### Are these words part of your leadership vocabulary?

- relationships
- communicate, communication
- share
- knowledgeable, flexible
- understand trends
- proactive
- quality, credibility, responsibility
- consistent, systematic
- priorities, risk
- data
- vision, goals
- patience, stamina

**Leaders are influenced by mentors.** Laurie Conzemius "had wonderful mentors as I developed my skills as a teacher and media specialist. These mentors instilled in me the responsibility to help others and also the courage to become a mentor to others. As a new member in MEMO, I received the support and information I needed to help me do my job well, and I felt an obligation to give back to MEMO."

**Leaders are on a mission to improve student achievement.** Library media specialists know they and their programs have much to offer; by working with others they can accurately plan material acquisition, curriculum strategies, and staff development workshops that help students achieve. Eric Bodwell, who works at an Illinois high school, was hired when administration learned that increased library media center staff and funding could lead to student achievement. Bodwell sees collaboration as key in his role of improving student achievement. "Without it, the work that my staff and I do would be irrelevant. To me, that means leadership from the middle, that is, helping teachers and everyone else, including students, do their jobs as effectively as possible." Bodwell observed that we don't "always take this concept far enough. I sometimes see colleagues take this to mean matching our current services and collections with the needs of our patrons. I think we have to move beyond that. My job in the school is to be a partner teacher. We are working on developing a collection development plan that will include collection mapping... My job is to help teachers get the resources and skills they need to most effectively help their students excel even if I can't help directly...And in a more traditional vein, it has meant starting to build special collections..."

## What Issues Concern Leaders?

No Child Left Behind (NCLB) and advocacy top the list. More than a few are concerned about the potentially negative impact NCLB is having on library media center programs. The pressures teachers face to meet Adequate Yearly Progress (AYP) shifts much of their energy into "drill and skill" teaching methods and test-taking strategies. Library media specialists say teachers are turning away from research and projects because it takes too much time. Another concern is the impact that online testing or practicing for state tests has on lab access, and library media specialists and library media center programs across the country face the danger of being seen as an extra instead of an essential part of the solution. Leaders ask, "What are *you* doing to help schools meet NCLB mandates?"

**Advocacy is the concern that won't go away**. Too many administrators are still wondering what library media specialists do besides check out books. Too many administrators and teachers, and even some library media specialists, don't see the possible roles in teaching and learning the library media center program can play. Many would agree with Harvey's comment that "too many of us get stereotyped by bad experiences administrators and teachers have or their lack of experience with a library media program. It makes it much too easy for them to

eliminate the library program because they don't see the value and the worth. It becomes crucial that every library media program be a dynamic and active part of the school, not only to help our students succeed, but also so that when a teacher in their building becomes a principal in another district without a library media specialist, he/she begins to demand it because of the positive impact they know it can have. Gierke added, "the constant issue is educating new administrators and the public...It takes strong leadership and persistent effort...Every bit of the effort is worth it." But, it's not always easy to make those efforts." Claire Sato described "...that stone wall that is called the 'culture' of the school...each school has its own belief about the library/librarian. Often times the new librarian must face incredible hurdles to begin to implement some of the ideals he/she learned about in library school...So often, they hit their heads against the wall and finally give in to the culture and lose the vision of what a library should be."

**Accountability and data collection are newer concerns**. Kirio mentioned the need to "validate [our] impact on student learning utilizing effective data collection strategies....At a time when budgets are being slashed and library positions are being cut, the only line of defense has been to present concrete evidence that directly correlates student achievement with library instruction. Although the issue is not new, librarians are realizing that an in-depth investigation and analysis is being required. Knowing how to conduct formative/quantitative methods of assessment, performing analysis, [and] interpreting and sharing our data has become not only a desirable skill, but also a job requirement."

**Shrinking budgets impact almost everyone.** Loss of dollars erodes staff, collection, programs, and morale.

**Technology continues to be an issue.** Not all library media specialists have embraced technology or become comfortable with it—a situation that hampers the perceptions other educators have of us. Technology policy and planning is a concern shared by those who are less involved than they would like to be. It's critical to proactively seek that level of involvement to

ensure that the needs of library media center programs are not ignored. Technology training and staff development needs still exist. Bodwell noted, "...most veteran teachers have moved beyond the basics of Microsoft® Office. Our newly hired teachers understand the technology and have gone to college with the Internet and other technologies. But the next step for all is to move into technology integration. We also need to help teachers discover and take advantage of new and old technologies like Wikis, organizing information with tagging (del.icio.us bookmarks), bookmark managers, and selective subject directories.

**Partnerships with other areas of education are critical.** Bodwell commented that it seems we are finally talking to others outside of our profession through efforts such as the 21st Century Literacy project by ALA or the Keith Curry Lance studies. But most teachers and other professionals don't know the extent to which we can help in areas such as reading and literacy. We need to redefine our role in this area.

## Conclusion

The why's and what's of leadership are intriguing and varied. Leaders give a lot and gain much in return. The leaders who generously shared their thoughts demonstrated an eagerness to share, motivate, and help.

"[We] possess knowledge and expertise that can be valuable for our colleagues. There we CARE . . . Collaborate, Assist, Relate, and Encourage." (Carolyn Kirio)

Becoming a leader takes "putting your heart and soul into being a school librarian, patience, observation of good teaching practices, calmness, a happy disposition, and dedication to learn and persevere when leading others." (Karen Muronaga)

"From my own experience, I know that when I have been in leadership, my life has been much more engaging and connected with people and processes that are important to me. It adds color and dimension to a life that could be flat, boring, and insipid. You could say it changes water into wine." (Wendy Larson)

The library media specialist profession has an abundance of opportunities for each of us to be leaders in our schools, districts, communities, and beyond. Get involved; each little step you take along the way makes a difference. Those small steps help build your program *and* your influence.

## Library Media Specialists Interviewed (through e-mail correspondence)

Eric Bodwell, Community High School District 94, DuPage, Illinois

Judy Bull, North St. Paul (Minnesota) Public Schools

Diane Chen, Hickman Elementary, Nashville, Tennessee

Laurie Conzemius, Sartell (Minnesota) High School

Carolyn Gierke, Sweet Home High School, Amherst, New York

Carl Harvey, North Elementary School, Noblesville, Indiana

Sara Kelly Johns, Lake Placid (New York) Middle/High School

Carolyn Kirio, Kapolei (Hawaii) High School

Wendy Larson, Farmington (Minnesota) Public Schools

Peggy Milam, Compton Elementary School, Powder Springs, Georgia

Karen Muronaga, President Abraham Lincoln Elementary School, Honolulu, Hawaii

Pam Nutt, Moore Elementary School, Griffin, Georgia

Claire Sato, retired, Honolulu, Hawaii

Susan Wilmes, Farmington (Minnesota) High School

## Library Media Specialists Not Interviewed but Mentioned

Jim Glazer, South Washington County Schools, Minnesota

Will Haines, Greece Athena Middle School, Rochester, New York

*Mary Alice Anderson is a media specialist for Winona Area Public Schools in Minnesota. She has been an active, involved member of her state's library media specialist organization for several years and has leadership roles in her district. She is a regular contributor to professional journals and available as a conference and workshop presenter. She is an online adjunct instructor with the Online Professional Development for Educators Program in the School of Education at University of Wisconsin–Stout where she teaches an advocacy class for media specialists and a course on using primary sources. Contact her via e-mail at maryalicea@mac.com.*

Anderson, M.A. (2006). Leadership: What makes us tick? *Library Media Connection, 24*(6), 14-19.

# The Power of Audience: Effective Communication with Your Principal

## By Gary Hartzell

Sooner or later, advocacy comes down to communication. No matter how good your ideas, no matter how strong your evidence, they count for nothing if you can't get them across to your target. The message is important, of course, but there is no message apart from the mechanism that carries it. How, then, do you maximize the odds that you'll be able to capture your principal's favorable attention? Organizational and communication research offers some useful suggestions. Consider these half-dozen ideas that might pay substantial dividends the next time you craft a proposal.

### 1. Lay Advance Groundwork

Before you think about how best to present your idea, develop support for it among a few of the people who might be affected by it. Before you go to the principal, spend time with key players at lower levels: teachers, lead teachers, department chairs, counselors, assistant principals. Target anyone you know who has the principal's favor. Circulating an idea to get people's input before you present it to the boss generally strengthens your position. Ask them, "What do you think? Would this be helpful? Is there something I'm missing?" It's important to get informal reaction, especially any that might be negative. Find out if others are bothered by some part of your proposal, and look for ways to accommodate any reasonable concern. Once you've sorted out those things, you can take your idea to your principal, knowing that some people in whom the principal has confidence buy into it. Informally eliciting and addressing concerns in advance raises the odds that your idea will not be shot down the moment you present it.

### 2. Decide on the Initial Format

Decide whether to make your proposal orally or in writing—or both. Research suggests that written presentations foster greater understanding, but face-to-face presentations are more effective in persuasion efforts. Clearly, you'll want to do both. Reinforcement increases both the richness and the accuracy of the information you want to communicate. The question becomes which method to use first when approaching your principal.

Peter Drucker, the outstanding organizational researcher and theorist, classifies managers as "readers" or "listeners." You need to know if your principal prefers written or oral presentations. The implications, according to Drucker, are clear. If the principal is a reader, send a written report first and follow it up with a face-to-face discussion. If the principal is a listener, brief him or her on the subject, or make a presentation (depending on the principal's preference), then send a written report afterward.

In making the presentation or submitting the report, you also need to know if the principal prefers succint or elaborate communications. Some principals want you to talk them through an entire idea; others want only a synopsis. Some want a full written report and others an executive summary. Your goal is to get your idea the most positive hearing you can. Delivering it in the format the principal prefers is the first step.

### 3. Speak Your Principal's Language

Remember that in many ways, the principal speaks a language different from your own. Once you learn it, you can more meaningfully translate your ideas to him or her. Every part of an organization develops its own particular lexicon. Teachers, counselors, librarians, and administrators all use different terminology. Sometimes even people within the same group have specialized vocabularies. Look, for example, at the varying vocabularies of special education, industrial technology, music, foreign language, English, and art teachers. This variation in disciplinary lexicon is a challenge to principals, who have to deal with people from all across the educational spectrum. It's one reason we so often hear about "developing shared meaning" in both goals and processes in the education arena.

How do you learn your principal's language? There are at least three things you can do. First, read through the administrative journals in your professional library, and pay close attention to the terminology. Second, take every chance you get to listen carefully to the principal, assistant principal, or any other decision-maker you want to influence. Ask yourself what their burning issues and concerns are. Pay attention to the buzzwords they're using. What metaphors do they frequently use? Do they describe schooling as sport, combat, construction, travel, or something else? Take in it as you would take in a second language if you were abroad, with the intention of using it.

Finally, another good way to learn how to frame your ideas in administrative terms is by getting some administrative education. That doesn't necessarily mean getting certified as an administrator, although that might be a good idea. In the long run, nothing would advance library visibility and support as quickly or solidly as former librarians becoming administrators. Assuming, though, that you're not going to make that career change, most universities do offer access to individual classes. Think about taking a class in the principalship as a way of acquiring both perspective and vocabulary.

In writing your proposal and marshalling your supporting arguments, assess your principal's personality. Communication research argues that individuals' personal characteristics affect their ability to be persuaded. Intelligent people are best influenced by communications that rely on strong, logical arguments. But it doesn't stop there. Authoritarian personalities, those who believe that status and power differences do and should exist among organizational employees, also are more swayed by authority. Logical arguments and clear evidence can carry the day with non-authoritarian types, but your odds of convincing an authoritative personality go up if you appeal to authority in your arguments. Appealing to authority helps you overcome what researchers call a "status incongruence" reaction. Such reactions occur when people of higher organizational status and an authoritarian personality (a characteristic of some principals) perceive themselves being pushed by people of lower organizational status (such as librarians). Citing higher authority—recognized names in the field, professional organizations, leaders in a number of other schools or districts, or researchers—reduces the focus on you as the compelling force behind the idea.

## 4. Frame Your Proposal from Your Principal's Perspective

One of my mentors long ago used to talk about the invariable importance of the WIIFM principle: **W**hat's **I**n **I**t **F**or **M**e? People have a tendency to see the world in those terms. One key to persuading people to support any proposal is to demonstrate "what's in it for them." This isn't easy to do. Because we naturally see things from our own perspective, we tend to speak and write from our own perspective rather than from the perspective of the person to whom we are trying to sell our ideas. The challenge is to put yourself in the other person's place, think about what he or she might be looking for, and then speak to that.

As you craft your proposal, ask yourself, "What motivates the principal (or the teachers or students involved)? What is in this for the *people* it will affect? Which of *their* problems will it address? What problems might it create for *them*? What benefits will *they* realize?" Rather than focus on how your proposal

might affect the library media program, analyze the potential savings, gains, or enriched opportunities that your idea offers to other school constituents—students, teachers, counselors, and administrators. Then link your proposal to those benefits. The greater the connection people can see between your idea and what *they* do, the greater the odds of support.

Don't talk about how your proposal might help the library media program. Principals tend to be "big picture" people. They're looking for ideas and operations that will enhance student achievement and school performance. Make one or both of those the leading edge of any proposal you advance. Never ask for anything for the library or the library program itself. Always couch it in terms of the needs of students, teachers, or a particular program.

## 5. Put the Bottom Line at the Top

A fundamental part of any good proposal is an executive summary paragraph right at the beginning. Provide an overview of your proposal, put it in context, and outline its costs and benefits. We often try to proceed in a logical fashion, putting our conclusions at the end because we want a chance to build our case before asking for support. This can be counterproductive in dealing with someone as busy as your principal. He or she is likely to either turn immediately to the last paragraph anyway, or see that the conclusion is not stated at the beginning, set it aside to read later, and never get back to it. The first paragraph may be all that your principal has time to read—so make it one he or she remembers.

## 6. Be Brief

Principals don't have time to read everything they receive. Pieces that are quick and easy to read make their way to the top of the pile. The first thing many busy people look at is a document's thickness or—if they open it—its length. The shorter it is, the more likely it is to be read. Length has to

vary with complexity, of course, but it's a good idea to try to keep proposals somewhere between one and three pages. Supporting documentation and implementation plans should be available on request—but don't add to the principal's paper load by submitting them with the proposal.

Brevity also is a function of medium. Time is the question here—your principal's time. You might be tempted to send your proposal via e-mail. In some instances and with some people, technological transmission may indeed be the way to go. However, it's a good idea to assess your principal and the situation before you do that. Some principals are adept at using the available technology; others are not. If your principal senses that your information is useful, he or she will likely print it out, regardless of skill level. However, it's neither your intent nor in your best interest to cause the principal work or frustration. You will have saved some of your principal's precious time if you've already taken care of that.

## Conclusion

Communication is a game of odds. Education is in such flux today and competition for resources so numerous that a favorable reaction from your principal is not guaranteed. You can raise the odds by proposing competitive ideas and getting the powerholder's attention through a well-crafted proposal.

---

*Dr. Gary Hartzell is Professor Emeritus of Educational Administration at the University of Nebraska at Omaha (Nebraska), Department of Educational Administration. He is the author of* Building Influence for the School Librarian *(Linworth Publishing, Inc.).*

Hartzell, G. (2003). The power of audience: Effective communication with your principal. *Library Media Connection,* 22(2), 20-22.

# Re-designing a School Library Media Center for the 21st Century

## By Mary Moyer and Rosalie M. Baker

How does a school library media center become a library for the twenty-first century? According to Myerberg, "the twenty-first century library will be a flexible work and social setting for multiple activities: simultaneously a classroom, computer lab, reading room, study hall, conference center, theater, lecture hall, teacher's lounge, community center, and a place for parents to meet" (12). The School Library Media Center at Delsea Regional High School was an attractively designed room that had been converted in 1996 from a gymnasium into a media center. It was a much larger facility than the previous library; it had more room for books, computers, and students. However, the room was not meeting the current needs of the students, staff, and community. The school library media specialists knew that a re-design of the library space was needed. However, just talking about the need for the library re-design was not very effective. They needed to stop, reconsider their needs, and come up with a plan for the re-design. This new thinking launched the plan that led to the re-design of their school library media center. The new design provides space for class instruction and large group presentations. It also allows greater visibility of the room while retaining its attractive, inviting atmosphere.

## Off on the Right Foot

The first step in the project was to decide on the objectives for the re-design. The first objective was to consider the traffic patterns and how specifically the room was used. One problem was that the seating area for students was split into three sections, and this was not conducive to instruction. The layout meant that some students always had their backs to the teacher. The library media specialists wanted all of the students facing in the same direction without having to move their chairs. In addition, when students

worked in groups there was no easy way for the teacher to move from group to group to check their progress on projects. The library media center was often host to guest speakers, and the tables and chairs always had to be moved so that more than one class could participate in the event. Again, having the students all facing the same direction to hear the guest speakers was important. Other large group meetings that were held in the media center included faculty meetings where the staff was spread throughout the room without any feeling of cohesiveness during the meeting. Additionally, the media center was used for community meetings in the evenings

> During this process, the media specialists learned to plan objectives, provide a scale drawing, and to involve key players as stakeholders in the redesign project. They also learned to be patient and flexible.

and on weekends. Local sports organizations, the local business alliance, parents' groups, and the athletic director often held meetings in the media center during after-school hours. The library media specialists' objective was to improve the setting for instruction and large group presentations. This gave them the concrete reasons for why it was necessary to rearrange the tables and move the bookshelves.

The second objective for the re-design project was to provide greater visibility in the room. With the split seating area and the reference shelves blocking the view, it was difficult to view the entire room. This was a problem because of study hall students and classes using the room at the same time; it was essential to be able to track the movements of all the stu-

dents. The library media specialists decided to use visibility as a safety issue for their second objective.

## An In-house Architect

Once the objectives were clarified, it was time for a new layout design. The library media specialists enlisted the help of the CAD teacher who assigned a student to provide a scale drawing of the proposed changes. The library media specialists explained their needs to the student and exactly where they thought the furniture and bookshelves should be moved. The student measured the shelving, the tables, and the space between the shelving and tables to ensure that what was proposed would fit in the new set-up. The student used a CAD program to provide two versions of the proposed changes in a scaled drawing. The professionally prepared design provided a detailed sketch of the entire room with all the tables, chairs, shelving, computer area, and circulation area clearly labeled.

Armed with specific objectives, the rationale for their suggested changes, and a detailed drawing of the new design the library media specialists were prepared to meet with their principal and supervisor to discuss the proposed changes. During the meeting with the principal and the supervisor, the instructional advantages to the changes were stressed and how having an open space for large group meetings would also benefit the school community. The principal immediately saw the advantages. He wanted to create staff togetherness during faculty meetings and he also liked the fact that he would easily be able to see his staff during a faculty meeting with the proposed arrangement. The principal gave the go-ahead to approach the superintendent with the plan.

## The Big Pitch

With the principal's support, a meeting was arranged with the superintendent. However, the library media specialists knew they needed to include another key player in the meeting: the maintenance supervisor. This was very important because the maintenance department would be needed to help move the shelving, and the library media specialists wanted to ensure their support. They had the scale drawings to show the superintendent, the proposed changes, and a time frame for how the work could be accomplished during the school year without interrupting library services. The maintenance supervisor was supportive of the idea and thought the shelving and furniture could be moved before the end of the school year. The meeting was a success and after the superintendent reviewed the plan with the school board, the library media specialists were given the "green light" to begin reconfiguring the media center.

Students volunteered to help move the books, clean the shelves and scan the books for inventory. (The library media specialists decided to begin inventory at this time. Since the books were already going to be moved once, the logical step was to begin inventory to save having to move the books a second time for inventory.) Students were very happy to be included in part of the project and often gave up study hall periods to help.

The process involved moving books from one section and placing them on book carts or on the tops of other bookshelves in the correct order so that they could easily be moved to their new location. Next, the maintenance staff was called to move the shelving to the appropriate area. Then, the books were moved back onto the relocated shelves. The process took approximately four weeks to complete. In addition, during this time the bookshelves were cleaned, and books were repaired, weeded, and inventoried. The reconfiguration involved moving the Reference, Fiction, and 000 - 398 sections. The project was all done without

closing the media center or inconveniencing the maintenance staff. Since the maintenance staff only needed fifteen or twenty minutes at a time to move each section, it was easy for them to fit the work into their schedules. During this project, the library media specialists had to divide their time between maintaining library media services and supervising student helpers and the maintenance staff with the redesign process. It was extra work during this time, but the results were well worth the effort.

## The Payoff

The new library media center is now a place where large group meetings can occur, classes can receive library skills instruction, teachers can monitor their students more easily, and all students

> The media specialists had to divide their time between maintaining library media services and supervising student helpers and the maintenance staff with the redesign process. It was extra work during this time, but the results were well worth the effort.

can be seen (there are no more "blind spots"). The new set-up of the room allows the classroom teachers to easily find their students when other students are using the room. Also the library media specialists can also see all of the students from any point in the room. In fact, students have commented on how well they can see one another, and the new configuration has eliminated the small areas where groups of students would congregate to chat. There is still a small group seating area as well as a leisure reading area. The students and staff are happy with the results. The library media specialists have received many positive comments including one from the athletic director. He was very

pleased to see the new layout of the media center because it meant that when he needed to use the media center for meetings, he would no longer need to move the furniture. In addition, even though the move was completed late in the school year (early May), there were still opportunities to use the room for large group programs. Two math classes utilized the new seating area to host guest speakers from a local bank, and the guidance department was able to make presentations to several classes regarding guidance services. Also, groups used the room to host special luncheons to honor returning alumni, members of an advisory committee, and a ninth grade English class held a medieval feast.

The redesign of the library media center was a three-year-project from the beginning of the idea that the library media center was not designed for effective use to the very last book being moved and placed in its new shelving location. However, during this process the library media specialists learned to plan objectives, provide a scale drawing, and to involve key players as stakeholders in the redesign project. They also learned to be patient and flexible. What was once a viable learning center has increased its usage and flexibility to benefit the school and the community. "Although, the media center at Delsea Regional High school only consumes five percent of the school's real estate, it truly does serve 100% of the school's teachers and students (Myerberg, 12)."

### Bibliography

Myerberg, Harry. "School libraries: a design recipe for the future." *Knowledge Quest*. September/ October 2002, Vol. 31, No. 1:11-13.

*Mary Moyer and Rosalie M. Baker are Media Specialists in the Delsea Regional High School in Franklinville, New Jersey.*

Moyer, M., & Baker, R.M. (2004). Redesigning a school library media center for the 21st century. *Library Media Connection, 22*(7), 24-25.

# Library Media Center Facilities Access: Do You Really Want Your Library Media Center Used?

## By Thomas L. Hart, Ph. D.

"Curb Appeal" is a buzzword usually reserved for selling a home. It is an essential element for a quality library media center. Too often we get so wrapped up with selecting, organizing, securing, and circulating the collection that we forget about attracting users, students, teachers, and, to a lesser degree, parents and administrators.

### What Attracts You to Use a Library?

Most of us with a Barnes & Noble bookstore in our communities have experienced the relaxed atmosphere and wonderful odors from the snack bar. How can this be replicated in a library media center? We need to look at the possibilities for meeting our students' and teachers' needs. Obviously, Americans seek comfort and coffee-house odors. Our family has been to two different Barnes & Noble stores at unusual times and days of the week; they are always busy. This example provides evidence of what attracts to a bookstore: an example which should help in arranging a library media center for improved access and use.

### How Should Students and Teachers Use Library Media Centers?

To grasp a glimpse of possible uses, consider the following examples:

#### Elementary Example

Four third graders dash through the library media center's doors and hurry over to their friend, Mr. Hamilton, a library media specialist intern. Their questions overlap, "Is it time for our conference yet? Can you help us get started? Will you look at the questions we've written?" Mr. Hamilton smiles at their energy and leads them to a nearby table where the books, videotapes, artifacts, and computer printouts about folktales are arranged. Together, they examine and polish the children's

questions. Finally, Mr. Hamilton announces, "Okay, I think we're ready." They all move to the conference corner of the library media center.

The children, barely able to sit still, perch on the edges of three small chairs while Mr. Hamilton adjusts the equipment in the corner. Suddenly, directly in front of them four more images appear, projected into the air, and the children begin a long-distance conference with four youngsters at an experimental U.N. school in Nigeria. Together, the eight trade folktales from their divergent cultures and explore the messages those tales convey. Mr. Hamilton directs the exchange when

> The rapidity with which technology is changing, especially the miniaturization of delivery systems, makes it difficult to predict what types of equipment and spatial accommodations will be needed in the future.

necessary, and when the 30-minute conference is over, sends the children back to their classroom to report their findings and share the videotaped conversation with their classmates. There, students will include the information in a chapter of the class book they are writing about folktales from around the world.

#### Secondary Example

After the last bell of the school day, a diverse group of professionals hurry into the library media center. Leonard Johnson, a library media specialist intern, starts the meeting. "We're here to begin planning the electronic term paper project for the eleventh grade U.S. history students. Let's start by reviewing what experiences the students in those classes have had

with locating and using information and with the production equipment." The two history teachers and their teaching intern describe the students' background.

Leonard hesitates when they finish, unsure of what to ask next. The library media specialist with whom he is working steps into the discussion. "Let's shift our thinking a little now and try to delineate the essential questions we want the students to address, the content and processes they will use, and the product we want them to create." As a part of this exchange, the technician in the group describes possible production activities. Students will be able to use the library media center's camcorder to videotape footage of interviews or local historical scenes, integrate those scenes with segments pulled from the U.S. history DVD, add their own narration, and create a computerized path through the information. This year, they will also be able to ask learning partners at schools around the world to videotape a specific scene and send it to them through the Web. Gradually the structure of the unit takes form. By the end of an hour, the group has a plan that divides teaching and preparation responsibilities among all the members and sets a tentative schedule.

#### High School Café Example

Josh and Alice agreed to meet at the café in the library media center at 10:00 a.m. They first selected their bagels and nutritious drink, found a table, and then began browsing through the paperback collection. Alice remembered that she needed to complete a part of her senior English project on changes in climate of the Antarctic. She checked out a wireless laptop from the circulation desk and began a search. Since the online information access system for the library media center popped up on the screen when topics were entered in the search engine, she copied down the call numbers for books on the Antarctic and other media sources. This led her to search the collection where she found three excellent resources.

### Wireless Access Example

Alex Holden has been browsing around the ethnic resources displayed in the lobby of the library media center as a part of the Ethnic Fair. He is intrigued by the Aztec symbols, which are part of the Hispanic exhibit. After going to the circulation desk and submitting his ID card, Alex receives a wireless laptop with a properly charged battery. He finds an empty spot at a table and begins searching the Web for Aztec information, finding wonderful photos, sites with virtual tours of Aztec ruins, and stories about Aztecs. This has whetted his appetite for more in-depth information and better graphics than he has found. The library media center's OPAC is available through Alex's laptop and he finds several interesting books listed. What a surprise as he goes to the 970s and finds beautifully illustrated books that he never knew were available. Alex also browsed further and found great resources on the Incas.

### Use of Interactive Video Example

A dozen young teenagers enter the library media center singly and in small groups and hurry to the adjacent distance learning room. The last trio arrives just as their teacher's image appears on a large video monitor in the front of the room and greets them in Japanese, the language and culture the class is studying. Because the students are clearly visible on the teacher's monitor at her broadcast site in a distant state, she is able to speak individually to each, asking for an update of their current project on Asian art. One 13-year-old girl speaks eagerly, directing her comments toward the monitor where unobtrusive television cameras photograph her and send the image to her teacher's location. "I got the most incredible video from a library in Michigan about the art of papermaking. I finally understand why it's an art form in the Orient."

"Great!" the teacher responds. "Mr. Hamilton, can you and Alice share part of that video with us during our next class?"

Leonard, the school library media specialist intern, sits slightly behind

the students but still within range of the cameras. As site facilitator, he provides logistical and informational support under the supervision of the library media center's professional staff. "We can do better than that! Alice has made arrangements with her art teacher to do a papermaking demonstration for the class. She'll use the video to give background information. Then, the next week if there is time, Alice hopes to have a speaker from the university, who will discuss the effect that the invention of paper had on China and later on Japan."

As this interchange takes place, several visitors at the side of the room watch and take notes. Two are from a rural, southern school district and have been asked by their superintendent to make a recommendation concerning two-way, televised distance education for their district. Another visitor is from the Florida Department of Education, who is evaluating the computer-controlled communication system recently donated by an educational corporation. A fourth visitor is gathering information for a research study on the social aspects of learning in distance education.

## What Are the Common Problems with Facilities Design?

Facilities design changes along with other aspects of society. Flexibility in design ensures that the physical facility will meet future program needs. We have no idea what changes will take place in the future; we just know from past experience that there will be change. Probably the same amount of total space will be needed, but how the space is configured will likely change frequently. Therefore, it is essential to design a flexible facility, with few if any load-bearing walls.

Rapid technological advances will continue to affect the procedures for locating information, as well as those for circulation, inventory, and delivery of information. These advances will also affect the classroom connections to the library media center. The rapidity with which technology is changing, especially the miniaturization of delivery systems, makes it difficult to predict what types of equipment and spatial accommodations will be needed in the future. However, here are a few predictions.

### 1. Arrangement for Access to Special Rooms within the Facility

Computer labs need to be located near or within the library media center so that students can get access to *print* resources. Too often they fall back on Google™ or some other finding aid when they should be consulting with a library media specialist on the appropriate resource.

### 2. Location of Circulation/ Information Area

This area should be adjacent to the main entrance, staff offices, and workroom. If periodical storage is needed (sometimes replaced by online subscription database collections), storage area for those materials should be nearby. A photocopy machine is usually located within or near this space. This space should also include a display case or area.

### 3. Color Schemes for Walls and Furnishings

Colors of walls, fabrics, carpeting and other flooring materials, painted surfaces, wood stain, and furniture should be selected to work together and add to the overall visual appeal of the facility. Avoid selecting "trendy colors" of the decade that will soon date the center. Architects many times insist on *dark* wood for library media centers (particularly secondary library media centers) because it "conveys authority." However, soft, muted neutral colors can add visual appeal.

### 4. Windows between Rooms within the Facility

Interior as well as exterior windows should begin at least 45" above the floor (allowing shelving beneath). They should be placed where the library media specialist can be seated and be able to view the reading room and other rooms used by students.

### 5. Line of Sight Control

The library media center should be designed to facilitate the visual supervision of student space(s). Can the library media specialist see what is going on? Eliminate blind areas that cannot be controlled.

### 6. Electrical Outlets

Eliminate the need for outlet strip cords or extension cords by providing additional outlets in all workspace areas, circulation counter area, computer clusters and workstation areas, and any section of the facility where equipment will be used. Use installed electrical outlet strips in high-use sections such as the circulation desk, computer sections, and work station areas. These should be mounted vertically to avoid the need for daily crawling and fumbling to connect moveable equipment. More permanent installations, such as computer areas, may incorporate "hidden" under-counter outlets but need supplemental outlets more conveniently placed for occasional equipment needs. Don't overlook parts of the facility, such as storage, that might be converted to workspace in the future. Designate the location of equipment that uses peak current loads such as the laminator and laser printer. Consider the need for surge protection and backup power supplies for critical computing areas.

### 7. Climate Control

A system for heating and air conditioning (HVAC) is essential to maintain a temperature range of 70–77 degrees and control humidity at 60 percent. The system for the library media center should be separately controlled, allowing the facility to be used when school is not in session. Maintaining temperature and humidity is needed for the storage and preservation of equipment and resources. HVAC is a big issue in the South—Mold, Bugs, Heat, etc!

### 8. Access to Elevator in Two-Story Buildings

A nearby elevator or ramp in multi-level buildings will facilitate access to the physically handicapped, as required in the ADA regulations, and simplify transportation of library media center equipment.

### 9. Floor Coverings

Install aesthetically pleasing, sound-absorbent, and durable floor materials. High quality, commercial grade carpet-

ing is most often used. Use carpet, cushioning/padding, and adhesives that emit low levels of volatile organic compounds (VOC): products that carry the Carpet and Rug Institute's "Green Label" rating. Acoustical vinyl or tile flooring is recommended for media production, equipment storage, maintenance rooms, and workroom areas. Where equipment is moved on rolling carts, floor treatment should be continuous and seam-free. Flooring should have extra padding in the circulation desk area. For more information, visit the following online resources:

**Carpet vs. Hard Surfaces in Schools**
<www.shawcontractgroup.com/html/html/downloads/markets/carpetsinschools01.pdf>

> Install aesthetically pleasing, sound-absorbent, and durable floor materials.

**Carpet: A Haven for Unwelcome Guests**
<www.shawcontractgroup.com/html/html/downloads/markets/carpetsinschools01.pdf>

**The Carpet and Rug Institute Healthy School Environment and Enhanced Educational Performance**
<www.carpet-rug.com/drill_down_2.cfm?page=15&sub=12&requesttimeout=350>

### 10. Lighting

Lighting should be adequate for the spaces (standards set by Illuminated Engineering Society of North America) and controls should be located in logical, convenient places. Dimming and down light controls should be used in those areas where multimedia presentations and resources will be viewed.

### 11. Resource Shelving

Select age-appropriate shelving that is strong, durable, and fits in with other

furniture selections. All shelving should be adjustable. Individual shelves should be sturdy and no longer than 3 feet. Many library media centers find it impossible to intershelve their resources because there is no flexible shelving.

### 12. Storage

Storage space is always an important issue since buildings are so expensive to construct. Those library media centers that have most of their portable equipment permanently assigned to classrooms may convert some of the equipment storage space into general library media center space. Is there a place to put the holiday decorations or the puppet stage when not in use?

### 13. ADA Needs

Carol Simpson asked her students in Texas to check on ADA requirements for all their building facilities (some of which have been built in the last 5 years) and *not one* passed! Go to the EnableMart™ (Technology for Everyone) assistive technology site for choices to help select equipment <www.enablemart.com/default.aspx?store=10>.

Consider all aspects of physical access including, but not limited to, elevators and ramps, aisle widths, floor space, entrances and exits, signage, furniture size and height, shelving, and restrooms. Identify needed adaptive technologies that include equipment, hardware, and software. Alternative information formats may include Braille, large print, digitized speech, books-on-tape, real-time captioning for online conferencing, and captioned video programming.

*Thomas L. Hart, Ph.D., is a professor emeritus of the College of Information at Florida State University.*

Hart, T.L. (2005). Library media center facilities access: Do you really want your library media center used? *Library Media Connection*, 24(3), 16-19.

# Planning Considerations for Library Media Center Facilities

## By Steve Baule

In the post-NCLB world, educational facilities must change to contribute to the new bottom line in the same way that library media center programs are under increased scrutiny. At the same time, school leaders are still trying to pack increases in technology into an ever-tighter budget. In many ways this places the library media center in the situation of being considered a "nice-to-have space" but not a core academic area. In the future, library media centers will have to fight for space against a wide variety of other competing interests from cafeterias and gyms to office space for guidance staff. What this means for library media centers is the need to have flexible spaces and utilize space more efficiently than in the past. Any new facility or renovation project must also be friendly to the two technology imperatives of ubiquitousness and mobility.

### Less Is More

In regard to space, newer facilities will normally have less square footage than the library media centers of years ago. Everything seems to be squeezing in on library media center programs these days. Staffing cuts, budget cuts, and even the encroachment of classrooms in the library media center happen with greater frequency and often without a real understanding of the impact on the school. Separate spaces for class-sized computer labs or "library classrooms" are out of vogue for both pedagogical and practical reasons. The desire to integrate both print and nonprint media makes the use of class sets of notebook computers a much preferred (and in my experience, a highly effective instructional) option. Those planners moving toward either carts or mailbox-like laptop checkout stations for students need to ensure that adequate, secure storage areas exist for the carts and that the necessary electrical wiring is available to recharge the laptops. At this time, except for the most extreme multimedia applications, wireless networking technologies within the library media center will meet the needs of both students and teachers. Wired workstations for library media center staff and any desktop computers for drop-in use should still be wired, if possible.

Besides the reduction of separate computer labs, separate library media center classrooms should be avoided; due to the present enrollment growth, those spaces too easily become regular classrooms. Instead, opt for an instructional space without walls that is clearly defined through the use of bookshelves and other furniture. In the same vein, try to avoid a library media center that is designed so that it would

> Shelving space can be reduced in most secondary library media centers to provide additional seating or production areas

be easy to add a wall and create a classroom, even a small special education classroom, by taking a chunk out of the library media center.

Providing video projection in this instructional space is necessary today. Video projectors should not be viewed as an extra. Eighty percent of our students labeled as "at-risk learners" are primarily visual learners. Video projection equipment is now inexpensive enough that it should be considered standard classroom—and library media center—equipment.

### The Study Hall Legacy

Throw out the need to seat 10 percent of your student body. That is a legacy of the library media center as study hall. Make sure you can seat two classroom groups in a library media center with a single library media specialist. In all other library media centers, plan for class seating areas for the number of certified staff plus one. The additional space allows for drop-in students or small groups to work without interfering with any direct instruction. I would love to posit that the library media center should also have a laptop cart or similar class set of laptops for each class area. I am not sure if that is realistic from a fiduciary perspective, but it is a sound instructional idea.

Another potential concern is the need for more control of lighting than was generally required in the past. Many architects still see the library media center as an area to use large amounts of natural light and potentially have large windows and even skylights. Though I love natural light, one must consider its effects on video projectors and computer screens.

### The Role (and Space) of Print

Meanwhile, some still look at the book as "old technology" although Amazon, Borders, and Barnes & Noble seem not to have been told that books are passé. As budgets get tighter, print material budgets are not nearly adequate. Many graduate students spend more a year on books than their local elementary school library media center does. Due to this and the continued explosion of good electronic resources, shelving space can be reduced in most secondary library media centers to provide additional seating or production areas. However, this in no way should be viewed as a license to grossly reduce shelving or further reduce print collections. A 10–15 percent reduction in print shelving is probably appropriate due to the reliance on electronic reference sources and nonfiction in many schools.

Wherever possible, try to get the library media center placed in the building in such a way that it can have its own outside entrance. Many schools are beginning to offer more parent programs and tutorial programs. The library media center may be the best site for these programs, which bring in our reluctant learners

## Five Core Considerations in Planning a Library Media Center

**Flexibility**—Spaces may have to serve multiple functions as square footage is at a premium. Try to consider that the size and nature of the collection may change over the next decades. We can never be "future proofed," but look to a future of larger electronic and smaller print collections. Don't read that as print is dead; I don't believe that for a minute. We will always have books with us. However, smaller print budgets are a reality, so don't plan for bookshelves that will never get filled. If possible, design the floor plan so that the furniture can be moved out of the way to host parents or other receptions. Having receptions in the library media center provides a chance to market your program.

**Accessibility**—Think about all possible constituencies and try to provide access for them. Ensure that the plan provide for ADA accessibility as well. Try to ensure that computer labs in new construction are near the library media center, so students working on reports or projects have ready access to print materials.

**Technology**—Prepare for the day of one-to-one computer access for students. Provide for both wireless and wired networking, if possible. Install video projection equipment in each instructional area. Ensure there is space for servers and other network equipment somewhere in the building.

**Lighting**—Natural lighting is still optimal for LMCs; however, it must be able to be more controlled than in the past to accommodate video projection. Be careful when placing skylights as the space below them may change function.

**Lines of Sight**—If possible, ensure that the library media center can be supervised from a single spot—the circulation desk. Ensure there are not significant dead zones where students can sit or work unobserved. Place shelving so that one can view down the aisles instead of through the stacks.

### What Not to Consider

Ignore the old 10 percent rule for seating. It is out of date in an era of library media center programs that teach children.

Don't rely entirely on wireless networking. Wire is still the standard and can be from 4 to 25 times the speed of wireless networks. Similarly, don't ever believe any vendor who states they can "future proof" the project. That cannot be done.

own computers or other digital devices. Provide electrical services and either data ports or wireless bandwidth beyond what you think you will need. In most cases, before the library media center is renovated again, one-to-one computing will most likely have become a reality in your school. However, that does not mean to eliminate all of the production desktop stations. As anyone who has tried to develop graphics on a normal laptop will know, the production, scanning, and other multimedia stations still have a lot of value. Similarly, don't forget space for servers and other network equipment. It is still often overlooked or stuck in corners that are not hardware-friendly or easy to get to when needed. If possible, include a phone in the server area and leave room for expansion of servers and the network.

State-of-the-art library media centers will be more flexible spaces with a rich mix of technology in the future. However, at their core, they will still be serving the same basic function that the library at Alexandria served nearly two millennia ago. They will provide information, and library media specialists will assist their students in using that information effectively.

*Steve Baule is superintendent of schools for the Westmont Community Unit School District 201 in Westmont, Illinois. He is the author of* Case Studies in Educational Technology and Library Leadership *(Linworth Publishing Inc., 2005),* Technology Planning for Effective Teaching and Learning, 2nd Edition *(Linworth Publishing Inc., 2001), and* Facilities Planning for School Library Media and Technology Centers, 2nd Edition *(Linworth Publishing Inc., 2007).*

Baule, S. (2005). Planning considerations for library media center facilities. *Library Media Connection, 24*(3), 14-15.

and our sometimes reluctant parents. Surrounding them with library resources is an excellent way to increase their interest in learning.

## Bring Your Own Technology

Besides the video projectors and wireless laptop services already mentioned, be prepared for students to bring in their

# Easy Data Mining for Library Media Centers

## By Colleen MacDonell

The No Child Left Behind Act has ushered in a new era of accountability based on cold, hard data. Quantifiable measures are in; qualitative reports are out. Administrators, school boards, and district supervisors are all singing the same refrain: *If you want funding support, show me your numbers.*

Library media specialists collaboratively assess student achievement with teachers using rubrics that depend on observation of student behaviors. These rubrics fit our focus on process rather than product. The problem is that they are not amenable to standardized testing. Doug Johnson has pointed out that "it is difficult, if not impossible, to measure the impact of an effective library media program on test scores" (34). So when modern-day Gradgrinds are demanding "facts and calculations," what numbers can a library media specialist offer? Plenty!

Debbie Abilock notes that library media specialists "passively accumulate more data than we use" (7). Vendor software, online catalogs, and servers track student and teacher use of library media center resources. As library media specialists in a number-crunching world, we need to mine these and other "data warehouses." Such numbers take surprisingly little time to produce, yet they can speak volumes about how well-used your library media center is. Schedule them into your agenda at the end of every month or school term.

Here's a list of simple statistics with maximum impact. I call these straightforward stats "fast facts." They are easy to produce and administrator-friendly. Why not give them a try?

**Automatic Data Generation** is the fastest way to compile numbers that will wow your administrator.

Online databases—You get them in your e-mail every month. Use them! Monthly usage reports offer everything from numbers of searches at school and off-site to detailed analyses of resources that are being accessed. Cut and paste the basic data and send it to your principal. Be sure to include a brief explanatory note that will underscore the significance of the numbers: "Access rates are higher than ever for our online databases! It is gratifying to know that our students are choosing quality information sources for their research assignments."

ESS—Electronic security systems automatically count people as they enter and exit the library media center. Note the number on the counter at the beginning of the school year. At the end of each month, do the math. It will give you a quick picture of how many visitors you received. If you wish, you can have your maintenance person reset the number to zero. Your counter may display two numbers: one for visits and the other for each time the

> *Administrators, school boards, and district supervisors are all singing the same refrain:* If you want funding support, show me your numbers.

alarm sounds. Test which is which by walking through the gates.

Web site counters—Have your Web master place a counter on your library media center page. Remember to set this page as your default on all library media center computers. This will encourage students to use your online catalog, databases, and forms. It will also boost your hit rate.

Online catalog—Pick a simple monthly loans report and generate it consistently. Technical staff or volunteers can be trained to do this. Again, a quick cut and paste will produce a timely e-mail report.

Online reference desk—High school students may appreciate an online reference desk. Create a simple feedback form and put it on your library media center page. When students hit the "Submit" button, their query will be sent to your e-mail address. After answering these questions, transfer each e-mail to a "Ref Desk" folder. If it is well used, count up the submissions at the end of every term and you've got a new statistic.

Online purchase request—This form is similar to the reference desk, but asks students to fill in information about an item they would like to see in the library media center. Our online purchase request is well used by both students and staff. (Consult my book, *Essential Documents for School Libraries*, for examples of these last two forms.)

**Manual Data Generation** obviously takes longer to compile. However, if you have reliable volunteers or assistants, another warehouse of information about your library media center is ready to be mined.

Reference books—A traditional approach to data generation in reference departments is to simply count the number of reference books that are picked up and reshelved every day. This can be done for the circulating collection as well. Have a policy in place that students are not to reshelve items—they often put books in the wrong place anyway—and have clear signage to this effect. Of course, if this data collection is to work, assistants need to be assiduous about counting and recording what they put back each day.

Magazines—Take the same approach as you have for books. Remember to put signs in the magazine area.

Collaborative lessons—Count the number of classes booked in the library media center within a given period. This takes little time if you use a weekly booking calendar. Leave details about the number of units and subject area focus for your annual report.

Special activities—Do you offer special activities that you are proud of? Count these and get the recognition you deserve. Do you offer booktalks throughout the school year? Do students attend a regular library media center club? Do you train volunteers? Do you offer regular inservice sessions to teachers? All of these activities are quantifiable.

Reference questions—You answer many queries outside of collaboratively planned lessons. It is easy to forget to make note of these during busy break periods. It helps to keep a sheet on a clipboard at the circulation desk. Whenever you answer a few questions, add a few ticks. Don't complicate things by discriminating between quick reference, in-depth, or directional questions; a question is a question. Make an effort to keep track of the questions, and you'll add one more number to a growing list of reports that prove just how much you are helping students.

You know that your library media center and program offer much more than numbers can ever express. Anecdotes and heartfelt stories about the good things that happen every day in your library media center are an important way to show parents, teachers, and administrators just how valuable you are. Stories have an immediate, emotional appeal that numbers can't compete with. But for some, numbers tell another story. If it will affect your perceived value within your school, show them the numbers!

## Bibliography

Abilock, Debbie. "Data Driven or Data Action? Data Mining or Data Designing?" *Knowledge Quest* May/June 2004, pp. 7–9.

Johnson, Doug. "A Data Mining Primer and Implications for School Library Media Specialists." *Knowledge Quest* May/June 2004, pp. 32–35.

MacDonell, Colleen. *Essential Documents for School Libraries: "I've Got It Answers" to "I Need It Now" Questions.* (Worthington, OH: Linworth Publishing, 2004).

*Colleen MacDonell is currently working at the Raha International School in Abu Dhabi and is author of* Project-Based Inquiry Units for Young Children: First Steps to Research for Grades Pre-K-2, *(Linworth Publishing, Inc., 2007) and of* Essential Documents for School Libraries: "I've Got-It" Answers to "I-Need-It-Now" Questions *(Linworth Publishing, Inc., 2005).*

MacDonell, C. (2005). Easy data mining for school libraries. *Library Media Connection, 24*(1), 38-39.

# Making Better Decisions by Using Better Data

## By Terrence E. Young, Jr.

Accountability is a hot topic in educational reform. Demonstrating the importance of library media center programs' service to schools and how effectively library media specialists are performing their jobs has become increasingly important. Making compelling arguments about the value of library media centers without the systematic collection of data is very difficult. Administrators, school board members, and voting citizens will only support library media center programs when the data shows a correlation with student achievement..

Today's library media centers offer a full range of learning resources and services. The library media specialist, whether in the role of teacher, instructional partner, information specialist or program administrator, plans collaboratively with other teachers to teach information literacy skills in conjunction with curriculum assignments. An effective library media center program ensures that opportunities are provided for students, faculty, and staff to become effective users of ideas and information and acquire lifelong patterns of learning. Library media centers are critical to meet schools' instructional goals and objectives. They promote literacy by developing and encouraging reading. But how do you know whether your library media center program is effective? What is a realistic vision for the library media center of the twenty-first century?

One of the goals for the library media specialist, under "Program Administration: Principle 6: Ongoing assessment for improvement is essential to the vitality of an effective library media program" in *Information Power: Building Partnerships for Learning,* is to "Make decisions based on the results of data analysis to develop plans and policies for continuous improvement of the library media program" (1998, pp. 108–109).

New research findings and the renewed emphasis on reading achievement and standards-based education have prompted many school districts and some states to begin examining their library media center programs and plan for necessary improvements. Often data collection and data analysis is required to evaluate the library media centers' services. We think that more is better—more data will lead to more useful information, which will produce more informed decisions and, therefore, a more effectively managed program of service. The underlying assumption is that data about library media center programs can be transformed into useful information, and that the information will become management knowledge.

## Collecting Data

Why do we collect data? Often data collection is imposed by school boards

> Making compelling arguments about the value of library media centers without the systematic collection of data is very difficult.

and accrediting institutions. Data is gathered automatically by library OPACs or supplied by online vendors. We collect data to:

- document trends in collection and user activity. Which areas of the collection are used year after year? Is a group of students (gifted, special education) new to the library? Is the collection current for topics such as national elections, national debate topics, and science fair projects?

- track progress toward strategic goals. Is our goal general or specific, such as increasing the number of books per student; updating the science reference collection; increasing the variety of reading levels in the state book collection; or analyzing subscription database usage in terms of cost? Is our public relations campaign working? Do we support local authors?

- document and understand user needs. Does the collection reflect the school's population as reported on the school report card? Do students find what they want, and if not, are you approachable so that they can inform you? Is the library media center atmosphere conducive to learning? Does the faculty recognize that you support their classroom assignments and activities?

- track user satisfaction. Are reports and projects completed by students acceptable to the teachers? Are students finding adequate and sufficient resources to complete assignments without having to go to the public library? Are the library media center's users informed about new resources, programs, and activities? Is the library media center open sufficient time before and after school to meet students' needs? Is the level of instructional support to teachers adequate?

- get answers and information. Can teachers and students find information and answers outside the library media center through ILL, networks, public libraries, consortiums, and databases? Is information in the "evening news" readily available for further investigation?

Information skills or information literacy is tested on most state mandated tests. In Louisiana, the Graduation Exit Examination for the 21st Century (GEE 21) includes information skills on the English Language Arts test. "Locate, select, and synthesize information" is one of six standards categories reported on students and schools' test results. As library media specialists, we have a professional obligation to longitudinally track "information skills" scores by grade level and design lessons to introduce, teach, and reinforce these skills as needed. The purpose of longitudinal tracking is to collect information annually and use this information to assess students' progress. A database that tracks student information skills data over time will provide a solid footing for choices that must be made in the areas of curriculum, instructional approaches, books, and materials. It will also allow you to make informed judgments about your role as a teacher. When you do your part as a library media specialist to improve student achievement, faculty and administrators view you as a part of the teaching faculty.

## What data are you collecting?

- Take a few moments and ask yourself: What is it I need to know about my library media center's users and programs? Before collecting data, perform a needs analysis by answering the following questions:
- What data do you collect or use now?
- How do you collect or use this data?
- How frequently do you collect or use this data?
- What problems do you encounter collecting or using this data?
- For what purpose(s) do you collect and use this data?
- How do you enter and access the data?
- How do you manipulate the data?
- Do you cross-correlate this data with other data? If so, what type of data?
- How do you present or want to present your data?
- How frequently do you generate reports on the data?
- What other issues, concerns or needs do you have about data gathering and analysis?

## What type of data should be collected?

To measure the effectiveness of your library media center program, collect data that relates to:

Access—is the library media center staff (professional and clerical) available throughout the school day? Can the students and faculty access library resources throughout the school campus and remotely from home? Is the library media center open before and after school to assist students who do not have remote access?

Suitability—Does the library media center collection support the curricu-

lum? Do library resources support the varied student learning styles and the teaching styles of the faculty? Is the technology available to meet learning and teaching needs?

Competency—Is the library media center staff competent? Do the resources and technology support all aspects of the curriculum? Can library media center assistants take the place of certified library media specialists? (Under the federal law, No Child Left Behind (NCLB), certificated education professionals in non-"core" academic subjects do not need to meet the new requirement of "highly qualified.") As a library media specialist, should I be concerned about funding for my position?

Why should I be interested in the collection of library media center use data?

> We must be concerned with the degree to which services and collections are important and make a difference for every student.

Collecting library media center use data allows library media specialists to:

1) assess the current library media center use on a more definitive and descriptive basis;

2) develop a more consistent, standardized, and complete range of detailed measures for assessing library media center services and usage;

3) identify the wide range of use, besides circulation, occurring within library media centers;

4) better justify library media center resource allocation (based upon volume of all types of use); and

5) identify both needed and successful library media center services and materials.

Identify successful programs in other library media centers and see if they are replicable in your library media center. For ideas and successful programs, visit What Works Clearinghouse (WWC) <www.w-w-c.org>. WWC gathers studies of the effectiveness of

educational interventions (programs, products, practices, and policies). If certain student subgroups are not using the library media center resources, how can you get them to?

## Quantitative or Qualitative?

Why aren't more science teachers using the library media center? Are boys or girls more interested in reading Young Adult novels? How long should the library media center be open? Often, data used to investigate such questions is qualitative. Quantitative data correspond to characteristics (quantities) that can be measured numerically. Quantitative data tell how much or how many of a particular characteristic or attribute is present in an object, event, person or phenomenon (such as the number of computers available for students to use, the number of volumes in the library media center or the number of classes using library resources). Qualitative data classify an object, event, person or phenomenon into categories with respect to the attributes by which they differ. Qualitative data is not arrived at through measurement, but rather through observation and survey. By looking beyond "how much" and "how many" to the attributes of the people, things, and activities being counted, library media specialists can have a more useful understanding of their library media centers and their work.

There are a number of implications about what we might do to change the situation from number-driven, efficiency conscious data collection and analysis to more context-sensitive, sense-making collecting and analytical techniques. All of these are offered not as alternatives, but as enhancements to the standard statistical data you presently collect.

| Less Emphasis | More Emphasis |
|---|---|
| Quantitative data | Qualitative data |
| Students as a generic group of users | Students' wants and needs |
| Number of books in the collection | Collection quality |
| Quick and simple inquiries | Higher-order thinking inquiries |

Look seriously at the genuine shortcomings of quantitative data collection and analysis and seek to incorporate qualitative methods that permit deeper understanding of library media center users, collections, programs, and services.

- Focus less on the students as a genus, and more on specific categories of students and profiles of their wants and needs.
- Focus less on numerical aspects of collections and more on acceptable indicators of collection quality.
- Focus less on simple student inquiries and more on the nature and level of these inquiries.
- Foster awareness among principals and school board members that efficiency and effectiveness are not equivalent concepts, and that effectiveness in the library media center is a greater good than efficiency.

An excellent report on school library media center programs and qualitative data is:
Zweizig, Douglas and Dianne McAfee Hopkins. *Lessons from Library Power: Enriching Teaching and Learning.* Westport, CT: Libraries Unlimited, 1999.

## Collection Analysis

Are you looking for an inexpensive, easy-to-use tool to evaluate the book collection in your library media center? Titlewise Collection Analysis from Follett® Software Company <www.fsc.follett.com> and BenchMARC from Sagegrush™ Corporation <www.sagebrushcorp. com> are free Web-based resources that analyze individual school collections. These programs make it easy to identify the strengths and weaknesses of a library media center collection and view or print reports, graphs, and charts that help you focus on the areas that need improvement. The resulting data can also be presented as a district aggregate to give an overview of the book collections district-wide. The process is simple: just export your MARC records with the holdings tag, copy information, and send them electronically to either vendor online. Your MARC records are analyzed and compared to recommended collections. A detailed report provides the information needed to improve your

collection, as well as help you find new titles that meet your needs. BenchMARC allows you to create your own age standard for your reports.

This type of collection analysis focuses on the quality of the collection (usually by matching holdings against "best" lists) and the completeness of the collection (usually matching against a list of issued items). The key assumption here is that larger collections are better collections, so size may be a proxy for goodness. Less popular, but receiving more attention today, are student-centered measures. These measures focus on the degree to which students find the collection to be useful. Surveys, interviews, and questionnaires, as well as focus groups, are used to query students. In particular, we must be concerned with the degree to which services and collections are important and make a difference for every student.

> By looking beyond "how much" and "how many" to the attributes of the people, things, and activities being counted, library media specialists can have a more useful understanding of their library media centers and their work.

## Who collects data?

It is not just individual schools or districts that collect data on library media centers and reading. State and federal governments are now keenly interested in getting a cumulative picture of how library media centers help students in their learning. Some agencies collect data to get a baseline report of the status of library media centers. Others sample schools with effective library media center programs to present a cumulative picture of what great library media centers contribute to the learning community.

A National Endowment of the Arts survey (July 2004) <http://www. nea.gov/news/news04/ReadingAtRisk.html> shows that reading in

America is declining. The steepest decline is in the youngest age group. This report is a must-read for all library media specialists who are interested in libraries, books, and the general intellectual health of the United States.

At the state level, Iowa Code 256.51(h) requires the State Library of Iowa to collect data indicating current conditions, growth, and development of library services provided in Iowa, and to disseminate this information in a timely manner to the citizens of Iowa. In 2002, Iowa's library media centers started collecting data and completing the annual survey. You can find detailed information, including the annual survey instrument, at <www.silo.lib.ia.us/for-ia-libraries/tell-library-story/school-library-surveyl.htm>.

On the national level, the U. S. Department of Education's Office of Educational Research and Improvement collects data on library media centers. Federal surveys of library media centers in elementary and secondary schools in the United States were most recently collected for the school year 1999–2000. The collection occurred in the school years 1993–94, 1985, 1978, 1974, 1962, and 1958. What information is collected on the library media centers survey? Data from the questionnaires provides a nationwide picture of library media center staffing, collections, expenditures, technology, and services. Detailed information on the Library Statistics Program: School Libraries is available at <http://nces.ed.gov/surveys/libraries/school.asp>.

In addition, recent results from the federally-sponsored National Assessment of Educational Progress (NAEP) provide evidence that students who read for fun every day have significantly higher reading achievement scores than students who read less frequently (NCES, 2002). The results of these studies provide convincing evidence that active library media centers promote students' reading achievement.

## Collecting Data

Library media centers collect different data, often in different ways. Please keep the following in mind when collecting data: *Consistency in data collection is essential.* Count the same things in the same way, regardless of when counted or by whom.

## Now that you have all this data, what do you do?

*Use your data to:*

- identify goals for improving the library media center program to better serve students and faculty;

- inform principals, school board members, and other stakeholders in order to gain support/advocacy for your library media center program;

- secure additional funding for books and periodicals by comparing your data to external data: see *School Library Journal*™ 2004 annual average book prices at <www. schoollibraryjournal.com/article/CA 386702> and EBSCO's 2004 Periodical Price History for School Libraries at <www.ebsco.com/ home/printsubs/priceproj2.asp>, state guidelines or standards, and accreditation association standards and benchmarks.

- develop an action plan that includes library media center resources and services to help achieve School Improvement Plan goals as required by NCLB.

## Presenting Data: Annual Reports

As the name suggests, the annual report is produced once a year, usually at the end of the school year. Annual reports provide a very effective way to demonstrate to the administration that you are improving the educational process. Be sure to keep a well-organized log of all library media center events; postponing documenting the information about the library media center can lead to activities being forgotten, especially those for which no data were collected.

The annual report is the main official document describing and defending the library media center's mission and how its goals were achieved throughout the school year. It relates aims and budgets to results and activities, and forecasts future actions based on a well-studied budget proposal. When a library media specialist begins working in a library media center, he or she should look for the annual reports and read them. They may provide background information, data, and areas of both weakness and success. Special programs are best described in more detail in occasional reports.

When writing the annual report:

- don't reinvent the wheel
- keep it simple
- sample where possible
- keep measures focused
- use data reported by your automation software whenever possible
- turn data into information by presenting it graphically
  - trend-lines
  - charts and graphs
  - PowerPoint
- present results-oriented measures based on users' needs
- be consistent to facilitate comparison
- turn results into actions

## Conclusion

We collect data to assess the state of our library media centers' programs and services and the policies that support and guide them. This data is used to describe library media center services, evaluate the library media center programs, and measure performance. We need to collect only meaningful, purposeful data. Often data collected for one purpose can be put to use in multiple ways; various data elements can be combined to create new insights. Don't ignore incremental changes. Change based on small measures often adds up to noticeable results.

We need to develop our skills to collect, analyze, interpret, present, and use data. When we present our data to principals and school board members, we must remember to make it understandable. Present the data with this goal in mind: library media centers can contribute to improved student achievement by providing up-to-date instructional materials aligned to the curriculum and instructional practices; collaborating with and supporting teachers, administrators, and parents; and extending their hours of operation beyond the school day. Finally, if we can learn from our successes and our failures, then we are well on our way to "Every Student Succeeds @ Your Library® Media Center."

*Terrence E. Young Jr., M.Ed., MLS is a library media specialist at West Jefferson High School in New Orleans, Louisiana and adjunct instructor of Library Science at the University of New Orleans. Contact him at bestman@att.net.*

Young, T.E. (2005). Better data......better decisions. *Library Media Connection, 23*(4), 14-19.

# Leverage Your Library Program: What An Administrator Needs to Know

## By Audrey P. Church

*t has been said more than once that library media specialists have the opportunity to work their hardest and be the best they can possibly be, OR they can slack off and do just what is needed to get by. Why is this the case? Because, for the most part, administrators do not know what we do! As Gary Hartzell, Patricia Potter Wilson, and others point out, few administrators have taken coursework in their educational leadership programs that alerts them to the contributions to be made by a dynamic library media specialist. Few administrators leverage their library program by setting high expectations and maximizing the potential that exists. This article is written, then, for, your administrator. Read it and share it. Watch the bar rise higher, and get ready to make a difference in your school.*

*—Carol Simpson*

If you presently serve as a school administrator, at some stage in your educational career, you have been a classroom teacher. While you know what to expect from a classroom teacher, you may not have a good idea of what to expect from your library media specialist. Take the following pretest to check your knowledge.

Did you answer True to each of these statements? If so, your school has a strong librarian and a strong library media program. If not, did any surprise you? Are these activities that you expect of your library media specialist? Research studies completed in Alaska, Colorado, Iowa, Massachusetts, Oregon, Pennsylvania, and Texas show that these activities improve student achievement.

What does the library media specialist do all day? What should you expect? Let's take a look at some key areas.

## Collaboration

Library media specialists of the 21st century are no longer isolated "keepers of the books." Today, library media specialists are full-fledged instructional partners actively involved in the total instructional program of the school (*Information Power* 4-5). They must be well-versed in curriculum and in content area standards in your school, your school district, and your state.

This knowledge allows the library media specialist to purchase resources supporting the instructional program of the school. With a thorough knowledge of content area standards and a willingness to partner, the library media specialist is available to plan, collaboratively teach, and co-evaluate with classroom teachers. Library instruction is completely integrated into the classroom content lessons since information-seeking is a natural, integral part of the assignment.

Classroom teachers, in most instances, are not accustomed to partnering with library media specialists for instruction. They tend to view the library media specialist as a resource person. You need to promote and support this collaborative instructional culture.

Does this collaborative instructional model make a difference in test scores? Faye Pharr, Principal of Lakeside Academy of Math, Science, and Technology in Chattanooga, Tennessee, shared this statistic at the June 4, 2002 White House Conference on School Libraries:

After the first year of flexible scheduling, with all library projects based on teacher/librarian collaboration, we found there was direct correlation between library usage and improved test scores. After running the end-of-the-year circulation report, it became obvious that the teachers who had the highest library usage also had the highest test scores. A detailed analysis revealed there was a direct link between library usage and test scores in the reference study and reading comprehension. For example, the classroom with the highest library usage had a mastery percentage of 86% in reference study and 81% in comprehension. The teacher who offered the most resistance to collaborative planning and library usage also had the lowest in mastery scores—19% in reference study and 52% in comprehension. (3)

## Information Literacy

Information literacy is defined as the ability to access information effi-

---

### Administrator's Pretest:

Respond to each of the following statements by answering True or False.

My school's librarian

_____ concerns himself with content area standards.

_____ actively participates in curriculum development.

_____ promotes reading.

_____ meets, plans, and collaborates with classroom teachers.

_____ teaches students how to access, evaluate, and use information.

_____ trains teachers in the use of information technology.

_____ promotes ethical and responsible use of information.

_____ takes an active role in the instructional program of the school.

_____ effectively manages the library collection and library program to make it an integral part of the school.

ciently and effectively; to evaluate information critically and competently; and to use information accurately and creatively (*Information Power* 8). The library media specialist insures that students acquire these critical information literacy skills by helping students construct focused questions that will direct the research. He teaches them to identify possible sources of information (encyclopedia, book, periodical, Internet) to select the best source for the information need, and to use Boolean logic for effective and efficient searching.

Next, the library media specialist teaches the students to evaluate the information found. Does it meet the information need? Is the information authoritative, accurate, unbiased, and current? Students need to ask these questions to become critical consumers of information.

Finally, the library media specialist assists the students in using the information to develop an authentic, creative product. Here communication and collaboration with the classroom teacher is key. When the assignment is developed, the library media specialist can suggest alternative products. A brochure, a newsletter, or oral presentation may be more appropriate than a written research paper.

## Information Technology

Technology abounds in our schools today. The library media specialist provides inservice for teachers in information technology—effective use of information in electronic formats. Teachers should be able to use the library's online public access catalog effectively. Staff development in the use of Boolean operators (combining terms using *and*, *or*, or *not*) is imperative, since Boolean logic is applicable in all electronic settings.

The library media specialist may offer a workshop on effective use of Internet search tools—search engines, subject directories, and metasearch tools. Beyond good search techniques, the library media specialist should teach teachers to judge Web sites for content, currency, accuracy, authority, and objectivity. Expensive, licensed databases will be more effectively utilized if teachers (1) know they exist, (2) receive training in their usage, and

subsequently (3) feel comfortable using them in instructional settings.

## Reading

Historically, libraries have been known for having collections of books and promoting reading. Yet as funding for libraries has stagnated, or has even declined, book budgets have suffered (Miller and Shontz 50). School libraries require adequate funds for collection development so that both print and nonprint needs can be addressed. Beyond having the books, though, your library media specialist needs to be sure to promote reading.

Various events, such as Read Across America, Teen Read Week in October, and Children's Book Week, lend themselves to reading promotion. Additionally, many library media specialists now sponsor book clubs, breakfast or lunch discussions, or literature circles for students.

> *It is critical that your library media specialist be a strong administrator for your school's library media program. Your library media specialist should have a vision for his program and a strategic plan.*

## Program Administration

Given these elements, it is critical that your library media specialist be a strong administrator for your school's library media program. Your library media specialist should have a vision for his program and a strategic plan. Goals and objectives for the program should dovetail with the mission, goals, and objectives of your school. He should be a member of the school improvement team or principal's advisory committee. This participation connects the library media program to the larger school picture and communicates its potential to key teachers in the school.

As a program administrator, the library media specialist is responsible for budgeting, staff, facilities, scheduling, policies, and procedures.

He must, in many cases, manage and supervise support staff—clerical workers, parent volunteers, and student helpers. He is in charge of and responsible for the library facility in which he works, and he develops policies and procedures that promote flexible and equitable access to library resources. Your library media specialist should also work to connect your school library to the larger learning community by participating in formal or informal conversations and cooperative ventures.

What else should you expect in the area of program administration? Your library media specialist should be knowledgeable in the area of copyright and should promote compliance with federal copyright law. Your library media specialist should explain the concept of intellectual property and encourage your faculty and students to practice ethical behavior in their use of information.

By realizing that students will search for information from the classroom and from home, your library media specialist understands the importance of providing virtual reference services, perhaps 24/7, and will have developed a Web page for the library media center.

## Leadership

You should expect your library media specialist to take a visible leadership role within your school. The library media specialist is, in almost every state, a teacher with additional licensure or with an advanced degree in library science (Perritt 50). Seeing the scope and sequence of curriculum, content, and instruction, he is a natural member of curriculum development and school improvement teams.

You should also expect your library media specialist to take a visible leadership role outside your school to raise library awareness of parents and the larger learning community. Once the larger learning community is aware of the activities and benefits of a strong school library media program—through newspaper articles, guest appearances at local civic clubs, and open houses in which community and business leaders are invited to visit to discover what today's school library media program is all about—support grows.

## And in Return......

What does your library media specialist expect from you, the administrator of the school? First, your library media specialist needs adequate resources. Second, he needs adequate staff: depending on the student enrollment and the level of library usage by the students and teachers, your library media specialist needs clerical assistance, and, perhaps, additional professional staff.

Third, your library media specialist needs no outside duties. Before school and after school, during lunch, and during class changes are times that the library media center should be available to students and teachers.

Fourth, and critical, your library media specialist needs time to meet, plan, and collaborate with classroom teachers. Collaborative planning opportunities connect library activities to classroom content and integrate information literacy skills instruction.

Finally, your library media specialist needs your support in the effort he is making to develop a dynamic, effective, student-centered library media program. Does principal support make a difference? Dr. Gary Hartzell, Professor of Educational Administration at the University of Omaha, Nebraska, shared the following thoughts:

We have enough research on the principal's role to know that the principal is a key player, perhaps the key player, in library media programs that make a difference. . . . The research evidence also is clear that teachers collaborate more with other teachers and with the librarian when the principal openly encourages it and makes schedules that facilitate it......opportunity rests in the principal's hands. The principal is an absolutely essential element in maximizing the return on library investment (6–7).

## Resulting In...

If your library media specialist is involved in these activities—and if you are willing to provide the support listed above in return—your library media program can be an integral part of the instructional program of your school. As library media specialists collaborate with classroom teachers; teach students information literacy skills;

- instruct teachers in the effective use of information technology;
- promote reading;
- administer the various essential program components; and
- display leadership within your school
- they actively contribute to student achievement, helping students become information-literate, independent, lifelong learners. You have leveraged your library media program to maximize its potential.

### References

American Association of School Librarians and Association for Educational Communication and Technology. *Information Power: Building Partnerships for Learning.* Chicago: American Library Association, 1998.

> *Your library media program can be an integral part of the instructional program of your school.*

Hartzell, Gary N. "What's It Take?" *IMLS: Publications Conferences & Resources: Conferences* 4 June 2002 <http://www.imls.gov/pubs/whitehouse0602/garyhartzell.htm>.

Lance, Keith Curry, Marcia J. Rodney, and Christine Hamilton-Pennell. *Good Schools Have School Librarians: Oregon School Librarians Collaborate to Improve Academic Achievement.* [N.p.]: Oregon Educational Media Association, 2001.

Lance, Keith Curry, Marcia J. Rodney, and Christine Hamilton-Pennell. *How School Librarians Help Kids Achieve Standards: The Second Colorado Study.* San Jose, CA: HiWillow, 2000.

Lance, Keith Curry et al. *Information Empowered: The School Librarian as an Agent of Academic Achievement in Alaska Schools.* Juneau: Alaska State Library, 1999.

Lance, Keith Curry, Lynda Welborn, and Christine Hamilton-Pennell. *The Impact of School Library Media Centers on Academic Achievement.* Castle Rock, CO: HiWillow, 1993.

Lance, Keith Curry, Marcia J. Rodney, and Christine Hamilton-Pennell. *Measuring Up to Standards: The Impact of School Libraries & Information Literacy in Pennsylvania Schools.* 2000. 15 May 2002 <http://www.statelibrary.state.pa.us/libraries/lib/libraries/measuringup.pdf>.

Miller, Marilyn and Marilyn Shontz. "New Money, Old Books." *School Library Journal* Oct. 2001: 50-60.

Perritt, Patsy H. "Getting Certified in 50 States: The Latest Requirements for School Librarians." *School Library Journal* June 2000: 50-72.

Pharr, Faye. "Reflections of an Empowered Library" *IMLS: Publications Conferences & Resources: Conferences* 5 June 2002 <http://www.imls.gov/pubs/whitehouse0602/fayepharr.htm>.

Rodney, Marcia J., Keith Curry Lance and Christine Hamilton-Pennell. *Make the Connection: Quality School Library Media Programs Impact Academic Achievement in Iowa.* Bettendorf, IA: Mississippi Bend Area Education Agency, 2002.

This article is abbreviated from *Leverage Your Library Program to Help Raise Test Scores: A Guide for Library Media Specialists, Principals, Teachers, and Parents*, Linworth, 2003.

*Audrey Church is Coordinator of the School Library Media Program at Longwood University in Farmville, Virginia, and can be reached at achurch@longwood.edu. She is also the author of* Leverage Your Library to Raise Test Scores: A Guide for Library Media Specialists, Principals, Teachers, and Parents *(Linworth, 2003) and of* Your Library Goes Virtual *(Linworth Publishing, Inc. 2007)*

Church, A.P. (2004). Leverage your library program: What an administrator needs to know. *Library Media Connection,* 22(6), 31-33.

# Perks, Rewards, and Glory: The Care and Feeding of Volunteers

## By Sheryl Kindle Fullner

A few years ago, I organized a community play recreating our town's holidays from one hundred years ago. This volunteer effort was an immense success, but I learned a very valuable lesson from the video tapes of the event. One volunteer was singled out for honors at the end of the theater run. She slouched up to the podium and received the corsage on a slumped shoulder. With a singularly churlish lack of grace, she accepted the praise and applause. The video tape caught it all. When I watched myself later (because of course I was the "dog-in-the-manger-ish" one), I resolved to accept any future awards with my head up and a big smile and even a Miss America wrist wave. That video gave me the clue that not all volunteers respond the same way to the same stimuli.

### The Many Forms of Reward

At about that same time, I read Gary Chapman's *The Five Love Languages*, which examines how people respond differently to praise, gifts, acts of service, quality time, or physical touch. Chapman provided some insight into respecting my volunteers. Some might respond best to a printed word of appreciation in a district newsletter, while others would value a book or pin as a gift. The best clue I had for discovering my volunteer's respect language was the language he or she used toward me: Were cookies brought? (Gift language); Were hugs offered? (Physical touch language); Were thank you notes given? (Words of affirmation). After I tried this for a while, I decided that I would just use a variety of respect languages and hope that most would hit the target. What follows are several ways to nurture volunteers in the library media center setting.

### Glory

*Star Girl* by Jerry Spinelli is currently very popular and one of the burning teen questions it addresses is "who gets the credit?" While most of us are glad to avoid blame, many of us live for credit. We don't admit it, but even as adults some of us like to be caught doing something good.

Honors can be free. Many schools have a newspaper or newsletter that could support a brief thank you article for one or more volunteers or local newspapers may print thank you notes on the op ed page. Many communities have a Man or Woman of the Year award. Simply nominating volunteers sends the message of how much they are valued. Local markets, banks, or your own school may be willing to run an electronic message on their reader boards so volunteers can see *their* names up in lights (instead of the temperature). Bulletin boards, sidewalk chalk art, even the dust on their wind-

> Some might respond best to a printed word of appreciation in a district newsletter, while others would value a book or pin as a gift.

shield can sport the sign of a heart, "Loved by the Library," which all add up to simple ways of giving credit. Local radio and television may also be possibilities for out-loud acknowledgment. Instead of calling the station to inquire if they will air a thank you (they probably will not), submit the thank you to the community calendar page of the station. Then rolling right across the screen will be seen:

Date: November 10
Event: Marcia Cratsenberg Appreciation Day
Place: Nooksack Valley Middle School

The principal can also sign a proclamation designed and prepared by the media specialist.

Create a specially decorated chair in the lunch room and offer an invitation to share lunch with the kids. Enlist the help ahead of time with cafeteria staff. Ask for a free meal for the volunteer. Bring a goblet from home and let students or library staff make a big deal of filling it with a school-proffered beverage while they have a towel over one arm like a waiter. A bud vase and a cloth napkin can complete the vignette, although the choir director or band teacher may also help by supplying a live student musician (Drumrolls are super). None of this costs any money; just a little preparation and cooperation. All of the props will fit into a small basket. This is the art of making a fuss with a minimum of fuss.

### Perks

Most libraries have rules and boundaries devised to maximize service to a wide variety of patrons. Think one small step outside those protocols as a way of rewarding volunteers. Our volunteers are encouraged to have first choice of check out when we receive new books. When offering a perk, it is important to describe it so that the helpers know they are getting something special. For example, one might say, "I appreciate all you do for our library and so I would like you to have the first opportunity to check out one of our brand new books for a week." Specifying the number of materials and the length of the loan helps to avoid misunderstandings or nagging. It would be horrible for a brand new Paulsen novel to languish in a family room somewhere for a month.

Volunteers are allowed to take home a magazine for one night between the time it arrives in the mail and before it is processed and shelved. Some librarians might prefer to offer the dibs after it is ready to circulate in order to keep track of it better, but I like to use that dead processing time when it might not otherwise be used.

Our library sometimes receives either duplicate or unsolicited magazines. Those are occasionally incorporated into prize packages for students, but more often made available to our volunteers. A wire or plastic basket labeled "Perk Bin: Please help yourself to one item" is a repository for perfume samples, stickers, magazines, posters, and magnets that either come in the mail or that are picked up free from store or convention displays.

The following perks need to be used judiciously by the librarian rather than directly by the volunteer because there is room for misuse. One can also offer the library laminator for a photo or clipping or the photocopier for an enlargement. I offer library mylar book coverings for one book. This can be justified with the district because the volunteer is offering many hours of unpaid help, which far outweigh the cost of the perk.

### Order Power

In our library, each volunteer is asked to nominate a book to be ordered for the library. When it arrives, a book plate with the volunteer's name and specialty (if any) is attached prominently. Rather than using commercial books plates, use a splashy font such Algerian 24 point to type: "Generously Donated in Honor of Volunteer: Brielle Hoffman—Data Entry Expert."

This is printed, trimmed, laid on the first empty page of the book and then covered with three-inch clear book tape. The process takes less than one minute and is very showy. Since all good librarians solicit book suggestions from patrons to round out collections, this is good library practice put to a pragmatic use.

### Rewards

Our library is in an economically depressed area. It has the highest tax payer levy in our county and the fewest businesses. We try to use national companies as the source for our rewards. *Books Are Fun* visits our school regularly. Staff member purchases often come with free or bonus items, which are designated for library use. If none of the books are appropriate for our collection, an item is chosen as a gift for our volunteers. These are accumulated until the end-of-the-year recognition ceremonies.

Keep a sharp eye out for free offers in stores or newspapers. Buy one, get one free offers and free rebate items are also stockpiled. The free rebate items

> *Learn the art of making a fuss with a minimum of fuss.*

require an initial outlay of money, but this is returned via check. It is possible to obtain gel pens, staplers, markers, writeable CDs, and other stationery gift items this way. Instead of spending $25.00 received from the PTO, consider using it over and over to purchase rebate items.

Thrift stores and garage sales frequently have like-new mugs for under a dollar. A cellophane bag filled with coffee beans, candy, etc. can be stuffed inside and tied with a ribbon for a total cost of $3.00. Since even that small amount has to come out of salary, we try to find alternatives. Small four-inch baskets with long handles that hang over a door knob are purchased (cost is usually 50 cents) over several months and then stored until May Day when they are filled with free garden flowers such as lilacs in a plastic cup of water for a very memorable reward. It may be easier to buy 59-cent primrose plants for the baskets than to wander about your garden pre-dawn with clippers.

Every few years I try to treat our PTO or other workers to a tea or garden tour at my home. Oddly enough it takes much less work and time to let people wander one's home eating store bought English chocolate biscuits than to phone people to bring cupcakes to school. And the gesture is magnificent.

### Is This Just "One More Thing"?

When reading about glory, perks, and rewards, it may seem like an overwhelming amount of work. It is not. It is a mindset that is alert to ways of inventively and quickly sending messages of appreciation and value to people who are worth infinitely more. The collective five or ten hours per year spent generating tokens of gratitude for free workers is miniscule compared to the hundreds of hours with which they bless our library.

---

*Sheryl Kindle Fullner is the Librarian at Nooksack Valley Middle School in Everson, Washington.*

Fullner, S.K. (2004). Perks, rewards, and glory: The care and feeding of volunteers. *Library Media Connection, 22*(4), 38-39

# A Practical Approach to Marketing the School Library

## By Amy Burkman

As school funding decreases and educational costs rise, auxiliary programs in public school face extermination. School librarians must respond quickly with efforts to prove library programs are vital to the success of the students. Practical strategies for marketing the school library are important to the success of the program. Without positive marketing the school library could fall victim to economic hardship.

## Target Audience

The first step to any marketing effort is targeting the audience. School librarians need to target several groups: administrators, teachers, students, parents, and the general community. Each target audience requires a different marketing strategy. It is important to remember that students are not the only audience in the school library. Librarians typically target students when marketing the program, but leave out the other groups.

## Marketing Programs

Librarians can take many approaches to designing a marketing program, including taking surveys to target needs, working with a cooperative group of librarians, and researching popular techniques used in other libraries. Time constraints create a challenge to marketing as most school librarians work alone in their libraries. This article provides practical tips on starting a marketing program.

## Administrators

The most effective way to prove library effectiveness is to keep data on student and teacher use of the library. Once a semester, take the data to the administrators and present the facts. Include all areas of usage:

- Circulated materials
- Number of students independently using the library
- Number of classes using the library
- Collaborative projects
- All weekly schedules

Make the presentation attractive and professional. Use graphs, charts, and PowerPoint presentations to show the administrators how vital library usage is to the education of the students. Leave copies of the data with all administrators as well as examples of lessons taught cooperatively with teachers. Concrete examples of activities explain best what goes on in the library (other than checking out books to students).

At the end of the school year collect test scores for the school. Compare the scores of the classes that utilize the library to the classes that do not. Chart the comparison and you will find a distinct difference. Take this information to the administrators when you present your end of the year statistics to administrators. Data from your campus proves the worth of the library far more than data from a journal article.

> At the end of the school year collect test scores for the school. Compare the scores of the classes that utilize the library to the classes that do not. Chart the comparison and you will find a distinct difference.

Campus administrators oversee dozens of programs during the school year. Unless an administrator has been a librarian, he will not know what you do unless you tell him. Do not be afraid to show the administrators what you do, or they may not realize the importance of an involved library program.

## Parents

Parents are another lost marketing audience for the school library. A school librarian's contact with a parent typically develops from volunteer opportunities or issues with library materials. Yet school librarians need to have relationships with parents concerning library programs that go beyond what is traditional.

Promoting the library to parents should include the whole family. Have a family night once a semester. Bring in parents for programs and special activities that will allow all of their children the opportunity to experience the school library. Many activities can be shared with the local public library. This promotes a cooperative program that extends family library use.

Parents need clear information about library policies and usage. Provide fliers to be sent home with students or to be passed out at an open house. Librarians should attend all evening activities when the school is open to the parents. Parents need to see the school library as an extension of the classroom. The atmosphere of the library should be welcoming and positive every time a parent enters.

Finally, advertise to parents. Send out announcements, flyers, and newsletters explaining upcoming events. Send invitations to each home when an activity is to take place. Invite the parents separately and they will feel like an important component of the library program.

## Teachers

Teachers are valuable partners in the school library. It takes teachers and librarians working together to create a solid learning environment. It is a challenge to most librarians to bring in teachers because teachers often hold preconceived ideas of what a library can do for them.

Have an opening breakfast. If you feed them, they will come. Teachers love to eat and talk. There is little time during the day for teachers to interact with each other. Provide books to preview, samples of cooperative lessons you have done, and copies of materials you would like to order. Invite the teachers to suggest books they would like for the library to purchase and/or topics they would like to see covered in the library collection. Create forms that teachers can use for these requests and suggestions. Leave these forms and instructions out on tables for the teachers to take after eating.

Another strategy for involving teachers is to attend department meetings. Take fliers and lists explaining available programs and library opportunities and invite teacher suggestions. Teachers decide the success or failure of the library. Creating opportunities for teachers will ensure students have reasons to use the library frequently.

## Students

Students are the easiest target marketing audience. The traditional focus of a school library is student use. Students need to use the library for school assignments and to get books to read recreationally. The difficulty lies in bringing in students who do not like to read and who do not always complete assignments that require reading or research.

The first marketing method is word of mouth. The librarian has to create an atmosphere of acceptance and fun in the library. Students need to feel accepted no matter their academic level and they need to feel that the library is a fun place to be. Once students start talking about the positive experiences they have in the library, reluctant students will utilize the library as well.

Second, it is important to have frequent contests that involve students. Creativity is required to find contests that do not always require reading. The library is more than a place to get a book to read. There are magazines, computers, graphic novels, and books on tape. Students who do not like to read will not participate in library programs that neglect the reluctant reader.

Have writing contests, or contests where students can draw or work in groups. Make all students feel involved.

Finally, advertise alternatives to traditional reading. Subscribe to e-books, order books on tape, buy graphic novels, and you will draw in students who do not "like" to read. Then advertise the availability of these items. Create special displays and do book talks during the school's daily announcements. Let students and teachers know what secrets the library holds.

> *If you feed them,
> they will come.*

## The Community

Marketing to the general community around the school is deceptively easy. Librarians need to create cooperative programming with schools that feed into the same high school. Creating chains of elementary, intermediate, and middle schools will ensure that all students in the feeder group know what to expect from the other library programs. It is also important to remember those people who live in the community and do not have children attending the schools. Have local radio stations and local newsletters run special public service announcements advertising programs and special events. This will reach all members of the community. Also invite business owners to participate in and donate prizes to contests held in the library. The community surrounding the school creates a network of seldom-used resources for the school library.

## Marketing Evaluations

The best way to evaluate marketing techniques is to monitor library usage. If marketing is done effectively, library usage should increase over a relatively short period of time. Another valuable evaluative tool is a survey. Survey parents, teachers, and students to discover new areas to market. Survey administrators to increase support of the library program. Open and frequent communication is the key to effective marketing.

## Discussion

Traditional library programs may fail because there is a lack of communication between the library and the people supporting the school. Without marketing, the school library will soon be replaced by computer labs and support staff who do not know how to create a positive library program.

When the librarian markets the library, no one can be left out. The administration, the teachers, the parents, and the students all have equal stock in the library program. Librarians need to put themselves out into the school population and be vocal about what they can do for the educational system. Librarians need to embrace change and market programs that are non-traditional. This is the only way to save the school library.

*Amy Burkman is a Library Media Specialist at Hillwood Middle School in Keller Independent School District (Fort Worth, Texas).*

Burkman, A. (2004). A practical approach to marketing the school library. *Library Media Connection, 23*(3), 42-43.

# Come to Capitol Hill !
# Be a Library Media Center Advocate!

## By Sandy Schuckett

On May 4–5, 2005, the Washington Office of the American Library Association will sponsor National Library Legislative Day in Washington, DC. Outlined here is a brief history and background of this exciting two-day event, and a play-by-play account of exactly what happens there. It is written to give LIBRARY MEDIA CONNECTION readers a feeling of what it's actually like to participate. By the time you have finished reading this short description, you'll want to attend!

### History and Background

In 1945 it became evident to the library community, and specifically, the ALA, that if libraries of all types were going to be adequately supported and funded by elected officials on the federal level, it would be a good idea to have a strong presence in Washington, DC. Thus, the ALA Washington Office was established. Today the office at 1301 Pennsylvania Avenue–NW, just a few blocks from the White House, buzzes with activity and acts as a link between ALA members and the federal government as it works to maintain communication between the library community and the elected officials in Washington.

The ALA Washington Office organized the first National Library Legislative Day in 1974. Today it is co-sponsored by the District of Columbia Library Association, and is usually held on the first Tuesday in May. Legislative Day brings 300–500 librarians, library trustees, board members, and other library friends to Washington, DC, to speak personally with U.S. senators and representatives or their staff members. Legislative Day provides an opportunity for librarians from all types of libraries to communicate with each other regarding the similarities and differences in their issues. It also provides the opportunity for them to support each other's requests where elected officials are concerned.

### National Library Legislative Day: You Are There

National Library Legislative Day has grown to a two-day event in recent years. Monday is an all-day briefing session with in-depth briefings by selected knowledgeable speakers on all of the issues that will be discussed with legislators on Tuesday, and an opportunity for participants to ask questions. Often there are breakout groups where specific issues, such as ESEA, the Library Services and Technology Act (LSTA), Copyright, and E-Rate, are discussed in greater depth. Each attendee receives a packet filled with Issues Briefs (each a one-pager printed on a different colored paper bulleting the important points to be made). Packets are provided for each legislator as well.

> If your state has a large congressional delegation, you will probably be trudging up and down the hill from building to building, and the weather in Washington in May could be anything from hot to rainy to wonderful!

A state coordinator is appointed by each state library agency to lead that state's delegation in Washington. Appointments have been made in advance with all of the congressional representatives and the state's senators, and a schedule shows which people are to visit which offices. The state coordinator picks up the packets for that state's legislators and distributes them to the library advocates who will be visiting each office. For a small state, such as Rhode Island, or a large state with a small population, such as Wyoming, participants will only have to visit a few offices, and the whole delegation may visit all of the offices together. But for a state like California, with 53 members of Congress to visit, quite a hectic day awaits, especially if there are a small number of Legislative Day participants. For this reason, the larger state delegations often schedule some of their appointments on Monday, in addition to Tuesday.

On Tuesday the whole day, until about 4:00 p.m., is devoted to visiting the congressional and senatorial offices. Depending upon the size of your delegation to Washington, one or more Legislative Day participants will accompany you on your visits. Usually the state coordinators divide their delegations—especially the larger ones—into two or three person teams. You will probably be paired with a public librarian, someone from your State Library, or a library trustee, friend, or other supporter. While walking to your appointments, you can decide who will say what and who will emphasize which points when the meeting actually begins. As the library media center advocate, your task will be to stress the specific points that relate to library media center funding, usually in connection with ESEA, and currently most significant in our effort to urge Congress to appropriate full funding for the Literacy Through School Libraries section of No Child Left Behind. (In 2001 this section was authorized by Congress to be funded at $250 million, but only a small fraction of that amount has actually been funded over the past three fiscal years.)

Wear comfortable shoes! The congressional offices are located in three buildings on Capitol Hill—which really is a hill—the Cannon House Office Building (CHOB), the Rayburn House Office Building (RHOB), and the Longworth House Office Building (LHOB). If your state has a large congressional delegation, you will probably be trudging up and down the hill from building to building, and the weather in Washington in May could be anything from hot to rainy to wonderful! Your trudging can be eased a bit by underground tunnels that connect the buildings. If you use these, you will walk through long, dull-looking hallways, but you will avoid getting wet or suffering from heat exhaustion, and the route is flat.

Once you enter the particular building, you will need to go through security just as you do at the airport. These buildings were built quite a long time ago, and there are all sorts of interesting statues, plaques, and other things of historical value to view. Their floor plans are quite interesting also, and, in some cases, not unlike a maze. However, they do have relatively good signage and maps, and it usually isn't too difficult to find a specific office. It's quite thrilling to walk through the halls. You may see media people gathered with their microphones and video cameras outside of one particular office, which usually means that particular member of congress is embroiled in some important or controversial piece of legislation. You might even see an interview in process being conducted by a national network Washington reporter! You get the feeling that important business is going on, and you realize that all of these men and women in Congress have been elected by their constituents to come to Washington to work for *them*.

In front of each congressmember's office is a large flag from his or her state. The flags are especially helpful if you are at the end of one of the long hallways; just look down the hall for your own state flag. The names of the members and their states, along with the room numbers, are emblazoned in gold leaf on the lush-looking oak doors.

Once you enter the member's office, look around. It's very interesting to note how he or she has decorated the reception area. Many congressmembers have artwork done by children, beautiful photos of points of interest in their states, awards or commemorative plaques, maps of their districts, or interesting pieces of art. Some of the offices are large and beautiful, with amazing views of the Capitol building across the street. Others seem to be quite tiny. A lot depends on seniority and committee membership. A television is constantly

playing in the reception area. It is either tuned to the session in the House if one is going on or to CNN.

Introduce yourself to the receptionist, and provide her with your business card, if you have one, and let those accompanying you do the same. If you are fortunate enough to meet with the congressmember, you will be ushered into his or her private office. This might happen immediately, or you might have to wait. In the inner office you will see more plaques and awards, often pictures of the member with the current or a past President of the United States, and more beautiful art. If you are meeting with a staff person, you may meet in the member's office if the House is in session, in a small conference room, or maybe just sit on a couch in the reception area. Sometimes you will be invited to a lounge or coffee area in another part

> Early on Tuesday evening, after all of the legislative appointments have been completed, the ALA Washington Office hosts a reception in one of the special reception rooms in a congressional office building.

of the building, and your meeting will continue there, and sometimes you will even meet just standing in the hallway outside the office!

When you are actually going over the issues you came to discuss, remember that time is of the essence, and you need to be clear, concise, and quick. Leave the packet containing the Issues Briefs, which was provided for you on Monday. You might want to point out specific pages to bring particular matters to the congressmember's or staff's attention. If you have business cards, be sure to leave one, along with an offer to provide additional information on library media centers should it be needed. This would be a good time to give a few pages with bulleted details showing the results of the many recent studies that have shown the connection between well-supported library media centers and

raised student achievement. When you are ready to leave, thank the member or staff for his or her time, and don't forget to thank the staff people in the outer office. Be sure to pick up a business card for each legislator or staff person with whom you've met. You will need these when you write your thank-you notes or letters after returning home.

Lunch on Capitol Hill is fun. Each of the buildings has a cafeteria/lunch room for its employees that is also open to the public. The lunchroom in the Longworth building is similar to a food court at the mall. There is always a feeling of excitement in the Longworth cafeteria, because you never know who will be eating there on any given day. Most of the congressional staff members eat there and you will often see some of the members of Congress themselves. You will also invariably see large groups of students of all ages on school tours—often wearing their school shirts or uniforms. There is also a House of Representatives gift shop next to the cafeteria where you can purchase all sorts of souvenirs with the House logo—anything from key rings to T-shirts to scarves and gorgeous bronze bookends to crystal paperweights.

If you are lucky, the schedule for your visits will have been arranged so that the congressional appointments are all in the morning, and the senatorial appointments in the afternoon, or vice versa. The Senate office buildings are all the way across the Capitol Complex on the opposite side of those for the House. Again, this is a substantial walk, but if the weather is pleasant you can enjoy the sights. As you walk across the Capitol Complex, you will pass by the impressive Library of Congress and the Supreme Court on your right, and the U.S. Capitol building on your left.

The senatorial offices are also in three buildings: the Russell Senate Office Building (RSOB), the Dirksen Senate Office Building (DSOB), and the Hart Senate Office Building (HSOB). Your visits to the senate offices will be similar to those in the congressional buildings. You will go through security, and once in the senators' offices you will follow the same procedures and use the same techniques. Again, be sure to thank everyone and pick up business cards as you leave each office.

At this point, you are probably dead tired, but your day isn't over yet! Usually, early on Tuesday evening, after all of the legislative appointments have been completed, the ALA Washington Office hosts a reception in one of the special reception rooms in a congressional office building. There will be welcome refreshments, and you will have the opportunity to mingle with library supporters from all over the country. You will also meet library media specialists from other states with whom you can chat and share stories about your library program or compare notes about your legislative office visits. The ALA Washington Office often presents awards at this reception to legislators who have been especially strong

library supporters, and since you are right there in the same room you can meet and thank them for their support. In 2004 Senators Russ Feingold (D–WI) and Bernie Sanders (I–VT) were presented with awards for their work in fighting against the US PATRIOT Act's encroachment on library users' privacy. You might also have a chance to meet other senators or members of congress since they are all invited, and there are always several who do show up—usually the strong library supporters.

Whether you arrived in the nation's capitol by plane, train, bus, or car, on the way home you can reflect on the National Library Legislative Day experience and feel a great sense of accomplishment since you will know you have played an important part in influencing the decision-makers of our nation. You

are one of a select few concerned citizens who has taken the time to fight for something you strongly believe in: your library media center and the students it serves. You are a true library media center advocate! (For further details on 2005 National Library Legislative Day, go to <www.ala.org/washoff> and click on "Events.")

*Sandy Schuckett is a veteran school librarian and the official liaison from the California School Library Association to the California Teachers Association. She is also the author of* Political Advocacy for School Librarians: You Have The Power! *(Linworth Publishing, Inc., 2004.)*

Schuckett, S. (2005). Come to Capitol Hill! Be a school library advocate! *Library Media Connection, 23*(6), 26-28.

# Tools of the Trade: Political Advocacy "Always" List

## By Sandy Schuckett

### I. ALWAYS BE HONEST

No exaggeration or embellishment of facts
Quote figures that are accurate

### II. ALWAYS BE COURTEOUS

Offer to help elected officials
If you disagree with their point of view, explain consequences to students
Do not threaten with "I will see that no-one votes for you."

### III. ALWAYS COMMUNICATE/COMMUNICATE/COMMUNICATE

Respond quickly to requests for information
Provide straight information: do your homework and be aware of the opposition
Visit legislators early with your list of issues and information
Prepare a one-page fact sheet related to your issues

### IV. ALWAYS REFRAIN FROM CRITICIZING OTHER LEGISLATORS

Concentrate only on the legislator with whom you are meeting
Your "enemy" may be their friend

### V. ALWAYS BE IMPORTANT TO LEGISLATORS

Become known as the "expert" on school libraries who can provide information
Relate with their staff also; they can be very helpful

### VI. ALWAYS BE SWIFT

Be bright/be brief/be gone!

### VII. ALWAYS BE UNDERSTANDING

Know their background/culture/politics
Patience is a virtue
Be able to compromise

### VIII. ALWAYS OFFER ASSISTANCE & BUILD COALITIONS

Educate others in the community
Let all know how a strong school library helps them

### IX. ALWAYS BE A CHEERLEADER

Thank-you letters are essential
Even after a "wrong" vote, thank officials for taking time with you

### X. ALWAYS DISPLAY PROFESSIONALISM

Do not be "uppity"
Be confident and maintain a sense of humor

This list and lots of other useful information can be found in Sandy Schuckett's book *Political Advocacy for School Librarians: You Have the Power!* (Linworth Publishing, Inc., 2004).

---

*Sandy Schuckett is a veteran library media teacher who worked for 38 years in elementary and middle school libraries in the Los Angeles Unified School District. She is the Vice President Emerita for Legislation of the California School Library Association, and a former chair of the Legislation Committee of the American Association of School Librarians. She has been an activist in advocating for school libraries in the local, state, and national arenas for more than twenty-five years.*

Editor's Note: Each issue will feature reproducible items that are designed for you to share with your school community. It might be a tool to help manage the library media center or an executive summary of an important library-related issue for your administrator or colleagues. Each carries permission for you to reproduce the material within the building in which you work.

Schuckett, S. (2005). Tools of the trade: Political advocacy "always" list. *Library Media Connection, 24*(1), 60.

# Budgeting: As Easy as 1-2-3

## By Gail Dickinson

Maybe it's the name that's the problem. Talk about budgeting, and the snoozing starts. Or maybe it's the perception that budgeting requires a lot of math skills. No one talks about wanting to become a school librarian because they were drawn to calculators and spreadsheets. Although the lack of a stable budget is a major constraint on the future of school library media programs, discussions of budget processes, budget development, and budget analysis just don't seem to draw cheering crowds and packed ballrooms.

This can change, although it won't happen overnight. There are few instances in which a principal or central office administrator claps a hand to his forehead as the light bulb appears and cries, "I have a great idea! Let's give more money to the library." We have to *ask* for the money our programs deserve. Asking, in budget terms, is defined as developing an evidence-based request for funds, presenting that request to those who have the authority to grant the funding, and then following up on the request to ensure that funds are included in the final budget.

### Why Budget

Budgeting is an important part of the program administration role of the library media specialist, and provides the tools for success in other roles. With a strong, stable budget stream, school library media programs have new technologies in good repair, a current collection of resources, and an attractive and inviting library media center facility. The development and presentation of a mission-based, instructionally sound budget request on an annual basis is a professional responsibility and a job role that cannot be ignored. It is also how school library media programs can achieve the level of budgeting required to create the programs that our schools, students, and staff need.

### The Three-step Process

The budget cycle, shown in Figure 1, is the basis for the budget process. This cycle has three parts: knowledge, planning, and implementation. Each part is equally important to creating a stable budget stream. This is not a linear process, achieved by completing each stage before moving on to the next. All parts of the budget cycle may happen simultaneously, or may overlap. While budgets are being implemented, the planning has already started for the next year. Knowledge of budget needs and processes is ongoing throughout the year.

### Knowledge

The first step in developing a budget is to have a sound understanding of the budget processes in the school and district. The school district budget manual may not be an exciting read, but it contains answers to essential questions underlying budget processes. Two of the most important questions focus on deadlines and budget control.

> There are few instances in which a principal or central office administrator claps a hand to his forehead as the light bulb appears and cries, "I have a great idea! Let's give more money to the library."

*Deadlines.* There is a sequence of events surrounding budget processes in schools. The deadline to have budget requests for the following school year may be as early as October of the current year. The budget requests will go through a series of stages before being printed into the final school district budget. The school library media budget needs to be developed and circulated well before the earliest deadline. A day late may literally mean a dollar short, or in the case of the library budget, thousands of dollars short. Submitting a budget request in March for the next school year may seem to be reasonably early, but in almost all cases it will be up to 5 months late. Learn the deadlines. It will be easier to attract the attention of administrators to your budget when their attention is already focused on budget planning.

*Budget control.* Although the superintendent most likely will be the person presenting the final budget to the school board and taxpayers, a variety of other central office or school-based administrators will submit the requests that make up that budget. A building level administrator may have complete control over funds requested for his or her building, or may have none at all. The budget control given to a site-based team may be simply allocating limited funds to a narrow set of pre-determined priorities, or the team could be responsible for creating the budget request. Other avenues for budget approval may be curriculum or testing coordinators, federally funded programs, or subject area administrators. The budget manual usually lists all administrators with budget responsibility and details the budget process. It may be surprising to learn the many avenues that will lead to a brighter budgeting future for the library media program.

*Budget History.* Past budget files will reveal important information about the school library program. A budget dollar figure that has remained the same for a number of years is actually a decrease in funding. The degree to which that has occurred can be surprising. A simple procedure to bring dollars up to today's currency equivalency is detailed in *Empty Pockets, Full Plates* (Dickinson, 28, 33-35). Also, there is a wealth of data that can be gathered on the state of the library program past and present. Surveys of students and teachers will results in lists of resources needed for instruction in the school. Collection analyses and curriculum maps can portray an accurate picture of the state of the resource collection.

Knowledge is power only when it is shared, and small drips of water over time have more effect than occasional floods. School administrators and busy classroom teachers need the sound bite approach to information sharing. By the time the budget is presented, the audience should already know every fact behind the budget rationale.

### Planning

Budgeting would be easier if the amount of money required to achieve excellence in school library media programming were available in a published list. Unfortunately, we do not know how much money that would be. How many books should elementary students read before they become accomplished readers? How many databases are enough for a high school? It's even harder to think in terms of dollars per pupil. Does a 2000-student high student need to have four times the budget of a 500-student high school? A very small rural school may have fewer than 100 pupils. An equal amount per pupil will result in an unequal ability to meet students' needs.

Building a budget request does not start with dollars, it starts with standards. It is necessary to have an understanding of the recommended components of a strong school library program. *Information Power* (AASL/ AECT, 1998) is always the best place to start, along with regional and state accreditation standards. The results of a collection analysis, the collection development plan, and a facility analysis are also good starting points for a list of the resources, staff, technology, and other expenditure-based items in the library media program.

Probably the single greatest cost item in the library media center program is personnel. Teaching is a hands-on business, and personnel costs are always the highest item in any education budget. Although it may be tempting to request salary increases based on extra work in the library program, it is probably better to use the salary line in the budget process to request additional staff hours. A full-time media assistant may not be reachable as a goal the first year, but it may be possible to request more staff hours.

An under-funded library media program is like a house in need of repair. The cost to bring it up to standard can be staggering. There is a cost for neglect, and the bottom line is always higher than it would have been to do the necessary maintenance in the first place. While a 3-year plan, such

as outlined in Figure 2, can help to spread out those costs, a neglected library media program will require substantial funding.

### Implementation

Budget presentations need not be formal PowerPoint-driven charts and graphs in front of a hushed audience. Budgets can be presented as formal reports or as simple newsletter articles. Regardless, the budget must have the following components:

Itemized dollar amounts. The bottom line will always be cost, and budget audiences will want to know that figure early in the presentation. The budget dollars can be given as a total, and then broken down by per pupil cost, or per use cost. The cost of an online database may be thousands of dollars, but a well-used database can be presented as costing pennies

> *School administrators and busy classroom teachers need the sound bite approach to information sharing. By the time the budget is presented, the audience should already know every fact behind the budget rationale.*

per use over the course of the year.

Itemize by type of item. Some grant agencies or end-of-year reports will want to know the amount spent on library books, technology, or other itemizations. The amount requested versus the amount received in each category may be the beginning of a budget request for the following year.

### Justify everything

"Mission-based", "instructionally sound"—these are the buzzwords for budget development. The mission of the school library media program in the school as outlined by *Information Power* (AASL/AECT, 1998) and the mission and goals of your school and district drive budget development. Every item requested must have a direct relationship to student achievement, either through improved teach-

ing or through direct benefit to students. There can be no other reason to spend money in an institution created solely for the education of students unless the request for funds can be shown to directly affect the educational process.

## Do I Have To?

Budget development is a necessary responsibility, but it is not one that all library media specialists may do. Time is probably one reason for this. Budgeting is a back-room activity. It can take time away from meeting the more direct and pressing needs of students and teachers. For school districts in financial difficulties, which these days probably describes many school districts, it is difficult to think beyond not getting the money. However, these real concerns do not absolve the professional responsibility to develop and prepare a budget. Instead of Frequently Asked Questions (FAQ's), frequent budget excuses are probably more aptly called FHW's (Frequently Heard Whines).

*I don't have any control over a budget, I am told how much money I have.*
You may not have had much control in the past over the budget you received, but you have total control over the dollar amount you request. It is an administrative task to say no to requests. A school library media specialist who does not formally request needed funds is denying the value of the library program, essentially vetoing the budget request *in vitro*.

*There is no money.*
Nonsense, there is always money. If the 1960's can be described as the golden age of school library media, then the 1980's and early 1990's could rightly be described as the dark ages. School libraries were closed, and school library media services at the state, regional, and district level were curtailed or eliminated. It was one of the lowest times for school library media expenditures. Still, during that same time period, school libraries went from card catalog and book stamp checkout to almost an entirely automated profession. Retrospective conversion, automation software, and OPAC stations are expensive, yet almost every school library is now automated. The money existed.

Even now as most school districts

plead poverty, there are new initiatives and new programs. It's not just new football fields and Olympic-sized swimming pools grabbing big dollars. Savvy school library media specialists watch the money flow, and learn how new programs rise and fall. They observe the direction of the district towards new initiatives, and plan their budget defense accordingly.

*They will just say no.*

Maybe, but that's their job, not yours. The basketball motivational quote, "You miss 100 percent of the shots you don't take" is very applicable to the budget process. It is quite possible that the amount of money it would take to fully fund the library program may not be well-received. Submitting an annual budget request is still a professional responsibility. It is the responsibility of the school district to decide whether or not to fund that request. Just because the school district is abdicating its responsibility is no reason for library media specialist to join in that abdication. We need to make them tell us no, and do it over and over again. Sooner or later, the answer will be yes.

*It won't work, and will be a waste of time I don't have.*

I will admit that one of least exciting assignments in my graduate school classes is probably budget development. Most students in my classes are practicing library media specialists, working towards licensure. I brace myself each time I make this assignment, ready for the inevitable "but we don't do a budget in our district," "so do you just want a list of what we buy," "the principal said not to ask for money," and other questions. I say the same thing each semester, "I make this assignment each year, and if done properly, about 1/3 of the class will receive an increase in funds, if not total funding." Within a month the e-mails begin coming: "I just got an additional $10,000," "My assistant principal asked what I was doing, and when I told her she left, then came back later and told me I could spend "$3000." I hear of facility development plans that are funded, extra money for collections based on collection analyses, and budget processes used to secure grants. Budget requests are not just a useless process learned in library

school and discarded in the real world. The budget process works.

## What's a Savvy School Library Media Specialist to do?

The budget cycle of knowledge, planning, and implementation can be condensed to three simple steps for budgeting:

### 1. Ask

Ask for the money needed to run the school library media program. Ask the person or persons who have the authority to grant the request. Base the request on defensible facts, current research, and instructional goals aligned with current initiatives of the school and district. Develop a written budget that is professional in tone, contains little emotion or hyperbole, and is concise and direct. Submit the budget to the proper channels. Repeat the process every year.

### 2. Gather Support

Tell others in the learning community who will benefit from the results of your budget work. This includes parents, teachers, support staff, students, and administrators. Confide in parents that you will be increasing the amount of fiction reading available for students. Tell the science faculty that you are including $15 per pupil to revamp the science collection. Discuss the need for maps and globes with the social studies department chair. Disclaim ownership of the library media center program, resources, and facility. Share authority with the Media Advisory Committee for budget development. Make sure that literally and figuratively, as many people as possible know the answer to the question "What's in it for me?"

### 3. Celebrate the YES inside the No.

Change takes time. Most change experts say that 3-5 years of hard work and effort are required before real change can occur. This can be discouraging. Analyze budget refusals. Is a negative answer the result of a lack of understanding about the library media program and its role in student achievement? Does the administrator understand the basic functions, but is unaware of how the library media center can achieve the priorities of the school and district? A "no" is not always a "no." Sometimes it is a promise for next year, or can set the stage for alternative fund-

ing such as PTA, special school district grants, or funding originally intended for other purposes.

## Budgeting = Advocacy

No doubt about it, budgeting and advocacy go hand in hand. One evaluative measure for the advocacy program could be the degree to which the library media program is supported by funding necessary for its continued survival and growth. Every advocacy activity that increases the perceived value of the library media program increases the chances that the library program will receive more funding. Showing up at PTA meetings is a budgeting strategy, as well as sponsorship of student clubs, writing a newsletter, presenting a staff development workshop, and other advocacy activities. The more that the library media program is perceived to have a role in academic achievement, the greater the chances that the library media program will be funded.

As John Dewey noted in 1915, "What the best and wisest parent wants for his own child; that should the community want for all of its children" (Dewey, 1915). Funding the school library media program is the best way for the community to be the best and wisest parent. The school library media specialist is the open door to make that happen.

### Works Cited

American Association of School Librarians / Association for Educational Communications and Technology. *Information Power.* Chicago: ALA, 2003.

Dewey, John. *The School and Society.* Chicago: Univ. of Chicago Press, 1915.

Dickinson, Gail K. *Empty Pockets, Full Plates.* Worthington, OH: Linworth, 2003.

*Gail Dickinson is an Assistant Professor at University of North Carolina at Greensboro. She is also the author of* Empty Pockets and Full Plates: Effective Budget Administration for Library Media Specialists *(Linworth Publishing, Inc., 2003).*

Dickinson, G. (2004). Budgeting: As easy as 1-2-3. *Library Media Connection, 22*(6), 14-17.

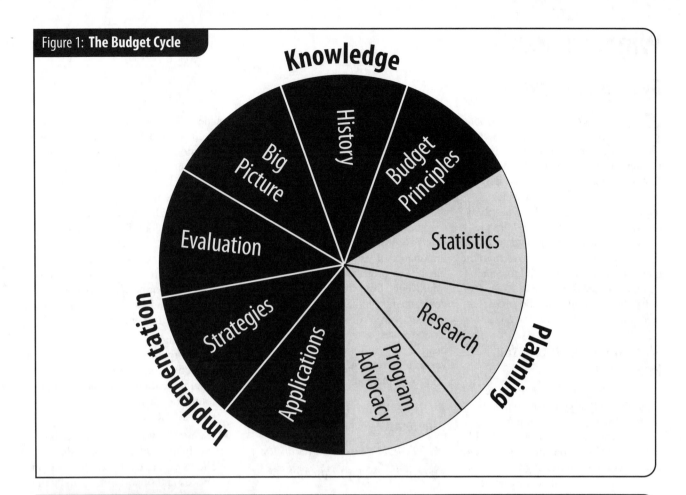

**Figure 1: The Budget Cycle**

Knowledge

Planning

Implementation

History

Budget Principles

Statistics

Research

Program Advocacy

Applications

Strategies

Evaluation

Big Picture

**Figure 2: Budget Worksheet**

| | Recommended to bring to standard | YEAR ONE | YEAR TWO | YEAR THREE |
|---|---|---|---|---|
| **Books** | | | | |
| **Audiovisuals** | | | | |
| **Facilities** | | | | |
| **Equipment** | | | | |
| **Staff** | | | | |
| **Electronic Resources** | | | | |
| **Other Types of Access** | | | | |
| **Other Materials** | | | | |

# Winning Grants

## By Parisa Tahouri

Can you count the number of grant alerts you have seen in a newsletter or on the Internet last month? After reading the details, how often did you fantasize about winning a grant but ended up feeling too overwhelmed to apply? Chances are you have heard about educators using grant dollars to supplement their schools' budget, but you are not sure how to join them in the quest. There is no big secret to winning a grant; the key is to have the courage to try! Start with finding the answers to *who, what, where, when,* and *how*.

## Who Will Benefit from Your Project?

Before starting, it's important to be clear about what you want to accomplish and who you want to help. The focus of your grant application should not be on the materials to be purchased; that's a common mistake grant writers make. For example, they present the purpose of the project as "to purchase X reading program for our students." That is not the purpose. In this case, the purpose would be "to increase reading test scores of failing students."

As a general rule, I believe that if you are part of an education agency, every project you attempt to get funded should be built around the children. If you lose sight of the fact that it has to benefit the children, you risk not making a compelling argument about the long-term benefits of your project. Be clear about the population you will be targeting and why. Remember to use accurate and up-to-date research to support your reasons. It will be hard for anyone evaluating grant applications to argue with valid data.

## What Makes Your Project Any Different from the Next?

We can all rattle off a laundry list of things we would buy for our programs if we had extra money. Avoid the habit of asking for things you want rather than the things you need. Sure, it would be great to have a computer for every student in your school, but can you do with 15 laptops on a cart that can be shared among classrooms?

Make certain that you are clear about the goals and objectives of your project and what you need to complete the project. A comprehensive project will have measurable goals aligned to the funder's requirements, as well as the organization's mission. You should always use statistics to demonstrate the importance of your project. For example, if your project is designed to improve the test scores of dyslexic students, then try to include data about: (a) number of dyslexic children in the United States, your state, as well as your district; (b) cost for early intervention versus long-term support services; and (c) proven methods for addressing the

> The focus of your grant application should not be on the materials to be purchased. If you lose sight of the fact that the project has to benefit the children, you risk not making a compelling argument about the long-term benefits of your project.

educational needs of dyslexic children.

You should also ensure the evaluators have a sense of your project's uniqueness. Remember that your project will be competing with others; it is crucial that you demonstrate not only the importance of the project, but also its long-term value and sustainability. If your project can be replicated at other schools, making that fact clear will help you gain a competitive edge. Keep in mind that no one wants to invest in something that is short-term or isolated when there are so many long-term projects that can benefit students for years to come.

## Where Should You Look for Funding?

The answer to this question is simple—the Internet! The Internet has made research as easy as click, click, and click. Your State Department of Education has a special section for grant announcements and applications, as well as training updates. Be sure to visit the site on a regular basis.

You might be asking yourself, "Where do I look for foundation grants?" The Internet remains a favorite starting point. There are several wonderful Web sites where you can sign up for newsletters that will alert you of upcoming deadlines. Here are a few of my preferred links:

- The Foundation Center—a non-profit organization focused on collecting, organizing, and communicating information on all foundation and corporation grants <www.fdncenter.org>.
- eSchool News Online—a grants-and-funding clearinghouse that allows you to explore ongoing grant awards and opportunities, and gain expert insight on grant-seeking <www.eschoolnews.com>.
- Fundsnet Services Online—a well-organized Web site that provides grant-seekers with information on financial resources available on the Internet <www.fundsnetservices.com>.

## When Is the Best Time to Start?

If you ask any professional grant writer about the best time to start your hunt for funds, the answer will most likely be last year! Believe it or not, you have to travel down a long, dark, winding road to get to the pot of gold; the last thing you want to do is wait until all the planets are aligned to submit a proposal.

To be successful, it will take time, motivation, persistence, and conviction. This is a competitive field, so staying focused at all times is a requirement. A successful organization will have a funding strategy in place with clear goals, objectives, and realistic expectations. You must devote a lot of time to research and planning. Many people become so focused on finding the next grant opportunity, they forget to research and plan. This results in higher rejection rates, which causes frustration, a sense of failure, and burnout. If you find yourself in an organization that relies on grants, you'll need to consider grant research and writing an ongoing task. Keep in mind that most grant applications will take anywhere from three months to a year to be reviewed and awarded.

## How Do You Prepare a Proposal?

Most grants have the same basic components. Although the components may vary from one opportunity to the next, you can expect to see the following on a regular basis. By familiarizing yourself with these, you'll avoid being intimidated by the application. The key components include:

- Executive Summary—an overview that summarizes all major components. Although this is the first section of a grant application, wait until the end to write it and remember not to introduce new information in this section.

- Organizational Overview—a succinct description of your school's mission, programs, students, and staff to show your ability to successfully implement the proposed project.

- Statement of Need—a clear and persuasive statement that is supported by facts, evidence, and statistics to communicate the need for the project.

- Project Description—a comprehensive roadmap of your implementation plan, including goals, objectives, activities, staffing, and evaluation.

- Budget—a breakdown of how the grant dollars will be used.

Keep in mind that a grant proposal is a persuasive document that sells your project to the funding agency. In order to be effective, make sure your writing is brief and simple. Although it's tempting, avoid educational jargon and complex vocabulary at the risk of intimidating your evaluator.

Remember the writing rules we learned in college? Let's review:

- Use strong, short, clear sentences.

- Present information in a logical order.

> *Grant writing is an ongoing, never-ending process, so make a list of "fundable ideas" with clear goals and objectives. Then start thinking about how you would implement them if you had the funds.*

- Simple words are your friends; avoid the urge to recite the dictionary.

- Opt for active language as opposed to passive.

- Don't use abbreviations. Usually they make sense to you, not to your evaluators.

- Don't plagiarize. If you are using research, then cite the source.

- Typographical errors happen! Make sure you proofread more than once.

- And most importantly, make sure your proposal is interesting to read. Add a little personality—it goes a long way.

## A Final Word for Grant Writers

Ever-increasing budget cuts have forced public school administrators to explore alternative sources to implement No Child Left Behind requirements and their existing programs. Today, grant writing is no longer optional; it is a requirement. A successful grant writer becomes a precious asset to any organization.

If you ask most grant writers how they got started, you would most likely hear that they were dragged into the world of grants without their consent and eventually got labeled the "grant writer" as soon as they won a couple of grants! If you decided to read the rest of this article after finishing the first paragraph, then chances are that either you are personally interested in grant writing or you have been selected as the lucky person to take it on at your organization. My biggest piece of advice for the beginner is to be proactive in your research and writing efforts. Don't wait for an announcement or application to force you to react. You can improve your grant writing, as well as your success rate, by ensuring you stay a couple of steps ahead of the game. I believe that grant writing is an ongoing, never-ending process, so make a list of "fundable ideas" with clear goals and objectives. Then start thinking about how you would implement them if you had the funds. Remember, every new project starts with an idea—so dream it, define it, and design a project around it!

*Parisa Tahouri is a national grants manager from Walnut Creek, California.*

Tahouri, P. (2005). Winning grants. *Library Media Connection, 24*(2), 46-47.

---

### Ouch! Your Proposal Was Rejected . . . Now What?

- Take the time to mourn—it's healthy!

- Channel those feelings in the right direction; refine, refine, refine!

- Pull out a pen and write a nice letter thanking the funder for taking the time to review your proposal. The key is to make a positive impression because relationships are important in the grant process.

- Ask for the evaluator's comments. Read them without getting defensive; the comments are the key to your future success, so put your feelings aside.

# Crying Over Spilled Milk

## By Gail Dickinson

Weeding is defined as the ongoing process of removing resources from the collection. What is also ongoing, unfortunately, is the recurring outcry from the public over weeded resources. Visions of headlines such as "Librarian Trashes Precious Books" and scores of parent protestors guarding school dumpsters can turn even the most determined library media specialist into an equally determined weeding procrastinator.

That strategy turns into a self-fulfilling prophecy, as the unpurged materials get older, mustier, and more in need of weeding. Unable to put the task off any longer, the library media specialist attacks the task in the heat of summer and in the early morning dumpster dusk. Of course, such activity rarely goes unnoticed, and the heat of summer becomes a self-fulfilling prophecy of the heat of unwanted and distracting phone calls, headlines, and outrage from overburdened taxpayers.

Gathering support from the library media center advisory committee, prominent PTA and other parents, and administrators is a good idea, and should be done on an ongoing basis. It is certainly easier, though, to discuss with committees and administrators the few books that are being weeded rather than the many thousand. This article contains a few strategies to streamline that process, as well as to give the timid weeder a few good reasons to begin.

## Weeding Basics

Weeding is a professional responsibility. It is what librarians in all types of libraries do. Abdicating this responsibility degrades the appearance of the collection and creates the opportunity to spread dangerous or misleading information. Much of the health and nutrition information from the 1960s and 1970s has been found to be completely false. Scientific facts have changed our perception of the world. Formats have disappeared from use. The library media center collection should not be an interactive museum of equipment, media, and information from past generations.

The act of weeding in itself creates opportunities to learn the collection. Because online catalogs abound, it is comforting to use more of the senses in working with resources. Great finds that could be miscataloged, need better subjects, or different classification numbers as the curriculum has changed through the years wait on every shelf. OPAC searches sometimes reflect cataloging skill rather than content.

## How to Weed

Weeding is selection in reverse—literally de-selection. Many mnemonic devices exist as guidelines, and the bibliography of this article gives some further reading for weeding how-to's and why-to's. The most common tools are the M*U*S*T*Y and C*R*E*W principles, as shown in Figures 1 and 2.

The CREW principles use the MUSTY guides with the added categories of the copyright date and the last checkout date. If the book fits the MUSTY standard, is of a certain age determined by subject category, and has not been checked out in several years, then that book will probably be weeded. Ramona Kerby takes the CREW standards and gives them a school media center slant in her 2002 article.

Weeding fiction is always more difficult. The guidelines shown in Figure 3 come from Merle Jacob's article subtitled "Should I Dump *Peyton Place*." The answer to each question is probably, "yes."

## Weeding Logistics

Because weeding is frequently far down on the to-do lists of student-centered library media specialists, there can be a buildup in important areas of the collection. This creates, as mentioned earlier, the chance that weeding could be a political process rather than a backroom program administrative task. One strategy is to turn weeding into an instructional event, with students evaluating the material as part of an information skills lesson (Davis, 2001) if that is seen to possibly relieve the political pressure rather than exac-

**Figure 1**

| | |
|---|---|
| **M** | Misleading information |
| **U** | Ugly |
| **S** | Superseded by better works |
| **T** | Trivial—may have been more valuable to the collection years ago |
| **Y** | Your collection has no use (irrelevant to curriculum, student or teacher needs |

**Figure 2**

| | |
|---|---|
| **C** | Continuous |
| **R** | Review |
| **E** | Evaluation (and) |
| **W** | Weeding |

*Source: Segal (1980).*

erbate it. However, it may be easiest simply to make weeding a continuous part of the administrative routine of the library.

Weeding is best done:

- *Continuously throughout the year.* This makes the weeding process a weekly task, not a summer project that may or may not get accomplished. Weeding continuously also takes less time. You can spare 15 minutes each week to weed. You may not have a free day or a free week.

- *In small numbers at a time.* Some of us became library media specialists because we love books. It's hard to see them go in the dumpster. Our patrons, whether parents, classroom teachers, or students, also think we love books. To think of us throwing books away is the worst kind of cannibalism. We are eating our young, in some minds, and it opens the door for other unflattering comparisons. Weeding

## Figure 3: Weeding Fiction

| WEEDING FICTION | |
|---|---|
| **Duplicates** | Was it once a class set used by teachers long retired? Once a bestseller? Do you need the extra copies? |
| **Poor Condition** | At one time, books were rebound in monocolor, with austere lettering. These books may not appeal to today's readers. Neither will books that are falling apart or look in poor condition. |
| **Obscure** | Some authors seemed up and coming at the time, but were one-hit wonders who are long gone. Some books may have once been wildly popular, but today's youth may not be able to identify with the characters, plot or setting. |
| **Genre fiction** | May have affected collection development at one time, but the collection should reflect current reading interests, not past. |
| **Short Stories** | Short story collections do not see heavy use usually, so they should be kept small and current. |

in small portions also lessens the likelihood that we will be targeted as wasting taxpayer money and destroying the hopes and dreams of a future generation.

- *In targeted small sections of the collection.* It's always nice to see progress. Instead of weeding randomly, keep your enthusiasm strong by noting how good the sports section looks after it has been weeded. Keep track of your progress.

- *Quietly and without comment.* Weeding Party! Come Help Weed! It's Time to Weed! Although this certainly spreads the responsibility of weeding over a large number of people, it also equates weeding with spring cleaning, harvesting, and other one-time events. Weeding is a continuous event, and a normal professional responsibility. Every so often, put your selection policy and weeding procedures on the agenda for the library media center advisory committee. Most likely, you will get through the discussion quickly before the yawns begin. Weeding is just what you do.

- *With support of the principal and library media center advisory*

> *Weeding, when viewed as a normal part of a library media center routine, does not involve shirtsleeves, hot summer days, or brown paper bags surreptitiously stored in the trunk of the library media specialist's car.*

*committee.* As noted, you need to review the procedures with the principal and library media center advisory committee. Before-and-after pictures help, as do student comments regarding "new" books that were just recent finds rather than recent purchases. Remember that you are not asking for forgiveness or permission, but rather informing the principal and advisory committee of a routine procedure that is part of developing and maintaining an adequate collection.

## Three-Step Weeding Process

When does anyone have time to weed every week? Everyone has 15 minutes

at some point during the week. Try this one-shelf-per-week procedure. (Total Time Required: 15 minutes)

- **Step 1.** Stand in front of the shelf, slightly pulling out the books that at first glance look like they might need to be weeded. (Time: 1 minute)

- **Step 2.** Look at each book you have selected, and apply the selection principles of accuracy and authoritativeness. Make the decision of whether or not to actually weed the books. (Time: 4 minutes)

- **Step 3.** Take the books that you have selected to the workstation, and delete them from the catalog database. Mark the books as weeded, remove markings, and complete any other tasks to take them completely out of the collection. Toss the books in the trash can. (Time: 10 minutes)

While it is true that this procedure will not weed every single book that needs to be weeded, it will find the most glaring examples of weeding readiness. Over time, you can get through the entire collection, and then repeat the process. It's quick, it's efficient, and it works!

## Trash or Trade?

Although it is general consensus that books and other resources that do not qualify to remain in one library media center collection do not qualify enough to be in anyone else's collection either, there are still those who seek to place weeded books anywhere but in the trash. The following analogy might help.

### The Milk in the Refrigerator

The milk in the refrigerator is past the sell date, has an odor, and is curdled and lumpy. Would you?

Keep it, because you don't know when you could get to the store to buy more?

Then why would you keep a book on the shelf with misinformation because you don't know when you could replace it?

Keep it, because otherwise your refrigerator would look empty?

Then why would you keep outdated books on the shelf to preserve a

## The Milk in the Refrigerator

| | |
|---|---|
| ■ *Milk is outdated, curdled, and lumpy* <br> ■ *Would you?* <br>    ■ Keep it because you don't know when you can get to the store? <br>    ■ Give it to a neighbor to keep in his or her house? <br>    ■ Keep it because otherwise the refrigerator would be empty? | ■ *Book is outdated, with misinformation* <br> ■ *So why would you?* <br>    ■ Keep it because you don't know when you can replace it? <br>    ■ Give it to a teacher for classroom use? <br>    ■ Keep it because if you weeded everything that should be weeded, the shelves would be completely empty? |

false collection size?

Give it to a neighbor to keep in his or her refrigerator?

Then why would you send outdated encyclopedias or other materials to a teacher for classroom use?

Donate it to a food pantry for hungry children?

Then why would you send outdated resources to be used by children in this or other countries?

The facts are simple: either the resources remain in the collection or they don't. When in doubt, keep it for another year. After all, the milk may not be all that spoiled; it may be still usable and have value.

The arguments commonly used to discourage weeding simply will not wash. Keeping resources to meet a books-per-pupil quota will not pass inspection. Just as spoiled milk can no longer be considered milk, spoiled information can no longer be counted as books. Try this argument with a principal or supervisor, "We will be cited either way. We can either be praised for having a well-developed

and well-maintained collection of resources but cited for it being too small, or we can be cited for having an old, outdated collection that does not meet the learning needs of students. Your choice." As to whether or not anyone would notice, just compare a weeded shelf with a non-weeded one.

> *Keeping resources to meet a books-per-pupil quota will not pass inspection.*

Trust me, they'll know.

Sometimes a library media specialist will claim that a principal has ordered that weeding not be done, or wants to review every book weeded—comply with this request. Explain the reasons that the books should not be on the shelf, constantly point out the increased usage that weeded shelves get, and ask to simply store the books somewhere other than the library shelves. Eventually, the books may even disappear.

## Git-R-Done

Although there are few occasions when a quote from Larry the Cable Guy will appear in a practice-based library media center journal, in this case, it may be appropriate. It is the professional responsibility of a library media specialist to weed. Weeding, when viewed as a normal part of a library media center routine, does not involve shirt sleeves, hot summer days, or brown paper bags surreptitiously stored in the trunk of the library media specialist's car. Plan to start your 15-Minutes-to-a-Better-Collection exercise routine today.

### Works Cited

Davis, Vivian R. "Weeding the Library Media Center Collection." *School Library Media Activities Monthly.* (Mar 2001): 26–28.

Jacob, Merle. "Weeding the Fiction Collection; or Should I Dump *Peyton Place.*" *Reference & User Services Quarterly.* 40(3) (Spring 2001): 234–239.

Kerby, Ramona. "Weeding your Collection." *School Library Media Activities Monthly.* (Feb 2002): 23–31.

Segal, Joseph P. *Evaluating and Weeding Collections in Small and Medium-sized Public Libraries.* Chicago: ALA. 1980.

*Dr. Gail Dickinson is a professor in the School Library Media Program, Department of Educational Curriculum and Instruction, Darden College of Education at Old Dominion University, Virginia. She can be reached at gdickins@ odu.edu . Gail is also the author of* Empty Pockets and Full Plates: Effective Budget Administration for Library Media Specialists *(Linworth Publishing, Inc., 2003).*

Dickinson, G. (2005). Crying over spilled milk. *Library Media Connection, 23*(7), 24-26.

# Professional Growth and Staff Development

## Introduction

Staff development is a phrase that strikes fear in the hearts and minds of many experienced educators. Workshops that are unconnected to the real world of today's schools, lectures by talking heads, busywork activities that keep everybody in the building long past time to go home in the afternoon are all symptoms of staff development that doesn't work. School library media specialists, who walk the talk and talk the talk of lifelong learning, have a real opportunity to facilitate useful and relevant staff development.  In "*Conducting Effective Staff Development Workshops*" Kay Bishop and Sue Janczak provide possible answers to the critical questions we need to ask as we plan workshops that teachers will actually want to attend. Two useful one-page "*Tools of the Trade*" follow. The first checklist, by Kay Bishop and Sue Janczak, provides an outline to follow in planning and conducting a staff development workshop, while the second is a workshop evaluation form by Julieta Dias Fisher and Ann Hill.

Staff development can actually be seen as an umbrella label for outreach activities directed at many of the communities we serve. "*Family Literacy Programs in School Libraries: Helping Parents Become Their Child's Best Teacher,*" by Jennifer Griffis, shows how media specialists can apply the same principles to promote family literacy while Janet Hopkins provides some specific tips for developing partnerships with special educators.

Professional growth is the flip side of staff development. Modeling lifelong learning and reflecting on changes in our school environments ensure that we will remain relevant in our schools. Not familiar with the smaller learning community concept? Liz Metzger provides the background information you need. Smaller learning communities (SLC) focus on building connections and school library media specialists need to develop strategies to strengthen their role as a teacher and instructional partner in the SLC model.

The final articles in this section focus on how you can document your commitment to lifelong learning and professional growth and explore one way you might be rewarded for this commitment. While school library media specialists are familiar with being evaluated by someone else, they may not be familiar with self-reflection and evaluation. A good way to start that process is by keeping a professional journal. In "*Journaling: Telling Your Professional "Story*," Donna Miller suggests easy first steps like finding a suitable place and time to write. Once you've started to use reflective journaling, you might formalize your product into an electronic portfolio. Marilyn Heath outlines the advantages and disadvantages of electronic portfolios in "*Are You Ready to Go Digital? The Pros and Cons of Electronic Portfolio Development.*" Media specialists have an opportunity to lead by example by developing their own electronic portfolios to document and demonstrate professional growth. By sharing these portfolios with their colleagues, media specialists can not only showcase their technology skills, they can also help educate others about the roles and responsibilities of a 21st century media specialist. For many media specialists the final step in documenting their own professional growth and best media program practices takes the form of seeking the status of a National Board Certified Teacher (NBCT). This rigorous process is described in articles by Sara Kelly Johns and Peggy Milam. Both outline the benefits of the process and offer suggestions to be successful. Whether or not you choose to become a NBCT, we all need to think about the future of our profession. Will there be a well-trained, dedicated media specialist ready to fill your shoes when you retire? In "*Mentoring the Next Generation of Library Media Specialists*", Christine Meloni highlights our role in attracting the best-of-the-best to our profession. Serving as a mentor for a media-specialist-in-training may be the best gift you can give yourself and your profession.

# Conducting Effective Staff Development Workshops

## By Kay Bishop and Sue Janczak

If you are like most library media specialists, your days are filled with countless activities to help provide quality library media center programs and collections for the students and teachers in your school. You know that some of your teachers are struggling with the use of new technologies, and you also realize that both students and teachers are in need of assistance with information literacy skills. So what can you do to help remedy such a situation? One possible solution is to conduct staff development workshops to help teachers learn how to integrate information literacy skills and technology into their curricula.

### Who Needs Staff Development?

We all do—teachers, administrators, staff, and library media specialists. Before we, as media specialists, are able to conduct effective staff development activities, we must first become comfortable with computers, Internet, and other technologies. We need to learn how to most effectively teach information literacy skills. A majority of teachers today have had little training in the use of new technologies. The need for educators to integrate technology and information skills into the curriculum is being increasingly emphasized.

### How Do You Select a Workshop Topic?

The best way to select a topic for your workshop is to discover the needs, as perceived by your teachers. Do this by sending out a survey with some possible workshop topics listed and include an item where teachers can write in their own suggested topics. You can informally ask for workshop topics at a faculty meeting or in your one-on-one encounters with teachers. It is also important to be observant of needs. Watching teachers with their students in the library media center can provide you with many hints related to needs. Perhaps a teacher never touches a computer, seems uncomfortable in searching for materials on the OPAC, or

allows students to include plagiarized materials in their assignments. All of these situations indicate needs that should be addressed. Another way to decide upon a workshop topic is to ask school administrators. For instance, a principal may be aware that his or her teachers require information relating to copyright even if the teachers do not perceive this need.

### Who Should Conduct the Staff Development?

The answer to this question might be you, the library media specialist, if it is an area in which you feel confident. However, it is impossible for a library media specialist to be an expert in all areas of technology and information literacy. Perhaps you know a classroom teacher or administrator in your school with particular competence or knowledge of a topic. Take advantage of these people when planning staff development.

If you are introducing a new software product or piece of equipment, the company from whom you purchased the item may be willing to provide personnel to conduct a workshop. This is particularly true of companies who market OPACs or computer management systems. Sometimes companies provide this assistance free while in other instances they have a fee that you might be able to negotiate. If you live near a college or university, try contacting the education or library science departments to see if they can provide names of consultants. Sometimes a department has a Web site that includes the faculty members' research interests and recent publications. Some colleges maintain databases of speakers with areas of expertise. Remember to ask such consultants for information relating to their charges for staff development activities. If someone is willing to come into your school as a service to the community, you should provide a small honorarium or gift. Also, be as specific as possible regarding your expectations and workshop objectives.

Don't forget to ask for assistance in conducting your workshops.

Classroom teachers, parents, students, and members of the community can all provide valuable help. Always consider having extra persons available if your staff development includes hands-on activities; their assistance frequently makes the difference between mediocre and successful experiences for the participants.

After you have conducted a workshop on a topic, consider sharing it with other schools, and ask other library media specialists if they will share their staff development workshops with your teachers. By dividing up topics of specialization, it becomes possible for each library media specialist to fully develop one or two workshops and consequently save hours of preparation time.

### What Is the Best Format?

The topic itself usually provides an indication of the appropriate format for the workshop. "One-shot" presentations can be used for topics such as learning how to operate a piece of equipment or how to evaluate a Web site. After-school workshops are appropriate for topics that will require 90 minutes or less. You will need half-day or all-day workshops for more complex topics such as learning how to use all the various aspects of PowerPoint or creating a Web page. In some instances, you may want to provide opportunities for participants to apply their knowledge between sessions, so a series of workshops on the same topic will be the best format.

### How Do You Plan?

Consider the following problems that you might encounter: time and scheduling constraints, perceived lack of need for the staff development, possible resistance to change or the introduction of anything new, and possible techno-anxiety that teachers may experience. Before you begin planning, it is important to learn all you can about your audience, including their knowledge and level of expertise on the workshop topic. If you are conducting staff development for teachers

Knowing how much time it takes to prepare staff development workshops, the authors have written the book, Staff Development Guide to Workshops for Technology and Information Literacy: Ready To Present (Linworth, 2004). An accompanying CD-ROM includes all the materials you will need (announcements, agendas, PowerPoint presentations with in-depth speaker notes, resource handouts, and evaluations) to conduct effective workshops on the following topics: copyright, plagiarism, use of digital cameras, designing classroom Web pages, inquiry-based Web projects, virtual field trips, and creating electronic portfolios. The materials on the CD-ROM can be adapted to fit your school's needs.

other than those at your own school, ask what grades the teachers teach, what their usual methods of instruction are, how much experience they have had with technology, and whether they have any particular school-wide projects. After you have sufficient knowledge of your participants, you can begin planning your workshop objectives, keeping in mind the length of time available for the workshop and the number of expected participants. When deciding on activities, include a good balance between lecture, demonstration, and hands-on activities.

All materials needed for the workshop should be ready well in advance of the presentation. Equipment needs to be checked; back-up equipment and items such as extra bulbs should be available. Prepare an agenda and gather and organize all the materials (pens, handouts, computer disks) that will be needed. If you are providing refreshments, order or prepare them ahead of time. Confirmation of orders on the day of the workshop is a good idea if someone else is preparing the refreshments.

Be sure the temperature of the room is comfortable, taking into consideration the number of participants and the workshop activities. A cool, empty room can quickly become too warm

when a large number of participants begin using computers. Provide as comfortable seating as possible. If any of your participants are arriving from other schools, have plenty of large signs to direct them to the workshop.

Provide ample time for set-up on the day of the workshop so you will not be overly stressed. If you are pressed for set-up time, use students or parents to assist. Being in a state of emotional relaxation and mental preparedness is important to your success in conducting the workshop.

## How Do You Get Teachers to Attend?

Most teachers are very busy and have numerous activities to fit into their days. Even though you prepare a fantastic workshop, it does not necessarily mean that your teachers will attend. Gaining the support of your administrators, who can either make the workshop mandatory, provide words of strong encouragement to attend, or let it be known that they plan to attend, is very helpful for attendance purposes. You also want to let the teachers know how their participation in the staff development will help them. Make creative flyers or invitations that not only announce the logistics of the workshop, but also include catchy questions or phrases relating to how teachers will benefit from the workshop. It is usually best to request RSVPs so you will have sufficient materials and equipment. Also, send additional reminders, perhaps by e-mail, as the scheduled workshop approaches.

## How Should the Workshop Be Conducted?

### Always provide copies of a written agenda. This will help keep you and your participants on task. Try to provide a time for socialization and refreshments before beginning the workshop—but stick to the amount of time allotted on your agenda. Let your participants know ahead of time that you will be supplying refreshments and a short time for socialization. Having refreshing drinks and a choice of both sweet and nonsweet snacks available when participants arrive is always appreciated.

### Begin and end your workshop on time.
This will involve some practice and preparation on your part before you actually conduct the workshop. You may have to remind your participants to stay on task during hands-on activities or group discussions. As anyone who has conducted staff development will tell you, it is often easier to manage students than a roomful of teachers!

### Utilize demonstrations. If you are demonstrating a piece of equipment, make certain everyone is able to view the demonstration. Have a large screen available when you are demonstrating computer applications.

### Include hands-on activities. Teachers generally love make-and-take-it projects, so whenever the workshop topic is conducive, consider having an activity in which the participants leave with an item they have produced.

### Be patient with your participants.
Provide generous praise and encouragement for the teachers' efforts and ideas. Showing a good sense of humor always goes a long way toward putting people at ease.

### Teachers love prizes and rewards. If you are able to get donations from merchants, offer door prizes. They do not have to be costly items—a popular book, an item with the school logo, or a small gift certificate can raise spirits, especially if the workshop is conducted after a long workday. A "fun" certificate for having learned a particular skill or for successfully completing the workshop is another possibility.

### Include some type of evaluation. Short surveys with well-constructed items can provide valuable information about whether the workshop objectives were achieved and whether the presentation could be improved. Evaluations should not be over a page long and not require more than five minutes to complete. You will receive more honest responses if you allow the surveys to be anonymous and provide a box or basket where the surveys can be placed, rather than having them handed to you.

### Offer follow-up activities. Encourage your teachers to continue working with the technology or information literacy skills you presented. Offer to

meet with them individually for further assistance. Consider sending out e-mail messages a week or so after the workshop to ask the teachers if they are using the newly acquired skills or knowledge in their classrooms. Ask teachers who successfully integrate the technology or information skills into their classrooms to share their experiences informally at faculty or departmental meetings. If administrators were not present at the workshop, provide them with a short, written report and thank them for any support they provided. Finally, remember to send thank-you notes or small gifts of appreciation to all persons who assisted you with the workshop.

---

*Kay Bishop is an Associate Professor and Director of the School Library Media Program at the State University of New York at Buffalo.*

*Sue Janczak coordinates the School Library Media Program at the State University of New York at Buffalo and teaches courses in management of school libraries and the use of technology.*

*The authors have written the book* Staff Development Guide to Workshops for Technology and Information Literacy: Ready to Present *(Linworth Publishing, Inc., 2004). An accompanying CD-ROM includes all the materials you will need (announcements, agendas, PowerPoint presentations with in-depth speaker notes, resource handouts, and evaluations).*

Bishop, K., & Janczak, S. (2005). Conducting effective staff development workshops. *Library Media Connection, 23*(7), 50-51.

# Tools of the Trade:
# Conducting Effective Staff Development Workshops

*By Kay Bishop and Sue Janczak*

- [ ] **Learn Participants' Needs**
- [ ] **Select a Workshop Topic**
- [ ] **Determine Who Should Conduct a Staff Development Program**
- [ ] **Choose the Best Format**
- [ ] **Plan the Staff Development**
- [ ] **Know Your Audience**
- [ ] **Plan Objectives (consider available time and number of participants)**
- [ ] **Select Activities**
- [ ] **Prepare Materials and Equipment**
- [ ] **Attend to "Creature Comforts"**
- [ ] **Market the Workshop**
- [ ] **Conduct the Staff Development**
- [ ] **Provide an Agenda**
- [ ] **Begin and End on Time**
- [ ] **Utilize Demonstrations**
- [ ] **Include Hands-on Activities**
- [ ] **Be Patient; Show a Sense of Humor**
- [ ] **Offer Prizes and Rewards**
- [ ] **Include an Evaluation**
- [ ] **Offer Follow-up Activities**

*Kay Bishop is an associate professor and director of the school library media program at the State University of New York at Buffalo.*

*Sue Janczak coordinates the school library media program at the State University of New York at Buffalo and teaches courses in management of school libraries and the use of technology.*

*The authors have written the book* Staff Development Guide to Workshops for Technology and Information Literacy: Ready to Present *(Linworth Publishing, Inc., 2004). An accompanying CD-ROM includes all the materials you will need (announcements, agendas, PowerPoint presentations with in-depth speaker notes, resource handouts, and evaluations).*

*Editor's Note*: Each issue will feature reproducible items that are designed for you to share with your school community. It might be a tool to help manage the library media center or an executive summary of an important library-related issue for your administrator or colleagues. Each carries permission for you to reproduce the material within the building in which you work.

Bishop, K., & Janczak, S. (2005). Tools of the Trade: Conducting effective staff development workshops. *Library Media Connection, 23*(7), 52.

# Tools of the Trade: Workshop Evaluation Form

## *By Julieta Dias Fisher and Ann Hill*

On the whole, the workshop met its objective.

◯ excellent      ◯ good      ◯ fair      ◯ poor

The instructor was well prepared and organized.

◯ excellent      ◯ good      ◯ fair      ◯ poor

The instructor assisted students on an individual basis.

◯ excellent      ◯ good      ◯ fair      ◯ poor

The workshop was appropriate to my computer skill level.

◯ excellent      ◯ good      ◯ fair      ◯ poor

The balance between instruction and time for practice was appropriate.

◯ excellent      ◯ good      ◯ fair      ◯ poor

I would recommend this workshop to other teachers.

◯ yes      ◯ no

I will use what I learned from this workshop.

◯ yes      ◯ no

The instructor should spend more time on:

_____

The instructor should spend less time on:

_____

I learned:_____

_____

_____

Fisher, J. D., & Hill, A. (2005) Tools of the trade: Workshop evaluation form. *Library Media Connection*, 23(4), 35.

# Family Literacy Programs in School Libraries: Helping Parents Become Their Child's Best Teacher

## By Jennifer Griffis

Parents are commonly described as their child's first and most important teachers. Over the past two decades, our society has experienced many changes that have kept some parents from fully undertaking this role in their child's life. Increases in both the mobility rates of young families and the number of single-parent households have reduced the number of adults available to contribute to a child's early learning experiences at home. Parents who did not complete their formal education or are non-English speakers may not feel confident assisting their child with homework or discussing their child's progress with educators.

In response to these trends, family literacy programs began to emerge in the 1980s (Family Resource Coalition, 1997). Legislation at both the federal and state levels has had a strong influence on many of these programs. A report by the National Center for Family Literacy provides details on the legislative activities of 11 states with regard to state-funded family literacy programming. According to this report, several other states are currently in the process of creating similar legislation (Peyton, 1999). Family literacy programs are growing rapidly. Library media specialists should be aware of the research behind these programs when considering the implementation of a family literacy program in their school.

### The Basics of Family Literacy

Family literacy programs are distinguished from other literacy programs by their intergenerational focus. The goal of family literacy programs is to increase the literacy skills of the entire family, thus helping the family to achieve self-sufficiency and enabling parents to become active participants in their child's education. Federal legislation, including the Adult Education and Family Literacy Act and the Reading Excellence Act, defines "family literacy services" as any program that integrates the following four components:

- Adult literacy education,
- Parenting education,
- Age-appropriate child education, and
- Interactive parent and child time.

Adult literacy education includes, but is not limited to, GED and ESL classes, as well as other participant needs such as job training skills or learning to use community resources. Parenting education seeks to network parents together and give them the skills they need to become active participants in their child's education. Specific instruction on child development and early literacy skills is also included. Age-appropriate child education includes programs such as Head Start and Even Start. The final component, interactive parent and child time, is the key to a successful family

> It is important to understand family literacy programs as a whole before looking at specific ways the library media center can and should be involved.

literacy program. During this time, parents have the opportunity to work with their children, practicing the skills they have learned during parenting classes. This interactive component is always a literacy-related activity, such as reading a story together (Schwartz, 1999; Peyton, 1999).

Together, these four components form a complete family literacy program. It is important to realize that not every family literacy program will include all four components. Programs should be tailored to meet the needs of the families they serve. If a program seeks to improve literacy skills through the context of the family, many believe it should be considered a family literacy program (Mulhern, Rodriguez-Brown & Shanahan, 1994). However, if a pro-

gram does not meet the federal or state definition of a family literacy program, it may not be eligible for federal or state funds, so the components included in the program should be carefully considered (Peyton, 1999).

### The role of the librarian

The library media specialist (LMS) should be considered an important member of the planning and facilitating team for family literacy programs. Collaboration is an important aspect of creating a successful program. The LMS may be responsible or partly responsible for only one component of the program. However, it is important to understand family literacy programs as a whole before looking at specific ways the library media center can and should be involved. This article will explore the characteristics of successful family literacy programs and barriers to be overcome when establishing these programs. It will conclude with specific program ideas for school libraries and a list of resources for more information.

### Characteristics of a Successful Program

Based on research and evaluations of family literacy programs, the most important characteristic of any successful family literacy program is respect and appreciation for the diversity of knowledge and backgrounds that the families will bring to the program (Mulhern et al., 1994; Brown, 1998; Family Resource Council, 1997; Schwartz, 1999). Families should be viewed from a resource model, acknowledging the variety of resources they can provide for the program, rather than from a deficit model that sees families as lacking the resources needed to be self-sufficient (Mulhern et al., 1994).

Successful family literacy programs also:

- Consider the needs of the participants. Invite participants' suggestions about content and topics they would like covered during the sessions.

- Demonstrate that home languages are valued. Provide translated materials if necessary.

- Build upon literacy behaviors already present in the home by encouraging shared literacy experiences. Provide ideas and materials for home extension activities.

- Encourage parents to participate in school activities before, during and after school hours.

- Hold meetings at a convenient location. Provide refreshments and child care for young children.

- Provide complete and varied literacy instruction for children and parents, including reading, writing and computer skills and activities.

- Include an interaction time between parents and children focusing on a wide range of literacy skills and activities.

- Provide access to information and resources (print and electronic) that will help families become self-sufficient. Take field trips to further explore community and educational resources.

- Collaborate with a variety of community partners to provide comprehensive resources and instruction.

Seeking to implement the characteristics listed above into a family literacy program is the first step to creating a successful program (Morrow, 1997, p.77; Schwartz, 1999). One program that embodies many of these characteristics is Project FLAME in Chicago. This comprehensive program was started in 1989 and has experienced dramatic success. Evaluations have shown that children whose families participated in the program consistently scored 30 points higher on standardized tests than their peers. In addition, they required fewer specialized services at school. However, the children were not the only ones benefiting from this program. Research has shown that after participation in the program, many of the parents made changes to improve their lives. Several acquired new jobs or began attending college. Others worked to improve the commu-

nity by participating on local school committees or writing letters to ask for better health care in their neighborhoods (Mulhern et al., 1994). Although this type of success is certainly possible for well-developed family literacy programs, there are still some barriers that may need to be overcome.

## Overcoming Barriers

Barriers of various types may present themselves during the early planning and implementing of a family literacy program, depending on the characteristics of the specific program. Almost all family literacy programs will encounter the following four challenges:

- Sources of funding,
- Attitudes of educators,
- Retention of participants, and
- Implementation in diverse communities.

*The most important characteristic of any successful family literacy program is respect and appreciation for the diversity of knowledge and backgrounds that the families will bring to the program.*

## Funding sources

As mentioned previously, federal and state legislation has created numerous sources for funding family literacy programs. This legislation has shown a strong belief in the effectiveness of these programs in meeting the literacy needs of the entire family. It is important to remember that family literacy programs may be required to have certain components to be eligible for this funding. Typically, the programs are given flexibility in the way they implement the components so that the needs of their participants can be met (Peyton, 1999).

Schools that receive Title I funds may also be allowed to use these funds for family literacy programs. Changes in the regulations regarding use of Title 1 funds now allow the

money to be used to meet the needs of all children in the school, not just those under the age of eight. Site-based decisions about the use of the funds and encouragement for parental involvement are other changes that support the use of these funds for family literacy programs (New Title 1 and family literacy funding, 2001).

Beyond the federal and state funding that is available, there are private organizations offering grants to develop and expand family literacy programs. One of the largest organizations is the Barbara Bush Foundation for Family Literacy, which awards approximately $500,000 a year to family literacy programs. In April 2001, 11 grants were awarded ranging from $17,300 to $50,000. Over 275 programs in 44 states have received grants totaling almost $9 million since the foundation was established in 1989 (The Barbara Bush Foundation for Family Literacy, 2001).

Local organizations are also sources of funds for family literacy programs. Smaller grants may be available from these organizations, or collaboration opportunities may arise that can increase not only financial resources but also information and staff resources. Research and legislation support the success of family literacy programs for all members of the family. Businesses and others seeking to develop a more productive community might be willing to support a family literacy program if given the opportunity.

## The attitude is everything.

Another barrier that may need to be crossed is educator attitudes. In a 1997 survey, conducted to explore the feelings of educators concerning issues of parent involvement in education, some disturbing attitudes were discovered. As expected, 92 percent of teachers surveyed believed that parental involvement in reading instruction was important or very important. The other eight percent were neutral. The remaining questions on the survey explored ideas about how parents should be involved, the quality of literacy activities that occur in the home, the competence of parents to have input with regard to reading instruction, the motivation behind parental involvement and methods of school-home collaboration.

Teacher responses in each of these areas indicated a limited view of how parents can and should participate in their child's literacy development. For example, when asked if parents should have a say in reading instruction in the classroom, 52 percent of teachers said no "because parents were not qualified to give input" (Fawcett, Rasinski & Linek, 1997). Another 30 percent said parents should have input, but only if they are "educated enough." When asked about parental motivation, many of the teachers felt that parents have little or no desire to help their children in school (Fawcett et al., 1997).

These responses do not reflect the trends in research regarding family literacy. While socioeconomic status may relate to parental involvement, it does not affect a parent's value of education. Many Latino and Asian parents see the teacher as the expert and do not want to interfere in school issues (Mulhern et al., 1994). Other parents may feel unable to participate due to language barriers (Brown, 1998). Before any family literacy program can succeed, it is important to educate teachers about current family literacy research and help broaden their perspectives about the variety of literacy opportunities families can and do provide for their children

## Keeping participation high

Another barrier to successful family literacy programs is retention of participants. Research has shown that attendance rates are typically higher in family literacy programs than adult education programs, sometimes by as much as 24 percent. One of the reasons for this may be the focus on creating a program that meets the needs of the participants. A program centered on their needs will encourage families to continue their participation. It is important to keep attendance records and talk to families who leave the program to be sure their reason for leaving was not related to the program or its content (Mulhern et al., 1994).

## Diversity may be a stumbling block

A final hurdle involves implementing a program in a diverse community. This becomes especially difficult in linguistically diverse communities. The focus in these situations should again be the needs of the participants. Smaller groups may need to be established, especially for the adult education component, to meet the language and education needs of the learners. For other components, participants should be brought together so they can share commonalities and learn from cultural and social differences. Many programs use the diversity of a community as an opportunity for a real-life literacy project, such as a multicultural cookbook. Although these situations generally involve more work and creativity on the part of the program facilitators, the interactions they provide have the potential to be more beneficial for everyone (Gadsden, 1996).

## Specific Program Ideas for School Libraries

The school library media center and the library media specialist can be a central focus for any family literacy program. Not only can the library serve as a meeting location, but it can also provide access to books, magazines and computers, which are vital components of the program. The LMS will probably be most involved with planning and presenting the parenting education and interactive parent and child time components because of their focus on specific literacy activities and sharing opportunities. Here are some specific ideas the LMS could use for these two components or for a separate program on family literacy through parents and children sharing literacy activities together.

Reading bags: Create interactive literacy bags parents and children can check out from the library. These should include a book, an extension activity and a response journal for participants to record their reactions to the story and activity. Parents and children could complete a story kit activity during the program and then be invited to take another one home. Similar kits can be purchased from some library vendors.

Children's writing: Provide parents with information about children's writing stages and how to promote writing at home. Allow time for parents and children to write together and then share what they have written with others.

Book sharing: Give parents practical strategies for sharing books with their children. Focus on the literacy interactions that naturally occur during these times. End the session with parents and children reading together.

Library visit: Take a field trip to the local library. Be sure to allow time for filling out library card applications and selecting books to check out.

Book fairs: Host a book fair where parents and students can purchase books. Provide Spanish books if needed and consider using coupons or other discounts.

Favorite food festival: Invite each family to bring their favorite food or snack to share. Collect the recipes and use them to create a cookbook for each family. Allow time at the end for parents and children to write about their experience.

Book selection: Inform parents about selecting quality books that fit the needs and interests of their children. Have examples of quality books available for reading and checkout.

Storytelling: Use wordless books to explore the wonders of storytelling. Parents and children take turns telling each other the story in their own words. Explain to parents that this technique can be extended to help nonreaders tell stories in favorite books using the pictures to support their stories.

Creative dramatics: After sharing a folk story together, provide parents and children with simple props or costumes and invite them to dramatize the story together or with a small group.

Family bookmaking: Guide parents and children as they explore simple bookmaking techniques. Allow time for writing and illustrating a book and provide bookmaking materials to take home.

Art response time: After sharing a story with their children, parents assist their children in an art project related to the story.

Home literacy centers: Give parents simple, inexpensive ideas for creating home literacy centers for their child. Discuss ways to use these centers to enhance their child's literacy skills and provide materials to get their centers started.

### Organizations

**The National Center for Family Literacy**
Waterfront Plaza, Suite 200
325 West Main Street
Louisville, KY 40202
502-584-0172

**The Barbara Bush Foundation for Family Literacy**
1002 Wisconsin Avenue NW
Washington, DC 20007
202-338-206

**International Reading Association**
800 Barksdale Road,
P.O. Box 8139
Newark, DE 19714-8138
302-731-1600
<www.reading.org>

### Web Sites & Online Articles

**Family Literacy:
An Annotated Bibliography**
<www.ed.gov/pubs/Family_Lit_2000/>

**Simple Things You Can Do To Help All Children Read Well and Independently by the End of Third Grade**
<www.ed.gov/pubs/SimpleThings/>

**Children's Literacy Development: Suggestions for Parent Involvement**
<www.ed.gov/databases/ERIC_Digests/ ed365979.html>

**Partnership for Family Involvement in Education**

**Strong Families, Strong Schools**
<eric-web.tc.columbia.edu/families/strong>

**Parents and Children Together Online**
<www.indiana.edu/~eric_rec/fl/pcto/menu.html>

**Parent Involvement Materials**
<www.indiana.edu/~eric_rec/bks/pim.html>

**Family Literacy Strategies to Support Children's Learning**
<eric-web.tc.columbia.edu/digests/dig144.html>

**Texas Family Literacy Center**

---

Family puppet show: Begin the evening with a puppet show. Engage parents and children in creating their own puppets from various materials. Encourage them to create their own puppet show at home.

"Meet My Family": After sharing several books on families, ask parents and children to write a "Meet My Family" book by answering questions about their family. These books can be shared with others in the group to foster friendships.

Reading strategies: Teach parents basic reading strategies to use with their beginning reader. Include the use of prediction, rhyming words and picture clues. Use early reader books to illustrate these strategies and allow time for parents to practice with their children.

These are only a sample of the many creative and innovative ways the LMS can use the library media center to encourage shared literacy

activities. When planning these activities, remember to be sensitive to participants' needs and be sure to provide interactive parent and child time in addition to parenting instruction as part of each session (Nespeca, 1996; Mulhern et al., 1994; Ermis, 1996).

In summary, research and the continued passage of state and federal legislation have supported the idea that family literacy programs work. Unlike other programs, family literacy programs can address a variety of issues including welfare reform, early childhood programs, education reform and parent involvement (Peyton, 1999). Much research in the cycle of poverty has shown that poverty and illiteracy are closely related. Family literacy programs seek to break the cycle of poverty by creating literate, self-sufficient families (Family Resource Council, 1997). These programs also provide a positive way for

schools, libraries and other organizations to help support parents as they seek to become their child's first and best teacher.

### References

The Barbara Bush Foundation for Family Literacy. (2001). National grant program. Retrieved July 17, 2001 from the World Wide Web: <www.barbarabushfoundation.com/nga.html>

Brown, B.L. (1998). *Family literacy: Respecting family ways.* (ERIC Digest No. 203). Columbus, Ohio: Ohio State University College of Education. Center on Education and Training for Employment. (EDO-CE-98-203).

Ermis, S. (1996). Once upon a time......families reading together: Promoting early literacy through parental workshops. *The State of Reading*, 11-16.

Family Resource Coalition. (1997). *Family support programs and family literacy*. Retrieved July 17, 2001 from the World Wide Web: <npin.org/library/1997/n00247/n00247.html>

Fawcett, G., Rasinski, T.V., and Linek, W. (1997). Family literacy: A new concept. *Principal*, 34-37.

Gadsden, V.L. (1996). *Designing and conducting family literacy programs that account for racial, ethnic, religious, and other cultural differences*. Retrieved July 17, 2001 from the World Wide Web: <www.ed.gov/pubs/FamLit/design.html>

Morrow, L.M. (1997). *Literacy development in the early years: Helping children read and write* (3rd ed.). Boston: Allyn and Bacon.

Mulhern, M., Rodriguez-Brown, F.V., and Shanahan, T. (1994). *Family literacy for language minority families: Issues for program implementation*. (NCBE Program Information Guide Series, Number 17). Washington D.C.: National Clearinghouse for Bilingual Education. Retrieved July 17, 2001 from the World Wide Web: www.ed.gov/pubs/FamLit/design.html>

Nespeca, S.M. (1996). Literacy begins at home: 25 ways to make sure reading runs in the family. *School Library Journal*, 26-29.

*New Title 1 and family literacy funding.*

Ohio Literacy Resource Center. Retrieved July 17, 2001 from the World Wide Web: <literacy. kent.edu/Oasis/Leg/title1.html>

Peyton, T. (1999). *Family literacy legislation and initiatives in eleven states.* Louisville, Kentucky: National Center for Family Literacy. Retrieved July 17, 2001 from the World Wide Web: <www. famlit.org/policy/states.html>

Schwartz, W. (1999). *Family literacy strategies to support children's learning.* (ERIC Digest No. 144). New York: Columbia University Teachers College. Institute for Urban and Minority Education. (EDO-UD-99-4).

*Jennifer Griffis is a Librarian at Rayburn Elementary in Grand Prairie, Texas, and can be reached at* jennifer.griffis@gpisd.org.

Griffis, J. (2003). Family literacy programs in school libraries: Helping parents become their child's best teacher. *Library Media Connection, 22*(1), 30-34.

# Extending Inclusive Learning: Library and Special Education Collaboration

## By Janet Hopkins

Inclusive education is not a new concept. No longer considered an educational trend, inclusion is a priority in school systems around the world. In the United States, the Individuals with Disabilities Education Act (IDEA) requires that "to the maximum extent appropriate," students with special needs be educated in the "least restrictive environment" (LRE).

### §§300.550 General LRE requirements.

*(b) Each public agency shall ensure—*
*(1) That to the maximum extent appropriate, children with disabilities, including children in public or private institutions or other care facilities, are educated with children who are nondisabled; and*
*(2) That special classes, separate schooling or other removal of children with disabilities from the regular educational environment occurs only if the nature or severity of the disability is such that education in regular classes with the use of supplementary aids and services cannot be achieved satisfactorily.*

*(Authority: 20 U.S.C. 1412(a)(5))*
[IDEA '97 Final Regulations. Subpart E—Procedural Safeguards. Least Restrictive Environment (LRE). IDEA '97 Laws & Regs <www.ideapractices.org/law/index.php>.]

Special education classrooms still provide important services within the school system. However, students with special needs are more frequently receiving some or all of their education in general education classrooms, as well as the library media center. The scope of inclusive education practice continues to evolve as new technologies and innovative instructional methods emerge. Inclusive learning is becoming more than facility access and expansion of the settings where special needs students join other students.

Beyond the physical and social inclusion of students with special needs lies the goal of reducing or removing barriers to learning and participation. Adapted and modified resources and educational and assistive technologies facilitate learning, participation, and access to the curriculum and library media center resources.

## Forging Library Media Center/ Special Education Partnerships

Library media specialists are in a strong position to support the expansion of inclusive learning opportunities for all students. Working closely with special educators to develop services and collections that support school-wide inclusion, library media specialists can enhance and promote the value

> *Special educators and library media specialists can launch a partnership to review special needs learning resources throughout the school.*

of both departments within the school. Collaborations between library media specialists and special educators offer exciting new opportunities. These opportunities include the identification of common ground for professional goal setting, achievement, and satisfaction.

Interdisciplinary collaborations build school resources, capability, and direction. Library media specialists and special educators share similarities, as both provide services that support classroom teachers. Often classroom teachers are challenged for time to locate or create specialized learning materials and lesson plans for individual students. Alternative learning resources available to students and teachers in an accessible library media center provide helpful options to support all students' learning needs

while reducing preparation demands on inclusive classroom teachers.

Library media specialists and special educators are skilled at meeting the needs of students and colleagues. However, library media specialists and special educators also need support for their own professional growth. Through collaboration, library media specialists and special educators can extend professional development opportunities by sharing expertise, enthusiasm, and professional development resources.

Partnerships lend themselves to strategic learning opportunities. Working together, collaborators can identify conferences offering mutually valuable special education and library-related sessions. These may include topics on inclusion, accommodations, learning styles, assistive technology, special needs educational resources, and information and communication technology. Collaborators can share handouts, resources, and ideas from conferences attended alone or together. Consider attending workshops or seminars that provide an opportunity to step away from the school setting and discuss inclusive services in a relaxed environment free of distraction.

## Meeting the Needs of All Learners

Special educators and library media specialists can launch a partnership to review special needs learning resources throughout the school. Assess the variety of curriculum and learning resources available to students in your school. Are print materials the dominant or only learning options available to your students? Are modified resources and curriculum materials available in alternate formats such as video, audiotapes, large print, or digital format? Is assistive technology available to students? Look for ways of expanding the options available to students to reflect the variety of learning preferences of students with specific learning needs.

While discussing the learning options available for students with special needs, examine the possibilities for delivering these options. In the elementary school environment, where students receive much of their education in a single classroom, it makes sense to maintain a collection of appropriate alternate learning materials and technologies in the classrooms of students with special needs. Educating students in the least restrictive environment at the elementary level often means within the regular classroom. However, the least restrictive learning environment must be determined on a case-by-case basis for each student.

At the secondary level, students typically receive instruction in many different classrooms. High school classrooms are often shared by a number of teachers. Some teachers are on the move from room to room as frequently as their students. As the high school learning environment is more dynamic and complex than the elementary environment, providing access to special needs resources and technologies in the least restrictive environment may be more challenging.

A high school classroom with desks, a blackboard, and a set of dictionaries is a restrictive learning environment for a student with special needs who relies on computer access to work efficiently. Without alternate materials and technology options, students with special needs may lack the tools that help them succeed in their high school studies.

How many enabling learning environments within the school are available to students with special needs? Must these students always go to the special education classroom to access the learning materials and technology they need? Are portable technologies and resources available? Is the library media center also prepared to accommodate the learning needs of these students?

"Inclusion considers that all students are full members of the school community and are entitled to the opportunities and responsibilities that are available to all students in the school." [Inclusive Learning Environments for Students with Special Needs. New Horizons for Learning <www.newhorizons.org/spneeds/inclusion/front_inclusion.htm>.]

In the upper grades, research becomes a standard requirement for projects across the curriculum. Students in high school need library research opportunities. Considering its range of resources, you can make a strong case that the library media center is the least restrictive learning environment of all for many students. It makes sense to extend services to students with special needs through the library media center so they can take advantage of a variety of resources and research options.

> *Considering its range of resources, you can make a strong case that the library media center is the least restrictive learning environment of all for many students.*

Some students prefer to use specialized resources and assistive technologies in a special education setting instead of the regular classroom. For students with considerable support requirements, the special education classroom may be the most appropriate environment during portions of the school day. However, many students with special needs may prefer to work alongside their peers and avoid special education settings. These students can be well served by a library media center that provides assistive technology and learning resources not available in the regular classroom. Flexibility is the key to delivering inclusive learning opportunities for all students. With the wide range of specialized hardware and software options now available, there's no reason for students with special needs to be stranded on the "have not" side of the digital divide.

Connecting students with special needs with technology and appropriate learning resources helps prepare them for educational transitions and career success. Having all of these available within the library media center also provides an accessible learning environment during breaks outside regular class time.

## Ten Steps Toward Building a Library Media Center/Special Education Partnership

*(These suggestions can be modified to suit specific partnership objectives.)*

**Identify Participants:** Which library media center, special education, counseling, teaching, support, or administrative staff should participate on the library media center and special education collaboration team?

**Conduct Research:** Review literature and online resources and seek input.

**Evaluate Facility Access:** Is the library media center accessible to all students and staff with special needs in the school?

**Evaluate Curricular/Information Access Options:** Does the library media center/school have a range of print and alternate format resources? Is a grade/subject listing of modified/adapted learning materials available for staff? Is it updated and circulated as new materials are acquired?

**Evaluate Assistive Technology Options:** Which high tech, mid tech, and low tech resources are familiar to staff and available for student use?

**Identify Professional Development Priorities:** Have library media center staff received disability awareness or professional development training?

**Establish Goals:** What are the objectives of the library media center and special education collaboration?

**Create an Action Plan and Identify Funding:** What will be done? How will professional development and implementation ideas be funded?

**Develop an Evaluation Plan:** How will the value of the initiative be measured and progress documented?

**Develop a Dissemination Strategy:** How will the initiative be shared with the school community?

Students with special needs who intend to pursue postsecondary education must develop efficient library and research capabilities. This is critical for students who need to develop competencies in accessing print and digital text resources through the use of assistive technologies. Students with special needs can be shown how to use built-in accessibility features on computer operating systems, scanners, and video magnifiers. Students with reading difficulties can boost comprehension with online literature summaries, auditory supports, such as screen reading software, and books on tape. Providing access to information about learning strategies and alternatives helps prepare students with special needs for independence.

## Meeting the Needs of Education Partners

Collaboration brings with it potential gains for library media specialists, special educators, and students. However, other education partners can benefit from a library media center prepared for diversity. Library media specialists are usually high profile staff members who report on resource acquisitions and library media center activities during staff meetings. At both elementary and high schools, students and staff have the opportunity to visit the library media center and observe the library media specialist. The library media specialist is often one of the most familiar faces within the school community. The status of the library media center and its staff can provide strong leadership toward the creation of inclusive schools.

By accommodating student diversity through technology support and varied library resources, the library media center expands its service value for classroom teachers. Teachers can assign project work and research for a wide range of students with library media

> *By accommodating student diversity through technology support and varied library resources, the library media center expands its service value for classroom teachers.*

center support. This doesn't mean that the library media center usurps the role of the special education department; it means that the library media center assists in reducing learning barriers for students and instructional barriers teachers encounter in traditional classrooms. It means strengthening the library media center–classroom relationship by expanding learning opportunities for all students and their teachers.

Library media centers that are prepared for diversity extend inclusive learning opportunities throughout the entire school. Library media centers that meet the needs of all learners demonstrate their versatility and value to administrators and the school community.

Library media specialists, educators, and institutions can collaborate to strengthen the culture of inclusion within a single school, as well as the extended education community. Partnerships have the potential to enrich learning experiences for students, education professionals, and education partners.

"Collaboration of the school with its surrounding community systems is a factor to help create positive educational change. Partnerships within and outside the school setting are essential to support education reform." [Inclusion of Students with Special Needs: Collaboration. New Horizons for Learning <www.newhorizons.org/spneeds/inclusion/collaboration/front_collab.html>.]

There's no limit to the collaborative learning opportunities that can be forged by motivated professionals. Extending inclusive learning opportunities for students with special needs brings with it the opportunity to share library media center experiences and expertise with other schools, districts, and regions interested in inclusive education.

*Janet Hopkins is the author of* Assistive Technology: An Introductory Guide for K–12 Library Media Specialists *(Linworth Publishing, 2004) and can be reached at AT_Consulting@Canada.com.*

Hopkins, J. (2005). Extending inclusive learning: Library and special education collaboration. *Library Media Connection, 23*(6), 17-19.

---

## Least Restrictive Environment (LRE) Resources on the Web

Least Restrictive Environment Clearinghouse <www.leastrestrictive.org> Funded by the Illinois State Board of Education, this site provides information for educators and parents about LRE issues.

ERIC Clearinghouse on Disabilities and Gifted Education <http://ericec.org/digests/e629.html> *The Least Restrictive Environment Mandate: How Has It Been Defined by the Courts?* This site provides information on legal cases related to LRE.

Wrightslaw LRE/Inclusion Page <www.wrightslaw.com/info/lre.index.htm> There are some very informative links on LRE and inclusion for educators and parents on this site.

National Information Center for Children and Youth with Disabilities/National Dissemination Center for Children with Disabilities <www.nichcy.org/Trainpkg/8ohs.pdf > This training package provides highlights on the key issues of LRE.

# Smaller Learning Communities: An Overview

## By Liz Metzger

Ask 100 different educators for a definition of "small learning communities," and you will likely get 100 different answers. However, lack of a commonly held definition does not seem to be slowing down the proliferation of SLCs across the country. Entire districts, from Los Angeles Unified to New Jersey, are reorganizing into SLCs; the phrase is appearing more frequently not only in professional literature and at educational conferences, but also in the mainstream press. Funders—including the U.S. Department of Education, and the Annenberg, Gates, Carnegie, and Annie E. Casey Foundations—have spent millions of dollars to help schools and districts build small schools, or to restructure existing large schools into smaller ones. And more than 15 years of research supports what many teachers, school staff, and parents have long held as conventional wisdom: Smaller schools are inherently safer and lead to increased student achievement and connectedness (Raywid, 1995; Hill, Foster, and Gendler, 1990; Hallinan, 1994; Klonsky, 1995; Meier, 1995a, 1995b).

Yet the research is also clear that size alone is not enough. Small schools researcher Kathleen Cotton points out that downsizing, when poorly done, will yield few benefits—a situation that could ultimately relegate SLCs to the "dead fad pile" (3). Gladden writes that " . . . smallness alone cannot create satisfying relationships or academic focus." (123, in Cotton 5). Visher, Teitlebaum, and Emanuel (1999) agree, though they continue that although school size alone is not enough to increase student achievement, it can act as "a facilitating factor for other desirable practices" (21), including increased collegiality, more personal teacher/student relationships, establishment of a collective responsibility for student learning, and increased teacher expectations of students.

Though new small schools and reorganized schools were initially most prevalent in urban districts with high minority populations and poverty rates, more recently the movement has taken root in large suburban schools and districts (Cotton, 50). One such school is Chico High, in rural northern California, where a variety of approaches to personalizing the learning environment embody the suggestion given by researcher Diana Oxley: " . . . the particularities of local practice are part of what makes an SLC successful—building on the school's unique character" (8). It is precisely that "building on unique character" and site strengths that make the SLC program at Chico High a blend of the traditional (small theme-based academies and mentoring programs) and the innovative (the Chico High library's "Booktalk" series, an ongoing after-school venue through which faculty and students share favorite books to audiences of more students and teachers).

> More than 15 years of research supports what many teachers, school staff, and parents have long held as conventional wisdom: smaller schools are inherently safer and lead to increased student achievement and connectedness.

## Chico: Profile of the School and Community

The Chico Unified School District (CUSD) is a rural California K-12 district that serves almost 14,000 students in 23 schools. Chico, a university town located 175 miles northeast of San Francisco in the agricultural Sacramento Valley, is typical of many California communities in its rapid growth over the past 15 years. As housing prices and the cost of living in California's metropolitan areas has soared, Chico's population has exploded from 40,079 in 1990 to 73,558 in 2005. Within the unincorporated areas immediately adjacent to the city limits, another 28,562 live, bringing the population served by the CUSD to 102,120.

This increase is evident to anyone walking through the halls at Chico High School (CHS), which crowds more than 2,000 students onto a campus built for fewer than 1,500. Since the fall of 1993, the population at CHS has more than doubled. Counseling caseloads are 400:1, nearly twice what is recommended by the American School Counselors Association. Class sizes of 35-38 are the norm in core academic courses. Elective programs such as art, music, and sports, which traditionally connect many students to school, face the constant threat of elimination, the casualty of a state budget crisis that has California almost last in per-pupil education spending.

## Smaller Learning Communities at Chico High: The Beginning

In part to address issues of disenfranchisement and increasing student academic need, Chico High implemented a smaller learning communities program in 2002 through a grant from the U.S. Department of Education. Chico High was already home to two smaller learning environments, each serving about 300 students K-12: a Coalition of Essential Schools affiliate (Chico High West) and a career academy (the Academy of Communications and Technology, or ACT). The decision to go schoolwide with SLCs as a means to address academic and affective need was partly prompted by the fact that these "schools-within-schools" regularly drew more applicants for admission than there were spots available.

Department of Education-funded SLCs usually restructure using *structures*, which create mini-units (such as houses, academies, "schools-within-schools," or other smaller units) within the larger school. In addition, *strategies* (such as freshman transition, academic teaming, mentoring, looping) are often used in conjunction with the structures and are designed to help personalize each student's experience. Chico High used both.

## Chico High Structures

In 2001 and 2002, four new SLC structures were designed and developed by teachers, in response to perceived student need. By 2004-05, 1,149 students were enrolled in SLC structures—56 percent of the student population. This included 64 percent of the freshman class, 68 percent of the sophomores, 42 percent of the juniors, and 50 percent of the seniors. These 1,149 students enrolled in seven distinct smaller learning communities:

- The *Academy of Communications and Technology (ACT)*, a California Partnership Academy with a career pathway in media communications.
- *Chico High West (West)*, an affiliate of the Coalition of Essential Schools.
- *SOUL*, a two-year transition program offering highly at-risk students the problem-solving strategies and academic skills they need to succeed anywhere.
- The *Chico Academic Transition Services (CATS)* program, helping special day class (SDC) and Resource Specialist Program (RSP) students achieve a successful transition to adulthood.
- The *Ag Barn*, offering both college prep and career pathway programs in animal science, plant science, horticulture, and agricultural mechanics.
- *STAGE*, a performing arts academy, offering a rigorous advanced-level humanities curriculum along with enrichment classes in drama, music, and dance.
- *M\*A\*S\*H* (Medicine, Athletics/Fitness, Science, and Health), providing a pathway for students interested in pursuing a career in health-related occupations.

## Chico High Strategies

Students within SLC structures, as well as those who opted not to belong, were supported through one or more of four central strategies. All of these, but particularly the first, have benefited from the support of the library media center.

- a campuswide *literacy program* (based on the philosophy that every

teacher at CHS is also a teacher of reading)

- the *Chico High Mentoring Program*, which provides academic, social, and vocational mentoring for students (in 2004-05, 115 students were matched in one-to-one mentoring relationships with adults)
- a *freshman transition program* called Challenge Days, with a goal of promoting tolerance and understanding
- a *parent and family involvement program*, which provides parent liaisons to the Latino, Hmong, and African-American communities.

## Results:

Outcomes from the first four years of the grant were encouraging: increased reading scores overall, a reduction in the achievement gap among students, and a tangible sense of community

> By the end of 2010, the goal is that every one of the 4,000 students on both campuses will be known well by at least one adult connected to school, who understands that student's goals and dreams, and can help him or her to achieve them.

campuswide. In 2005-06, Chico High applied for and received a second round of funding (in conjunction with sister high school Pleasant Valley) to expand the scope of work to both schools. By the end of 2010, the goal through this new grant is that every one of the 4,000 students on both campuses will be known well by at least one adult connected to school, who understands that student's goals and dreams, and can help him or her to achieve them.

However, several lessons learned from the first round of funding will help inform work in the second—and perhaps can serve as words of advice to other schools looking to restructure in this way:

- *Stay focused on results:* The effective side of SLCs—creating a sense of community, providing

individual supports through mentoring and freshman transition, and other strategies—are important, but keep in mind that they are means to an end: improved student academic achievement.

- Provide multiple entry points to the work, for students and staff. Avoid the trap of thinking that reform can be "one size fits all." Effective SLCs allow students and staff to choose how (and whether) to be involved in SLCs.
- *Never underestimate the importance of ongoing communication.* Any change like this has the potential to create divisiveness, and a feeling of "haves" and "have-nots." Communication doesn't eliminate that, but it can help.
- Support teachers with resources including time and professional development. Teacher burnout goes with the territory in establishing SLCs, as with most other educational reforms. Time to plan, to meet together, to share results of student work, and to build professional capacity are essential.

The library media center and its staff have an important role to play in ongoing small learning community development and implementation. At Chico High, this has included providing links and literature related to SLCs, offering support for students and teachers, helping with SLC Web page design to facilitate communication, and securing SLC mini-grants to sponsor programs such as "Booktalking." The SLC program at Chico High is truly a community effort.

## Works Cited

Cotton, Kathleen. "New Small Learning Communities: Findings from Recent Literature." Portland: Northwest Regional Laboratories, 2001.

Gladden, R. "The Small School Movement: A Review of the Literature." In *Small Schools, Big Imaginations: A Creative Look at Public Schools.* M. Find and J.I. Somerville, eds. Chicago: Cross City Campaign for Urban Reform, May 1998, 113-133.

Hallinan, M. *Restructuring schools: Promising practices and policy.* New York: Plenum Press. 1994.

Hill, P.T., Foster, G.E., & Gendler, T. *High schools with character*. Santa Monica, CA: The RAND Corporation. 1990.

Klonsky, M. (1995). *Small schools: The numbers tell a story. A review of the research and current expectations*. Chicago: Illinois University.

Meier, D. *The power of their ideas: Lessons for America from a small school in Harlem*. Boston: Beacon Press. (1995a).

Meier, D. Small schools, big results. *American School Board Journal, 182*(7), 37-40. (1995b, July).

Oxley, Diana. "Smaller Learning Communities: Implementing and Deepening Practice." Portland: Northwest Regional Laboratories, 2004.

Raywid, M. *The subschools/small schools movement—taking stock*. Madison, WI: Center on Organization and Restructuring of Schools. 1995.

Visher, M.G, Teitlebaum, P., and Emanuel, D. "Create Small Learning Environments Enabling Students and Teachers to Work Together." *Key High School Reform Strategies: An Overview of Research Findings. New American High Schools: High Schools at the Leading Edge of Reform*. Washington, DC: Office of Vocational and Adult Education, March 1999, 19-26 (ED 430 271). Available http://ericae.net/ericdc/ED430271.htm

*Liz Metzger is an English teacher and grant writer at Chico (California) High School. She can be reached at emetzger@chicousd.org*

Metzger, L. (2006). Smaller learning communities: An overview. *Library Media Connection, 25*(1), 22-23.

# Journaling: Telling Your Professional "Story"

## By Donna Miller

Some of us remember keeping a diary when we were younger. Anne Frank's poignant words to her diary-friend Kitty provided continual encouragement and inspiration to me as I wrote to my diary-friend Katie, especially during my turbulent adolescent years! Some adults maintain this practice as a tool for reflection, self-improvement, emotional release, recording and preserving the family history, keeping track of important milestones and events, or for other purposes. A journal is similar to a diary, but there are some important differences. According to James E. Miller, a diary is "a day-to-day record of how you spend your time" whereas a journal focuses instead on "the writer's interior life--how you feel about something at the moment, or what you think about some matter that has grabbed your attention" (Miller, p. 9). This article addresses a specific type of journal writing, i.e., professional journal writing. Although recording events and emotions will certainly be appropriate, the focus of this type of journal writing is somewhat different from that of personal journal writing.

So what are the differences between professional journaling and personal journaling? The most obvious difference, of course, is that a professional journal is used to record events, emotions, milestones, and other items that relate to one's career. Beyond that, the techniques for writing in a professional journal can be very similar to those used for personal journal writing. Such devices as prompts, questions, reflections, free writing, and other tools can be used in both types of journals. The message rather than the medium differentiates the two types of journals. Tools, strategies, and devices that apply to all types of journals as well as those items that primarily apply to professional journal writing are relevant to and important for library media specialists.

## Protect Your Thoughts: The Importance of Privacy

It is especially important in the case of professional journals that the author find a place to keep the journal to facilitate maintaining privacy. Miller advises that journal writers keep their journals "out of obvious sight" and even perhaps hide or lock them away (p. 21). Although this advice may sound extreme, in the case of a professional journal keeping your journal away from prying eyes is very important. In fact, unless the professional journal is to be included as a part of your evaluation portfolio, it might be best to keep the journal away from school or your library. As with e-mail messages that are sent, received, and stored at the work place, a journal could be considered to be the property of the school or district for which you

> You will need to carefully assess how you plan to use the journal before you decide upon the best format.

work. If the journal entries include sensitive information—especially entries in which you express negative thoughts, feelings, or opinions about administrators, teachers, or other staff, it is best to store the journal at home.

## Format is Fundamental: Types of Journal "Books"

In the forthcoming book *Day by Day: Professional Journaling for Library Media Specialists,* by Miller and Larsen (Linworth), various types of journals and the benefits of each are described. The kinds of journals are numerous and include everything from Web-based ones to plain old paper steno pads. Each particular type of journal has its own peculiarities, so you will need to carefully assess how you plan to use the journal before you decide upon the best format. For example, if you intend to curl up in bed and write, you may not have ready access to the Internet. Thus, a Web-based journal might not fit your

needs. If, on the other hand, you prefer to write at a desk and want to be able to edit quickly and neatly, a word processing program or a Web-based journal may offer you the perfect format. The best way to determine which type of journal to use is to think about how, where, and when you plan to write and then see which format best fits with your particular style.

## Quill or Cursor: With What Will You Write?

Do you have a favorite pen, pencil, marker, keyboard, or other writing utensil? If so, you probably realize how important using just the right writing instrument can be—especially for those of us who are kinesthetically oriented. Permanent ink is usually better than pencil lead if the writer intends the journal to last for a long time. Once you become dedicated to the practice of writing in a professional journal, the importance of using a comfortable writing utensil will become apparent. Also, know that your preference of writing/word processing instrument may change over time, so do not be afraid to transition to another tool as you realize you prefer another writing instrument.

## Steps to Start: Preliminary Efforts for Effectiveness

### 1. Determine your purpose.

Having a purpose may be the single most important factor in successful professional journal writing. Your purpose serves as a catalyst for you to continue making entries, and this purpose will assist you in maintaining a focus so that the journal is a productive and beneficial tool. As with the types of journals available, the purposes for writing in a professional journal are numerous. These purposes can include but are not limited to:

- Time management
- Assessing strengths and weaknesses
- Goal setting
- CYA tool (cover your anatomy)

- Working through professional problems/situations
- Analyzing and improving relationships with co-workers or supervisors
- Identifying "what went wrong" in professional situations
- Identifying successful practice for the purpose of replicating it
- Professional growth
- Getting published
- Combinations of the above
- Others

### 2. Find a suitable place to write.

Just as the location for storing the professional journal is important, so is the location for writing in the journal. You probably will not find it feasible to write in your journal in a full, busy, and productively noisy library media center. Since privacy is important, it might be best to make journal entries at home. However, sometimes it is best to capture at least the essence of an event immediately following it, so you may want to jot down brief impressions, thoughts, and feelings about the event while at work and then "flesh out" the journal entry later at home.

Such features of the location as lighting, furnishings, colors, and décor can be important. For example, if you need to feel calm and rested when you write, a room with vivid yellow walls and fluorescent lighting might not be the best choice. On the other hand, if you want to feel energized when recording a successful situation, a colorful room might be perfect!

### 3. Determine the best time to write.

The best time of day for writing is as individual as are the writers of journals. Some people are "morning persons" and others are "night owls," so it is important that you decide what time of day or evening works best for you. Of course, it may not always be possible to write in the journal at the optimum time of day due to the pressures of family, household chores, community or church obligations, or other factors, but as much as is possible, it is advantageous for you to select a time during which you are most productive. It is, in fact, a good practice to "schedule" your writing and make it a priority.

### 4. Be as comfortable as possible when writing in your journal.

Tight, restrictive clothes, extreme heat or cold, loud noises, uncomfortable chairs, and other factors can negatively impact journal writing. Although this may seem apparent, it is sometimes tempting to simply find the nearest corner in which to sit and begin writing—especially if you are using the journal for catharsis. You will find it more effective to take the time to be comfortable and relaxed so that your entries can be useful in helping you to meet your purpose(s) for writing.

### 5. Just write!

This edict is not always easy, but if all you do is simply write whatever words come to mind in an effort to

> You will probably not find it feasible to write in your journal in a full, busy, and productively noisy library media center.

begin the journaling process, that is sometimes better than trying to find just the right words to describe an event, develop a goal, or express the exact feeling that was experienced in a professional situation. Using some writing devices as described below to jumpstart your writing will eventually result in you being able to more easily capture the specific words and feelings you want/need to express in order to fulfill your writing goal for the day or for a writing session.

## Diary Devices: Tools to Jumpstart Your Writing

Sometimes sentences, phrases, or words can be used as catalysts when the proverbial writer's block occurs. Barbara Woodard includes a lengthy list of these types of sentences in her book *Journal Jumpstarts: Quick Topics and Tips for Journal Writing*. Although her book is written to be used with students, some of these prompts such as "Who

are you—really?" and "What is the greatest lesson you have ever learned?" are generic enough to be beneficial for all journal authors, including those writing a professional journal (p. 19).

In her book *The New Diary: How to Use a Journal for Self Guidance and Expanded Creativity*, Tristine Rainer provides a list of devices to bring to journal writers awareness of "the range of ways to write in a diary" (p. 52). Some of these devices that are most applicable for professional journaling include:

- Catharsis
- Description
- Reflection
- List
- Unsent Letter
- Dialogue

Rainer describes each of the above and many more devices thoroughly and tells writers how to use them. Although some are not necessarily appropriate for professional journaling, most of these devices can serve as helpful tools for professional journal writers. For example, one device you could use for a professional journal is a list. When you are developing goals for your library program, you could make a list of the components of the library program that are important and then write these as goal statements.

## So What's In It For Me? The Benefit to Library Media Specialists

The Miller/Larsen book previously mentioned includes daily pages with helpful hints from the Tips and Shoptalk columns in THE BOOK REPORT and LIBRARY TALK magazines, journal prompts specifically for library media specialists; reminders about necessary tasks such as preparing materials orders and weeding; notices about special days, authors' birthdays, and holidays; and finally, humorous and inspirational quotes from a great variety of people. The prompts, tips, reminders of special days, and other items included in the book can be used to help you plan, set goals, reflect, and improve your practice, as well as inspiring you to write in your journal.

After doing your homework by reading various resources and then deciding how and why you want to begin the exciting and fulfilling journey of journaling, what is next? How can the journal actually be used to improve practice and promote professional growth? The specific use for your journal again goes back to your purpose. If you want to use your journal to help you maintain a professional portfolio for your annual evaluation, capture your thoughts and experiences in your journal as needed to help you remember significant accomplishments, examine your weaker areas so that you can begin to work on them, and articulate your goals to your principal.

If your purpose is to better manage your time, you could use your journal to list the tasks you perform each day with a notation beside each task indicating the time spent. Then you could begin to analyze how you are spending your time and make adjustments as needed. Tracking various tasks to be completed throughout the year can help you identify recurring tasks and learn to be more efficient in planning for and completing them.

Library and education publishers are always looking for new authors who can share fresh ideas with their colleagues. We library media specialists usually are certified teachers as well as credentialed librarians, so we have much knowledge and experience to contribute. If you are an aspiring writer, use your journal to capture your good ideas and inspirations. Getting published is not as daunting as it might seem, and a professional journal can make this process even easier. The uses for your professional journal are only limited by your time, commitment, and imagination! We library media specialists are very familiar with the power and importance of stories, and a professional journal is, after all, the story of your career as an educator. What an important story that is! Carl Jung says it best:

"Thus it is that I have now undertaken, in my eighty-third year, to tell my personal myth. I can only make direct statements, only 'tell stories.' Whether or not the stories are 'true' is not the problem. The only question is whether what I tell is *my* fable, *my* truth."

*Donna Miller is Library Media Coordinator for the Mesa County Valley School District in Grand Junction, Colorado, and is the author of* The Standards-Based Integrated Library: A Collaborative Approach for Aligning the Library Program with the Classroom Curriculum, *2nd Edition (Linworth Publishing, Inc. 2004), and co-author, with Karen Larsen, of* Day by Day: Professional Journaling for Library Media Specialists *(Linworth Publishing, Inc. 2003).*

## Works Cited

Miller, James E. *The Rewarding Practice of Journal Writing: A Guide for Starting and Keeping Your Personal Journal.* Fort Wayne: Indiana: Willowgreen Publishing, 1998.

Rainer, Tristine. *The New Diary: How to Use a Journal for Self Guidance and Expanded Creativity.* New York: Jeremy P. Tarcher/Putnam, 1978.

Woodard, Patricia. *Journal Jumpstarts: Quick Topics and Tips for Journal Writing.* Fort Collins, Colorado: Cottonwood Press, Inc., 1994.

Miller, D. (2003). Journaling: Telling your professional "story." *Library Media Connection, 22*(2), 32-35.

# Are You Ready to Go Digital?
# The Pros and Cons of Electronic Portfolio Development

## By Marilyn Heath

Do you have a professional portfolio? Increasingly, portfolios are being required of educators for university graduation, licensure, employment, and evaluation. Professional portfolios provide an authentic tool for evaluation. Portfolios provide a unique, in-depth look at an educator's knowledge, skills, practice, beliefs, and attitudes by means of self-selected artifacts and accompanying reflections. In addition, portfolios provide a valuable record of an educator's growth over time.

Professional portfolios may be developed for different purposes, but they share many common attributes. Generally speaking, a professional portfolio is *an organized collection of self-selected artifacts and self-generated reflections, developed for a specific purpose and audience, which demonstrate the author's professional knowledge, skills, dispositions, and growth over time.* So whether a portfolio is used as a resumé, an assessment instrument, a showcase, or a professional development vehicle, it should contain each of these defining elements to display the educator's professional expertise in the best possible light.

Whether or not you currently have a professional portfolio, it might make sense to consider developing one in an electronic format. Electronic portfolios have many advantages: they are easier to distribute, can be duplicated quickly and easily, and portray the dynamics of the teaching life more accurately than any traditional portfolio. They do, however, have their limitations: they can be time-consuming, expensive, and stressful. Nevertheless, an electronic portfolio can be well worth the investment of time and energy. Here are some points to consider as you decide if an electronic portfolio is right for you.

## Benefits of an Electronic Portfolio

Primary benefits of electronic portfolio development include:

*Much of what educators generate—word documents, slide presentations, Web sites, statistics, and reports—is already in electronic format.* Instead of printing out paper copies, organizing them, preparing them for a binder, and printing reflections, it is much easier to leave the artifacts in digital format, add digital reflections, and organize them electronically.

Once the portfolio is created this way, it is easier to maintain, edit, and update. Artifacts and reflections can be edited, removed, or rearranged with a few keystrokes instead of the time-consuming tasks of editing, printing, and replacing that a binder would require.

*Much of what educators do does not communicate effectively on the printed page.* Because working with

> Portfolios provide a unique, in-depth look at an educator's knowledge, skills, practice, beliefs, and attitudes by means of self-selected artifacts and accompanying reflections.

students is dynamic, creative, and stimulating, educators need a vehicle that adequately conveys these characteristics to their portfolio audience. An electronic portfolio that employs a variety of media can present artifacts in ways that convey the vitality of the profession. Text, graphics, audio, and video can be combined in a variety of ways to present a more accurate picture of what transpires in classrooms and library media centers, whether it is orienting new students to the library media center, storytelling, reenacting a famous historical event, or conducting science experiments. Activities such as these, although typical in the professional lives of educators, can sometimes be difficult to accurately portray within

the confines of a standard evaluation instrument or a traditional portfolio.

*Electronic portfolios can support complex organization for effective documentation.* A major limitation of traditional paper portfolios is that they can be organized only in a linear fashion. There is no getting around it—one page must follow another. However, that is not the case with electronic portfolios. Authors can choose a linear organization if that works best, but most often the structure of an electronic portfolio is hierarchical. Through the use of hyperlinks, electronic portfolio developers can organize their portfolios to show relationships between major headings. Supporting artifacts can be linked to more than one heading and to each other, if necessary, to accurately reflect the complex relationships that exist in our professional practice (see Figure 1).

*Electronic portfolios are much easier to reproduce, distribute, and access.* A traditional portfolio in a binder is usually limited to one copy, which can be large and unwieldy. Sharing it effectively with more than a few people at a time is difficult. Distributing it to selection committees, prospective employers, or various administrative personnel is prohibitive, not only because of its bulk, but also because of the time and cost involved in duplicating and distributing it. In addition some items, such as original student work, cannot be satisfactorily reproduced in the traditional paper format.

Electronic portfolios on a portable storage device can be easily and quickly reproduced and distributed. Portfolios published on the Internet can be accessed by a virtual audience at the click of a mouse. This feature is especially important when the portfolio will have a wide distribution. New teachers, for example, can make their portfolios available to multiple prospective employers in advance of an interview instead of bringing their portfolio with them. Similarly, teach-

Figure 1

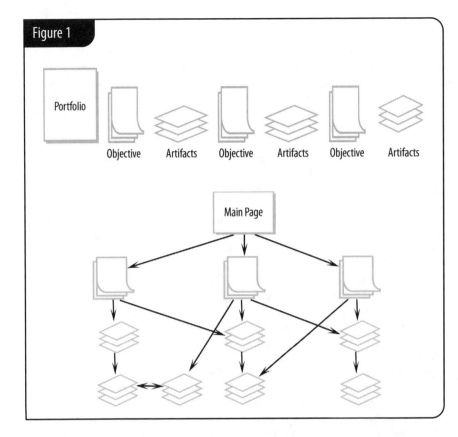

assessment and are used by classroom teachers at all levels. It makes sense that teachers and instructors should be able to model electronic portfolio development for their students, other teachers, and administrators.

*Electronic portfolios are inexpensive.* When created with available software and hardware, development costs can be reduced to the price of a few CD-ROMs or other storage medium. True, if the author decides to master new software or needs a scanner, digital camera, or other hardware, costs can rise significantly, but by using what is already available, an electronic portfolio can be created for pennies (see Figure 2). By using hardware and software that have already been mastered, the portfolio developer reduces his or her learning curve significantly.

## Disadvantages of an Electronic Portfolio

If all this sounds too good to be true and you can't wait to jump on the electronic portfolio bandwagon, then you should first know that there is a downside to electronic portfolio development as well. Seriously consider the following issues to make a truly informed decision whether or not electronic portfolio development is right for you.

*Electronic portfolio development takes time.* The creation of any pro-

ers submitting portfolios for board review for a grant, award, tenure, or other achievement can easily supply each member with a copy of their electronic portfolios.

*Electronic portfolios are an effective way to demonstrate technology skills or learn new ones.* Many educators have come a long way in technology skills development in the last few years. For most, Word documents, PowerPoint presentations, and spreadsheets are an integral part of lesson planning, record keeping, and instruction. These types of programs can all be used effectively to produce an electronic portfolio. For educators who want to expand their technology skills, developing an electronic portfolio is an excellent incentive for doing so.

In addition many states and local school districts are developing or already have in place technology standards for educators. Electronic portfolios can be an excellent venue for exhibiting technology proficiency to administrators.

Finally, developing an electronic portfolio is another way to model technology skills for administrators, colleagues, and students. Student portfolios continue to be a popular means of

*The decision to create a portfolio is not one that should be made in haste, and the portfolio itself should not be made that way either.*

### Figure 2: Cost comparison between traditional and electronic portfolios

*The cost of one tradional portfolio, at $25.95, is more than multi-packs of any of the electronic media except for the new memory key. Prices were taken from Office Max® and Best Buy® Web sites, and are subject to change.*

| Traditional Portfolio | | Electronic Portfolio | |
|---|---|---|---|
| **Material** | **Cost** | **Material** | **Cost** |
| 3" 3-ring binder | $7.99 | CD-ROM 30@17.98 | $.60 } $1.10 |
| | | Jewel case 10@$4.99 | $.50 |
| Paper | $3.99 | Floppy disk 10@$3.99 | $.40 |
| Sheet protectors—50 | $9.98 | Zip disk—250 MB | $7.49 |
| | | 2@$14.98 | |
| Index dividers for laser printer—5 tab | $3.99 | Memory key— 128 MB | $49.99 |
| **Total Cost—Single** | **$25.95** | **Total Cost—Multipack** | |
| | | CD-ROM + Jewel case | $22.97 |
| | | Floppy disk | $3.99 |
| | | Zip disk | $14.98 |

fessional portfolio, whether traditional or digital, takes time. Portfolios are both a product and a process. If sufficient time and thought is not devoted to the process, the final product will suffer as a result. The decision to create a portfolio is not one that should be made in haste, and the portfolio itself should not be made that way either. This advice holds true for any portfolio, but you can be sure that developing an electronic portfolio will take substantially more time than a traditional one. In order to develop a portfolio of exceptional quality (Would you want any other kind?), be sure that you have sufficient time to devote to the process.

*Electronic portfolio development can be expensive.* It is certainly feasible and desirable to create an electronic portfolio with the hardware and software at hand. Nevertheless, there is often a great temptation to use electronic portfolio development as the rationale for buying that really cool digital camera, the latest version of Web authoring software, or both. Beware of such dangerous thinking, which can turn a money-saver into a substantial expense.

*Electronic portfolio development takes technology skills.* This statement might seem like a no-brainer, but it warrants discussion. Although it is true that learning new technology skills is not necessary for portfolio development in most cases, the fact still remains that some technology skills are necessary. Portfolios can be created with computing skills so basic that even those who do not know much more than how to open and save a file can create an electronic portfolio. Bells and whistles are not mandatory. However, your level of technology expertise is an important factor in planning and developing your portfolio. If your technology skills are modest, keep your portfolio plan modest as well.

*Electronic portfolio development can be stressful.* Anyone with any technology experience at all knows that, at times, technology can be frustrating, mystifying, and just plain uncooperative ("Why won't it do what I want it to do?"). Times like these lead to stress and then more stress. If you ignore the preceding cautions and allocate insuffi-

cient time, buy expensive hardware or software that you now must learn how to use, or plan a portfolio far beyond your technological expertise, you might send yourself over the edge.

Electronic portfolio development should be a time of professional learning and growing. This important truth can easily be overlooked if you have to rush through the process or if you spend most of your time learning new skills. Stress does not lend itself to the clear and careful thinking necessary for organizational and selection decisions, and it surely will detract from any reflective thinking you might attempt.

*An electronic portfolio might not meet your needs.* In spite of all the sound reasons for electronic portfolio development, authoring one might not be in your best interest in a particular situation. For example, if you are a veteran teacher and decide to complete the application process for national board certification, you can expect to submit a substantial professional portfolio. At this time, however, the requirements specify a paper portfolio and submitting anything else would likely result in it not being scored. It is important, therefore, in any situation, to comply specifically with any instructions or requirements that pertain to your portfolio submission.

## The Technology Factor

By now you have several aspects of electronic portfolio development to consider as you decide whether developing one is right for you. Before you make that decision, one more discussion of the technology factor is in order. This one centers on the issue of priorities.

Keep in mind that the number-one priority of portfolio development is content. Whether electronic or paper, a flashy presentation cannot redeem a portfolio that is poorly designed, carelessly constructed, and lacking in authentic reflection. However, even the best portfolio can be undermined by a flawed presentation. Herein lies the crux of the issue: finding and keeping a desirable balance between portfolio content and portfolio technology.

Yes, the technological skills that you employ in constructing your portfolio speak to your level of expertise. Since technology is an increasingly

necessary skill for educators to possess, it is desirable to present a portfolio that displays your technology skills in the best possible light. Displaying one's technological expertise is one of the benefits of electronic portfolio development. However, these skills should never overshadow the content of the portfolio.

This situation can easily occur if you are learning new technology or if you are a technology whiz. In the first instance, you can expend far too much time and attention on mastering new hardware or software. Since there is presumably a limit to the amount of time you can devote to your portfolio, some other aspect of your portfolio will probably be neglected. Unfortunately, that aspect is often the reflective elements, artifact selection, or some other critical element of portfolio content. If you are a technological wizard, you might be tempted to pull out all the stops and make your portfolio so flashy that the technology overpowers the content. Even though your artifacts are excellent and your reflections truly insightful, they might become lost in all the glitz.

Hence, there is a need for balance between portfolio content and portfolio technology. *Content is always more important than the technology used to create it.* Remember, technology, as marvelous or aggravating as it can be, is merely a tool, a means to an end. The process of portfolio development, complete with reflections, should lead to professional growth as an educator. Focusing on portfolio content will allow that process to happen.

Can you do it? Of course you can if you choose your development tools carefully and keep the scope of the portfolio within your level of expertise. Proceed wisely and you will have a tremendously satisfying professional development experience and a portfolio that makes your practice shine.

### Additional Resources

Barrett, H. *Electronic Teaching Portfolios: Multimedia Skills + Portfolio Development = Powerful Professional Development.* 2000. ERIC ED444.

Campbell, D., P. Cignetti, B. Melenyzer, D. Nettles, & R.

Wyman, Jr. *How to Develop a Professional Portfolio.* Boston: Allyn and Bacon. 2001.

Kilbane, C. R., & N. B. Milman. *The Digital Teaching Portfolio Handbook: A How-to Guide for Educators.* Boston: Allyn and Bacon. 2003.

Kimball, M. A. *The Web Portfolio Guide: Creating Electronic Portfolios for the Web.* New York: Longman. 2003.

Van Wagenen, L., & M. Hibbard. (1998). "Building Teacher Portfolios." *Educational Leadership.* 55(5) (1998): 26–29.

*Marilyn Heath is a Library Media Specialist at Belton-Honea Path (South Carolina) High School. She is also the author of* Electronic Portfolios: A Guide to Professional Development and Assessment *(Linworth Publishing, Inc., 2004).*

Heath, M. (2005). Are you ready to go digital? The pros and cons of electronic portfolio development. *Library Media Connection, 23*(7), 66-70.

# It Takes Connections to Be a NBCT!

## By Sara Kelly Johns

The process for becoming a National Board Certified Teacher (NBCT) seems on the surface to be a lonely one. After all, when you are going through the process, it is about YOUR teaching, YOUR knowledge, YOUR achievements. It is not a measure of a strong school library media program; it is a measure of you as a teacher of library media.

However, in my opinion, you can't achieve that distinction without having "connections" and using them well.

### 1. Connections to a sound program of information literacy:
The 10 Library Media standards are intertwined with *Information Power* <http://www.ala.org/ala/aasl-proftools/informationpower/informationpower.htm>. Information literacy is your curriculum, interwoven with your school's subject content. You teach both collaboratively and independently, both your students and your staff, and while your program is not what is being measured by the certification, it needs to be strong and grounded in *Information Power*.

### 2. Connections to classroom teachers:
When you send in the videotape of your teaching, that teaching must be collaborative. The standards were written so that, while flexible scheduling is considered a best practice in our profession, it is certainly possible to become certified while working in a fixed schedule. But you do have to identify teachers with whom to collaborate in whatever framework of scheduling you have and you want to connect with other good teachers. Your best choices may well be other teachers in the building who have or are going through the NBCT process themselves; they will certainly sympathize!

### 3. Connections to your school community:
You will need to demonstrate connections to students' families and the community. Have you done newsletters, community service projects, PTA presentations and projects, a blog, workshops in technology use or Internet safety, or refreshments in the library during Open House? Public relations or marketing, it is part of our job as accomplished teachers.

### 4. Connections to good professional resources:
You will need to look over your own professional library. Make sure you have *Information Power* and the *IP Planning Guide* from ALA, and then shore it up with a couple of books on the NBCT process like Peggy Milam's and Gail Dickinson's and then books on the best practices of our profession. If you put them in author order, your bookshelf should read like a *Who's Who* in the library profession: Berkowitz and Eisenberg, Dickinson, Everhart, Harada, Hartzell, Johnson,

> The people you meet through professional involvement are smart and like-minded and the exchange of solutions to problems is invaluable.

Kearney, Koechlin and Zwaan, Krashen, Kuhlthau, Lance, Loertscher, Milam, Simpson, Stripling and Hughes-Hassell, Stripling and Pitts, Turner and Reidling, Valenza and Woolls and as many others as you can afford, borrow, or interlibrary loan. Try not to rack up too many overdue fines!

### 5. Connections to a friend/editor:
You are probably a good writer by this stage of your career, but it is wise to have a friend who is patient and kind enough to read everything you write to make sure you write what you mean to say and that you answer the question. This friend doesn't have to be a librarian or even a teacher, but does need to be a good editor and pay attention to details. Buy the friend a copy of the new illustrated Strunk and White (Penguin Group, 2005) and *Eats, Shoots & Leaves* (Penguin Group, 2004), and then send flowers, wine, or 6-packs regularly.

### 6. Connections to your professional organizations:
You will need to demonstrate your leadership and professional development. What we do has changed drastically in the last 20 years; it's crucial to stay current on educational trends, new technologies, and issues of the profession and to reflect, assess, and work continuously to have a leading-edge library program. To do so takes leadership and involvement. What conferences have you attended, boards have you sat on, workshops have you done, committees have you served on, offices have you held? The people you meet through professional involvement are smart and like-minded and the exchange of solutions to problems is invaluable.

### 7. Connections to your students:
Understanding child development and learning styles and how to use that in your teaching is part of being an accomplished teacher. Being a school librarian keeps you young and vital as you work with students as learners and, especially, as readers. They need to care about your quest and to understand what you are trying to accomplish when they are videotaped. A friend's students were sure they contributed to her success because they talked loud enough for the microphone to pick up when they talked about what a good teacher she is. They cared.

### 8. Connections to literature:
Even in these days of the Internet, it is crucial for students to be good readers and, hopefully, love to read. You need to know the literature of your students and promote student reading vigorously and constantly. The thrill of matching the right student with the right books continues to be the most satisfying part of the job for most of us. You will be asked to demonstrate your knowledge of children's or young adult literature in the assessment center and your leadership in the promotion of reading. Participation in teaching reading and writing skills will demonstrate your excellence as a teacher librarian.

**9. Connections to technology:** Janet Shaw, a middle school LMS from Delaware, told me that NBCT candidates need a good optometrist and a good computer, preferably a laptop with a wireless connection since you get really tired of sitting in the same spot! Besides your personal technology, you'll need access to a video camera for the taping of your teaching and even a video coach. While your library is not required to have all the latest technology now available, good library teaching means being able to use and teach technology with your students and your staff, in groups and one-on-one.

**10. Connections to support systems— electronic discussion lists (listservs), support groups (cohort), teachers in your district or area who have already completed their certification:** Besides that editor-friend, I highly recommend being a part of the electronic discussion lists for NBCT candidates, especially one for library media candidates. Many state education departments and associations or university programs have cohort groups of people going through the process at the same time. It's too easy to be isolated while immersed in the process, and the suggestions and encouragement of others will get you through it a lot easier, especially during those times when you're facing that brick wall. Is it worth it all to take the leap, make those connections, and work through the process?

Being recognized as an accomplished teacher is personally satisfying and professionally uplifting as the administrators and other teachers in your school see you as one of the best of the best TEACHERS in the school. The time invested will sharpen your already good teaching for the rest of your career, benefiting all the students you will ever have.

### Yes, it's worth it.

*Sara Kelly Johns, library media specialist at Lake Placid Middle/High School, was one of the writers for the Library/ Media Standards for National Board Certification and, as such, she could not try to be certified for five years. She had decided to try for it if she wasn't elected as AASL President-Elect. She was elected! She'll look at it again in three years. Sara can be contacted at johns@northnet.org.*

Johns, S. K. (2006). It takes connections to be a NBCT! *Library Media Connection,* 25(2), 22-23.

# Now More Than Ever: Why National Board Certification in Library Media Is Vital

## By Peggy Milam

The last decade has ushered in dramatic changes to the responsibilities and workloads of school library media specialists. New technologies, online resources, automated circulation systems, and increasing amounts of patron databases to maintain have stretched the duties of school library media specialists to near breaking points in some districts. At the same time, severe budget cuts, rising costs of print materials, increased demands for technology resources, and personnel cuts have added additional stress to the job. With all the changes in the profession, school library media specialists who simply do their jobs day to day are pretty remarkable. Those who "shine" while doing their jobs are truly exceptional.

So, what practices signify "exceptionality" or "accomplishment" in the field? The answer is complex. In my book, *National Board Certification in Library Media: A Candidate's Journal* (Linworth Publishing, Inc., 2005), I wrote, "An accomplished media specialist is one who has not only kept up with the changes in the field, but has been a change agent and a role model for peers, particularly with integrating technology, information literacy, literature appreciation, ethics and access, and so on. And most importantly, an accomplished media specialist, while exemplifying exceptional practice, also makes a significant contribution to student achievement."

### Why Seek National Board Certification in Library Media?

You may ask, "What is National Board Certification anyway, and why would anyone want to pursue it?" I pondered the very same questions and I found some interesting answers. As I explained in the introduction to my book, "After twenty-two years of teaching, I had begun to wonder if I was truly making a difference in student achievement. As I listened to reports of budget cuts and job losses nationwide, I wondered what my next performance

review might say. I worried about the comments from my co-workers who grumbled that I didn't have papers to grade and parent conferences. I was beginning to lose satisfaction with my job and with my role as a vital member of our learning community."

As I considered my options, I noticed other media specialists who were making a difference in their profession. I read the results of national research studies that repeatedly showed media specialists were making a difference in student achievement, but no one in my district seemed to notice. I decided I needed to make a visible difference in my home school. I embarked on the greatest professional development experience of my life; I began to pursue National Board Certification in Library Media.

### What Is the Vision of the National Board?

The vision of the National Board for Professional Teaching Standards is to

"retain, reward and advance accomplished teachers through a system of advanced certification." I explained in my book that, "while state boards of education set the minimum standards for teachers to become certified in that state, the National Board had defined rigorous standards of professionalism for teachers, and has initiated a voluntary certification process to identify teachers whose practice exemplifies the National Board vision for accomplished teaching. National Board Certification is the highest degree of certification awarded nationwide to certified professionals with three or more years of experience who are accomplished in their field."

In most areas, it takes a bit longer to become a state certified school library media specialist than it does to become a certified teacher. So a state certified media specialist might wonder why anyone would want to spend a year or more working toward obtaining National

---

### What Does Research Say About National Board Certified Teachers?

According to recent research in Arizona, students of National Board Certified teachers score higher than other students in 35 out of 48 measures of student achievement on the SAT-9. See <http://epaa.asu.edu/eppa/v12n46> for a copy of the report. See also the University of Washington report at <http://www.nbpts.org/research/archive_3.cfm?id=158>, which indicates that the certification process does identify more successful teachers.

#### What You Can Expect as A National Board Candidate

*National Board Certification in Library Media: A Candidate's Journal* offers tips and explanations of the process of candidacy from start to finish. It clarifies the reason why it is a significant achievement. "The National Board Certification

process is unique in that it not only measures the knowledge teachers have about their field, but it also measures how effective they are at communicating that knowledge to their students. This assessment process is inherently complex and involves many examples of accomplished teaching from written essays, to videotapes, to student work samples, to responses to timed test questions. The idea of the National Board Certification process is to examine as many aspects of a teacher's practice as possible to get a broad picture of how a candidate measures up to standards for that field. Of course, teaching conditions and students vary from one region to another, so the sampling helps to level the playing field while still maintaining high and rigorous expectations."

---

## Current National Board Certified Library Media Specialists by State

| State | #of NBCTs as of 2004 | Lib. Media NBCTs as of 2004 |
| --- | --- | --- |
| North Carolina | 8280 | 278* |
| Florida | 6364 | 200 |
| California | 3080 | 17 |
| Ohio | 2374 | 20 |
| Georgia | 1780 | 79 |

North Carolina currently leads the nation in NBCTs in all certificate fields.

Board Certification. Besides the bonus checks and other perks of obtaining it, National Board Certification has a big payoff in clout. Recent research indicates that National Board Certified teachers do, in fact, make a significant difference in student achievement.

## Implications for Practicing School Library Media Specialists

Obtaining National Board Certification makes a powerful statement for the profession. It is a credential that proves media specialists know the principles of library and information studies and how to teach them to our students. It proves that we are leaders, learners, and instructional partners in our work. It verifies that we are committed to professional growth and ethics, equity, and diversity, and that we are making a difference every day in student achievement at our jobs.

## Is National Board Certification Right for You?

At the very least, the process requires candidates to closely examine their teaching practice and to reflect on their strengths and weaknesses. No candidate can complete the process without improving the content and quality of his or her daily practice. No candidate comes out of the process without growing both personally and professionally. Moreover, the process helps to develop practices that lead to accomplishment whether or not a candidate earns certification

immediately. As a result of my candidacy, I experienced a revolution in my career, becoming vocal, visible, and vociferous. I learned new practices that led to more powerful instruction such as thoroughly analyzing student work samples, collecting evidence to inform instruction, and reflecting on my practices with a goal of continuous improvement. I have had opportunities to speak professionally, to mentor others, to present at conferences, and to publish as a result of becoming National Board Certified.

## Benefits of Becoming National Board Certified in Library Media

The candidates who do achieve certification find there are many benefits beyond the initial exhilaration of having attained the required 275 points on the score report. Many districts offer their National Board Certified Teachers (NBCTs) a bonus check, and many states offer a salary supplement to NBCTs for the life of their certificate. Some states reimburse expenses occurred in obtaining certification, and the majority of states guarantee portability of licensing from state to state. As of this writing, legislation has been enacted in all 50 states and around 544 school districts to recognize and reward NBCTs.

More than 1000 school library media specialists have obtained National Board Certification since the credential was first offered in the field in 2001. The more certified library media specialists there are in the field, the greater the chance for us as a group to make our voices heard and our influence felt, particularly in this era of budget cuts and job shuffling. I highly recommend that state certified media specialists with three or more years of experience in the field seek National Board Certification. Obtaining certification allows us to make a powerful statement of advocacy for our credentials

and our importance in improving student achievement.

You may decide National Board Certification is not for you right now, but you can support others who decide to pursue it. At the very least, you might be interested in reading more about the process and what it can do for you and your career in library media. For more information, check out the list of resources below.

*Peggy Milam is a national board certified media specialist at Compton Elementary School in Powder Spring, Georgia.*

Milam, P. (2006). Now more than ever: Why National Board Certification in library media is vital. *Library Media Connection,* 25(2), 24-26.

# Mentoring the Next Generation of Library Media Specialists

## By Christine Meloni

Try to remember how you felt the first time you stood in front of your library media center classroom. Were you excited? Confident? Terrified? When I look back on my first year as a library media specialist, I cringe. I went straight from a public library setting to a school setting—without first serving an internship. I was nervous about teaching and unsure about many aspects of library media center management. The simplest task seemed daunting because I had no prior experience. I remember once feeling terribly inadequate because my aide had to show me the proper way to tape a plastic cover on a book. Like many elementary library media specialists, I felt isolated. I was the only library media specialist in my school and rarely had an opportunity to meet with the other library media specialists in my district. I would have benefited from knowing a veteran library media specialist who was willing to show me the ropes; someone to whom I could show my weaknesses. Even so, after many mistakes, I somehow survived my first year.

Today, years later, I find it satisfying to fill the role of that supportive library media specialist I so desperately needed as I was starting out. How do I do this? Every year I volunteer to be a cooperating teacher to a future library media specialist.

With the new state requirements, many library media specialist students will be required to complete an internship that is more like the traditional student-teaching program. To obtain certification, in addition to their coursework, they may have to complete over 300 hours in a library media center classroom setting. For many students, especially those from outside the field of education, success as a library media specialist is directly related to what is mastered during the internship service. Without the opportunity to work with a mentor who can be a teacher and coach, an ongoing struggle with the core issues of library

media center service may result. On the other hand, an intern will be forever benefited by a mentor who is enthusiastic and passionate about the craft of librarianship.

By becoming a cooperating teacher, you can help the next generation of library media specialists master the skills they will need to be successful. The first point to consider when deciding to become a mentor is the amount of time you have to spare. Mentoring will require you to share many prep and lunch periods, planning with your intern, so if you are currently renovating your library media center, now might not be the best time. In the course of a single semester, as

> By becoming a cooperating teacher, you can help the next generation of library media specialists master the skills they will need to be successful.

the intern progresses and accepts more responsibility, the mentoring process will go through three stages: instructor, coach, and finally, colleague. If you have the time and the interest, the following suggestions will help to ensure a positive experience for the mentor and the mentee.

## Mentor As Instructor

To build trust, you must show that you are genuinely concerned with the intern's feelings and professional growth. To ease the nerves of him or her on the first day, have lunch together in the library media center. By giving your intern a chance to share the goals and expectations of the internship, an essential bond will be formed that will, hopefully, produce a feeling of comfort in being able to ask any question and take risks.

A few simple things ensure that your intern will feel comfortable in

your school, as well as in your library media center. Although your intern will only be working in the library media center for one semester, provide some physical space—a drawer, a shelf—a place to organize personal things. Also, during the first week, take your intern on a tour of the school and point out important locations such as the teachers' lounge and the main office. Share information about your school dynamics: the school philosophy, safety procedures, and the school community. As your intern will eventually participate in collaborative projects with the staff, be sure to include an early introduction to the staff and the students.

Remember that this will be the first time your intern will take all the knowledge gained during graduate school and put it to practical use. In the first phase of the internship, the mentor's role is to instruct the intern on how the process of balancing the day—between running a library media center and teaching—actually happens. This is best done through modeling. During the first few weeks, your intern will observe how you structure your program, paying special attention to your teaching style and how you organize the library media center. Be aware of all the teaching moments. For example, when you are deleting a book from your shelf list, demonstrate the process and explain why it is done that way. Reading about managing a library media center differs from actually performing the operations, so don't assume that the intern already-knows how to do something.

Take the time to share little tricks of the trade. Even things that may seem too small to you—preparing for a substitute or putting covers on books—are important. By explaining the nuts and bolts of daily life as a library media specialist, you will foster your intern's readiness to take over a library media center.

During the first few weeks, I invite my interns to watch me teach and after each lesson we discuss what I did and why. I value the intern's opinions and always encourage suggestions on what may strengthen the lesson. The objective of having the intern observe many different types of lessons is exposure to a variety of teaching strategies. I also make it clear that there are many different ways to be effective and that what works well for me may not work as well for others.

## Mentor As Coach

During the second stage, your intern is now ready to accept more responsibility. Perhaps the biggest part of this is creating and implementing lessons. It is the mentor's role to guide the intern through this process. When your intern is ready to stand in front of the library media center classroom, I suggest beginning with co-teaching. For example, for a first grade lesson on safety, using the book *Officer Buckle and Gloria,* I greet the students and settle them down in the story section. My intern then introduces the theme of safety tips and reads the story to the students. After the story, I hand out paper stars while my intern explains to the students that they are each to write a safety tip on a star. After the writing activity, I lead the class as they transfer to book exchange.

By co-teaching, your intern knows that there is a supportive person right there who is going to jump in if something goes awry. After a few weeks, your intern is ready to teach almost all of the library media center lessons alone, and it is amazing to watch the development of personal style. When your intern begins to create lessons, you can provide assistance by sharing reflections on decisions and by always supplying positive feedback.

By the middle of the semester, most interns understand how to manage a library media center and are ready to take over many of the routine daily operations: teaching, collection development, and cataloging. For some of us, relinquishing responsibility may be difficult, but it is necessary to ensure the success of our intern. The mentor's role is to be a good coach—by being encouraging and positive that your intern will succeed, and by providing guidance when questions arise. At some point in the semester, your intern may become frustrated and feel overwhelmed. Your assurance that even the most veteran library media specialists have felt the same way can be given by sharing your success stories and the ways in which you overcame problems. These stories will build confidence and provide inspiration.

## Mentor As Colleague

As the semester enters the last few weeks, we reach the third stage—the intern metamorphoses from a trainee to a colleague—skills have been developed to successfully teach, maintain the library media center, and handle all library media specialist functions. Before your intern leaves your library media center in search of one of his or her own, be sure to give the assurance of your continuing support.

The greatest reward of mentoring is the building and maintaining of relationships, so I always encourage remaining in contact. I have also told all of my interns that I would be happy to provide a reference as they begin their job searches.

If you are now inspired to take a library media specialist student under your wing for the next semester, contact your local graduate library school and ask to have your contact information kept on file.

*Christine Meloni is a library media specialist at J. W. Dodd Middle School in Freeport, New York.*

Meloni, C. (2006). Mentoring the next generation of library media specialists. *Library Media Connection,* 24(4), 32-33.

# Where Do We Go Next?

## Introduction

To know where school library media centers are going in the future, it's always good to take a look back at where we've been. Since their inception, now over 100 years ago, school libraries have relied on standards to shape school library programs and on the leadership of individuals in the school library field to implement the standards. With each change in the school library field, standards have detailed the implementation of each new technology, new medium, new educational initiative, or new information skills issues. School library leaders have both smoothed the path to widespread acceptance of each change and have acted as leader-models for the school library programs and for the broader field of education.

And so it will probably always be. New technologies will always appear. Some will stay, evolve, and grow to be a mainstay of the school library program. Some, like filmloop projectors or Betamax videorecorders, will appear to be promising but will not stand the test of time. New educational initiatives will appear, loom large on the horizon, and melt away like the open schools that were supposed to encourage collaboration, but instead just encouraged creative ways to make walls.

It is easy to predict the past and say what should have been, what could have been, and what opportunities were missed. It is much harder to predict an unknown and unknowable future. We can identify some attributes of the current educational system that probably will stay with us for the foreseeable future. We can also spot some trends that have been with us always, and will probably not go away. Jo Ellen Priest Misakian starts off this section doing just that with her article looking at standards in the library media program.

One of the most powerful influences of the past several years is accountability. Accountability goes beyond the need to justify our existence to decision-makers in the library world. Instead, accountability is about program improvement, by providing opportunities for school library media programs to documents ways in which they impact on and improve the teaching and learning processes in schools, and to focus on areas in which they can increase their impact on student achievement. Dr. Ross J. Todd, Carl A. Harvey II, and Jody Howard and Su A. Eckhardt provide a balanced and thorough look at the issue of accountability in schools.

We also have to believe that technology in its many forms and formats will make even more of an impact on the library program, and that the most pervasive format will be virtual. Mary Alice Anderson starts off this section with a look at how technology impacts the role of the school library media specialist. The impact of specific technology is first detailed in Laura Brown's look at the possibilities of video streaming, then by Terence Cavanaugh's analysis of using e-books in the library program and Theresa Embrey's overview of handheld computing.

The educational arena can be a true battleground with a limited amount of turf as well as limited money, energy, and time. School librarians will most likely always have to battle for their place in the sun and also seek ways to strengthen alliances within the school community. Betsy Ruffin provides the transition between technology and leadership with her article on librarian technologists. Neil Krasnoff and Fitzgerald Georges continue that discussion with their articles in this arena.

We close this chapter with David Warlick's look into the future of school librarianship. Our evolving profession has never forgotten its past yet is not afraid to lead educational practice into the future.

# The Synergistic Attributes of Library Media Center Standards

## By Jo Ellen Priest Misakian

Chances are if you have had any substantive conversation concerning education lately, the word standards has been a large part of that dialogue. While every profession strives to maintain a certain degree of excellence using benchmarks as measurements, the education community seems to have taken it to another level. Standards drive pedagogy, curricula, and instructional interventions. Federal and state mandates attempt to make certain that specific methodologies are being used by schools to achieve predetermined student performance levels. Designing curricula around the standards, with clearly delineated strategies, expectations, and evaluative procedures, is thought to assure that growth in student achievement may be tracked. While this process can sometimes be nebulous, one thing is certain: clearly understanding what is involved in reaching a degree of excellence and determining when and if growth in student performance has been achieved is fundamental. The library media center community is not exempt from this process, nor should it be.

To remain a vital part of the educational system, library media center personnel must join with the rest of the community in understanding and using state content standards. Library media specialists must help teachers link state content standards to curriculum and encapsulate them fully into the library media center program. In addition, library media specialists must have a set of standards specific to the library media center program to which they adhere and stand ready to share with and defend to their school community. An effective library media center program will reflect standards of educational excellence based on benchmarks of quality.

## Library Media Centers and Standards

Library media center personnel have a variety of standards from which to draw direction and inspiration. The most significant philosophy and methodology for designing a vital library media center program rests within the pages of *Information Power: Building Partnerships for Learning* (ALA, 1998). The library media specialist profession is also guided by teacher education and library education state and national credentialing standards. Two organizations of special interest are the National Board for Professional Teaching Standards (NBPTS) and the National Council for the Accreditation of Teacher Education (NCATE). While national standards are extremely important and useful, state and local standards fit the needs of a particular

> *Recognizing and conforming to established criteria for excellence in school libraries will result in consistent, high-quality library media center service across and within our states.*

state or district. California has joined the list of state library associations providing excellent library media center standards. Other states with standards include Texas, Massachusetts, Illinois, Kansas, Oregon, Minnesota, Missouri, and Kentucky.

Despite—or perhaps because of—the fact that shrinking state dollars precipitated a dramatic decline in funding for library media center materials and a spate of staffing reductions, library media specialists in California recently developed a comprehensive set of standards and guidelines for improving library media centers across the state. Thanks to a generous grant from Greg Worrell, President of Scholastic Library Publishing, a copy was sent to every school superintendent and California School Library Association (CSLA) member in the state.

Scholastic's contribution not only helped the project along monetarily, but it also brought renewed spirit to the whole process. Their faith in the importance of this document helped drive the project forward. Information about the document (including an order form and sample pages) is available at <www.schoolibrary.org/pub/Standards_publication_order.htm>.

## Statewide Impact

*Standards and Guidelines for Strong School Libraries* (CSLA, 2004) has not been officially recognized by the state legislature or the state department of education, but it is still has a positive impact on library media center programs across the state. The document presents the educational community in California with comprehensive qualitative and quantitative measures for library media center programs. Administrators are able to quickly determine if their library media center is *Exemplary*, *Making Progress*, or *At-Risk*—in terms of the quantity and quality of personnel, the teaching of information literacy skills, number and quality of print and digital resources, current technology, and appropriate facilities. An extensive bibliography and supporting documentation point to appropriate research authenticating the standards and guidelines in the document.

This publication provides both direction and renewed hope to those managing library media centers in California at a time when the state library media centers have been disproportionately affected by the state budget crisis. Library media teachers (LMT)—a California professional designation—have used the document to share with their school communities a clear image of the type of library media center programs that should be available to their students.

LMTs throughout the state use the document to "educate" their school communities on the value of and requirements for maintaining a strong library media center program. Library media center personnel now have a complete set of tools with which to approach the decision makers in their districts. They have concrete and concise standards and guidelines for building an exemplary library media center program. Every aspect of the library media center program is described and defined: information literacy, staffing, facilities, print and digital resources, and technology, along with an extensive body of research references to back up the included criteria. The document can be used to examine the library media center program holistically or in segments. And that is just what is happening all over California.

## Holistically Speaking

The categories of *At-Risk, Making Progress,* and *Exemplary* allow for a quick assessment of the current library media center program. Examining library media center services in this light is an illuminating experience. Some school personnel are shocked to discover that their library media center does not even meet the *At-Risk* range in some or all categories. After the shock wears off, they begin to realize that they now have some definitive benchmarks upon which to build a decent library media center program. Instead of awkwardly moving along from year to year, often at the mercy of changing winds and lines of support, well-defined standards assist in the development of a plan that can map out a future for the library media center program.

Some LMTs are using the document as a point of reference covering the spectrum of library media center service and a baseline of excellence. Some are planning to add a certain number of resources or higher degrees of service each year in the journey toward the *Exemplary* category.

Mary Helen Fischer, a district library coordinator in the Buckeye Union School District, Shingle Springs, California, decided to present the whole document to her school board, but instead of trying to cover the entire document in one sitting, she wisely chose to present it in "bits and pieces." This knowledge-management

strategy increased understanding of each segment as the entire document was gradually explored. Fischer is not only sharing important information with her school board, she is also engaged in impressive advocacy tactics. Her success was affirmed when the board actually requested that she continue to include pieces of the standards in the weekly information packet they receive from the district.

Fischer says, "I am thrilled, to say the least, to have gotten such an enthusiastic, positive response to what I thought was just a new way of saying some of the same things I've been saying for years. That professional published document carries great authority with it and we must not underestimate its power."

> Instead of awkwardly moving along from year to year, often at the mercy of changing winds and lines of support, well-defined standards assist in the development of a plan that can map out a future for the library media center program.

## Information Literacy Skills

The document includes a complete K–12 continuum of library media center skills, furnishing library media center personnel, classroom teachers, parents, and administrators with a blueprint for determining what skills are introduced, reinforced, and mastered at what grade levels. Knowing what skills students should possess at a particular point in their educational journey may be intrinsic to most library media center personnel; however, for those who are not quite sure, it is wonderful to have them laid out in an easy-to-read grid. Even if one does not agree with the specifics, it becomes very easy to adapt the designation of skills to fit a school population.

Tom Kaun, an LMT in Southern Marin County, California, and his library media center colleagues, classroom teachers, and community members are using the document to develop

a scope and sequence of information literacy skills, based on the Standard's continuum of information literacy skills for grades K–14. Kaun is not only working within the K–12 framework, but has extended the *Standards and Guidelines for Strong School Libraries* sphere of influence to include the local community college. Representatives from these entities are working together to spread the word about the importance of students acquiring information literacy skills as they align and coordinate curriculum between the district and the local community college.

## Staffing

In just about every state, library media specialists are reeling from a budget crunch. Few states have a plentiful work force in the library media center. And yet, the kaleidoscope of duties and responsibilities in library media centers continues to increase. The *Standards* document helps explain to others what professional library media specialists are expected to do as part of their management and teaching duties in the library media center. The complete set of professional standards outlines responsibilities of library media center personnel in positions at the site, school district, and county offices of education. In addition, a section is included on what is expected of the paraprofessional library media center staff.

Lenn Schwartz, LMT for Firebaugh Unified School District, a small district in the San Joaquin Valley, California, sat down with his superintendent, Dr. Wayne Walters, to explore expectations of professional performance. Dr. Walters acknowledged the fact that Schwartz, as the lone library professional in the district, could not possibly meet the professional performance standards delineated in the document. Dr. Walters promptly asked Schwartz to develop a proposal to present to the school board requesting them to hire an additional LMT for the district. Dr. Walters states, "A good district library media program is essential to the success of a standards-based curriculum."

Susie Goodin, an LMT in Berkeley, California, reports that the Friends of the Berkeley Unified

School District Libraries used the document to create a staffing table, showing library media center staffing at below the *At-Risk* level. This was used as justification for proposing that a share of the property tax increase, presented to voters on the November ballot, be used for improving staffing in their library media centers. Following the success of the initiative, schools got 16 percent of the monies designated toward increased staffing. Goodin says, "People got it when they saw the figures in black and white!"

## Facilities

Detailing criteria for the physical space was an amazingly difficult undertaking. Many issues must be factored into the equation. Barriers include the actual space allotted to the facility, the money set aside for the building or renovation, and working with those in charge of the actual design. If we agree that form must follow function, then library media specialists must be included in the planning at the outset because no one understands the functions of a library media center better than those who work in it every day. Although the standards may supply specific suggestions for a structure of merit, they are meant only to be guidelines. The standards provide some worthy help and may be useful to architects who often do not understand the complexities involved in designing a library media center.

Vicki Rondeau, an LMT who oversees 11 library media centers in the Natomas Unified School District, Sacramento, California, articulates her take on the document:

*Whether you're constructing a new library or remodeling an older one, don't forget to use standards and guidelines. I took* [Standards and Guidelines for Strong School Libraries] *into a facilities meeting the other day to start work on another new library in our ever-growing district. It covered every aspect of library infrastructure with specific recommendations for space, shelving, resource areas, etc. The architects were very impressed!*

## Resources

How many books should a library media center provide for students? What role does technology play in formulating resource needs? What is available digitally? The benchmarks provided in the resource section give specific numbers for consideration. Some schools may have more than enough while others are struggling, but each school can adjust the recommendations to fit its particular need. For instance, a school could decide to increase the number of books by three to five per child the first year, another three to five the next year, and so on, maintaining a concerted effort to construct a set of resources to meet the requirements for their students. Understanding precisely what is involved in offering current, pertinent resources in all formats to students helps articulate necessities to others.

## Conclusion

Recognizing and conforming to established criteria for excellence in library media centers will result in consistent, high-quality library media center service across and within our states. Standards and guidelines provide a framework from which to build the type of library media center service students deserve. Developing a library media center plan with these documents in hand is straightforward and fruitful. Seek out your own or other state standards and use them along with national guidelines to build a quality library media center program—one that is designed to meet the needs and wishes of your specific school community.

*Jo Ellen Priest Misakian is director of the Library Media Teacher Credential and Master of Arts in Education with an emphasis in Library and Information Technology program at Fresno (California) Pacific University in Fresno. She is also the author of* The Essential School Library Glossary *(Linworth Publishing Inc., 2004).*

Misakian, J.E.P. (2006). The synergistic attributes of school library media center standards. *Library Media Connection, 24*(4), 22-24.

# School Libraries and Evidence: Seize the Day, Begin the Future

## By Dr. Ross J. Todd

"The hallmark of a school library in the 21st century is not its collections, its systems, its technology, its staffing, its buildings, BUT its actions and evidences that show that it makes a real difference to student learning, that it contributes in tangible and significant ways to the development of human understanding, meaning making and constructing knowledge." (Todd, 2001)

## Introduction

During my role as a school library educator, I have had a wonderful opportunity to speak to many school librarians around the world. No matter the educational setting, no matter the country, no matter the educational context, school librarians understand the importance of providing high quality information services to the school community. Our school library profession has a sense of common purpose and commitment that transcends national boundaries and cultural differences. One school librarian I spoke to recently from Australia expressed it so eloquently:

*"We employ our information management skills to manage information and knowledge across a whole spectrum of formats. We are at the forefront of taking information technology from a frightening specter to place it within the context of education in a controlled and meaningful way. We look at the curriculum needs, and work with teachers to plan their courses and lessons, then set about finding the best information in whatever format, including Web sites, and applying the most suitable information technology—from simple pathfinders on a Web site to highly complex Web quests. We then teach teachers and their classes how to use it. Schools and teachers are convinced that we know what we are doing because we use*

*every opportunity to be involved in curriculum planning and to sell our skills to the school community: on councils, meetings, inservices, assemblies, workshops. We use our Web sites to best effect for the school and to present our knowledge and information management to the school and the broader community. We monitor education and librarianship e-mail discussion lists and channel relevant e-mails to our colleagues. We publish good news about our libraries in every venue possible. We send our library staff to as many professional development sessions as possible."*

Several things struck me as I listened to this dynamic school librarian speak about her role. There was such urgency and passion, focus and commitment.

There is no question that the quality of the professional experience of school librarians is vitally important for the future and continuity of the profession. It is important to discuss these issues, and to work towards solutions.

But I was left with one burning question: So what? Why does all of this matter? What if all of this energy and all of this work never happened? What if it stopped happening now? Who would care? Who would notice? Who would lose out? From a perspective of having been involved with our profession and its research for well over two decades, the answers to these questions are very simple. The learners would be the losers. Learners as losers? It is a frightening thought. As I thought more about what that school librarian said, I saw clearly a focus on "doing," and indeed, some very important doings—collaboration,

curriculum support, professional development, information literacy, advocacy—all important dimensions of an effective school library. But what does this mean in terms of students "being" and "becoming"? How does an effective school library help them? How does it empower their learning in and out of school? What does an effective school library enable students to do and to become? What difference does an effective school library make to students and their learning? In my view, these questions are some of the most important questions facing school libraries today. It is a matter of outcomes. It is a matter of evidence.

Sometimes it is so easy to see the professional barriers, rather than the outcomes. As I travel around the world, I hear these barriers expressed so often in so many forums. Like a common set of purposes that drives our profession, these barriers too seem to be common, despite national boundaries and varied cultural contexts. They tend to center on fiscal deficits: budgets, resources, technology, and time; as well as value deficits: perceived lack of understanding of the nature and dimensions of the role; perceived lack of value, importance, and appreciation; negative perceptions of the role of school librarians by others; and perceived low status. There is no question that the quality of the professional experience of school librarians is vitally important for the future and continuity of the profession. It is important to discuss these issues, and to work towards solutions. There is no question about that. But I want to gently suggest that too often these barriers become the public face of the profession—an advocacy for redressing the fiscal and value deficits: those things we believe to be essential in providing effective information services to our school community. My view is that we need to move beyond this advocacy/sell/public relations approach to our future, and to focus on an evidence-based practice approach, and make this the public voice of the profession.

## Evidence: The Voice Of The Future

The strong voice of the profession has to tell the story of how an effective school library makes a difference to the learning outcomes of students. This is not just other school libraries, but YOUR school library as well. How does your school library make a difference to student learning outcomes? If your local newspaper phones you and says, "We want to do a story on your school library and how it really helps students learn," what would be your response? Could you quickly draw on a portfolio of actions and evidences to build your case? If your school board, in its efforts to distribute a meager budget amidst budget cuts, asked you to give a clear summary of how your school library has had an impact on the students in your school in order to help its deliberations, what would you say? And how would you know this? If your principal or superintendent asked you to provide an overview of the current research on school libraries and their impact on meeting curriculum standards, technology standards, on independent and lifelong learning, what would be your response? This is the mindset of evidence-based practice. Key stakeholders, educational policy makers, and funders sometimes do not convincingly see the links between what school librarians espouse and do on a day by day basis, and how that enables the learning outcomes of students. It is a question of evidence-based research and evidence-based practice.

## Evidence-Based Research and Evidence-Based Practice

Evidence-based research and evidence-based practice ask three things of each of us working in school libraries. First, it asks us to have a very clear and precise knowledge of and insight into the research of our profession that demonstrates the differences that an effective school library makes to the learning goals of the school. Second, it asks us to mesh that knowledge with our own wisdom and experience to build professional work practices that enable us to achieve significant student learning

outcomes. Third, it asks us to look at our own school communities and work towards providing the evidence of how our local school library makes a difference—it asks us to articulate clearly and unequivocally how our school library helps students learn. Sometimes the most convincing evidence comes from the local school, rather than from complex research undertaken in distant places. Principals, teachers, and parents want to hear of local successes and local improvement; they want to know how *their* students *in particular* are benefiting, more so than how other schools or districts are doing. Local outcomes matter. Local improvements are watched, listened to, and clearly factored into decisions relating to staffing and budgets. As part of the context of

> If your local newspaper phones you and says: "We want to do a story on your school library and how it really helps students learn," what would be your response? Could you quickly draw on a portfolio of actions and evidences to build your case?

evidence-based practice, Oberg (2001) makes this timely comment: "Many people, including educators, are suspicious of research and researchers. Research conducted closer to home is more likely to be considered and perhaps to be viewed as trustworthy."

## Evidence-Based Research

The school library profession today is actively engaged in research directed to understanding the multi-faceted way that the school library contributes to learning. This is a worldwide phenomenon. A recent study published by Clyde (2002, p. 61) shows that the U.S. led in the publication of research articles and papers from 1991-2000 (41.5%); countries such as Australia (17%), Canada (9%), the United Kingdom (6%), South Africa, and Israel also contributed to this endeavor.

Underpinning best practice in leading professions is the conscientious, explicit, and judicious use of current best research evidence in making decisions about the performance of the day by day role. It is about using research evidence, coupled with professional expertise and reasoning to implement learning interventions that are effective. And school librarians surely want their profession to be perceived as a leading profession in the education of young people for the information age.

Yet there is one disappointing twist to this idea. As a researcher, I know that communicating research findings effectively and developing effective practice on the basis of these findings is not an easy task. There is some recent research that shows that library professionals in the main do not read research (McClure & Bishop, 1989). Often the argument is raised that busy school librarians do not have time to read the research literature, or too quickly dismiss it because it is "out there" in a world "removed from practical reality." Such a stance both devalues the profession as a thinking and informed profession, and cuts off the profession from advances in knowledge which shape sound practice. A profession without reflective practitioners willing to learn about the advances in research in the field is a blinkered profession, one that is disconnected from best practice and best thinking, and one that, by default, often resorts to advocacy and position as a bid for survival. As part of their own ongoing professional development, it is important that school librarians continue to engage with this research as it provides a rich understanding of the dynamics of the learning process when students engage with information sources, as well as practical insights into how local evidence might be gathered, analyzed, and utilized to position the school library as central to the learning process. In a recent study published in *School Library Journal* (Lau, 2002, p.53) which explored principal's perceptions of school librarians, it was found that only 37% of principals said that the school librarian made them familiar with current research of library programs and student achievement, and only 35% of principals were made familiar with current research on reading development. It seems that there is an opening here for not just engaging with the research, but actively sharing the findings. *Carpe Diem.*

Of course, there is a clear message here as well for researchers generating evidence-based research. Those of us undertaking such research have a major responsibility to present findings in ways that enable and empower practice, and there is some research evidence to suggest that this may not be done as effectively as it could be. Turner's New Zealand study (2002) found that applied research that seeks to resolve operational concerns is most widely used; that research is not consulted because it is perceived to inadequately address the real concerns of practice; or that it is not presented in ways that foster understanding and application. One of the challenges that exists is the disparate spread of this research, and the need to analyze and synthesize this research into meaningful generalizations with practical utility, and librarians, as the information literate experts (and presumably with information literacy competencies centering on the ability to analyze, organize, synthesize, and evaluate information, and especially the information of their discipline) can surely play a central role here, bringing insights as the reflective practitioners to the research and its outcomes for practice.

## A Look at Some of the International Research

While the research agenda in relation to school libraries has taken shape only within the last 20 or 30 years, a number of summaries and syntheses of this research have been published (Loertscher & Woolls, 2002; Callison, 2001; Haycock, 1992, 1994; Oberg, 2001a, b). Within this corpus of research, Callison (2001) identifies important themes, such as instructional role, instructional methodologies, intellectual freedom, information search process, students' use of online technologies, program evaluation, and student achievement. Clyde (2002, p. 66) identifies growth from 1991-2000 in the focus on national surveys, information literacy, information technology, principal support, and reading promotion.

Some of the most prominent work comes from the U.S., and hopefully is well known to us all. The statewide studies undertaken by Keith Curry Lance and colleagues have involved hundreds of primary and secondary schools, and include: Colorado I (1993), Alaska (1999), Colorado II (2000), Pennsylvania (2000), New Mexico (2001), Oregon (2001), and Texas (2001). A similar study has been undertaken by Baughman (2000) in Massachusetts. These important studies have sought to empirically establish the relationship of school library programs to student achievement, and support several common findings. These include: professionally trained school librarians do make a difference that affects students' performance on achievement tests; in order for school librarians to make this difference, the support of the principals and teachers is essential, as well as the availability of support staff who can free the librarians from routine tasks to undertake their curriculum role; school librarians have a dual instructional role of teaching students in facilitating the development of information literacy skills necessary for success in all content areas and as inservice trainers of teachers enabling them to keep abreast of the latest information resources and networked information technology services within and beyond the school library. These are very significant outcomes, and hopefully they should motivate and inspire school librarians to pursue their instructional role, or at least to question and reflect on their own practices if they do not include this strong instructional role.

The longitudinal research of Carol Kuhlthau (1991, 1993, 1994, 1999) provides some of the fundamental building blocks for the collaborative instructional role of the school librarian centering on information literacy development. This research provides evidence of the nature and dynamics of inquiry-based learning centering on the information search process, and the nature of information literacy pedagogy. With a strong focus on knowledge construction through effective engagement with a variety of information sources and formats, Kuhlthau's research establishes the cognitive, behavioral, and affective dimensions of the search process. Her Information Search Process (ISP), found to occur in seven stages: Initiation, Selection, Exploration, Formulation, Collection, Presentation, and Assessment, also provides a framework for gathering evidence on the learning journey of students as they progress from the time of the initiation of their research task to the time they complete it and reflect on its outcomes.

## Scotland Also Leads the Way

Some very rich research on the impact of school libraries and learning is being undertaken by the Council for Museums, Archives, and Libraries in Scotland. Leading this research has been Professor Dorothy Williams of the Robert Gordon University in Aberdeen, Scotland. The research was conducted in secondary schools in Scotland between August 1999 and February 2001, and involved focus groups with teachers and students in selected schools across Scotland. Both groups shared a common perspective that the school library can contribute to learning. The collective perceptions of the impact of the school library were: the acquisition of information and wider general knowledge; skills development in the areas of finding and using information, computer technology skills, and reading skills; higher achievement in school work; development of a study and reading habit that encouraged independent learning; the ability to use these skills confidently and independently and the ability to transfer these skills across the curriculum and beyond school; and the development of interpersonal and social skills, including working collaboratively (Williams & Wavell, 2001, p. i).

On the basis of these areas of impact, the study also generated impacts in terms of Motivation, Progression, Independence, and

> *We need to move beyond this advocacy/sell/public relations approach to our future, and to focus on an evidence-based practice approach, and make this the public voice of the profession.*

## Learning Outcome Indicators

| Outcome | Indicators |
|---|---|
| Motivation: student enjoyment and participation and absorption in the set tasks | Verbal and written expressions of enthusiasm by students<br>Student willingness to participate in the activity set<br>Student appreciation and absorption in the task<br>Willingness of students to continue their work by returning to the library, or at home<br>A change in attitude towards work over a period of time |
| Progression: an awareness of or ability to use specific skills associated with finding information and sometimes the use and presentation of information | Knowledge of and success in applying specific information skills related to finding, using, and presenting information<br>The use of new knowledge in work or discussion of new knowledge<br>Personal achievement or quality of work<br>The ability to apply skills or knowledge to a new situation |
| Independence: where students appeared to have mastered a skill and were seen to have the confidence and competence to proceed and progress unaided, either in or out of class sessions | The ability and confidence to continue and progress with a task unaided<br>Awareness of the need for help and the confidence to ask for it<br>Use of initiative<br>Increased self-esteem |
| Interaction: where discussion and interaction took place--with peers and teachers | Discussions with others about the task<br>Peer cooperation<br>Ability to mix with other groups<br>Use of appropriate behavior |

(Williams & Wavell, 2001, p. ii-iii)

Interaction. The table above shows some of the indicators of learning outcomes identified in this study.

One of the important contributions of this study is approaches to evidence-based practice. Evidence-based practice involves critically analyzing the accumulated data on the basis of indicators, and deriving statements about student learning outcomes. What is important is that such evidence is cumulated, analyzed, and synthesized so that a learning outcomes profile of students engaging in library learning initiatives can be constructed. In the Scotland study, the school librarians interviewed were aware of what they were trying to achieve, but were not sure whether their objectives were being met. Their study identifies some potentially useful tools for school librarians to monitor the impact on learning. These include: student observations of their activities and learning in the school library; discussion with and questioning of students about their work during and at the end of their activities; analysis of submitted work to identify learning gains; discussion with other members of the teaching staff about work, attitudes, and related incidents; and examination of reader records.

## Australian Research

There is also a considerable amount of smaller research studies that examine more closely the many different dimensions of the relationship between student learning outcomes and school library programs. One of Australia's journals, *Scan*, has regularly published research on the impact of school library programs since 1996. An analysis of some of these papers (Todd, Lamb & McNicholas, 1993; Todd, 1995; Jones, 1996; Moore, 1996; Hawkes, 1997; Grant, 1998; Lewis, 1999; Gordon, 2000; Maxwell, 2000; Rich, 1999) suggests similar patterns to the findings in the U.S. and elsewhere.

- A process inquiry approach, focusing on the systematic and explicit development of students' abilities to connect with, interact with, and utilize information to construct personal understanding results in improved performance in terms of personal mastery of content. This is shown in examination and assignment grades, and through the mastery of a wide range of particular information skills;

- Successful information literacy programs are ones that set clear expectations and manageable objectives, establish realistic timelines, and provide opportunities for students to reflect on their successes and failures with finding and using information;

- The systematic and explicit development of students' abilities to connect with, interact with, and utilize information to construct personal understanding results in:

more positive attitudes to learning; increased active engagement in the learning environment; and more positive perceptions of students themselves as active, constructive learners;

- When students master a range of information processes—technical, critical, evaluative—they are empowered to learn for themselves; there is a strong relationship between an effective school library and personal agency;

- Active reading programs encouraged by the school library can foster higher levels of reading, comprehension, vocabulary development, and language skills;

- When there is access to diverse reading materials, more reading is done and literacy development is fostered.

Some research currently under way in Australia also focuses on the strategies and processes that school librarians might use to document their school library's contribution to learning. The goal here is to be able to provide rich, diverse, and convincing evidence that demonstrates that the library is a vital part of the learning fabric of the school. In our climate of uncertainty, particularly fiscal and staffing uncertainty, this must be a high priority. Data has been collected from 39 school librarians in which they have identified a range of strategies and processes that they use to document the contribution of their school library to student learning outcomes. These center around:

- **Assessment tasks:** not just assessing student work, but analyzing the output of students' products more thoughtfully to identify learning outcomes, in terms of new knowledge gained; evidence of skills application, evidence of reflection, and use of a range of information sources;

- **Feedback tasks:** collecting evidence of gains in knowledge and skills through simple checklist strategies where students indicate their perceived levels of skills and viewpoints before and after learning tasks—so that improvements can be specified. Even getting students to take a few minutes to record the most important things

they have learned through the library classes will provide rich insights;

- **Rubric measures:** where students are first scaled according to a set of criteria that clearly defines what the range of acceptable to unacceptable performances and information products looks like, and then where the school librarians analyze and synthesize this evidence to create a set of statements about student learning through the particular activity;

- **Interview measures:** regularly setting up informal discussion and review activities where students provide some input on how they have engaged with their learning, the processes and skills they have learned, and the benefits they see in relation to their classes and beyond;

- **More formal school surveys:** this can be any shape or form, and does not need to be a major research study, but solicits feedback on the learnings that are taking place. Creating a simple feedback checklist that the students can submit online at the end of their library-based units would cumulate a lot of benefits;

- **Portfolios:** with students' permission, you may wish to build up a portfolio of examples of outstanding work that shows mastery of information literacy skills;

- **Using available school data:** taking the time to thoughtfully review your schools' national, state, school, or grade-wide testing program results, as sometimes it is possible to establish how actual classes have performed, and correlate these with information skills or reading programs conducted by the library;

- **Undertaking small action research projects:** this is where a learning problem is identified, such as low motivation for reading, plagiarism, weaknesses in information analysis, World Wide Web use, and a cycle of collaborative planning, acting, evaluating, and reflecting is implemented to address it. This is a structured, focused way of getting feedback on learning gains.

- **Seize the Day.** The poet Michael Cibenko seemed to understand this. He wrote: "One problem with gazing too frequently into the past is that we

may turn around to find that the future has run out on us." Working with the evidence-base of our profession that research provides us, and using this to shape and inform our practice is part of building a strong future. Also part of building a strong future is providing the evidence in our schools and districts that our school libraries make rich and transformative contributions to the learning and lives of our students. Then the future will continue to smile on us.

---

*Dr Ross J. Todd is Associate Professor, School of Communication, Information, and Library Studies at Rutgers, The State University of New Jersey.*

## References

Baughman, J. (2000, October). *School libraries and MCAS Scores.* Paper presented at a symposium sponsored by the Graduate School of Library and Information Science, Simmons College, Boston, MA. Retrieved April 14, 2003, from http://artemis.simmons. edu/~baughman/mcas-school-libraries/Baughman%20Paper.pdf

Callison, D. (2001) The Twentieth-Century school library media research record. In A. Kent & C. Hall (Eds.), *Encyclopedia of Library and Information Science* (Vol. 71, Supplement 34, pp. 339-369). New York: Marcel Dekker.

Clyde, L. (2002). Developing the knowledge base of the profession: Research in school librarianship. In: D. Singh et al (Eds.), *School libraries for a knowledge society. Proceedings of the 31st Annual Conference of the International Association of School Librarianship and the Sixth International Forum on Research in School Librarianship* (pp. 55-75). Seattle: International Association of School Librarianship.

Gordon, C. (2000). Putting the learner in charge: Are information literacy skills enough? *Scan, 19*(1), 32-39.

Grant, V. (1998). Information skills and their impact on learning: A New Zealand study. *Scan, 17*(2), 50-54.

Hawkes, J. (1997). Views from the top: the information skills process and senior students. *Scan, 16*(3), 47-52.

Haycock, K. (1992). What works: Research about teaching and learning through the school's library resource center. Seattle, WA: Rockland Press.

Haycock, K. (1994). Research in teacher-librarianship and the institutionalization of change. *School Library Media Quarterly 23*, 227-233.

Jones, E. (1996). The value of research assignments. *Scan, 15*(3), 45-48.

Kuhlthau, C. (1991). Inside the search process: information seeking from the user's perspective. *Journal of the American Society of Information Science, 42*(5), 361-371.

Kuhlthau, C. (1999). Student learning in the library: What Library Power librarians say. *School Libraries World Wide, 5*(2), 80-96.

Kuhlthau, C. (1993). *Seeking meaning: a process approach to library and information services.* Norwood, NJ: Ablex.

Kuhlthau, C. (1994). *Teaching the library research process: A step-by-step program for secondary school students.* Metuchen, NJ: Scarecrow Press.

Kuhlthau, C. (1999). Accommodating the User's Information Search Process: Challenges for Information Retrieval System Designers. *Bulletin of the American Society for Information, 25*(3), 12-16.

Lance, K. (2001). *Proof of the power: Recent research on the impact of school library media programs on the academic achievement of U.S. public school students.* ERIC Digest. Syracuse, N.Y.: ERIC Clearinghouse on Information & Technology.(ERIC Document Reproduction Service No. EDO-IR-2001-05)

Lance, K., Hamilton-Pennell, C., & Rodney, M. (2000). *How school librarians help kids achieve standards.* Castle Rock, CO: Hi Willow Research and Publishing.

Lance, K., Hamilton-Pennell, C., & Rodney, M. (1999). *Information empowered: the school librarian as an agent of academic achievement in Alaska schools.* Anchorage, AL: Alaska State Library. Retrieved April 14, 2003, from http://www.educ.state.ak.us/lam/library/dev/infoemp.html

Lance, K., Rodney, M., & Hamilton-Pennell, C. (2000). *Measuring up to standards: The impact of school library programs and information literacy in Pennsylvania schools.* Harrisburg, PA: Pennsylvania Department of Education's Office of Commonwealth Libraries.

Lau, D. (2002). What does your boss think about you? *School Library Journal*, September, 52-55

Lewis, E. (1999). Science instruction and information literacy: Information is power. *Scan, 18*(1), 49-53.

Loertscher, D. & Woolls, B. (2002). *Information literacy research: a review of the research: a guide for practitioners and researchers.* 2nd ed. Castle Rock, CO: Hi Willow Research and Publishing, 2002.

McLure, C. & Bishop, A. (1989) The status of research in Library and Information Science. *College & Research Libraries, 40*, 127-143.

Maxwell, E. (2000). Integrating information skills and exposition texts into the Year 7 science program. *Scan, 19*(2), 27-31.

Moore, P. (1996). Information literacy: The importance of questions. *Scan, 15*(1), 43-46.

Oberg, D. (2001a). Demonstrating that school libraries improve student achievement. *Access, 15*(1), 15-17.

Oberg, D. (2001b). Research indicating school libraries improve student achievement. *Access, 15*(2), 11-14.

Rich, W. (1999). Enhancing the participation and achievement of girls in school science. *Scan, 18*(2), 46-50.

Todd, R. (2002). Evidence based practice II: Getting into the action. *Scan, 21*(2), 2002, 34-41.

Todd, R. J. (2001). *Transitions for preferred futures of school libraries: knowledge space, not information place; connections, not collections; actions, not positions; evidence, not advocacy.* Keynote address: International Association of School Libraries (IASL) Conference, Auckland, New Zealand. Keynote paper, IASL conference 2001 virtual session. Retrieved April 14, 2003, from http://www.iasl-slo.org/virtualpaper2001.html

Todd, R., Lamb, L., & McNicholas, C. (1993). Information skills and learning: some research findings. *Access, 7*(1), 14-16.

Turner, K. (2002). *Do information professionals use research published in LIS journals?* Paper presented at the 68th IFLA Council and General Conference August 18-24, Glasgow, Scotland. Retrieved April 14, 2003 from http://www.ifla.org/ IV/ ifla68/ papers/ 009-118e.pdf

Williams, D. & Wavell, C. (2001). *The impact of the school library resource center on learning: a report on research conducted for Resource: The Council for Museums, Archives and Libraries.* (Library and Information Commission Research Report 112). Aberdeen, Scotland: The Robert Gordon University.

Todd, R.J. (2003). School libraries & evidence: Seize the day, begin the future. *Library Media Connection, 22*(1), 12-18.

# Impacting School Improvement

## By Carl A. Harvey II

Across the country, school improvement plans and school improvement committees are the guiding forces in our schools. As school improvement plans are created, revised, and evaluated, library media specialists have an opportunity to demonstrate how they can play a critical part in the team that strives to increase student achievement in their building. Administrators are focused on increasing student achievement with less funding. If library media center programs are not seen as part of the solution, it will be easy for them to be eliminated.

The goals and strategies in the school improvement plan are the responsibility of every teacher in the building to execute in his or her classroom—including the library media specialist. The subject or grade level does not matter because the school improvement plan provides a centralized focus on what areas need to be improved. Library media specialists should not only be aware of the school improvement plan, but should also be part of the development, implementation, and evaluation. By being an active participant in the process, the library media specialist articulates how the library media center program can support and enhance the school improvement plan.

### The School Improvement Committee

At a minimum, the library media specialist should be a member of the school improvement committee. Most schools have teachers, administrators, parents, and community members serving on the team. The library media specialist is especially positioned to be a valuable voice at the table, since he or she works with every teacher in the building and provides resources and instruction at all grade levels to help meet curriculum and standards. Too often, committee members get wrapped up in their own specific grade level or subject area. In contrast, the library media specialist has a global perspective and is aware of issues and concerns that affect the whole school.

Schools differ on how the school improvement team is formed. The members may come from principal appointments, or perhaps the teachers' union is responsible for selecting the committee members. In all instances, the library media specialist should clamor to be first in line to volunteer. The role a library media specialist plays on the school improvement team can vary. Possibilities include data collection and analysis, technology integration, professional development, or chair. The talents and strengths of the library media specialist will dictate what role he or she plays on the team, but the important thing is that the library media specialist is part of the process.

Data collection and analysis is the heart of the school improvement plan. Data determines areas that need improvement, instructional strategies to be used, and provides documentation in determining if the strategies worked or failed. Collecting and organizing data is not always a simple task. The library media specialist who is skilled in organizing information can work to develop spreadsheets and data collection tools to help make the process easier. Library media specialists can also use their information-seeking and information-gathering skills to find research to help make informed decisions on what instructional strategies to implement.

Most school improvement plans must also demonstrate how technology can help reach the goal. Library media specialists, who are catalysts for technology integration in their schools, should be guiding and aiding in brainstorming ideas of how technology can help meet the school improvement goals. In this area, an opportunity exists for library media specialists to ensure information literacy strategies are included in the plan.

The school improvement plan provides direction for professional development. Library media specialists, especially those who attend professional development meetings in their field, can be especially adept at finding people to lead professional development seminars that will help further the school improvement plan's objectives. A library media specialist's knowledge of the staff and curriculum make him or her attuned to the needs of the building. The library media specialist's role as a teacher also makes him or her a prime candidate to provide training to teachers as well.

One of the goals of the library media specialist is to be seen as an instructional leader in the building. By working with every teacher and administrator, library media specialists build trusting relationships. This level of trust is crucial for successful collaborative projects and activities. Any library media specialist who has built these positive relationships of respect and trust will be recognized by administrators as an effective leader who can guide the staff through the school improvement process.

### The School Improvement Plan

The school improvement plan focuses on areas where a school needs to make improvement. School improvement plans should contain goals and data to support those goals, instructional strategies for meeting the goals and data to support those strategies, methods of evaluation, a technology component, and a professional development component.

Most goals will fall into two main areas: literacy (reading and writing) and mathematics. School improvement dictates that the goals will vary as individual schools pinpoint specific areas that need improvement. Ideally, as the plan is developed, the library media specialist will have an opportunity to introduce instructional strategies for consideration. For each goal the school improvement team adopts, the library media specialist should develop specific instructional strategies that the library media center program can do to help the students reach their mark. Examples of possible library media center strategies for literacy and math are provided in Tables 1.1 and 1.2.

**Table 1.1 Examples of Literacy Library Media Center Strategies**

| |
|---|
| Use of an incentive program to support reading |
| Use of audiobooks and other library media center resources |
| Use of appropriate Internet resources |
| Collaboration with the library media specialist for activities and lessons |
| Use of Library Catalog/ILL to find materials that correlate to Indiana Academic Standards (e.g., multiple copies of books needed for literature circles) |
| Use of booktalks to promote a variety of authors, genres, and new books |
| Use and promotion of resources in the Parent Collection |

**Table 1.2 Examples of Mathematics Library Media Center Strategies**

| |
|---|
| Collaboration with the library media specialist for activities and lessons |
| Use of Library Catalog/ILL to find materials that correlate to Indiana's Academic Standards |
| Use of library media center resources such as math games |
| Use of appropriate Internet resources |

With the prevalence of technology in education, school improvement plans contain specific ways that technology will be used to help meet a goal. As mentioned earlier, this is a prime location for the library media specialist to include information literacy strategies in the actual plan. The library media specialist should be part of developing the technology strategies and can help guide the group to broaden their ideas of media and technology strategies that include library media center strategies.

However, if that is not successful, library media specialists should still be ready to take the plan and make a list of instructional strategies. Even if inclusion in the official plan is not possible, library media specialists should share the list of library media center strategies with administrators and teachers. Make it clear how the library media center program can play an important part in the school improvement process. Collect data on the strategies suggested and provide reports to the administration. Let them know what is working and what is not working. Be flexible and make adjustments as necessary.

## Why Should the Library Media Specialist Be Involved?

We all have plenty to do. So, why does the library media specialist want to be involved in one more thing—school improvement planning? The answer is simple. Library media specialists are not *needed* if they don't play a part in the vision of how to improve the school.

In my district, four of the six elementary schools have had the library media specialists as one of their school improvement chairs. Each building has specific library media center–related strategies to help reach the goals set out in their plan. In addition, all the library media specialists meet and share ideas and projects centered on our school improvement plan. Last, but certainly not least, each library media specialist has taken on added responsibilities—whether it is leading professional development in writing, or helping create a resource room of leveled books for teachers to use in guided reading. Some of these roles might be seen by some as being beyond the responsibilities of a library media specialist. However, participation demonstrates commitment on the part of library media specialists to the school improvement plan and shows how we can play a part in the school improvement process.

The school improvement plan can be a justification for staffing, funding, scheduling, and many other elements important to a quality library media center program. If the library media specialist demonstrates that having support staff, funds for materials, and time to collaborate has an impact on school improvement, he or she has a stronger position when discussing with administrators the need to increase or add these items. A library media specialist needs to take the initiative in sharing how he or she can help school improvement. Often library media specialists are perceived as being "whiny" when they say, "I need more money for books. I need more staff." Administrators are far more likely to listen if a library media specialist states, "I need additional funds to provide books to support our goal of increasing the recreational reading of our students."

It is vital to the survival of the library media program that administrators have no doubt the program is an essential part in reaching the school improvement goals. With every decision, an administrator's focus has to be on school improvement. As administrators look at staffing, material budgets, facilities, technology, and staff, they must be certain they are helping student achievement. By being proactive and a part of the school improvement process (whether administrators realize we need to be there or not), library media specialists *can* have an impact.

### Resources

NCTM: Mathematic Standards <http://nctm.org/standards/>

US Department of Education: NCLB Legislation and Guidance <www.ed.gov/policy/landing.jhtml>

NCTE and IRA: Standards for the English Language Arts <www.ncte.org/about/over/ standards/110846.htm>

American Association of School Libraries: *Your School Library Media Program and No Child Left Behind* <www.ala.org/ala/aasl/aaslissues/n clb/nclb.htm>.

*Carl A. Harvey II is the library media specialist at North Elementary School in Noblesville, Indiana and is co-author, with Marge Cox and Susan E. Page, of* The School Library Media Specialist and the Writing Process *(Linworth Publishing, Inc. 2007).*

Harvey, C.A. (2006). Impacting school improvement. *Library Media Connection, 24*(6), 20-21.

# Why Action Research?
# The Leadership Role of the Library Media Specialist

## By Jody K. Howard and Su A. Eckhardt

Being a library media specialist is not for the fainthearted! The role is defined in *Information Power: Building Partnerships for Learning* (AASL & AECT, 1998) as encompassing the areas of learning and teaching, information access, and program administration. The leadership role that is embedded in the job is often neglected. *Information Power* encourages library media specialists to be members of the leadership team, organize learning opportunities for members of the learning community, develop curriculum, and work for the advancement of the profession through holding offices in professional organizations. What a job! All of these tasks assume that the library media specialists are leaders and have leadership skills. But leadership is intangible. Warren Bennis and Burt Nanus (2003) indicate that leadership is like love . . . everyone knows it exists but people have trouble defining it. Our responsibility as library media specialists is to develop our leadership skills so the members of the learning community will recognize us as leaders. This recognition will assist us in developing our library media center program and the school program, which both enhance the achievement level of our students. There has never been a doubt; *this* is our job.

In today's world of data-driven decision making, the library media specialist must develop the skills to work with his or her staff in using data for program improvement. Understanding the concept and process of action research will prepare the library media specialist to take a leadership role in improving both the library media center and the entire school program.

Action research is the process of reflective problem solving conducted at the school level. This process allows us to identify an issue we want to study to determine if we can change our process or procedures to improve our program. Action research leads to program improvement and increased academic achievement for our students. Daily we are faced with situations that need our attention. These situations can be "fixed" through action research. This research applies to each individual school setting for the improvement of the students in that learning community.

After reflecting on what improvements can be made to strengthen a program, a process is developed to collect data to determine what changes need to be implemented. This research is not like traditional state and national research; action research only applies to the site where the research is being conducted. The results of action research do not need to be *adapted* to your

> Our responsibility as library media specialists is to develop our leadership skills so the members of the learning community will recognize us as leaders.

school; they are *about* your school.

The action research method of problem solving is a continuous process, a spiral that lets the library media specialist reflect on a problem, analyze the problem through the collection of data, implement an improvement to that problem, and then begin the process all over again—reflect, analyze, and implement (see Figure 1). Using these three processes, the library media specialist will be constantly improving his or her program. Action research can be used for improving the library media center program or analyzing a problem affecting any area of the school.

The process of action research can be accomplished in seven easy steps.

### 1. Determine a topic and develop specific questions.

Having reflected on the effectiveness of a library media center program, the library media specialist probably already knows what area he or she needs to explore. Elementary school library media specialists may want to look at integration of information literacy and see how they can increase collaboration with classroom teachers or move toward a flexible library media center schedule instead of a fixed one. One possible problem in high school library media centers is the student use of the library media center during lunch periods. In some instances the library media center becomes more of a commons area, rather than an academic area.

The topic you choose should be one where you have the authority to affect any changes if your research shows that changes are necessary. For example, if you look at a staffing issue in the library media center and the research results show that an additional library media specialist or another paraprofessional is needed to impact the achievement level of the students and you do not have authority over the staffing of the school, then your research may have been for naught. In other words, don't spend time spinning your wheels on something you cannot change.

The process of action research is very effective if conducted in a collaborative manner. The library media center program is the heart of the school; as the library media specialist looks at changes that will improve the program, he or she should work with students and other members of the staff who will be impacted by the changes. Working collaboratively with members of the learning community will enable the library media specialist to analyze the problem, narrow the issue, and develop a research question that can be used to conduct the research. Working collaboratively in this role will also help the other staff members see you, the library media specialist, in a leadership role.

## 2. Review the literature.

Once your research question is determined, it is a good idea to look at the professional literature to see if anyone else has conducted research on a similar problem. A review of the professional literature will assist in finding related research that gives some background on the topic and helps narrow the research question.

## 3. Look at the learning community environment.

Before beginning the actual data collection, the library media specialist and the action research team should review the makeup of the learning environment: the school community, the school structure, and the library media center program. Reflecting on these three components helps the team become aware of any background information needed as they begin the project. If the project is explaining how to best communicate with ESL students, then data on the number of students this impacts would be relevant. If the project is evaluating a school-wide program, it would be helpful to understand the dynamics of the staff and the effectiveness of the principal's leadership. If the project is analyzing an aspect of the library media center program, then all members of the research team need to understand the current library media center program; this is a great way for others to understand more about what you actually do!

## 4. Collect the data.

The next step in the action research process is collecting the actual data. The most common data collection tools include questionnaires or surveys, interviews, observations, and archival information from the library media center or school records. Each of these tools has good and bad points. The library media specialist needs to determine which tools will be effective in collecting the necessary data.

Questionnaires and surveys provide a significant amount of information in a short time span since the survey can be distributed quickly to a large number of respondents. If the questionnaires are anonymous, then the respondents will be comfortable expressing their ideas. Unfortunately, using a questionnaire

does not allow for any follow-up or clarification of the questions. Interviews, on the other hand, require a significant amount of time and coordination of schedules to be conducted. The element of anonymity is lost; the interviewees may not be as comfortable expressing their ideas in a face-to-face setting. Interviews allow the library media specialist to ask follow-up questions and clarify items mentioned during the interview. Observations provide a good assessment as to what is occurring at a definite time period, but the results may be subjective. Archival data, such as student test scores or statistics, can be used effectively if it will support your research question. If your timeline to collect data is limited, we suggest using surveys. Electronic surveys, such as Zoomerang® or SurveyMonkey.com, are effective and easy to use.

> Using this method of reflective problem solving will illustrate that the library media specialist is truly a leader. This library media specialist is able to conduct his or her own research for the improvement of the library media center and can lead others through the process of program improvement.

## 5. Check for validity and reliability.

When the library media specialist designs the research study, he or she must triangulate the data. Simply put, this means the researcher uses three different data collection methods to answer the research question. Triangulation of data supports the research project's validity (truthfulness of the data collected) and reliability (accuracy of the data). Educators are familiar with the concept of reliability through the standardized tests they have administered to their students. The testing conditions must be the same for all groups taking the test if the results are to be reliable. This concept is also true with the collection of action research data. If the researcher

is using observation as a data collection tool, then he or she must account for the items being observed. The terms must be defined so that the researcher will know what "engaged in research" looks like and assure the reliability of the data collected.

## 6. Organize and interpret the data.

After the library media specialist has collected the data, the fun begins! The researcher should organize the data that has been collected from all three data sources and see what conclusions can be made. If the researcher finds the same answer to the question in three different ways through the triangulation, then a clear direction for program improvement can be determined.

## 7. Implement the changes.

Now the time has come for the library media specialist to determine what plan can be implemented to improve his or her program based on the data collected. The researcher should share this data with his or her staff to brainstorm the method of implementing the necessary changes. For example, let us revisit the circumstances of a high school library media center being used as a commons area instead of an academic location during the lunch periods. The library media specialist conducts his or her research through interviews with specific students and teachers, administers surveys to students in the library media center during the lunch periods, and conducts observations of the students using the library media center during the lunch periods. The data shows that the library media center is being misused during the lunch periods and both teachers and students are unhappy with this situation. The library media specialist shares the results with his or her advisory team and, through their brainstorming, they decide to implement a "pass" system to the library media center during the lunch periods. This system will allow the students to come to the library media center when they need to use it for their studies. The library media specialist and the research team will next approach the principal and the entire staff to share the timeline and procedures for implementing the needed changes.

This is action research. Isn't it a simple process? The example of a library media center during lunch periods illustrates how action research can be used to solve a problem in the library media center. The same process may be used for analyzing a problem occurring in another area of the school community; the steps for conducting the research are the same. In learning how to conduct action research, the library media specialist will be equipped with the skills needed to conduct data-driven problem solving. Using this method of reflective problem solving will illustrate that the library media specialist is truly a leader. This library media specialist is able to conduct his or her own research for the improvement of the library media center and can lead others through the process of program improvement. Staff members may not be able to state what makes the library media specialist a leader, but using action research will enable the staff to see the library media specialist in a leadership role. As Bennis states, "Leadership is like beauty, it is hard to define, but you know it when you see it" (Popper & Lipshitz, 1993, 23.)

### References

American Association of School Librarians (AASL) & Association for Educational Communications and Technology (AECT). (1998). *Information Power: Building Partnerships for Learning*. Chicago: American Library Association.

Bennis, W., and B. Nanus. (2003). *Leaders: Strategies for Taking Charge*. (2nd edition). New York: HarperBusiness Essentials.

Popper, M., and R. Lipshitz. (1993). Putting Leadership Theory to Work: A Conceptual Framework for Theory-based Leadership Development. *Leadership & organization Development Journal*, 14(7), 23–27.

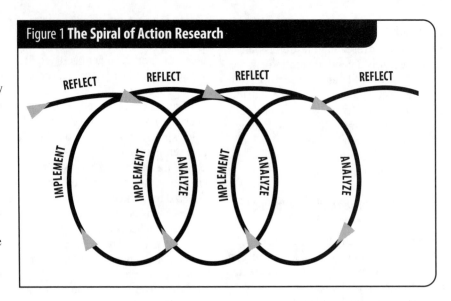

Figure 1 **The Spiral of Action Research**

REFLECT    REFLECT    REFLECT    REFLECT

IMPLEMENT   IMPLEMENT   ANALYZE   IMPLEMENT   ANALYZE   ANALYZE

*Jody K. Howard is the School Library Program Manager at the University of Colorado–Denver and Health Sciences Center, Denver, Colorado and may be reached at Jody.Howard@cudenver.edu. Su A. Eckhardt is the District Librarian at Cherry Creek School District, Centennial, Colorado and may be reached at seckhardt@cherrycreekschools.org. Jody and Su are also the authors of* Action Research: A Guide for Library Media Specialists *(Linworth Publishing Inc., 2005).*

Howard, J.K., & Eckhardt, S.A. (2005). Why action research? The leadership role of the library media specialist. *Library Media Connection*, *24*(2), 32-34.

# Technician or Technologist?
# Technology and the Role of the Library Media Specialist

## By Mary Alice Anderson

Long before classes begin, the doors to the library media center open, students rush in to complete multimedia projects, update their class project Web site, access their server space, search the online catalog, edit a video project, review lessons in their online math textbook, download a homework file they e-mailed themselves, or just hang out because the library media center is a cool place to be. Soon the weekly news broadcast begins; by the end of first period, three classes have used the library media center's computers to both search for and present information. Throughout the day, teachers stop by to borrow resources, ask for tech assistance, or plan instructional activities with library media center staff. The principal brings visitors on a tour of the library media center; an adult education teacher stops by to make arrangements for using facilities. At day's end, more students stop by to complete assignments while faculty attend an informal staff development session. Typical? Yes. In schools where students have good access to good technology, this is the norm. In other schools it's unimaginable.

It's been more than a quarter of a century since automation made it more exciting and motivating for students to search for books, and more than a decade since the Internet entered the educational mainstream. Today there are countless technology-infused library media center programs operating in schools of all sizes with varying student populations, funding, and facilities. It's been 15 years since *Information Power* (AASL & AECT, 1988) defined our roles as staff developers, curriculum partners, and technologists. Yet technology is still not pervasive in all library media center programs. Some library media specialists still see technology as a threat; others see it as just one more thing to do. Literature still draws many into the profession; reading promotion is undoubtedly an important role in this era of No Child Left Behind. However,

literature and books are just one part of our multifaceted jobs—technology is equally integral. Library media specialists must take proactive roles in making technology an essential part of their jobs, dispel myths about what they do, and use technology to create a vibrant learning community.

## Why Technology?

Technology has a prominent role in *Information Power,* our national guidelines. In fact, technology has been mentioned in the guidelines for quite some time. *Media Programs: District and School* (AASL & AECT, 1975) addressed production, television, computerized instruction, and telecommunications stating, "technology presently enables the learner to participate in different environments and will increasingly do so." Technology is identified as a major tenant of *Information Power: Building Partnerships for Learning*; "Three basic ideas—collaboration, leadership, and technology—underlie the vision of library media programs. These ideas provide unifying themes for building the effective library media specialist and for infusing all the activities, services, and function of an effective, student-centered program" (AASL & AECT, 1988).

No Child Left Behind requires every child to be technology literate by the end of 8th grade. The ISTE (International Society for Technology in Education) NETS (National Educational Technology Standards for Students, 2002) address technology productivity tools, communication tools, and research tools. NETS complement our profession's *Information Literacy Standards for Student Learning*. The seamless blend of a technology-enhanced library media center and strong curricular integration supported by a library media specialist can help all students achieve these goals. It can even occur in the absence of formal district approved curriculums when the library media specialist pro-

vides proactive and strong leadership.

Library media center program impact studies show a direct correlation between student achievement and library media centers that provide access to information in both print and electronic resources, and information technologies. The Ohio study points to the importance of "state-of-the-art technology to acquire, organize, create, and disseminate information." The study recommends that library media centers provide a learning-centered space supported by a strong technology infrastructure" (2003). *The Minnesota School Library Media Census* found "up to-date technology and access to fee-based information sources and the Internet" makes a difference in student achievement (Metronet, 2003). The North Carolina study also reported a connection between spending more money on electronic access to information and student achievement (Burgin, 2003). Keith Curry Lance found in three studies, including Alaska, Pennsylvania, and Colorado, that "the increasing high-tech environment in middle and senior high school libraries was contributing to academic achievement" (Loertscher, 2002). Studies with similar findings in 14 states can't be wrong.

Information is format-neutral and should be easily accessible in print and electronic formats. Every child using a library media center should have the capability of accessing information without having to stand in line to use a computer or go to an isolated lab down the hall. The same student should be able to move seamlessly back and forth between searching for information and producing his or her own information whether it is a basic word-processed document, a Web page, or a multimedia product.

Placing technology in a central location, which is generally more accessible than stand-alone computer labs, makes economic sense. Technology in the library media center is a good way to capitalize on a school's potential to reach all learners and help a school receive a good return on one of its largest investments. It is a leveling factor, providing opportunities for students of all abilities and learning styles to succeed while offering challenges for those who need or want them. Technology helps bridge the digital divide; quite likely a high percentage of students using a library media center's technology before or after the school day are students who do not have access at home because they live in a rural area or family finances prohibit it (PEW Internet and American Life Project, 2004).

Technology helps library media specialists reach today's digital natives who are more likely to access the Internet away from school than they are in school. Many students believe their teachers do not take advantage of what the Internet has to offer education. Millions of children and young adults have their own Web pages, use text messaging, and assume technology is a way of life (PEW Internet and American Life Project, 2004). This does not mean adopting their way of doing things; it means acknowledging technology, accepting change, and working to provide a learning environment that meets their needs and learning styles while also continuing and encouraging traditional best practices of information access and use.

Finally, technology helps us "build influence" and change perception as Dr. Gary Hartzell so often urges us to do. Technology calls attention to what we do and broadens our sphere of influence, putting us in contact with more staff, students, and the broader learning community. Technology in the library media center helps change people's perceptions of your role. One library media specialist described having visitors in her school; when she asked them which computer software they used in their district, they were amazed a "librarian" asked that question. These visitors had a far different perception of what a library media specialist would be concerned with.

Your technology skills will make you indispensable, especially when you provide assistance to teachers or do the jobs no one else knows how or wants to do. Principals want a tech-savvy library media specialist— someone who knows technology, keeps things running in top shape, keeps track of everything, and keeps things "humming." It's about more than hardware and software skills— it's about leadership and management. It's about managing technology, or someone who does will step in and take over your job.

## Making It Happen

Library media specialists are good managers. Good skills applied to managing print resources can transfer to managing technology resources and access to technology. The management component of our jobs is no less important than our teaching and collaborative roles. Good management skills make us valuable employees as schools struggle financially. Good technology management skills also enhance our teaching and collaborative roles, helping provide quick and efficient access to resources.

Access, access, access! Administrators, parents, and community members expect it. It's worth repeating: Good access to information in all formats is essential to student achievement. Successful library media center programs provide and support equitable, transparent, and quality access to technology. Without it, students will take their information business elsewhere. Every student who uses the library media center deserves the right to access current and up-to-date information in multiple formats. This means more than the OPAC® and a few computers for accessing online encyclopedias and state-provided databases (Simpson, 2002).

Computer labs in the library media center or computers throughout the library media center are a natural fit (Anderson, 2000). Technology helps promote constructivist learning as students can both access information and create their own information. Last winter, one of our science teachers asked her students do a little research project that was entirely book-based. Halfway through the day, I suggested they could create a computer timeline depicting the information they were gathering about events in space travel. Within minutes, the students and their books had moved to one of the library media center's labs. There was an observable improvement in the students' interest, attitudes, and abilities to stay on task. We've long noticed that students are quieter and better behaved sitting at a computer than when working at tables. Technology is not messy and it doesn't promote misbehavior.

If labs in the library media center are not possible due to limitations of finances, infrastructure, or space, make it a goal to strive for, and work within the current realities. Innovative people can do a lot with a little. Financial and infrastructure issues cannot always be readily resolved, but they can be addressed through proactively documenting and supporting the need. Space issues can often be creatively solved. Our first computer lab was on an old stage; the remainder of the library media center had been an auditorium. Schools have knocked a wall out to add labs and an entire new look to their library media centers. A library media specialist in a 1,400-student high school had a dilemma. The library media center could only accommodate a class of 30. There was no space for a lab or many desktop machines. She solved the problem by establishing a wireless lab in the library media center. Students can use the computers at their normal table space or sit on the floor.

## Will Technology Take Your Place?

Regrettably, wireless access is sometimes seen as a threat. In one Minnesota school, a library media specialist was cut when the school acquired several wireless labs. The administration assumed she would no longer be needed. Active involvement in planning and deploying wireless labs (or other labs) is crucial. Take mobile computers to classrooms or resource centers to extend access to the library media center and resources. Mobility, increased access, and our involvement will help make the library media center the true core of the school's learning environment, expanding, rather than eroding, our role and the viability of the library media center.

Technology will help make the library media center a place where students, especially teens, want to be. In "Teenager Users of Libraries" Loertscher and Woolls (2002) cite research showing the top three reasons teens use public libraries are to research, volunteer, and use the Internet. Make your library media center a place where kids want to be—remove the barriers to access.

Print and online can easily coexist. Many library media specialists, myself included, encourage a balanced use of print and online by putting books and note taking forms on carts that can be moved where the kids are: at the computers. It's a practice we reluctantly began, believing students needed to learn how to look for books on their own. We've since learned that easier access encourages more use of print.

Learning activities that integrate technology must be planned and scheduled the same as more traditional activities. The presence of technology affords library media specialists opportunities to model the use of technology and work with both students and staff. Technology is a hook for reaching out to digitally native teachers. Make it a practice to schedule with teachers; discourage the habit of just letting them "sign up" for labs or computers without co-planning. Joint planning encourages dialogue about both instructional and technology needs and can help you plan for optimal curriculum enhancement. For example, do the computers have the necessary plug-ins? Is everything working properly? Is a projector needed? Are students working in groups or individually? (Anderson, 2003).

Technology is a tool to enhance access to reading and motivate reading. Customized, enhanced online catalog records help identify special collections and curriculum resources. For example, library media center books that support a district reading curriculum can be appropriately identified. No Child Left Behind and reading achievement make it imperative that the capabilities of online catalogs are fully utilized.

## The Role of the Web

When technology is widely accessible, you can more readily promote the use of subscription databases provided by your district or state. There is a general belief among library media specialists that few teachers are aware of these resources and do not encourage their students to use them. Library media specialists should be at the forefront of both instructing teachers and students in the use of these tools, and providing easy access to them on the library media center Web sites. Sadly, this doesn't always happen. A Florida study revealed some disconcerting information about library media center Web sites. Only 20 percent of them link to SUNLINK, the state's union database of library media center resources—despite the fact that more than 85 percent of the schools provide access to these resources (Baumbach, 2005). A bit of good news from the study: "Higher achieving schools, as measured by the Florida Comprehensive Assessment Test, were more likely to have a school and a library media center Web site."

A Web site—is it one more thing to do, or the ideal tool for promoting access to your library media center program? Forward-thinking library media specialists view a Web site as the ideal tool for "one-stop searching" and expanding their program's influence. Link the library media center's Web site and core resources directly and prominently on the school's home page. Don't have a Web site? Start small even if it means only providing information about library media center hours and links to core resources. Develop the site to include subject-specific resources, program information and advocacy, reading promotion, special events, parent information, and whatever makes your program unique. Take control of your library media center Web site; make sure its content and focus is in your hands. Parents increasingly turn to the Web for information about their child's school. Make sure the library media center is one more place parents visit when they look at the school's Web site.

## Giving, Not Just Taking

Access to technology in the library media center is about more than expanded access to information; it's also about producing information, offering students opportunities for authentic, engaged, active learning. Technology encourages effective use of real-world, authentic tools such as spreadsheets, career exploration resources, and multimedia authoring or editing systems. Make sure your students have access to a full suite of productivity software, including photo and movie editing software, and tools such as graphics software. Create spaces for group work and utilizing peripherals such as scanners and digital cameras. Helping students do more than "find" information gives library media specialists more occasions to be part of more phases of the information process and ultimately more collaborative planning.

Enhancing access may mean allowing students to bring in their own laptops, handhelds, flash drives or other portable storage, or accessing a file they e-mailed themselves from home. Often our own or district policies prevent moving forward with improved access. For example, many acceptable use policies do not allow students to use e-mail at school. With the absence of disk drives on most computers, e-mail may be the only way students can move a file between home and school unless the district provides remote access to the district's server space. It may be time to re-examine your policies and loosen up to better meet the needs of today's learners. As one library media specialist commented, "I might as well let them do e-mail; otherwise they would have been in during noon hour throwing paper airplanes or talking loudly."

## Managing the Stuff

Your level of responsibility for managing hardware, peripherals, software, and supplies will vary with district staffing, policies, and how much you want to be involved. Consistency and standardization will make it easier to manage both hardware and software. With the exception of specialized software and peripherals (e.g., scanners, photo editing software), management will be simpler if all the computers are set up identically; students shouldn't have to guess if the computer they go to has what they need. Work with technical support to create images of a standard installation so it can be imaged to each computer. Have a plan for what is installed where and keep track of it. Keep a procedures book up-to-date so you can refer to it as needed. Utilize your automation system, spreadsheets, and databases to manage technology just as you use them to manage print resources.

## Working with Technology Staff

It's quite possible that as a library media specialist you are also your school or district technology coordinator and support staff. More likely, you work with information systems or tech support staff. Ideally, you are all part of the tech team, working to ensure good access to resources and supporting students and teachers. Unfortunately, library media specialists are not always part of the team and conflicts between tech support staff and library media specialists are not uncommon. Typical complaints are not being allowed to add content to a Web site, access servers, or get beyond security software. A Texas library media specialist vented her anger. "I had hoped to break down some barriers for students to get help from at least the librarian!" A Massachusetts library media specialist described a typical situation. "I often have to rely on the network administrator's assistance, because I'm locked out of the network management area for trouble-shooting purposes. I'm often frustrated because much of what I do depends on the other professionals in my building doing their job in a timely manner. When the people you depend on do their job well, you soar; when they don't, you crash and burn." (personal communication, February 2005) Library media specialists can lessen conflicts and potential problems that ultimately impact students by working with technology staff to model and develop practices that remove barriers, enhancing rather than impeding use. Lessen the impact of current or future problems by modeling good communication practices and showing tech support staff that you are a knowledgeable, professional team player. Finally, remember that they often take a lot of criticism from staff and need your support, too.

## What If You Don't Want to Be a Technician?

Quite likely you are still the first line of routine daily tech support in your building. In this role, you have the ideal opportunity to work with a broader array of staff and provide on-the-spot tech support for a smooth curricular experience. Just in time tech support is something you can learn through experience. It does not make you a technician, but it makes you a hero to the busy teacher you help. It never hurts to do a job that that no one else wants to do. Be the tech-savvy library media specialist in your building. Word spreads and dividends are high!

## Conclusion

Did reading this article affirm your library media center as integral to the school and student needs? Did it encourage you to strive for more? Or, did it leave you angry, upset, and thinking, "No way is this for me." If so, take a look at the programs that are thriving, merely surviving, or disappearing. Open your mind to other possibilities and newer ways of providing access for today's learners. Our mission remains the same; what's different is the expanded choice of tools. Student achievement is still the bottom line.

### Works Cited

American Association of School Librarians (AASL) and Association for Educational Communications and Technology (AECT). *Media Programs: District and School*. Chicago: American Library Association, 1975.

American Association of School Librarians and Association for Educational Communications and Technology. *Information Power: Building Partnerships for Learning*. Chicago: American Library Association, 1988.

Anderson, Mary Alice. "Computer Labs and Media Centers: A Natural Fit." *MultiMedia Schools*. 7(5) (Oct 2000): 20–23.

Anderson, Mary Alice. "Tools of the Trade: Tips for Using the Internet." *Library Media Connection*. 21(7) (Apr/May 2003): 49.

Baumbach, Donna J. "The School Library Media Center Web Page: An Opportunity Too Good to Miss." *Knowledge Quest*. 33(3) (Jan/Feb 2005): 8-12.

Burgin, Robert and RB Software and Consulting. *An Essential Connection: How Quality School Library Media Programs Improve Student Achievement in North Carolina*. <www.rburgin.com/index.html/>, 2003.

Hartzell, Gary N. *Building Influence for the School Librarian*. Worthington, OH: Linworth Publishing, 1994.

International Society for Technology in Education (ISTE). *National Educational Standards for Students*. <http://cnets.iste.org/students/s_stands.html>, 2002.

Loertscher, David and Blanche Woolls. "Teenage Users of Libraries." *Knowledge Quest*. 30(5) (May/Jun 2002): 31–35.

Metronet. *Check It Out! The Results of the School Library Media Program Census*. <http://metronet.lib.mn.us/survey/index.cfm>, 2002.

Ohio Educational Library Media Association. *Student Learning Through Ohio School Libraries: A Summary of the Ohio Research Study*. <http://www.oelma.org/StudentLearning/SLFindings.asp>, 2003.

PEW Internet and American Life Project. "Demographics of Internet Users." <www.pewinternet.org/trends/DemographicsofInternetUsers_12.20.04.htm>, 2004.

Simpson, Carol. "Information Technology Planning: Computers in the School Library—How Many Are Enough?" *Knowledge Quest*. 31(1) (Sep/Oct 2002): 51–53.

### Recommended Reading

PEW Internet and American Life Project. "America's Online Pursuits: The Changing Picture of Who's Online and What They Do." <www.pewinternet.org>, 2003.

Scholastic Research Foundation. *Research Foundation Paper: School Libraries Work!* <http://Scholastic.com/go/libhp/lbr_schlib.htm>, 2004.

*Mary Alice Anderson is the lead library media specialist at Winona (Minnesota) Area Public Schools. She can be reached at maryalicea@mac.com or <www.rschooltoday.com/winonamiddle/maryaliceanderson>.*

Anderson, M.A. (2005). Technician or technologist? Technology and the role of the library media specialist. *Library Media Connection, 24*(1), 14-18, 109.

# Streaming Video–the Wave of the Video Future!

## By Laura Brown

Times and technology are always changing. At one time teachers used slide projectors, filmstrips, and 16mm films. Today educators are slowly making the shift from videos to DVDs. Videos and DVDs do give teachers more flexibility, but there is a new choice that teachers, students, and librarians are excited about.

## The Next Wave

Streaming is the next "big thing" in audiovisual materials. Streaming enables educators to view videos on demand via the Internet. It works through the simultaneous transfer of digital media, which is video and voice data that is received in a continuous real-time stream. Real Media, Quick Time Player, and Windows Media Player are some of the applications with which users are able to display the video data. Windows Media is an application for PCs while Quick Time Player is an application for Macs and PCs.

## Why Stream?

Streaming solves all types of current problems with videos and DVDs. Videos and DVDs can be expensive and in certain subject areas, like science, are quickly outdated and downright boring. Often more than one teacher wants the same video or DVD at the same time. Videos and DVDs can be damaged, lost, stolen, and take up precious storage space. VCRs that are used frequently by teachers often stop functioning properly, are sometimes dropped when moved from one location to another, lose cables or get damaged, and are sometimes stolen if not properly stored and secured.

Streaming eliminates the problems librarians and teachers face using videos and DVDs. Streamed videos are always available for use. Streaming does require robust Internet access, but to overcome that limitation users can download videos to their computer desktops, save to a disk, or burn them on CDs. This allows teachers to insert the video clips into slide shows, or show them as they are. They can even be e-mailed if copyright considerations allow.

## What Can Streaming Video Do for You?

Distance learning is one way to use streaming video. Students who are absent can have instant access to content so they do not fall behind. Home schoolers may one day be able to take advantage of this technology for specific classes. High schools, community colleges, and universities that have television production classes and studios use streaming to reach a larger audience. Son Educational Outreach <www.son.washington.edu/dl/who.asp>

> *Streaming allows teachers to show a video in its entirety or pick and choose specific clips of the video. The length of each video and clip is listed so teachers know exactly how to plan their lessons.*

is an organization that specializes in using streaming for distance education.

Web casts are streamed by museums to promote their collections, exhibits, and upcoming events. This allows teachers and students to visit a museum without ever leaving the classroom. Find out more at <www.archimuse.com>. Web casts are also used for professional development for educators. Teleconference rooms that have been used in the past for training can be upgraded for digital video, which makes real-time transmission of information and ideas more effective.

## How Can Streaming Be Used for Instruction?

Presentation and timing are vital aspects of instruction. Teachers are always looking for ways to enhance instruction to further engage their students in the learning process. There simply may not be enough time, or need, in a class period or unit to show a complete video. Streaming allows teachers to show a video in its entirety or pick and choose specific clips of the video. The length of each video and clip is listed so teachers know exactly how to plan their lessons.

Streaming videos can be presented to the entire class on a television using a scan converter connected to the television and computer. To show videos to larger groups the computer can be connected via cables to an LCD projector and projected onto a large screen.

Streaming is also an information resource for students. Students are no longer turning in the traditional essay or written report. Many school districts now require students to be computer literate. In an effort to ensure that this happens, teachers are now requiring students to turn in reports and make class presentations electronically. This often includes a slide show. Students can use streaming to locate images and video clips to insert into their slide shows. This allows students much more flexibility and validity when making their production.

## Streaming Providers

Unitedstreaming <unitedstreaming.com> has an ever-increasing database of videos and video clips for educational use. This company was founded in 1954 as United Learning. United Learning brought full-motion, high quality educational content into the classroom. Unitedstreaming is United Learning's next step to providing videos to educators. The videos available are from companies that librarians currently patronize such as United Learning, Weston Woods, TV Ontario, Environmental Media, and Rainbow Educational Media.

Customers search for a video just like they search for a document. Searches can be done via keywords, subject area and grade level, or state curriculum standards. Advanced searches can be done in the same manner. All videos and video clips are indexed, which makes searches fast and successful. The results of a search include the title, summary, production company, copyright date, grade levels, and duration of the video, listed in order of relevance. Unitedstreaming has more than 2,000 video titles and more than 20,000 clips, and an image library, with indexed database, with more than 650 standards-based photographs in high-resolution. The subject areas include science, social studies, mathematics, language arts, children's literature, health, and guidance programs. Features that teachers will find extremely helpful are their state curriculum standards outlined for each video, teachers' guides, quizzes, and games, all based on the video selected and which can be printed for distribution. Finally, users can keep a record of all the clips they use on their account and not use their hard drive to save videos.

Real Player <www.real.com> is another streaming provider that schools use. This database allows its clients to put their own digital productions on the Internet. It also streams a variety of commercial videos that may not be appropriate for students. Real Player allows clients to view music videos and network and cable programming online. Real Player offers a 14-day free trial for prospective clients.

Many states, including Georgia and Rhode Island, have contracts with vendors to provide streaming services to public schools. Check with your state department of education to see what is available for your state. An example of a district-wide effort comes from Montgomery County, Maryland. Montgomery County Public Schools (MCPS) provides a variety of online services to its schools through the Maryland K12

Digital Library Grant. The grant allows the school districts to act as one client, in turn making them a more powerful buyer, and guaranteeing fair pricing for all systems.

## What Features and Services Should I Look for When Considering Subscribing to a Streaming Vendor?

A free trial period is important. Thirty days is standard. This will give educators an opportunity to use the product and see if it will meet their needs. Be proactive when introducing a new product to teachers and administrators during your trial period. Set up a time for a demonstration. Depending on the size and grade level of your school, a faculty meeting or an in-service day may be appropriate, but in a large departmental-

> *Streaming eliminates the problems librarians and teachers face using videos and DVDs.*

ized high school, the best strategy is to create a slide show for each, or at least the largest, departments and show it to them during departmental meetings, followed by a short training session. If the site is easy to use and teachers like it, then it will be much easier to secure it for your school. License agreements and use policies should be designed to meet the demands of the users. This includes school and home access for teachers and students.

The most significant deciding factor in selecting a streaming video vendor will be the service provided in terms of its cost. Sales representatives must be informative and work with individual schools and districts to offer discounts and the lowest competitive price possible. Librarians know and talk to each other and recommend products that produce results. When

dealing with vendors make it very clear what you want and expect from them. Ask them for the contact information of clients in your area so you can talk to them to get their feedback on the service and ask them how much they are paying for it.

They also must be responsive to teacher requests for media in areas in which the schools lack resources. Every vendor has areas of strengths and weaknesses. The service you select should have a large database that the majority of your teachers can find video clips from, but be sure that the company will provide videos upon request where there are gaps in the database.

Technical support is the final piece of the puzzle. A user-friendly site, with access to helpful technicians will make site users feel more comfortable. The service number should be toll free and the hours of support should extend beyond the school day. E-mailing responses to questions also is very helpful. Service providers must handle technical problems in an accurate and timely manner.

## Conclusion

Securing educational materials for instructional use has been and will always be a challenge. School budgets are constantly being stretched to meet more demands without necessarily being increased. The costs of products that support the educational process are always increasing. More than ever before librarians are forced to make the difficult decisions about which materials to purchase. Streaming isn't a difficult choice, but a right one.

*Laura Brown is a media specialist at Paint Branch High School in Burtonsville, Maryland and may be reached at Laura_J._Brown@fc.k12.mcps.md.us.*

Brown, L. (2004). Streaming video—the wave of the video future! *Library Media Connection, 23*(3), 54-55.

# eBooks: Expanding the School Library

## By Terence Cavanaugh, Ph.D.

### What Is an eBook?

eBooks are books or other forms of text in digital form: an enhanced book without the paper. At little to no cost, using technologies that are already available at most schools, it is possible to expand the library media center's collection of books, at the same time making many books more accessible to students. Digital libraries can be created on a stand-alone computer, made part of the school network, or placed on the Internet. As part of the school network, students have access to the electronic text portion of the collection from networked computers throughout the school. An additional benefit is that books that have passed into the public domain can be given to students at no cost. As of 2004, the Million Book Project had digitized over 80,000 free eBooks.

### Why Have eBooks in the Library?

- Shelf space saved
- Book budget not impacted
- Public domain books don't have to be returned
- Home access is expanded

eBooks contain many features, some of which can be classified as accommodations. The eBook itself has three different components: an eBook file, software to read the eBook, and a hardware device on which to read it (computer, laptop, or handheld). eBooks are available through online libraries, bookstores, or they can be created from common forms of electronic text with readily available programs (often available free). Examples of accommodating features include: light weight (in comparison to other texts), adjustable text size, highlighting, bookmarking, note taking, interactive dictionaries, and even reading aloud. By using these features, instructors can create pre-accommodated eBooks for student reading using items such as advance organizers and reading guides. Reading is considered to be one of the basic activities in all educational situations, and as such it is one of the most common activities requiring accommodations or modifications for special needs students.

### eBook Formats

eBooks come in a variety of formats, some of which are platform or device-specific while others are cross-platform. HTML or text-based eBooks are ready to use in standard browsers. Using browser capabilities, readers can adjust text style, size, and color. With html or text, it is possible to search for terms within the book, and copy and paste selected text to other programs. The Adobe® PDF eBooks format allows for page navigation, multiple viewing options, adding bookmarks, and searching. Many consider the Adobe Portable Document Format (PDF) a standard for electronic distribution worldwide, as pdf files are compact and can be easily shared, viewed, navigated, and printed. Palm eBooks can be read on computers and Palm handheld devices.

| Figure 1 | | | | | |
|---|---|---|---|---|---|
| | **Web (html/xml)** | **Text (txt)** | **Adobe Acrobat Reader (pdf)** | **Microsoft Reader (lit)** | **Palm Reader (pdb)** |
| **Windows desktops** | Yes | Yes | Yes | Yes | Yes |
| **Windows laptops** | Yes | Yes | Yes | Yes | Yes |
| **Windows tablets** | Yes | Yes | Yes | Yes | Yes |
| **Windows handheld devices** | Yes | Yes | Yes | Yes | Yes |
| **Apple desktop platforms** | Yes | Yes | Yes | Yes | Yes |
| **Apple laptops** | Yes | Yes | Yes | Yes | Yes |
| **Palm handheld devices** | Yes | Yes | Yes | Yes | Yes |

| | Web (html/xml) | Text (txt) | Adobe Acrobat Reader (pdf) | Microsoft Reader (lit) | Palm Reader (pdb) |
|---|---|---|---|---|---|
| Portable device | Yes | Yes | Yes | can be used on laptops and Pocket PC devices | can be used on your Palm, Pocket PC or laptop |
| Reader cost | free download | free built-in | free download | free download | free download (Pro version approx $15) |
| Printing | Yes | Yes | while the system has the ability, most publishers block this option | No | No |
| Number of titles that can be stored | unlimited, depending on memory size  1 copy of Tarzan takes up: 496 KB  a 1.44 floppy could hold 2 copies  129 copies on a 64 MEG card | unlimited, depending on memory size  1 copy of Tarzan takes up: 479 KB  a 1.44 floppy could hold 3 copies  v133 copies on a 64 MEG card | unlimited, depending on memory size  1 copy of Tarzan takes up: 331 KB  a 1.44 floppy could hold 4 copies  193 copies on a 64 MEG card | unlimited, depending on memory size  1 copy of Tarzan takes up: 238 KB  a 1.44 floppy could hold 6 copies  268 copies on a 64 MEG card | unlimited, depending on memory size  1 copy of Tarzan takes up: 219 KB  a 1.44 floppy could hold 6 copies  292 copies on a 64 MEG card |
| Word/text search? | Yes | Yes | Yes | Yes | Yes |
| Bookmarking | No | No | Yes | Yes | Yes |
| Highlighting | No | No | Yes (if allowed) | Yes | Yes with pro version |
| Note taking | No | No | Yes (if allowed) | Yes | Yes |
| Text-to-speech | No | No | Yes | Yes | No |
| Synchronized highlighting with "read" text | No | No | No | Yes | No |
| Adjustable text size | Yes | Yes | No (only zoom) | Yes | Yes |
| Display pictures and art | Yes | No | Yes | Yes | Yes |
| Draw in eBook | No | No | No | Yes | No |
| Interactive dictionary | No | No | Yes (if online) | Yes | Yes with Pro version |
| Remember where last stopped | No | No | Yes | Yes | Yes |
| Display | scroll | scroll | page at a time | page at a time | page at a time |
| 2-page display | No | No | Yes | No | Yes with Pro version |

The Palm format allows users to select various fonts and font sizes, which controls the amount of text on the screen. Microsoft® Reader eBooks are compatible with Windows (95+) operating systems for desktop and laptop computers, as well as handheld devices.

While there are over 25 different formats of eBooks, the charts on the previous pages compare what I consider to be the big five: Web (.htm/.xml); Text (.txt); Adobe Acrobat Reader (.pdf); Microsoft Reader (.lit); and Palm Reader (.pdb).

## A Personal Choice

The format of eBook that I have found to have the greatest number of features for ease of use and most advanced interactive abilities is the Microsoft Reader eBook. MS Reader uses a display format called "ClearType," which makes text displayed on a screen look like words in a printed book. Some of the other features of MS Reader include a graphic that displays the reader's location within the book, a navigation system that remembers where the reader stops reading, and the last place that was viewed allowing for instant return. The text is adaptable, allowing users to select from a variety of sizes and font styles to set the most comfortable display for the user. The MS Reader eBook also creates an annotation file that stores reader-created bookmarks, highlights, drawings, and notes. It also has interactive dictionaries, and searching within the book for specific words and phrases. Along with these interactive features, the page display of the

eBook itself is well designed, including margins to increase reading comfort, and a portrait page layout that displays a whole page at a time (no scrolling), with the option to blackout the rest of the computer screen. The ability to carry books, references, notes, and other resources electronically allows users to make better use of the information, along with the additional just-in-time learning advantages of options such as the interactive dictionaries.

## How to Create a Digital Library on a Computer

Questions to consider when constructing an eLibrary:

- Does the school have Internet Web space?
  If yes, you can make your eLibrary available to the world for download and reading. If not, you are limited to your school network or a stand-alone computer.

- Do have access to the Internet at school?
  If yes, you can access books from your own Internet library or from other libraries. If not, you only have access to the books you save and place on your system.

- Is there a school network with server access to the computers in the classroom?
  If yes, students and teachers can access the books from anywhere in the school. If not, people will have to go to the library media center or stand-alone locations to access or download books.

## Constructing an eLibrary

First decide if you want links to other library media center's eBooks, or you want to have the eBooks files located locally. If you are connecting to other libraries, there is a chance that the library link will change. Also the book files might not be compatible with your users' devices or software. Consider that your school system's Internet may not always be available. If you decide to publish the books on the Internet, they will be accessible to users to either read online or download, and you will know that those eBooks are always there. Library media centers without Internet access can make eBook files available on an Intranet, school network (doesn't connect out), or stand-alone computer eLibrary station.

Next evaluate and select books that match or support the school reading list and curriculum. To do this, you will need a reading list and a list of common curriculum topics. Then you will need to peruse the existing public domain libraries for books that you can use. Just because they are already in your collection shouldn't stop you from obtaining "extra" copies, especially as these are ones you can give away without the worry of return. Consider going past the required reading list to including other books by required authors. For an example set of eBooks to support science, see <www.unf.edu/~tcavanau/ presentations/SciRead/index.htm>.

Convert your books to the needed formats (see more below). Start by downloading the sharable eBooks in as

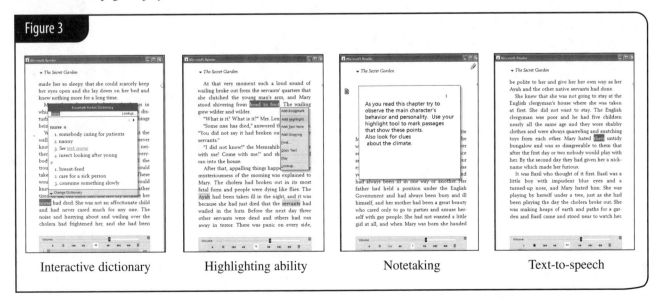

| Interactive dictionary | Highlighting ability | Notetaking | Text-to-speech |

Figure 3

many formats as possible, and then convert them to any other desired formats. Providing eBooks in multiple formats ensures that they are readable with familiar or available tools, especially for home use. Try for all of the big five and any others that you might want.

Create a Web site with links to each of your collection's eBook files. This Web site method will work even for offline book browsing. Any computer will run a Web page even if it is not on the Internet. A more advanced option is to create an eBook database of the eBook files and then link it with a Web authoring system (.asp/.php). eBook databases can be stored in several places: your school's Web site, on a file server, or on a database server such as SQL server or Oracle® server.

Don't forget to include links to reader software on your library media center site. If you are creating a stand-alone computer station, install software for all the formats on that computer. If you are creating an eBook library CD, make sure to download the installation files onto the CD.

Now publish your collection. Place your eBook eLibrary online so that everyone gets access.

It is also possible to buy a complete eBook library and then use it as the base to build your own. For example, Blackmask <www.blackmask.com/catalo/default.php> sells DVD copies of its 12,000 copyright free books for $30 per format. You could then use the book files from that DVD to start your library media center's eBook collection. Baen Science Fiction <www.baen.com> includes a large number of its current titles on CD for free sharing if you buy their hardbacks with the CD inside. Remember, don't share unless you have permission or it is in the public domain.

## Making eBooks

Many tools are available at no cost to convert existing electronic text into eBook formats. For example, Microsoft distributes for free a plug-in for MS Word 2000+ that allows users to change any MS Word document into eBook file formatted for the Microsoft Reader. Palm has a similar system with DropBook, which is a program for Windows and Macintosh that allows conversion of a text file to the Palm Markup Language for reading with the Palm Reader. ReaderWorks allows users to convert documents, publications, Web pages, and books into MS Reader (.lit) format. There is even a form of ReaderWorks online, called eBook Express, where users can convert their documents and then download the converted files. You can use these converters to add original student writing to your eBook library.

### Free Resources for Converting eBook Files

Text: any word processor just "Save As" text (.txt)

Web: FrontPage Express

Web: Netscape Communicator

Adobe Acrobat: <www.gobcl.com/convert_pdf.asp>

MS Reader—eBook Express: <http://www.ebookexpress.com/>

MS Reader—Word Add-in: <www.microsoft.com/reader/developers/info/rmr.asp>

*Dr. Terence Cavanaugh is an assistant professor at the University of North Florida, teaching Educational Technology. Terence is the co-author of* Teach Science with Science Fiction Films: A Guide for Teachers and Library Media Specialists *(Linworth Publishing, Inc., 2004) and is the author of* Literature Circles Through Technology *(Linworth Publishing, Inc., 2006).*

Cavanaugh, T. (2005). eBooks: Expanding the school library. *Library Media Connection, 23*(5), 56-59.

# Open Walls to a Larger World: What Handheld Computing Can Do for School Libraries and Media Centers

## By Theresa A. R. Embrey

Handheld computers have moved from a useful tool of the business world and individuals into the classroom. They have been used as a classroom resource by a number of innovative schools such as Illinois' District 230 in Orland Park and Michigan's West Hills Middle School in Bloomfield Hills. But library media specialists have a larger challenge. Handheld computers come in a variety of styles, sizes, and capacities. They have the potential to unlock doors and break down walls giving students access to the larger world of information beyond the classroom.

### To Be Wireless, or Not to Be Wireless?

Much of what the handheld computer can do depends on the handheld itself, as well as whether the school has rolled out a wireless network to support laptop and handheld computing applications. Wireless access allows students real-time access to all the network's resources, including downloading eBooks and documents, searching the library media center's catalog, and searching databases to which the library has subscribed.

However, much of this same functionality is still available without wireless. Without wireless access, students must sync the devices or beam data to gain it. This may be problematic due to potential security and device issues.

How does one tackle the security and policy issues within the library media center? Some vendors make or distribute printers that can have documents beamed to them. These printers vary in their methods, but they do help to cut back on the security and device incompatibility issues. General PDA users' Web sites, such as PDABuzz and infoSync World, are an informative resource for reviews and information on enterprise products. They provide help with security issues and a resource for newly marketed devices and general software applications.

In a non-wireless environment, it is important to remind handheld users to be aware of what and to whom they sync or beam. Beaming and syncing only to known users helps to control possible security problems (e.g., viruses), regardless of your library media center's networking environment.

### Decisions, Decisions

Once a decision on whether to go wireless has been made, it's time to consider which handheld computing devices the library media center can support. Handheld devices come in myriad styles and operating systems. While the Palm OS™ is the most popular with schools at present, other operating systems one may wish to consider include WinCE and Linux.

> *Wireless access allows students real-time access to all the network's resources, including downloading eBooks and documents, and searching the library media center's catalog and databases.*

The operating system or systems the library media center supports will have an impact on which software applications can be supported. This is vitally important when it comes to eBook readers, which are available for every operating system. Numerous sites provide free eBook titles for eBook readers and palm devices, such as the MemoWare site. Some of these new eBooks are audio files and use new standards like SALT. A large selection of audio eBooks can be found at Audible's Web site.

Aside from operating systems, one must also consider how to handle media. Handhelds can now display video and audio with remarkable clar-ity. Will students be encouraged to take and swap photos with their handheld devices for use in class projects? Lessons on respecting digital rights can quickly become important in such a fluid environment.

### Support IS an Issue

Students and colleagues often look to their library media specialist as their first contact for technology support. As a library media specialist, where can you go for help? Aside from the handheld computer vendor Web site and the PDA general information sites, there are also specialty handheld computer support sites such as PDAparts—formerly known as GetHighTech. At this site you can get detailed instructions to repair devices, buy or sell parts for devices, and find additional technology support information. Sites like this one are best used once the manufacturer warranty has expired.

Connecting to your library media center's online catalog is now possible. Some library automation vendors such as TLC /CARL and Innovative Interfaces have products and solutions to make wireless access easier. For library media center catalogs that use SQL as a database underneath the front end, a computer programmer developed a solution. Using SQL Anywhere® Studio, you may be able to extend your access to students and faculty. Be sure to check with your automation vendor to see if it has a wireless access product. Also, before encouraging handheld use of the online library media center catalog, check to see how it displays on a variety of devices. It may display differently on one device due to differences in the handheld's screen size, screen resolution, or connectivity issues.

Another opportunity to assist one's colleagues and students as they explore the larger world with handheld computing is to direct them toward lesson plans and projects on the Web that involve shareware and eBooks. The major handheld computing vendors have sections of their support Web sites dedicated to educational support. Palm has also published special advertising inserts with lesson plans in educational technology magazines such as *Technology & Learning*. So, reach out and explore!

## Glossary

**Beam.** The act of transferring data between a handheld and another device (a second handheld, printer, etc.) using the device's infrared port.

**Handhelds.** Computerized devices that are small enough to be carried in the palm of the hand or a pocket and are designed for mobile computing applications.

**Linux.** An operating system that is sometimes found on handheld devices.

**Palm OS**. The operating system used by PDAs and other handhelds that have licensed this operating system from PalmSource™, Inc.

**Palms**. The informal term used by users of handheld devices that use the Palm OS to describe those devices.

**PDA**. An acronym for personal digital assistant, which is a particular type of handheld.

**RFID**. An acronym for Radio Frequency Identification. RFID tags are an alternative to bar code technologies.

**SALT**. A newly developed standard that would allow you to use your voice to activate handheld devices.

**Sync**. The term used to describe the action of synchronizing data between a handheld and any other device, such as a laptop or desktop PC.

**Symbian OS**. The operating system used by smart phones and other handhelds that have licensed this operating system from Symbian, Inc.

**WAP**. The Wireless Application Protocol is the standard protocol that describes the display interface for many handheld devices.

**WinCE**. The operating system created by Microsoft® for its line of handheld devices, especially its personal digital assistants.

**Wireless**. A method of computing that is accomplished without wires or cables. It is most often used to refer to work with handheld computers and cell phones.

### *Useful Web Sites and Links*

Audible
<http://www.audible.com/adbl/store/welcome.jsp>

District 230, Orland Park, IL
<http://www.d230.org/adcenter/technology/Techhome2001.htm>

Education@PalmOne™
<http://www.palmone.com/us/education/>

Handheld Librarian
<http://www.handheldlib.blogspot.com>

infoSync World
<http://www.infosync.no/>

Learning in the Palm of Your Hand (Center for Highly Interactive Computing in Education at the University of Michigan)
<http://palm.hice-dev.org/>

MemoWare
<http://www.memoware.com/>

PDABuzz
<http://www.pdabuzz.com>

pdaED.com
<http://www.pdaed.com/vertical/home.xml>

PDAparts.com
<http://www.gethightech.com>

Technology & Learning Magazine
<http://www.techlearning.com>

West Hills Middle School, Bloomfield, MI
http://www.bloomfield.org/westhills/images/handhelds.mov

---

*Theresa A. R. Embrey is an independent consultant from Berwyn, Illinois.*

Embrey, T.A.R. (2005). Open walls to a larger world: What handheld computing can do for school libraries and media centers. *Library Media Connection, 23*(4), 56-57.

# Librarian-Technologist: Ready for the Future

## By Betsy Ruffin

Once upon a time, being technology savvy at school meant knowing how to work the film projector and the mimeograph machine. Now it's copiers, faxes, digital equipment, and most of all, computers! Most librarians have had to learn about technology as their jobs increasingly involved high tech equipment and cyberspace resources. So, why not use those skills to improve your visibility and increase your usefulness at your school? You can be a vital part of a program of skills upgrades for teachers and students.

## Upgrading Your Own Skills

Being a technologist, of course, means you first need to have the basic skills and be willing to continue learning as computers and all the peripherals involved change so quickly. Start by knowing your own computer and operating system well. Read the manuals or help menus to find out those little known details that can make use easier. Be willing to try out new programs or dig a little deeper into familiar programs so that you know what is available and how to use it.

Get involved in the technology community. You can start by making sure you know, and are on good terms with the primary computer folks in your school or district. They can be a wonderful source of information. Most of them have been through their own learning curve in this matter, so do not hesitate to ask questions about what you do not understand for fear of sounding foolish. Also, watch them at work. You may not follow all they do, but you will begin to pick up tips and tricks to try later.

If there are computer workshops available in your area, plan to go to them. Talking with the instructors and other participants can be as valuable as the hands-on training you receive. Again, do not hesitate to ask questions or share experiences. You are there to learn. Take full advantage of it.

Some states have groups dedicated to educational technology. Find out about these groups and join them. Take advantage of conferences when you are able. You will not only gain from the seminars given, but will find the vendors and their exhibits useful in keeping up with the latest.

## Learning Online

Another way to get involved is online. There are many useful places that can help you augment your skills. Tutorials are available for programs such as Windows and other Microsoft products, for use of the Internet, and more. Use a search engine to browse for free or low-cost instruction in areas you want to know more about. Forums and knowledge bases are good for troubleshooting help. Most programs will have a searchable knowledge base for their product. Some will have links to online forums, a group dedicated to discussion of a particular topic. Non-company forum Web sites exist that include FAQs (frequently

> Start by knowing your own computer and operating system well.

asked questions), helpful links, experts, and much other useful information available, along with the ability to post a question. For most computer areas, you will find that if you are wondering about it, someone else has wondered also and will be happy to share what they have learned.

Listservs are another resource. These groups are dedicated to a particular topic, but messages are sent to your e-mail address rather than being posted on a Web site. If you sign up for a listserv, make sure you keep any instructions that are sent. These usually include information on signing off, stopping mail during vacation, how to post a message, or other such items.

Finally, recognize that you will need to keep on learning. Technology changes fast, and even updates for familiar programs could entail some learning updates on your part.

## Helping Teachers Learn

Once you've gained those valuable computer skills, how do you pass them on to your teachers so that they can benefit?

Start by letting them know you are willing and able to help. Bibliographic instruction in the library may involve technology. This can start your staff thinking of you as tech-savvy. Keep your ears open for lunchtime or hallway discussions about computer needs and offer to assist, with a smile of course.

School e-mail can be used to provide your own listserv of sorts. Gather tips that were useful to you as you learned, then pass them on once a week in e-mail form to the staff as "Tech Tips." Topics could include computer files maintenance (e.g. defragmenting, emptying the recycle bin, cleaning out old documents), identifying troubles to help the tech department diagnose difficulties (e.g. unusual sounds or sights, checking connections for network issues), program or operating system helps (e.g. keyboard shortcuts, changes after upgrades, tricks and tips to enhance use of programs). The list is as long as your teachers' needs. Just keep listening to them, and you will have ideas for Tech Tips throughout the school year.

While you're e-mailing, how about helping them stay up-to-date with a once a month listing of useful Web sites (you could call it "Web Wanderings")? Librarians are skilled in finding, evaluating, and using information, including what's online. Use monthly holidays, themes, and special needs or units as a place to begin searching. A search engine, such as Google, AltaVista, or Yahoo, can help you find sites. Use the advanced searches or look for tips that can help you narrow the number of hits so that you find good material more quickly and easily. Once you've got your list, read the blurbs to assist you in deciding whether the site fits your needs. Evaluate sites chosen by checking the sponsor or author of the site, testing links for currency, noting reading and interest level of material, look-

## Books

### From Linworth Publishing, Inc.

*Indispensable Teacher's Guide to Computer Skills, the 2nd edition* by Doug Johnson

*Information Technology for Schools, 2nd edition* by Katherine Toth Bucher

### From Dummies.Com (for Dummies Books)

*Microsoft Office 2000 for Dummies* by Wallace Wang and Roger C. Parker

*Troubleshooting Your PC for Dummies* by Dan Gookin

*Macs for Dummies* by David Pogue

There are also many other helpful computer oriented books in this series.

### From Nerdy Books

*Just the Tips, Man*™ series, including titles for Word, PowerPoint, and Excel Windows ME

More titles are forthcoming.

## Web sites

### Tutorials

http://www.internet4classrooms.com/on-line.htm — various programs

http://www.microsoft.com/education/ ?ID=Tutorials — Microsoft products

http://www.atomiclearning.com/applesamples?noCache= 290;1059182514 — Macintosh /

### Apple products

http://www.pccomputernotes.com/ — hardware

http://www.k12.hi.us/~tethree/00-01/ resources/intap.htm — various programs

http://www4.district125.k12.il.us/webmeisters/cchausis/tutorial/default.html — arious programs

### Forums and Helps

http://www.komando.com/ — good email newsletter and tips

http://www.annoyances.org/ — forums

http://www.winnetmag.com/forums/ —f orums

http://www.computing.net/ — most operating systems covered

http://www.macfixitforums.com/ — forums

http://www.zdnet.com/ — downloads, reviews, more

http://www.pcmag.com/ — various helps

### Teaching Teachers

http://cnets.iste.org/ -- National Educational Technology Standards

http://www.cde.mathstar.org/standards_teacher_us.html — National Teachers Technology

### Proficiencies

http://www.electronic-school.com/0398f2.html — winning teachers to technology

### Listservs

http://www.h-net.org/~edweb/ — EdTech

http://www.classroom.com/community/email/ — Connected Teacher

http://www.coweta.com/Internet/list.html — Ednet

### Web sites for teachers

http://teachers.teach-nology.com/

http://www.sitesforteachers.com/

http://www.educationplanet.com/

http://www.education-world.com/

### Integrating Technology

http://www.4teachers.org/4teachers/intech/index.shtml

http://www.ridoe.net/teachers/technology.htm

http://www.siec.k12.in.us/~west/slides/integrate/

http://www.wtvi.com/teks/

### Student Tech Team

http://www.kent.k12.wa.us/staff/epeto/tech_team/index.html

http://www.intel.com/education/newtotech/tech_teams.htm

http://www.elco.k12.pa.us/High_School/clubs/STAT.html

### Technology Night

http://www.nku.edu/~education/technology/tlt/partners/act2.pdf

http://www.highlandpark.org/sherwood/Memories9899/imctechnight.htm

---

ing for bias or other prohibitive ideas, and other assessment techniques. Having found your sites, type up the URLs in appropriate categories. Note age levels and give a description of the sites to aid teachers in using the list more easily. Word processing and e-mail programs allow you to insert hyperlinks (a link to a site or networked file) into your document. This can help you in preparing the list more easily; simply click the link icon, find the site, go back to the program and the link is ready for you to insert. By inserting these as hyperlinks, you will enable your staff to check the sites right from your e-mail simply by clicking on the Web address.

## Formal Tech Training for Teachers

Passing on what you've learned about computers to teachers may also take the form of mini-sessions or longer inservices. Mini-sessions, lasting 30-45 minutes, can be held after school. Topics should be those that teachers need and request most. These might include working with Windows or Mac operating systems, using programs like Microsoft Office, or use of databases and Web sites such as Gale Group resources or the Marco Polo site. Some of these may need to be broken down into smaller sections. This can not only keep you within your time frame, but also prevent teachers from feeling overwhelmed with material. It also allows them time to practice what they have learned before the next segment.

Small groups are best as this allows you to give more individual help when needed. Remember to allow time for questions as well as giving ample "wait time" when stating instructions. Handouts detailing these step-by-step instructions will be handy for both you and teachers as an aid to memory in learning. If you have access to a projector-computer setup, take advantage of it. A picture, combined with the thousand words, is even more valuable.

A final note: offering teachers certificates that can be placed in their personnel folders may encourage more to come, especially as schools focus more on these technology skills. Most publishing or word processing software has certificate templates available that can easily be customized for your needs.

Summers and other inservice days are a good time to tackle those items that need longer stretches. More time-consuming topics would be covered here. This could include designing a class Web page, using Office or other integrated programs to make record-keeping easier as well as planning how to use them in students' lessons, or learning and planning the use of new programs and databases. You may have to have larger groups, so handouts, question times, projector set up, and practice times will be needed even more here.

## Passing It on to Students

You and your teachers are now ready, willing, and able technologically. Now, it's time to get your students prepared with the skills needed in coming years. Providing follow up help to your teachers after their sessions can make it easier for them to integrate new skills into their instruction. Use your Tech Tips

and "Web Wanderings" mailings to help. Newsletters, emailed or otherwise, can be used to feature technology-integrated lessons and other ideas for computer usage in the classroom. Form and maintain a good relationship with your computer skills teachers. Try team-teaching some lessons that combine information skills with computer skills. Topics such as using databases for research, evaluating information found on the Internet, or using programs to present information are possibilities for collaborative work.

## The Tech Team

Forming a student tech team can be a great way to help the entire school community. Students in 4th grade and up can help with a variety of tasks such as routine file maintenance on computers, cleaning keyboards and screens, assisting classmates and teachers with program use, and simple troubleshooting. Younger students could begin with the more simple tasks and work their way up the learning ladder. Older students can, of course, take on more responsibility according to their skill level.

Stress the importance of the work of the tech team from the beginning by requiring interested students to fill out an application, complete with signatures required from teachers as a recommendation. A hands-on test can give a further idea of the skill levels of your applicants. After viewing applications and test results, students are chosen for membership. The number chosen will depend upon sponsors and resources available; 20 to 25 is a suggested number for good manageability and usefulness.

Once the team members are chosen, meeting times are set up and parent permissions obtained. The first meeting should involve some basic rules for computer use, such as those found in most acceptable use policies. Courtesy should also be stressed. Students should be reminded to state their business to teachers before starting an assignment and ask the teacher if it is a good time to perform the task. If not, they should request an alternate time. It is also important to stress kindness when helping fellow students.

After that, two types of sessions may be held: working and instructional. Each meeting should begin with students checking in at the meeting site. Then, at working meetings, assignments will be given to teams of two students. The teaming increases accountability and provides an immediate source of assistance if needed. Tasks should be designed so that they can be completed within 20 to 30 minutes. It is also helpful to provide your team members with badges or cards designating them as tech team members so that teachers know these students are "on the job" when they come to that classroom.

Instructional meetings may be used to teach students the skills needed for a particular upcoming job or may be used to increase proficiency with software or databases. Students should have a pocket folder to hold handouts and assignments and should bring it to all meetings.

The tech team can also be an integral part of a technology showcase during an open house or other parent meeting. Team members may be stationed in the computer lab ready to demonstrate what is being taught in classes, showing how to use resources available on the school network, and explaining use of information skills for online sources.

## Forward

As the 21st century progresses, more and more jobs will require some level of computer knowledge. Librarian-technologists can help students be ready for this future and assist teachers in being prepared to teach those students what they need to know. Help your school's technology program go forward by using your own hard-won and special knowledge as part of a complete plan for a computer upgrade, including skills.

*Betsy Ruffin is a librarian-technologist in the Cleburne (Texas) Independent School District. She can be reached at betsy. ruffin@cleburne.k12.tx.us*

Ruffin, B. (2004). Librarian-technologist: Ready for the future. *Library Media Connection, 22*(7), 47-49.

# Library.com: Adding Customers to Your Library Web Site

## By Neil Krasnoff

As a first-year Library Media specialist during the 2001-2002 school year, I made it my mission to move students from Internet search engines to subscription databases accessed through my library Web site. In pursuit of that objective, I built the best Web site I could and advertised it at every opportunity (usually with classes meeting in the library). Throughout the year, the Web statistics I collected indicated modest progress toward that goal. While the Web site and databases saw an increase in traffic, the majority of students did not visit the library page without a verbal reminder from library staff, and very few visited the library page without being directed by their teachers.

As I observed students' search strategies, I found that two search strategies were especially prevalent. The single most popular search engine was Ask Jeeves. When not using Ask Jeeves, students would construct their search queries using natural language, and often their searches were comical. The most memorable was, "I'm looking for facts about toilet paper use in the United States." Many students simply skipped the search step and went straight to the "dot com" hunt. For example, a student looking for information on important Civil War battles would try going to "gettysburg.com," "battleofgettysburg.com" or "civilwar-battles.com." While this strategy was successful enough to encourage repetition of the behavior, it often failed to produce relevant, reliable results. From these observations I deduced that the library needed to compete directly with Ask Jeeves, and the library needed its own "dot com" address.

### Launching Rebelslibrary.com

The new domain name (derived from our school mascot), <www.rebelslibrary.com>, was launched at the start of the 2002-2003 school year. This launch was to be more than simply changing the URL of the Web site, but a full-scale ad blitz. The first audience was teachers. For one hour during the beginning-of-year inservice, I worked with small groups of faculty to demonstrate the advantages of directing students to the library instead of Google, Yahoo!, and AskJeeves. The second stage of the ad campaign occurred during freshman library orientation during the second week of school. For this 45-minute session, I coined a catchy slogan, "Better information faster," which provided the lesson's theme. Freshmen didn't just listen to librarians talk about the benefits of the library, but experi-

> "Better information faster."

enced a controlled product demonstration that had students compare the library databases with their favorite search engine. In a solid majority of cases students stated that the library databases could provide the more consistent, factual and reliable information on teen-friendly topics ranging from Ford Mustangs to makeover tips.

The kickoff promotion activities were completed by the end of August. During September, I was able to evaluate the impacts, which exceeded my wildest expectations. I was hoping to see a 50% increase in Web traffic over the average month from last year. Instead, I observed a tripling in traffic (300% increase) over the average month and an 85% increase over the busiest month of the previous school year (see graph). On a single day (September 17, 2002), the Web site delivered 780 page views, more than it did during the entire month of December 2001. Though traffic was down slightly during October, that month's total was still well above the highest point prior to the introduction of rebelslibrary.com. Use of online databases went through the roof during this period, with over 3,000 documents retrieved during the first two months of school. This represents more than one document for every student and teacher.

The 2001-2002 school year was characterized by continual

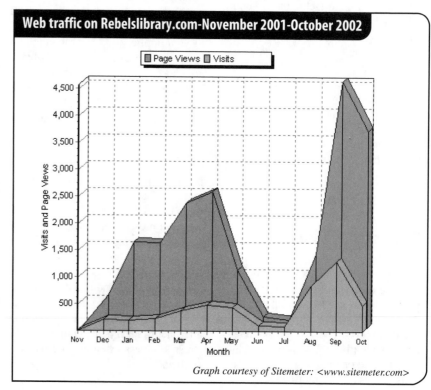

**Web traffic on Rebelslibrary.com-November 2001-October 2002**

*Graph courtesy of Sitemeter: <www.sitemeter.com>*

attempts to market the Web site and build traffic, yet growth in library Web traffic was uneven and sometimes stagnant throughout the year. The extraordinary gains appear to be attributable mainly to the new domain name.

## The Advantages of a "Dot Com" Domain Name

Many of the early pioneers of Internet commerce, including Yahoo! and Amazon, understood the importance of name recognition. At the peak of the Internet craze, companies spent millions of dollars to buy the rights to the "right" domain name, which often succeeded in generating brand awareness, Web visitors, and sales.

Teens are certainly brand conscious, and having a brand for the library generates awareness of the library Web site and makes it easier to compete with Yahoo! or Ask.com. Getting students to the library Web page has never been easier. Last year, the students had to be directed to the "Favorites" menu of the Internet Browser in order to locate the library Homepage. It was a two-step process, that took some time to explain and few students ever thought to do this on their own. With rebelslibrary.com, it is very easy to direct students to the page, and as the school year progresses, more are getting there on their own or with only brief reminders. During busy periods at the library, these factors can combine to make a big difference in the number of students one can assist during a class period.

Additionally, having a marketable brand has been very motivating for me, and I am always looking for ways to promote my product. As a librarian, this has improved my outreach to both students and teachers.

## Technical Advantages of Your Own Domain

In many conversations and correspondence with fellow school librarians, I discovered that few, if any, librarians have direct access to their District's Internet server. Thus, librarians are forced to go through a middleman to modify, add or remove Web pages. This process is highly inefficient, as technology departments at the District level are often understaffed and overwhelmed with requests. It is often not possible get a Web page live on short (less than 24 hours) notice. Furthermore, once on the server, it may be difficult to make necessary corrections or additions in a timely manner. When a librarian has a direct connection to the server, he or she can create pages and add them instantaneously, which allows for many more opportunities to serve teachers, who may not be able to plan more than a week ahead.

In addition to the time element, selecting your own Internet host opens up a whole range of technological possibilities. For example, as a first-year librarian, I wanted to have a password-protected section of the Web site for databases, something that would

> *Teens are certainly brand conscious, and having a brand for the library generates awareness of the library Web site and makes it easier to compete with Yahoo! or Ask.com.*

require a special directory on the server called a cgi-bin. Use of a cgi-bin also requires cooperation from the server administrator, so that the password program could work. With the private server that I use for the library Web page, I resolved all of the technical issues via e-mail within 48 hours.

I also wanted to set up some forms that would e-mail information to the library and a dynamic calendar that would show when the library was available to teachers. Each of these valuable features were easily established using freeware ASP programs that run on Microsoft Internet Information Server (IIS). While I do not endorse IIS or ASP as the only tools that can accomplish these tasks, I was able to find the necessary resources to make the program work. Since my district does not run IIS on its server, I personally could not have created these features as easily (see section below for a brief discussion of these technical terms).

## Getting Started

Running your own "dot com" Web site is not for everyone, especially if you are just learning the fundamentals of Web design. However, if you consider yourself ready to move to the intermediate stage of Web development and are motivated to learn new programming skills, you may be ready!

The first step is to decide how you want to develop your Web site. For instance you may want to develop your site in Microsoft FrontPage, in which case the server of your host needs to support FrontPage Extensions for the version that you use. If you use any other development tool, you still must decide which type of server to use. The two most important server types are Microsoft NT (IIS) and Unix. The server you choose will determine which types of scripts (programs) will work. There is some excellent information about these two systems at <http://www.stylusinc.net/technology/scripts/asp_cgi.shtml>. Ultimately, your choice needs to depend on your own strengths and preferences.

Once you decide on a server, you need to find the best deal on a host. For a fee, the hosting companies will register your domain name. Fees vary considerably from host to host. The pricing schemes for Web hosts are as varied and as complicated as calling plans for wireless phones. Price depends on storage space, bandwidth used, and numerous other factors. There are many places to shop for Web hosts, including Hostcompare.com <http://www.hostcompare.com>. This Web site also offers good basic information on Web design and contains links to other information sources.

You will also need an FTP (File Transfer Protocol) program, which helps organize your Web site and transfer files to the server from your computer. A detailed comparison of FTP programs can be found at Zdnet <www.zdnet.com>. Just type in "FTP" in the search box and look for results. FrontPage users may transfer files using that software and may not need an FTP program.

Once you have your domain, server and FTP software set up, the real learning process of site design and redesign begins. The possibilities for Web design are endless and it is important to discuss technique and technical issues with a variety of experts.

## Conclusions

The results of my venture into the "dot com" world were an unqualified success. While this move required considerable commitment, the efforts have clearly paid off. Dramatic increase in usage of electronic library resources is only one measure of success. More importantly, I feel more empowered to serve the teachers of my school and promote the library with greater zeal. With empowerment came stronger motivation to improve my Web development skills, which, in turn, drive more innovation and then more promotional activities. It has been a true upward spiral.

*Neil Krasnoff is a Librarian at Jack C. Hays High School in Buda, Texas.*

Krasnoff, N. (2003). Library.com: Adding customers to your library web site. *Library Media Connection, 22*(1), 20-22.

# Information Literacy, Collaboration, and "Killer Apps": New Challenges for Media Specialists

## By Fitzgerald Georges

### Information Literacy Defined

Information literacy is a set of abilities requiring individuals to "recognize when information is needed and have the ability to locate, evaluate, and use effectively the needed information."

An information literate individual is able to

- Determine the extent of information needed
- Access the needed information effectively and efficiently
- Evaluate information and its sources critically
- Incorporate selected information into one's knowledge base
- Use information effectively to accomplish a specific purpose
- Understand the economic, legal, and social issues surrounding the use of information, and access and use information ethically and legally

*Definition taken from the Association of College & Research Libraries, Information Literacy Competency Standards for Higher Education* (http://www.ala.org/Content/Navigation Menu/ACRL/Standards_and_Guideline s/Standards_and_Guidelines.htm)

### Information Literacy in Action

Research conducted by organizations like the American Association of School Librarians, the Association of College and Research Librarians, and statewide studies in Colorado, Alaska, and Pennsylvania all espouse the need to teach information literacy skills. The power of the information literacy paradigm is evident, especially in light of the explosion of the Internet. Students are exposed to more information today than ever before and it is getting worse. Information overload and the propensity for students to use Internet search engines as sole sources for their research needs is driving poor student work and encouraging academic dishonesty.

The role of the school library media specialist is clear. Providing bibliographic instruction, collaborating with classroom teachers to create standards-based (content specific) information literacy skills and activities, and conducting faculty workshops are just a few of the strategies for setting a standard of information literacy skills integration in any learning setting. Although the value-added leadership of a certified, highly competent school library media specialist is critical to the success of an information literacy initiative, the role of the classroom teacher and school administration are just as critical. The relationship parallels the interdependence of the three legs on a three-legged stool. If one leg breaks, the stool is useless.

> *Information overload and the propensity for students to use Internet search engines as sole sources for their research needs is driving poor student work and encouraging academic dishonesty.*

Librarians and information specialists have historically fought uphill battles defending their value to learning organizations. While the information literacy paradigm is seen by most educators as essential to the development of 21st century lifelong learning skills, lip service to information literacy programming has often been the rule. Why haven't information literacy standards been fully embedded across the curriculum in K-12 schools? One reason is that classroom teachers in practice do not consistently seek to integrate research activities that facilitate the learning of information literacy skills.

Many school library media specialists lay the blame on the reluctance of teachers to allocate precious class time to set up appointments in

the Library Media Center. Others blame their school administration for failing to embrace flexible scheduling and collaboration sessions between faculty and school based personnel. Nevertheless, there are schools where "optimal" conditions exist, and information literacy is dead. Theoretically, every unit of instruction in any subject curriculum has an opportunity for a problem- or inquiry-based learning component that requires data, information, and knowledge, yet there hasn't been a wholesale "buy in" to the initiative. Two primary historical developments may be to blame. The work of school library media specialists has never been fully appreciated and is often misunderstood. Some school library media specialists haven't worked hard enough to systematically add value to our organizations with innovative programming. We have failed to insinuate our skills and expertise whenever and wherever possible. We don't grasp for leadership and policymaking power. We have allowed the silly stereotype of an (unwelcoming) horn-rimmed, spectacled old woman to pervade. Ground breaking, research-based advocacy that legitimized and validated the work of school library media specialists all over the world has yet to be fully appreciated and realized. We must take responsibility for this failure in order to drive the change management process. Secondly, the onslaught of high stakes testing continues to rear its ugly head. The consistent pressure on school officials and teachers to meet escalating demands for higher test scores under difficult conditions has redirected school programming efforts away from holistic education services like fine arts, technology, and, of course, information literacy. Lock step, test prep, content volume-based regimen of instruction has become the rule. Failing schools that are desperately, periodically (systematically) revamped with new leadership and new reform initiatives with little or no success continue to perpetuate the cycle of failure. The common denominator is generally a non-existent library program and more importantly the absence of a certified, motivated, highly trained school library media specialist. The power of the school library media specialist can be far reaching. Unlike a classroom teacher, school library media specialists have the opportunity to positively impact the academic lives of all members of the school community. To make this happen, the school library media specialist has to create the equivalent of a series of "killer applications" to drive their information literacy program. Listed below are a few strategies for instilling your school's information literacy programming with "killer applications."

**Public Relations.** Talk up your program like a "predator." Get involved anytime and anywhere: curriculum committees, department meetings, student government, technology, shared decision making, new teacher orientation, faculty meetings, cabinet meetings, PTA/PTO.

**Professional Development.** Add value to your organization; partner with staff developers, get involved with Teacher Centers and offer in-service workshops or tutorials on technology and information literacy. District-wide staff development conferences provide opportunities to conduct workshops on that day which can be an instant eye opener and legitimize you and your message immediately.

**Library Programming.** Conduct programs and events that add value to the school community. Provide software fairs, technology fairs, and multicultural events. Host and present at PTA/PTO events and student government events. Coordinate AV showcases, literature appreciation programs, and speakers on library and information literacy issues.

**Fulfillment.** Litter teacher mailboxes with ready-made activities and lesson plans that combine information literacy skills development and subject specific content. Become a resource for the latest developments in teaching and learning practices. Systematically share that information with faculty, administration, parents, and students.

Create and propose a credit-bearing course to teach library skills, print/non-print resource use, and research project process in the context of the information literacy paradigm.

Get actively involved in local, state, and national library and technology associations. Teach courses at the college level. Share your experiences and expertise in writing and get published. Create a personal or professional Web site to get your message out to others.

Become a proficient grant proposal writer. The No Child Left Behind Act has awarded millions of dollars for library and technology initiatives.

> *Every unit of instruction in any subject curriculum has an opportunity for a problem- or inquiry-based learning component that requires data, information and knowledge.*

These strategies will take you a long way in the design of an effective information literacy program. However, in order to sustain a program that grows and becomes institutionalized long after you're gone, you must set an expectation for collaborative practice. First let's settle on a definition for collaboration.

## Collaboration Defined

"Collaboration is based on shared goals, a shared vision, and a climate of trust and respect. Each partner fulfills a carefully defined role; comprehensive planning is required; leadership, resources, risk, and control are shared; and the working relationship extends over a relatively long period of time. The teacher brings to the partnership knowledge of the strengths, weaknesses, attitudes and interests of the students, and of the content to be taught. The media specialist adds a thorough understanding of information skills and methods to integrate them, helping the teacher to develop resource-based units that broaden the use of resources and pro-

mote information literacy. Additional benefits include more effective use of resources and teaching time, integration of educational technologies, and a reduced teacher/student ratio. Teachers with experience in collaborative planning and teaching view the role of the library media specialist more positively and welcome continued collaboration. Participants believe that the results of a collaborative process are more powerful and significant than the results of their individual efforts" (Russell, Shayne. *Teachers and Librarians: Collaborative Relationships. ERIC Digest.* ERIC Identifier: ED444605 - Publication Date: 2000-08-00).

## Collaboration in Practice

The Readers Digest Foundation created and funded a public library, school library, and classroom initiative called "Tall Tree" several years ago. At the core of the program was the development of collaboration practices and principles that were essential to the success of the initiative. Developing a systemic approach to problem solving, meeting mandates, and driving positive reform helped identify the two key elements of successful collaboration:

**Identification of Common Needs.** Most collaborative exercises will fail if participants do not collectively believe that the needs exist, do not feel that the program will meet these needs, or do not feel they will gain by the collaboration. Participants must define core issues and agree about how these issues are to be addressed.

**Program Leadership.** Collaboration brings together multiple individuals from differing organizations. To ensure success leaders must influence stakeholders to relinquish some autonomy and willingly accept input from professionals outside of their domain. Clear lines of communication set the tone for acceptance and positive sharing among all stakeholders.

## Collaboration v. Cooperation.

Understanding the difference is critical to the program's efficacy and the belief that the program can achieve positive change. Collaboration is a rigorous activity that is much more demanding than cooperation. Collaboration will most likely require organizational changes on the part of stakeholders to achieve expected outcomes. This may become the sticking point as egos and personal agendas creep to the surface. Potential barriers between teachers and school library media specialists can be avoided by recognizing differences in training and instructional practices. For instance, school library media specialists may emphasize student exposure to literature and audio/visual connections to literacy whereas teachers may emphasize reading skills strategies. Barriers based on work culture are generally due to a lack of understanding of the norms and demands of each other's profession. Teachers are constrained by blocks of instruction based on time. School library media specialists are pressured by the varied needs of many students and faculty. These different demands represent unique work cultures that will affect collaborative practices.

In the end, The Reader's Digest Foundation's collaborative model demonstrated that classroom teachers and school library media specialists have much to share in improving the educational climate for students. Through effective and open communication, a collaborative blueprint combined with "killer applications" can build capacity for a productive and exciting information literacy program.

*Fitzgerald Georges is the Library Chairperson at Great Neck (New York) North High School Library.*

Georges, F. (2004). Information literacy, collaboration, and "killer apps": New challenges for media specialists. *Library Media Connection, 23*(2), 34-35.

# Setting the Stage: A Future Fiction

## By David Warlick

This is a work of future fiction. I do not call it science fiction, because I have every reason to expect that schools can change this much, and that it could happen during my career. If they do not, it will not be because the technology is not available, but because we did not have the courage or vision to make such dramatic changes in the way that we prepare our students for their future.

Some of what you read in this short story will seem unbelievable. However, if you are aware of the advances in computers and networking over the past ten years, it will not be the technology that surprises you. It will more likely be what learners and educators do while they are engaged in teaching and learning. So let us remove the veil of our own industrial age upbringing for just a few minutes and see one possibility. Welcome to The Bacon School, 2014.

Sally Crabtree sits at her desk as her A2 students amble out of her classroom, most talking in pairs and threes, some glancing at their tablets for messages from friends, parents, or project collaborators. Sally crosses her legs, lays her tablet in her lap and begins dragging icons around on the smooth bright surface using the stylus she slides out of the holder on the edge of the information appliance. As she busily works at her device, the information on the large plasma display at the front of the room begins to change, some sections of text and images moving around, new ones appearing, and others disappearing. Blocks of information slide down into view illustrating weather conditions, Web-cams in other parts of the world, and finally Arabic music, care of a Baghdad radio station.

Outside her classroom, students stroll down the hall toward their next class, B2 (B period, 2nd day of the week), or huddle in groups, talking, drawing at their tablet displays with fingers or styluses. Most of the conversations are simply social exchanges between newly pubescent middle-schoolers. However, a significant number of the interactions are discussions of the class projects in which teams of students are constantly engaged. Projects are the primary activity of Bacon School, and most other schools in 2014.

As she prepares for B2 to begin, Sally thinks back to her drive to school that morning with her young and excitable friend Isaac Johnson, one of the school's media center managers. Earlier in the Morning:

*Sally had just picked Isaac up at his small rental house, almost exactly half way between her family's home and The Bacon School. She had been listening to John Grisham's latest book being read to her in a Mississippi accent by her tablet. She touched the **Stop** icon on her tablet, as her nearly silent hybrid car glided to the curb in front of the refurbished mill house. Isaac, who had been sitting on*

> Projects are the primary activity of Bacon School, and most other schools in 2014.

*the porch scanning the news on his tablet while sipping his customary breakfast cola, dropped his tablet into his canvas messenger bag, jumped off of the porch, and slid into the passenger seat. As Sally pulled out onto the road again, their conversation went directly to Sally's beloved Reptiles, one of her student teams. Isaac was aware that they would be making their project presentation that morning during B2, since he works intimately with most of the school's teams on a daily basis. She had especially enjoyed the Reptiles, since that day at the beginning of the year when they chose their name. It was Alf's idea, but each of the other members had come up with a particular reason why the name fit.*

*The team is uniquely diverse in terms of academic characteristics. Two members, Desmone and Johann, are random thinkers and attention deficit. Samuel is a high achiever with an excellent memory and an analytical mind. Alf remains emotionally traumatized by the unfortunate, vicious sepa-*

*ration and divorce of his parents a year ago. Neither of the parents have much interest in supporting their thirteen year-old son through his turmoil, each too engaged in their own bitterness and adjustment. Regardless of this odd diversity, the team had jelled into an exciting force for producing surprisingly insightful work.*

*Isaac described how the team had been working after classes, with Desmone and Samuel completing the text version of the project and Johann and Alf polishing up the audiovisual. He added that Alf had just as often been working by himself on another component of the project that remained a mystery.*

*"Finding the resources for their visuals was not a problem," Isaac said, "but, validating them was a useful challenge." Each of the team members took a section of earth history, and created Web shelves in their personal information libraries with resources that they identified. They shared their Web shelves and used the information as a basis for their evaluation. It was an interesting learning experience for the team. I've asked if components of their shelves might be included in the Media Center.*

*"It was brilliant requiring Johann to handle the audiovisual editing and telling Samuel that he could only support him verbally." Isaac continued, admiringly. "Frankly, I was afraid that I would be pulled into supporting Johann more than I would like, but I found that he called on Samuel at least as much as he called on me. Also, he grasped the concepts and developed his skill, and he really seems focused on the communication, not technique."*

*Sally smiled at the reference to her scheme. "Thanks for supporting me on this, Isaac."*

As the B2 bell rings, Isaac sits at his desk in the media center and touches icons on his tablet causing a white document to appear on the display—a diagram of the Bacon School campus. He then taps with his finger the location on the map corresponding with Sally's classroom. Suddenly a full motion, real-time video of the classroom appears on his tablet, captured by a camera that is mounted in the back of the room near the ceiling.

An additional document slides out of the video window that lists the owners of about 50 computers that are also monitoring that classroom. There are often five to ten viewers of any one class, usually parents who wish to see what their children are doing and how they are behaving. Some pop in just to learn. However, when there is going to be a team project presentation, many more parents, other residents of the community, and teachers and students from other schools drop in to watch. All teams maintain Web sites that represent the progress of their work, including their work logs, considered resources, defenses, and their presentation dates.

As the students begin entering Sally's classroom, Isaac thinks back to an encounter he had with Desmone this morning just before A2.

Earlier in the Morning:

*Ms. Shuni, the other Media Center Professional, had just walked into their office area from one of the classrooms, where she had been consulting with a teacher. "Conichiwa," she said as she passed Isaac's desk. Is it Japan week?*

*"Conichiwa, Margaret-san," John replied, with a prayer bow gesture.*

*The 32-year library media specialist walked over to her desk, fit her tablet into its cradle, and touched the print login surface of her keyboard with her thumb, causing a virtual connection between the two devices through the room's wireless network. As she began typing an e-mail message, a group of students ambled into the media center. Isaac rose from his desk and strolled out into the larger room to see if he was needed.*

*Desmone, a member of Sally's Reptiles, said something to the group she was with and then walked over to Isaac. She was visibly anxious. "Mr. Johnson, Alf got in trouble again last night." The young man motioned to a nearby unoccupied work area, and they both walked over and sat. "Have you heard from him? Have you seen him here at school yet? Will he be here for our presentation today?"*

*Isaac asked the girl for her tablet and then pressed the print login with his index finger so that the information appliance could reconfigure itself for*

*his access. He then pulled up the school's information system, and learned that the boy's nametag had not been registered for the day. "He isn't in the building – yet," said Isaac.*

*The library media specialist then accessed the call-in register to see if Alf's mother had called indicating that he would not be in school that day. "His mother hasn't called in. Right now, it looks like he will be here." After a pause, Isaac said, "Just a minute!"*

*He pulled up the work folder for the Reptile's project and accessed Alf's video presentation, the part of the project in which he had been most engaged. Isaac touched the icon for the student's file, then touched the menu bar at the top of the display to select "Info" from the drop down list of options. A small white document appeared with statistical information on the file including its size, type, loca-*

> All teams maintain Web sites that represent the progress of their work, including their work logs, considered resources, defenses, and their presentation dates.

*tion and other data. Isaac touched the word "history" and a second document sprang out. After reading the list of entries there, he looked up at Desmone and smiled. He handed the tablet back to her after touching an icon to erase his configuration, and said, "I think Alf will be here today!"*

*As she reached for her tablet, Desmone noticed that her friends had gathered their things and were headed out of the room. She quickly thanked the educator, and, with some uncertainty, turned to join her friends.*

At the ring of the bell, Sally rises and walks over to the door, shaking the hand of each student as he or she enters the room. She smiles as she sees Alf walking rapidly down the hall to join the group as it enters her classroom. Alf is a tall young man with uncombed curly brown hair, the dark complexion of a boy who spends a lot of time outdoors, and the customary awkwardness of a teenager who is growing too fast. He shakes

Sally's hand, but does not look up at her, moving away and toward his seat in the rear of the room.

As she turns to her classroom, she recalls the morning visit from Mr. Ball, their balding and portly principal.

Earlier in the Morning:

*Sally looked up in mock irritation as the 31-year educator spun one of the rolling student desks over to her work area and sat heavily in the seat without consideration of his greater than average size. Sally and Mr. Ball had been friends for all of the eight years that he had been the chief administrator of Bacon, both professionally and personally. Their long friendship and professional relationship did not require niceties. He began with the heart of the problem. "Alf Greeley was taken in by the police last night for vandalism," he said.*

*Sally sighed and replied, "It was probably another fight with his mother. He is still hurting so much from their split, and she simply does not know how her reaction is making things worse for her son."*

*"All we can do is to try and keep him engaged in his projects and help him in anyway that we can." Mr. Ball said. "I just thought you should know, so that you can handle things accordingly."*

*"His team, the Reptiles, is making their ecology movement presentation today." Sally finally smiled at her friend and boss. "If you were to casually come in to watch, it would be an encouraging gesture."*

*Mr. Ball stood and said, "Send me a message when they are getting started and I'll do what I can!"*

*As the principal shoved the abducted seat back in the direction of the other desks, Sally pulled up her e-mail utility, addressed a message to Mr. Ball, and wrote the note, "Reptiles are starting their presentation! -SC-". She set it for delayed delivery, to be sent directly to his pocket tablet upon her click of a **Send** icon that suddenly appeared in a corner of her tablet.*

Sally returns to her desk, picks up her tablet and glances at the attendance document that automatically appears, indicating that one of her B2 students is not present, but that he is on the campus. Attendance remains a political necessity, but teachers no longer have to call the roll since the campus proximity system knows the location of all students and faculty on campus by their nametag chips.

A series of checks also appear by the student names on her class roll, indicating that they have submitted their class assignments. Some checks indicate initial submission of the work, others indicate that submitted work has been reviewed by the teacher, reworked by the student, and re-submitted. One student name has no check by it, but one suddenly appears as she is scanning the list. She looks up at the youngster, who blushes and returns his attention to his tablet.

She touches with her finger the **Send** icon at the corner of her information appliance, and the short message, written earlier in the morning, is sent directly to Mr. Ball's pocket tablet.

Sean, the missing student, walks quickly into the room, shakes Sally's hand distractedly and finds his desk. Then Sally announces, "As you know, today the Reptiles ("Slither, Slither" the members murmur at the mention of their team name) will make their presentation. I have to say that I am very excited about this presentation. Johann, Desmone, Alf, and Samuel have all worked very hard on their report, and I think you will learn a great deal from this presentation."

Sally continues, "But before we get started, I want to mention that you have an assignment posted on your calendars. I want you to read a short story written by a teenager from Croatia. A2 read it yesterday, and we had some very interesting discussions about the story today. Mr. Johnson also contacted the author and she sent a video file, in which she explains why she wrote the story. You are welcome to access A2's discussion and Nadia Kaufman's video file from the school's video archive."

"Now, without any further adieu, I introduce to you the Reptiles."

With the team's customary "Slither, Slither" chant, the room darkens and the front display board goes black, as Johann manipulates icons on his tablet with a glowing stylus. As the room turns dark, the classroom door opens and closes softly as Mr. Ball walks quietly in and sits in a seat toward the back of the room. From the center of the room, Desmone speaks, "The Institute of Ecosystem Studies' definition of ecology is 'Ecology is the scientific study of the processes influencing the distribution and abundance of organisms, the interactions among organisms, and the interactions between organisms and the transformation and flux of energy and matter.'" White text of the definition gradually brightens into view on the large display with key terms shifting to red. Then the definition gradually fades away into black.

Desmone continues, "There are no guarantees. The world is in flux. Conditions change, and the ecological balance teeters here and there, sponsoring the loss of some species, and the introduction of new ones. Some weaken, and others become stronger…"

While she speaks, images of now extinct species surface into view, and then fade again. In the background,

> *Attendance remains a political necessity, but teachers no longer have to call the roll since the campus proximity system knows the location of all students and faculty on campus by their nametag chips.*

and watermarked to about half brightness, two videos impose on each other. One displays a group of cheetahs chasing down a wildebeest that has been taken by surprise. The other shows a pride of lions failing to catch three gazelles that rapidly dart left and right out of reach. Desmone continues to speak, describing specific species of both animals and plants that have disappeared or changed dramatically, and the environmental conditions that seem to have caused the change.

Finally the images fade to a map of the world done in negative relief, appearing as it did millions of years ago. A timeline appears to the right of the map beginning at about 200 million years ago. A citation also appears in off-white indicating a Web site that was the source of the data. Immediately, a pointer, starting at the bottom of the timeline, starts to move up slowly. Simultaneously, land-masses begin to move in a motion with which the students are already familiar. Many of them have also used this animation from the Smithsonian Institute's Web site.

The team is not downgraded for using the familiar animation. However, the class becomes noticeably more interested as splotches begin to fade in and out in specific locations on the map. Numbers are imposed over the splotches as they gradually expand and become more opaque and then shrink to transparency. Soft but intense music plays in the background, credited to a talented student who had attended Bacon school two years earlier through a short citation appearing in the lower corner of the display. Samuel speaks over the animation and music, describing periods in the planet's relatively recent history of mass extinctions and seemingly spontaneous rises in species diversity.

"Each rise and fall has corresponded with some dramatic change in global conditions: ice ages, planetary collisions, volcanic or seismic calamities…" Samuel speaks on eloquently.

As he continues, Sally is taken back to a conversation she had with the boy during their work on the ecology project. Samuel is thought by many to be a technical genius. He has a genuine gift for understanding and using technology. He also has a flair for using these tools to communicate persuasively. She had convinced Samuel, however, not to handle the programming and data manipulation for this project, but that he leave that up to Johann. Samuel could give Johann verbal directions. She had also asked Samuel to do more of the copy and script writing on this project, an activity that she knew would be a challenge for him.

Several Days Earlier:

*Sally entered the school media center, a faint electronic click registering her entrance from the chip in her nametag. She stepped aside, so as not to block the doorway, and surveyed the room. The media center has far fewer books than it did when she went to middle school in the middle 1980s. There is a section in one corner that consists of shelves with books of vari-*

ous sizes and colors. They are almost exclusively fiction books that students check out for pleasure and for assignments in their humanities classes. These books remain because it is a deeply held belief that students appreciate the experience of reading a story without the benefit of electronic appliances. Regardless, most reading is done with tablet computers and smaller pocket text and audio readers.

The biggest portion of the room is devoted to work areas that Isaac calls "Knowledge Gardens." Most of these workspaces consist of a table, with a 19-inch display, attached to a folding cradle that can swivel 360º. The display can be assigned to any tablet in its vicinity when the owner touches the print login pad. Scattered around the table are small, but efficient, keyboards, each of which can also be assigned to any tablet with the touch of its print login pad.

There are also two small stages with 4x8-foot display boards where teams can practice their presentations. She sees a number of work areas that are much more casual, with homey lamps, bean bag chairs, low sofas, and assorted pillows. The media center is set up for knowledge construction, not just information accessing. Students come here to work, and mostly to work in small groups. It is rarely a quiet place.

Sally found the Reptiles and walked over. All four were together discussing their defense of one of the information resources they are using. She caught Samuel's eye and asked if he would join her for a minute. She had read through the talented young man's text document for the project, which was comprehensive and well organized. It appeared, though, that he had paid very little attention to grammar and sentence structure.

They sat down at an unoccupied table and she laid her tablet down, saying, "I wanted to talk for just a minute about your report."

"I'm not finished with it yet, Ms. Crabtree." Samuel immediately replied, somewhat defensively.

The veteran middle school teacher ignored his plea. She had expected a reaction from the young man who was more comfortable writing computer code than prose. "I

wanted to discuss something anyway. It is a good time in your process."

The youngster resigned himself as Sally reached over and touched her index finger to the print login on the table's 19" display. Immediately her tablet display was mirrored to the larger device. She pulled up a comments file that had been sent regarding a project from the previous year by another team. Sally continued by complimenting the boy on his thoroughness and the overall organization of the document, specifically pointing out the logical flow. Then she said, "I want you to read these comments from an architect, concerning the introduction of a project last year to design a school campus of the future."

As Samuel read, Sally followed, reading it again. The architect had first applauded the students on their insights and technical abilities, but then criticized them brutally on the quality of their writing. She (the architect) explained, "Poor written communication conveys a lack of respect for an audience, the product being described, and a lack of respect for the writer himself. Poor communication puts a blemish on the entire message or product that is difficult or impossible to remove again."

Isaac had walked up and was reading over their shoulders, having planned this meeting with Sally. Isaac said, "Writing text for people to read is a lot like writing computer code. Computer code is text that is written for a computer. You write it to convince the machine to do what you want it to do. If the syntax of the code is wrong, then the computer does not perform as you intended." He continued, "You write for people in order to affect them in some way, to inform them about a topic or event, or to cause them to behave in some way. If your syntax is wrong, then you can fail in what you want to accomplish."

Samuel cocked his head slightly, a personal gesture indicating he was considering what the adults had said. He admitted that he had never thought about grammar in that way and would be interested in a recommendation for some instructional software to improve his intuitive grammar skills.

Sally is drawn back to the presentation as Alf rises and walks to the front of

the room. As he turns to face the audience, he nods to Desmone, who begins the multimedia presentation. Sally could tell from the expression on her face that Desmone is nervous about controlling the presentation since she had not yet seen it.

The large screen goes black again, but in rising volume, music begins to play, a very slow and eerie piece with cellos, wooden blocks, and low flutes. A citation surfaces into view at the bottom of the screen in white, crediting the music to Alf Greeley. Sally's eyebrow rises as she acknowledges a new talent for this young man.

As the citation fades away again, a map of the world returns with a timeline to the right that covers a three thousand year range. The timeline pointer moves up the centuries and more splotches of red began to expand out becoming opaque, and then receding back into transparency. As the visuals proceed and the music fades back, Alf begins to speak, casually walking across the front of the room, identifying various periods of social turmoil and listing the number of people killed in violence as the labels and numbers impose themselves over the splotches.

As the timeline marker enters the later part of the second millennium, Alf describes the Protestant Reformation, the Spanish Inquisition, the fall of Imperialism, the American Civil Rights Movement, and the American War on Drugs. Alf finally says, "And the war on …" but stops abruptly.

Surfacing on top of the world map, a video clip materializes and shows the beating of Rodney King in 1992. Other videoed examples of violence by the police or military surface, play, and fade out of view, and as this occurs, Alf finishes his sentence, "…daring! Daring to be different, daring to resist, daring to celebrate or to mourn. Daring to be yourself in a world where fitting in makes things run smoother, but makes people run cold."

Then he stops, and walks back to his seat. The room is silent, and even Desmone remains motionless, until she smiles to herself and then turns and smiles at Alf. It was a powerful presentation, and there was also the provocation of Alf's video clips.

There would be much discussion of this presentation from the community, and many opportunities for the team to defend their work.

Later, after lunch, Sally sits in her classroom office reviewing the Reptiles' presentation. Her classes are over and she has the afternoon to engage in planning and other professional activities including: review of student work, research for her own presentations, meetings with students and teams on their progress, and online meetings with other professionals and collaborators. All class performances are recorded and available through the school's video archives. She has isolated the Reptiles' morning presentation into a separate file, which she is now annotating with comments.

Beneath the video is another document displaying the rubric that had been agreed upon by the team. In most objectives, each member of the team received excellent marks. For Alf, the objective that called for compelling communication was an "A" easily. She checked him at "Exceeded Expectations". It was a striking presentation and the quality of the video editing was exquisite. He had never demonstrated such skill before, and if she did not know that scores meant little to Alf, she might have suspected unethical use of copyrighted information. The presentation would provoke reactions from the community. Sally noticed that the outside comments bin was already filling up. She would spend a sizable part of the afternoon screening them for the students.

After reviewing the evaluations of the rest of the class and assessing the additional materials including student reflections on their project, Sally writes her initial comments for the team's review and then sets to writing her customary letters of thanks to the members. As she finishes her letters, Alf Greeley walks into the room. "Alf, how are you?" The teacher asks with genuine interest.

"I'm fine, I guess." The moody boy replies. Then he adds, "Ms. Crabtree, about the violence in my video…"

The teacher knew that this was coming. There is a hard rule in all presentations, especially images and video, that there be no violence demonstrated.

"You could have stopped the presentation right then, but didn't." Alf continued.

"The reason for the policy is to avoid the glorification of violence. You weren't glorifying violence. You were using it to very effectively make a point. Your examples were not that different from the examples of the lions and the cheetah, which were also violent."

Alf nods his understanding and then looks directly at Sally and sincerely says, "Thanks!"

Meanwhile, Isaac's workday has entered its more intense period as the large media center fills up with students and student teams working on their projects. All of the knowledge gardens are occupied by groups consulting with each other or working individually on specific components of their presentations. Many wear headphones as they consult with other team members or collaborators via teleconferencing or work with musical keyboards composing and editing background music or sound effects.

Isaac notices Desmone standing by the bookshelf, apparently waiting to talk with him. He commends the students he is sitting with on their work and excuses himself, walking over to the waiting teenager.

"I was just curious, Mr. Johnson," she begins as he approaches, "How did you know that Alf would be here today?"

The young educator smiles at Desmone. "Do you remember when I checked Alf's work files?" She nods. "His last work was done on a computer whose owner was labeled as Sgt. Jonathan Frick. I know Sergeant Frick. He works the night shift for the police department. Evidently, Alf finished up his part of your project from the police station."

Desmone cocks her head, not understanding.

Isaac continues, "Do you think Alf would have been working on his project at the police station if he had not fully intended to be in class for the presentation today?"

Desmone smiles, "Oh!" She immediately locks eyes with a friend across the media center, and looks back to the media coordinator. "Thanks, Mr. Johnson!"

"You're quite welcome!" Isaac bows slightly.

---

*David Warlick is the owner and principal consultant of* The Landmark Project, *and he conducts workshops and conference presentations around the world. He is also the author of* Redefining Literacy for the 21st Century *(Linworth Publishing, Inc., 2004).*

Warlick, D. (2004). Setting the stage: A future fiction. *Library Media Connection*, 22(6), 44-49.

# Appendix: Other Resources

## General Resources

American Association of School Librarians. AASL position statements. Retrieved September 1, 2006, 2006, from www.ala.org/ala/aasl/aaslproftools/positionstatements/aaslposition.htm

American Association of School Librarians. AASL resource guides. Retrieved 9/1/2006, 2006, from www.ala.org/ala/aasl/aaslproftools/resourceguides/aaslresouce.htm

American Library Association. (1995, June 28, 1995). ALA Code of Ethics. Retrieved September 1, 2006, 2006, from www.ala.org/ala/oif/statementspols/codeofethics.htm

Hartzell, G. (2003). *Building influence for the school librarian: Tenets, targets & tactics* (2nd ed.). Worthington, OH: Linworth.

Haycock, K. (1992). *What works: Research about teaching and learning through the school's library resource center*. Seattle: Rockland Press. Updates can be found at: http://www.teacherlibrarian.com/tltoolkit/works.html

Hughes-Hassell, S. & Wheelock, A. (2001). *The information-powered school*. Chicago: ALA.

Johnson, D. (1997). *The indispensable librarian: Surviving (and thriving) in school media centers*. Worthington, OH: Linworth.

Library Research Service: Research and statistics about libraries. Retrieved September 1, 2006, from www.lrs.org

The Librarian's Bookmarks
http://www.hopkintonschools.org/hhs/library/librarian.html

LM_NET on the Web.
http://www.eduref.org/lm_net/

Resources for School Librarians.
http://www.sldirectory.com/

Woolls, B. & Loertscher, D. (2004). *Whole school library handbook*. Chicago: ALA.

## Section I: Before You Start

Bradburn, F. (1988). School library media advisory committee: Key to quality. *North Carolina Libraries*, 14-16.

Loertscher, D.V. (2000). *Taxonomies of the school library media program* (2nd ed.). San Jose, CA: Hi Willow.

MacDonell, C. (2005). *Essential documents for school libraries: "I've-got-it" answers to "I-need-it-now" questions*. Worthington, OH: Linworth.

Misakian, J.E. (2005). *The essential school library glossary*. Worthington, OH: Linworth.

Nebraska Educational Media Association. (2000). *Guide for developing and evaluating school library media programs*. Englewood, CO: Libraries Unlimited.

Roys, N. K., & Brown, M. E. (2004). The ideal candidate for school library media specialist: Views from school administrators, library school faculty, and MLS students, *School Library Media Research*, 7. Available online at http://www.ala.org/ala/aasl/aaslpubsandjournals/slmrb/slmrcontents/volume72004/candidate.htm

Santa Clara County Office of Education. (2000). *Where do I start? A school library handbook*. Worthington, OH: Linworth.

## Section II: The Big Ideas

Callister, T.A. & Burbules, N.C. (2004). Just give it to me straight: A case against filtering the Internet. *Phi Delta Kappan*, 85, 648-655.

Shannon, D. (2004). The education and competencies of school library media specialists: A review of the literature. *School Library Media Research*, 7. Available online at http://www.ala.org/ala/aasl/aaslpubsandjournals/slmrb/slmrcontents/volume72004/shannon.htm

Harada, V. H. (2005). Librarians and teachers as research partners: Reshaping practices based on assessment and reflection. *School Libraries Worldwide*,11(2), 49-72.

Hartzell, G.N. (1997). The invisible school librarian: Why other educators are blind to your value. *School Library Journal*, 43(11), 24-29.

McGhee, M.W., & Jansen, B.A. (2005). *The principal's guide to a powerful library media program*. Worthington, OH: Linworth.

Miller, D. P. (2004).*The standards-based integrated library: A collaborative approach for aligning the library program with the classroom curriculum*, (2nd ed). Worthington, OH: Linworth.

Turner, P.M., & Riedling, A.M. (2003). *Helping teachers teach: A school library media specialist's role.* Westport, CT: Libraries Unlimited.

## Section III: Program Administration

Barron, D. D. (2001). School library media facilities planning: Physical and philosophical considerations. *School Library Media Activities Monthly*, *18*(1), 48-50.

McGregor, J. (2006). Flexible scheduling; implementing an innovation, *School Library Media Research*, 9. Available online at http://www.ala.org/ala/aasl/aaslpubsandjournals/slmrb/slmrcontents/volume9/flexible.htm

Thelan, L.N. (2003). *Essentials of elementary library management.* Worthington, OH: Linworth.

Valenza, J. (2004). *Power tools recharged: 125+ essential forms and presentations for your school library information program.* Chicago: ALA.

## Section IV: Professional Growth and Staff Development

Bauer, P. T. (2006). Changing places: Personnel issues of a joint use library in transition. *Library Trends*, *54*(4), 581-595.

Harvey, C. A. (2006). As good as we are, we can always get better. *School Library Media Activities Monthly*, *22*(7), 24-26.

Keller, C. A. (2006). The "buzz" about creating a professional e-portfolio. *School Library Media Activities Monthly*, *22*(7), 56-58.

## Section V: Where Do We Go Next?

Eisenberg, M.B., & Miller, D.H. (2002). This man wants to change your job. *School Library Journal*, *48*(9), 46-50.

Feili Tu, F.S. (2004). Virtual reference service and school library media specialists. *School Library Media Activities Monthly*, *20*(7), 49-51.

Harris, C. (2006). School library 2.0. *School Library Journal, 52*(5), 50-53.

Johnson, D. (2005). When your job is on the line: Strategies for assisting library media specialists whose positions are in jeopardy. *Library Media Connection, 23*(5), 44-46.

Owen, A., et. al. (2006). The impact of wireless on schools and libraries. *Knowledge Quest, 34*(3), 18-19.

Oatman, E. (2005). Blogomania! *School Library Journal, 51*(8), 36-39.

Pappas, M.L. (2005). Virtual school library media center management manual. *School Library Media Activities Monthly, 21*(5). Available online at http://www.schoollibrarymedia.com/columns/management/index.html

# Author/Title/Subject Index